Building in Words

CLASSICAL CULTURE AND SOCIETY

Series Editors
Joseph Farrell and Robin Osborne

Emotion, Restraint, and Community in Ancient Rome
Robert A. Kaster

Making Mockery: The Poetics of Ancient Satire
Ralph M. Rosen

Readers and Reading Culture in the High Roman Empire:
A Study in Elite Communities
William A. Johnson

Apollonius of Rhodes and the Spaces of Hellenism
William G. Thalmann

The Captor's Image: Greek Culture in Roman Ecphrasis
Basil Dufallo

Aratus and the Astronomical Tradition
Emma Gee

Gift and Gain: How Money Transformed Ancient Rome
Neil Coffee

Mosaics of Knowledge: Representing Information in the Roman World
Andrew M. Riggsby

Building in Words: The Process of Construction in Latin Literature
Bettina Reitz-Joosse

Building in Words

*The Process of Construction
in Latin Literature*

BETTINA REITZ-JOOSSE

Oxford University Press is a department of the University of Oxford. It furthers
the University's objective of excellence in research, scholarship, and education
by publishing worldwide. Oxford is a registered trade mark of Oxford University
Press in the UK and certain other countries.

Published in the United States of America by Oxford University Press
198 Madison Avenue, New York, NY 10016, United States of America.

© Oxford University Press 2021

All rights reserved. No part of this publication may be reproduced, stored in
a retrieval system, or transmitted, in any form or by any means, without the
prior permission in writing of Oxford University Press, or as expressly permitted
by law, by license, or under terms agreed with the appropriate reproduction
rights organization. Inquiries concerning reproduction outside the scope of the
above should be sent to the Rights Department, Oxford University Press, at the
address above.

You must not circulate this work in any other form
and you must impose this same condition on any acquirer.

CIP data is on file at the Library of Congress
ISBN 978-0-19-761068-8

DOI: 10.1093/oso/9780197610688.001.0001

1 3 5 7 9 8 6 4 2

Printed by Integrated Books International, United States of America

Contents

List of Figures	vii
Acknowledgements	ix
Bibliographical Abbreviations	xi
Introduction	1
1. Making Memories: Representing Construction in Rome	13
2. Debating the Draining of the Fucine Lake	63
3. Writing Cities, Founding Texts: The City as a Poetological Metaphor	100
4. Engineering Poetry: The Aesthetics of Construction in Statius's *Silvae*	136
5. Walls of Song: The Myth of Amphion	173
6. Conclusion: Construction in Reverse	199
Epilogue. Constructing *Romanità*: The Obelisk at the Foro Mussolini	214
Bibliography	233
Index locorum	255
General Index	263

Figures

I.1. Building site at Ground Zero, New York City, in July 2010. Photo: author.   2

1.1. Cippus of Nonius Datus, reconstructed at Béjaïa (Algeria). Photo: wikinm, CC BY-SA 2.0, https://commons.wikimedia.org/wiki/File:B%C3%A9ja%C3%AFa_-_Cippe_romain.jpg.   21

1.2. Base of the Column of Trajan. Photo: author.   23

1.3. Latin inscription on the base of the Obelisk of Theodosius. Photo: Prioryman, CC BY-SA 3.0, https://commons.wikimedia.org/w/index.php?curid=12067146.   26

1.4. Base of the Obelisk of Theodosius. Photo: Dennis Jarvis from Halifax, Canada - Turkey-03233, CC BY-SA 2.0, https://commons.wikimedia.org/w/index.php?curid=66987705.   30

1.5. Obelisk of Theodosius, north-east side. Photo: Diego Delso, CC BY-SA 4.0, https://commons.wikimedia.org/w/index.php?curid=8538566.   32

1.6. Obelisk of Theodosius, obelisk-raising scene. Photo: Derzsi Elekes Andor, CC BY-SA 4.0, https://commons.wikimedia.org/w/index.php?curid=36978670.   33

1.7. Obelisk of Theodosius, detail of capstan in obelisk-raising scene. Photo: Dosseman, CC BY-SA 4.0, https://commons.wikimedia.org/w/index.php?curid=76721423.   34

1.8. Tomb-crane relief from the tomb of the Haterii, Vatican (Museo Gregoriano Profano), Rome (cat. 9997). © 2021. Photo Werner Forman Archive/Scala, Florence.   36

1.9. Relief of buildings in Rome from the tomb of the Haterii, Vatican (Museo Gregoriano Profano), Rome (cat. 9998). © 2021. Photo Scala, Florence.   38

1.10. Building scene from the Basilica Aemilia frieze, Curia Iulia, Rome. Photo: author. Courtesy of the Ministero per i beni e le attività culturali e per il turismo, Parco Archeologico del Colosseo.   40

1.11. Building scene from the Esquiline frieze, Museo Nazionale Romano, Rome. Photo: author. Courtesy of the Ministero per i beni e le attività culturali e per il turismo, Museo Nazionale Romano.   41

1.12. Scenes XI–XIII, spiral relief of the Column of Trajan. Photo: Anger, Neg. D-DAI-Rom 91.155.   44

viii   FIGURES

1.13. Digger's basket (detail of Figure 1.12).   46

2.1.   Schematized map showing the location of the tunnel. From Thornton and
Thornton (1985), 117 (detail). Courtesy of Ares Publishers, Inc.   69

2.2.   Drawing of longitudinal section of the tunnel, indicating vertical shafts
('pozzi') and tunnels ('cunicoli') and types of soil and rock encountered.
The ratio between vertical and horizontal scales is 20. After Brisse and de
Rotrou (1872), plate IV, and Thornton and Thornton (1985), 118.
Original image courtesy of Ares Publishers, Inc.   70

2.3.   Drawing showing the overlapping of the ancient and the nineteenth-century
tunnels between 2,400 and 3,600 metres. Brisse and de Rotrou (1872), Plate V.   71

2.4.   Torlonia relief, panel 2 (city and landscape). Castello Piccolomini: Collezione
Torlonia e Museo d'Arte Sacra della Marsica, Celano. Courtesy of the
Ministero per i beni e le attività culturali e per il turismo, direzione
regionale Musei Abruzzo.   76

2.5.   Torlonia relief, panel 1 (lake, ships and capstans). Castello Piccolomini:
Collezione Torlonia e Museo d'Arte Sacra della Marsica, Celano. Courtesy
of the Ministero per i beni e le attività culturali e per il turismo, direzione
regionale Musei Abruzzo.   76

2.6.   Possible reconstruction of the Fucine Lake relief, with the positions
of known fragments, including panel 2 (Marruvium?) at the bottom left,
and panel 1 (lake) in the centre. From Giuliani (2003), fig. 70.
Reproduced courtesy of Prof. Cairoli Fulvio Giuliani.   77

6.1.   The statue of Saddam Hussein is toppled in Baghdad's Firdos Square,
9 April 2003. Photo by Gilles Bassignac/Gamma-Rapho via Getty Images.   204

E.1.   Mussolini wielding the *piccone*. Photo: Istituto Luce.   216

E.2.   Obelisk as it stands in the Foro Italico today. Photo: author.   217

E.3.   Obelisk in the quarries of Carrara in 1928. From Opera Nazionale
Balilla (1937), 238.   218

E.4.   Erection of the obelisk. From Opera Nazionale Balilla (1937), 241.   219

E.5.   Benito Mussolini and Renato Ricci at the inauguration of the obelisk.
From Opera Nazionale Balilla (1937), 7.   220

E.6.   Demolition of the concrete structure used for erection.
From Opera Nazionale Balilla (1937), 242.   223

Acknowledgements

The initial inspiration behind this book was a number of tutorials in Roman Art History which I received from Jaś Elsner as an undergraduate student at Corpus Christi College, Oxford. These tutorials left me with a fundamental desire to investigate the relationship between Roman literature and material culture – a desire which has been the central theme of my research ever since. I also owe a particular debt of gratitude to Ewen Bowie, Stephen Heyworth, and most of all to Stephen Harrison, who set me on my path as a literary scholar of Latin literature and who invited me back to Oxford for research stays which proved instrumental in finishing this book. As a PhD candidate at Leiden University, my supervisors Joan Booth and Caroline van Eck supported me in every possible way, from my application to the day of my defence and beyond. They have been an inspiration to me, not only as scholars, but also through their supportive and constructive style of supervision.

Many friends and colleagues read parts of my manuscript at various stages, commented on drafts, or helped me develop my ideas. I thank in particular Myrthe Bartels, Susanna de Beer, Sarah Cullinan, Jan-Willem Drijvers, Miko Flohr, Jo Heirman, Maarten Jansen, Casper de Jonge, Michiel van der Keur, Han Lamers, Christoph Pieper, Thomas Riesenweber, Kelly Shannon-Henderson, Ineke Sluiter, and Christina Williamson. I would also like to thank my dissertation examiners (Ruurd Nauta, Harm-Jan van Dam, Jaś Elsner, and two anonymous readers) and the anonymous reviewers for the press, all of whom read the manuscript with great care and had many valuable suggestions to offer. Of course, all remaining mistakes are entirely my own responsibility.

I gratefully acknowledge the financial support of the Nederlandse Organisatie voor Wetenschappelijk Onderzoek (NWO), which funded my doctoral position at Leiden for four years (project number 021.002.078). In subsequent years, further funding from Ineke Sluiter's Spinoza prize and an NWO Veni award (project number 016.164.057) supported the development of my dissertation into a book. A Niels Stensen fellowship allowed me to spend an inspiring year at the University of Pennsylvania under the aegis of Joe Farrell and to benefit from the lively scholarly debates at its wonderful

X ACKNOWLEDGEMENTS

Classics department. Several stays in Rome were also instrumental: many ideas in this book originated at the City of Rome course at the British School at Rome under the direction of Robert Coates-Stevens, and a number of productive research periods were spent at the Royal Netherlands Institute at Rome. The epilogue of the dissertation also formed the beginning of a joint research project on Italian Fascism with Han Lamers, and I want to thank Han for many years of inspiring collaboration.

Hylke de Boer provided invaluable assistance during the editing and production process and Evelien de Graaf at proof stage and with indexing. It has been my privilege to work with such promising young scholars. I would like to thank Professor Cairoli Fulvio Giuliani for the generous permission to reproduce his reconstruction of the Torlonia relief, and all other museums and holders of rights for allowing me to print images of their objects.

My family, and especially my parents, have inspired and supported me in many ways during the writing of this book. While my children Felix and Maria cannot be said to have sped up its publication, they are the delight of my life and make it all worthwhile. My greatest debt of gratitude is to my husband Albert, and I dedicate this book to him with love.

Bibliographical Abbreviations

AE (1888–), *L'Année épigraphique*, Paris.

CIG (1845–53), *Corpus Inscriptionum Graecarum*, Berlin.

CIL (1863–), *Corpus Inscriptionum Latinarum*, Berlin.

CLE Bücheler, F., and Lommatzsch, E. (1895–1926) (eds.), *Carmina Latina Epigraphica*, Leipzig.

Donderer Donderer, M. (1996), *Die Architekten der späten römischen Republik und der Kaiserzeit: Epigraphische Zeugnisse*, Erlangen.

Enc. Virg. Della Corte, F. (ed.) (1984–1991), *Enciclopedia Virgiliana*, Rome.

Harder Harder, M. A. (2012), *Callimachus: Aetia: Introduction, Text and Commentary* (2 vols.), Oxford.

ILS Dessau, H. (1892–1916), *Inscriptiones Latinae Selectae I–III*, Berlin.

IRT2009 Reynolds, J. M., and Ward-Perkins, J. B. (2009) (eds.), *Inscriptions of Roman Tripolitania, enhanced electronic reissue by Gabriel Bodard and Charlotte Roueché*, available at http://irt.kcl.ac.uk/irt2009/.

KSt Kühner, R. (1914^2), *Ausführliche Grammatik der lateinischen Sprache, 2. Teil: Satzlehre, bearbeitet von C. Stegmann* (2 vols.), Hannover.

LIMC (1981–2009), *Lexicon Iconographicum Mythologiae Classicae*, Zurich/Munich/Düsseldorf.

LSJ Liddell, H. G., and Scott, R. (eds.) (1940^9), *A Greek-English Lexicon, revised and augmented throughout by Sir H. Stuart Jones with a Supplement* (1968), Oxford.

LTUR Steinby, M., et al. (1993–2000), *Lexicon Topographicum Urbis Romae*, Rome.

OCD Hornblower, S., Spawforth, A., and Eidinow, E. (eds.) (2012^4). *The Oxford Classical Dictionary*, Oxford.

OLD Glare, P. G. W. (1969–82), *Oxford Latin Dictionary*, Oxford.

PCG Austin, C., Kassel, R. (1983–) (eds.), *Poetae Comici Graeci*, Berlin; New York.

Pf Pfeiffer, R. (1949–1953) (ed.), *Callimachus* (2 vols.), Oxford.

RE Pauly, A., Wissowa, G., and Kroll, W. (1893–1980), *Real-Encyclopädie der classischen Altertumswissenschaft*, Stuttgart.

TLL (1901–), *Thesaurus Linguae Latinae*, Leipzig/Stuttgart/Munich.

TrGF Snell, B., Kannicht, R., Radt, S. (1971–2004) (eds.), *Tragicorum Graecorum fragmenta*, Göttingen.

xii BIBLIOGRAPHICAL ABBREVIATIONS

Abbreviations of ancient authors and works follow the fourth edition of the *Oxford Classical Dictionary* (*OCD*), and, where not available, the *Oxford Latin Dictionary* (*OLD*) or the Greek-English lexicon by Liddell, Scott and Jones (*LSJ*). I have occasionally extended an abbreviation for easier comprehension. All journal abbreviations follow the conventions of *Année Philologique*.

Introduction

During a visit to New York City in the summer of 2010, I walked past the building site of Ground Zero. What I saw was a huge area of activity, with some twenty cranes of different heights and sizes, and a few structures of steel and concrete, as yet of modest height. While the nascent structures themselves did not look particularly impressive, the spectacle of the huge, bustling building site has stayed with me to this day. The powerful impression it made on me was partly due to my awareness of the destructive event that preceded and necessitated this new construction. The activity at the building site, in its awe-inspiring dimensions as well as its mundane details, was not only overwhelming in its visual and aural impact, but also had the power to speak to me about the resilience of the American people and about their 'constructive' response to a senseless attack (Figure I.1).

There is every reason to suppose that ancient Roman building sites were no less annoying, noisy, impressive, or emotionally evocative than modern ones. The building site of the new One World Trade Center may in some ways be compared to that of the temple of Jupiter Optimus Maximus on the Capitoline. This most sacred of Roman temples had been destroyed in the course of fighting between the supporters of Vitellius and Vespasian in AD 69—a traumatic event for the citizens of Rome.[1] The beginning of the rebuilding seems to have been impressively staged, with the emperor Vespasian himself carrying away the first bucket of rubble on his neck (Suet. *Vesp.* 8.5, Cass. Dio 65.10.2). Reconstruction work continued all the way through the reign of Vespasian, and, after another destruction by fire in

---

[1] Ancient accounts of the destruction are Plin. *HN* 34.38, Joseph. *BJ* 4.648, Tac. *Hist.* 3.71.2, Cass. Dio 64.17.3 (see further Scheithauer (2000), 127). The events on the Capitoline are analysed by Wiseman (1978) and Wellesley (1981), 179–87. Darwall-Smith (1996), 41–7, collects literary and archaeological material for the temple; see 41–3 on its destruction. The traumatic impact of the destruction is famously analysed in Tac. *Hist.* 3.72: see e.g. Edwards (1996), 74–82; Ash (2007); Shannon (2012), 763–5. Cf. also p. 201.

Building in Words. Bettina Reitz-Joosse, Oxford University Press. © Oxford University Press 2021.
DOI: 10.1093/oso/9780197610688.003.0001

Figure I.1. Building site at Ground Zero, New York City, in July 2010. Photo: author.

AD 80, through the reigns of Titus and Domitian.[2] The emotional impact of the construction activity, highly visible on top of the Capitoline, must have been considerable, offering—like Ground Zero—tangible, physical assurance of repair and new creation to accompany emotional healing.

Even building sites that are less emotionally charged cannot be other than conspicuous: they are full of movement, look different every day, cause noise, dirt, and disruption. Not many people would describe a building site as beautiful. And yet, the disruptive nature of construction and its impact on all of our senses force us to respond to it. This book considers such responses to construction in the ancient Roman world: what they may have been, how they were expressed, how they could be influenced, what they meant. In order to answer such questions, I focus on written accounts of construction in the Roman world.

---

[2] Darwall-Smith (1996), 43–5. After the fire in AD 80, Titus yet again began reconstruction works (Scheithauer (2000), 128, esp. n. 14), but since Domitian completed them, ancient authors are conspicuously silent about these activities.

INTRODUCTION   3

Building in Ancient Rome

Roman builders have left a mark still very much visible today in the city of Rome, throughout Italy, and in much of the vast Roman Empire, and Roman architecture has been studied keenly and deeply for many centuries.[3] Thomas, in an insightful and provocative macro-analysis of the field, argues that, for a long time, 'the priority of most researchers [has been] to understand "how it was done", rather than why': to investigate the technology, logistics, materials, and workmanship of Roman architecture.[4] Nonetheless, in recent decades, Roman buildings have also been increasingly investigated in terms of their social functions and cultural meanings. For example, Roman monuments and urban spaces have been interpreted as embodying and communicating the complex ideologies of political power.[5] In these and other ways, scholars have attempted to understand 'what these structures meant to those who conceived or used them'.[6] The investigation I undertake in this book is based on my conviction that questions of the 'how' and the 'why' of Roman architecture are not, in fact, separable. The process of creating architecture is integral to understanding its impact and meaning. Ideologically potent or impressive structures did not simply appear, complete with sophisticated decorative programmes. Rather, viewers walked past loud, busy building sites for years, were inconvenienced by the transportation of building materials, and only slowly saw the walls of the new structure rise. Those events of creation played an important part in creating the 'meaning' of these structures.

Such processes of construction in the ancient Roman world have become ever more tangible in recent years, thanks to much innovative research into the technical, economic, and logistical side of construction.[7] Investigations

---

[3] The particular way in which the discipline of Roman architectural history evolved may also be related to the considerable influence that the (selective) reception of Vitruvius's *De Architectura* has had on approaches to Roman architecture since the Renaissance: see Payne (1999) and Thomas (2010), esp. 844–5. See also p. 11 and n. 31.

[4] Thomas (2010), 839–40.

[5] On architecture as a vehicle of political ideologies, see e.g. the important studies of Zanker (1987) and (1997) on Augustan Rome; Boatwright (1987) and (2000) on Rome and cities in the empire under Hadrian; or Thomas (2007) on the 'social language' of architecture under the Antonines; and Ewald/Noreña (2010).

[6] Thomas (2010), 840.

[7] Dessales (2017) announces the 'archaeology of construction' as a new disciplinary orientation, while Russell and Wootton (2017) argue for a new 'archaeology of making' inspired by the anthropological turn to making (e.g. Ingold 2013). For stone-working specifically, the website produced by the 'The Art of Making in Antiquity' project aims to 'enhance our understanding of the physical process of working stone in the Roman period and to investigate the relationship between the surviving

4 BUILDING IN WORDS

of the mid-republican urban economy have thrown light on the logistics of construction for a period for which our evidence is particularly scant and problematic.[8] Between the first century BC and the first century AD—the period from which most of the literary texts discussed in this book derive—the changing political circumstances, as well as a number of huge technical innovations, significantly altered the way construction worked and looked. Scholars have mapped these changes in considerable detail: the responsibility for managing public building was increasingly centralized and put into the hands of a permanent bureaucracy;[9] new marble quarries were opened and the transport of marble streamlined under imperial control;[10] brick production was expanded,[11] while technical advances in vaulting and the use of concrete allowed for ever-larger structures and ever-faster construction.[12] Quantitative analyses allow us to imagine something of the manpower, cost, and organization connected with the very largest imperial building sites. For example, according to DeLaine's calculations, the building site of the Baths of Caracalla was manned by around 10,000 workmen at a time.[13] In order to drag the very largest blocks of stone that were used in construction through the city to the building site, 300 pairs of oxen were needed.[14] Such figures give us an impression not only of the economic impact, but also of the visibility and the spectacular nature of large-scale imperial construction. Ambitious building projects were always in progress somewhere in Rome, and often carried out at astounding speed. They regularly involved large workforces, impressive feats of transportation and lifting, and radical reconfigurations of

---

objects, the techniques of production and their makers' through the analysis and presentation of a range of visual material: http://www.artofmaking.ac.uk/.

[8] Bernard (2018).

[9] Anderson (1997), 75–95.

[10] Anderson (1997), 166–79; the overview of Fant (2008), 125–32 with further bibliography; and now, extensively, Russell (2013).

[11] Anderson (1997), 151–65; Wilson (2005).

[12] Mogetta (2015) (on the 'invention' of concrete); Torelli (1995); Lancaster (2005) on the so-called 'concrete revolution'; Lancaster (2008), 260–6, for an overview with bibliography. On innovative vaulting techniques across the empire, Lancaster (2015).

[13] DeLaine (1997) calculates that a workforce of at least 7,200 men would have been employed on the building site of the baths of Caracalla at any one time during the four years of construction, with up to 13,100 during peak periods (193).

[14] DeLaine (1997), 100–1: 'The supply of marble . . . was designed as a display of imperial power'. Carts were not allowed into the city of Rome for ten hours after sunrise, with the sole exception of carts supplying public building sites or demolition works, thus focusing the attention of the population during this time exclusively on the constant and sometimes spectacular transportation of building materials (see Robinson (1992), 73–6). On the logistics of heavy transport, see also van Tilburg (2007), 81–3; Bernard (2013), 99–122. On its impact, see also Russell (2018).

urban landscapes, providing spectacular displays of control over manpower, resources, and nature.[15] In Italy and the provinces, too, large-scale building programmes temporarily turned entire cities into building sites.[16]

What was the impact of such processes on those who experienced them first-hand? Some recent archaeological research attempts to answer this question. For example, in a pioneering article, DeLaine draws on a variety of visual, epigraphic, and literary sources to reconstruct Roman attitudes toward high-level construction, arguing that exceptional feats of construction were viewed 'as a source of wonder and as a symbol of civilisation'.[17] Favro's fresh look at a well-known monument, the Arch of Septimius Severus in Rome, demonstrates how the construction of the arch and the associated traffic caused significant inconvenience and obstruction on the Forum Romanum but that, at the same time, the transportation and the lifting technologies conveyed propagandistic messages about the strength of the emperor and his dynasty.[18] More recently, Favro's digital interpretation of archaeological data using procedural modelling has further advanced our understanding of the impact of a large number of synchronous construction projects in the city of Rome.[19]

In addition to such sophisticated reconstructions, we may also speculate about ancient responses to construction on the basis of our own experiences of construction processes—an intuitive, though methodologically fraught approach. For example, I opened this chapter with a personal account of just such an experience at Ground Zero, and Zanker, in his landmark study on Augustan Rome, writes that 'anyone who has experienced the building programme of the Fascists and National Socialists knows that the emotional impact of scaffoldings can hardly be overestimated'.[20] In an epilogue to this book, I shall argue for the essential validity and even necessity of such transhistorical comparisons, and explore some of their challenges and implications.

---

[15] See also Taylor (2003), who relies on a number of case-studies to 'evoke, if only hypothetically, the cultural and cognitive processes involved in the act of creating buildings' in ancient Rome (6).

[16] See Dirschedl (2003) on different examples of 'die Stadt als Großbaustelle'; cf. also especially Thomas (2007), esp. 107–61 on the 'monumentalising' programme of the Antonines throughout the empire.

[17] DeLaine (2002), 205.

[18] Favro (2011).

[19] Favro (2017), with a focus on marble construction in Augustan Rome. This article forms an important complement to Favro (1996).

[20] Zanker (1987), 159: 'Wer die Baupolitik der Nationalsozialisten und Faschisten erlebt hat, weiß, daß man die emotionale Wirkung von Baugerüsten kaum überschätzen kann'.

6   BUILDING IN WORDS

Writing about Roman Architecture

Research like that of DeLaine and Favro shows how we can, in different ways, fruitfully attempt to capture a sense of the 'lived experience' of Roman construction in progress. But the process of construction, impressive or disruptive as it was, was essentially ephemeral in a way that the resulting monuments were not. In this study, I shall focus on a medium which responds to the ephemerality of this process and its experience by creating a permanent record of the process of creation: textual representations of construction.

Roman literature contains a wealth of diverse literary (re-)creations of architecture. Descriptions of finished or planned individual buildings, complexes, and engineering projects, especially in conjunction with material evidence, have usually been investigated for what they can reveal about the structures themselves, as well as their social and political significance.[21] But literary texts not only 'respond' to what is there: they also actively and creatively participate in giving meaning to monuments and to the built environment. These dynamics of the interaction between texts and monuments have been explored in most detail with regard to the city of Rome, a city entirely 'crowded with meanings and associations' stemming partly from the relentless literary engagement with it.[22] I aim to engage with and add to this rich field of enquiry by focusing specifically on literary representations of the processes of building and construction. I argue that, in describing such creations, authors participate in a complex discourse about the meaning, impact, and aesthetics of architecture. In order to map this discourse, I analyse a wide range of literary depictions of construction. I investigate their representational strategies by offering close readings of the texts themselves, while considering them in their material, cultural, intellectual, and literary context. I also analyse epigraphic and visual representations of construction, as a means of contextualizing literary depictions, and especially where inscriptions or visual representations can be understood in a dialogue with literary texts.

---

[21] An example is Scheithauer (2000), who collects all literary testimonies for imperial building projects in Rome, with the main object of assessing ancient reactions to them (11), and Horster (2001) for the provinces.

[22] Edwards (1996), 1. Besides Edwards's seminal investigation of the 'literary resonances in the city and . . . the city's resonance in literature' (2), there are countless studies of different authors, genres, monuments, or features of the urban landscape, among them Jaeger (1997); Boyle (2003); Welch (2005); Larmour and Spencer (2007); Rea (2007); Rimell (2008); Roche (2011b); Vout (2012); Mundt (2012); and Schmitzer (2016). Spencer (2018) provides an up-to-date overview of (only English-language) bibliography.

INTRODUCTION 7

I consider the (literary) making of structures that had a physical existence outside the text (for example the construction of the *Via Domitiana*), of mythical structures (such as the walls of Thebes built by the mythical founder Amphion), and of largely imaginary ones (like the poetic temple in Vergil's *Georgics*). Although it can be fruitful to consider only one category at a time, more often, as will become apparent, these categories are not clearly distinguishable. A literary version of a 'real' building is always a fictionalized, tendentious recreation of it, a construction designed to fit the requirements of the text. On the other hand, a fictional structure is never devoid of all connection with the material world in which it functions and from which it derives its meaning.

Extended descriptions of architecture also hold a special interest for Roman writers. They can serve, like descriptions of artworks, as a means of reflecting figuratively, within the text, on the author's own literary artifice.[23] Describing a finished work of architecture in a literary text (one type of what is conventionally called 'ecphrasis') allows an author to stage the effect of it on the fictional viewers, thereby directing or problematizing the readers' response to art in general and to his own text in particular. Ecphrases can also be used to stress certain aesthetic or ideological features or implications of the author's literary work.[24] Investigations into the theoretical framework underpinning the working of ecphrasis have underlined the potential of an approach that recognizes the interaction of the verbal and the visual.[25] Furthermore, such investigations have now increasingly moved beyond 'traditional' ecphrasis to explore, for example, the importance of rhetoric or ornament for the interaction between verbal and visual domains.[26]

Despite the fact that the study of ecphrasis and of the interaction between the verbal and the visual in antiquity is now a very large and sophisticated field of research, representations of *processes* of creation cannot thus far be said to have taken centre stage in the field, especially where architecture is

[23] On this phenomenon, sometimes called 'mise en abyme', initially Dällenbach (1977). For an overview, see Heerink (2015), 29–30 and esp. n. 30.

[24] This applies especially to descriptions of architecture with artistic decoration, such as the temple of Juno in Vergil's *Aeneid*. A concise introduction to the literary possibilities of ecphrases in Latin literature, drawing on the temple of Juno as an example, is Elsner (2005), 312–17.

[25] E.g. Squire (2009), 191, arguing that ecphrasis is 'not a purely textual phenomenon' and advocating a 'model of competition and collaboration between visual and verbal media'. See also the overview of the history of ecphrasis scholarship in Squire (2009), 140–6, and (2015). Other important contributions include Fowler (1991); Laird (1996); Böhm and Pfotenhauer (1995); Becker (1995); Elsner (1996a, 2002); Goldhill (2007, 2020); Squire (2013); Dufallo (2013); Webb (2009) on ecphrasis as a rhetorical term; and Roby (2016) on technical ecphrasis.

[26] Elsner and Meyer (2014) on art and rhetoric, or Dietrich and Squire (2018) on ornament.

8 BUILDING IN WORDS

concerned.[27] I propose further to enhance our understanding of the dialogue between architecture and literature by analysing the literary representation of architectural processes: construction and, at the end of this study, demolition. For the purposes of this analysis, I rely on the term 'madeness', by which I refer to (a viewer's sense of) how a monument—or indeed any artefact—*was made*: designed, created, and constructed in the course of a process that required creativity, initiative, money, manpower, material, skill, and time. The 'madeness' of an artefact is activated when its audience is prompted to consider its process of creation, for example by means of a literary representation of it.[28]

Structure

This book consists of two complementary parts. Its first two chapters analyse how representations of the process of construction strategically influence a viewer-reader's reaction to finished structures. Representations of construction can also be a means of encouraging the reader to consider the production of the text itself, especially in terms of ambition, aesthetics, and durability, and this is considered in the book's second half (chapters 3, 4, and 5).

Chapter 1 deals with representations of construction in three different media and explores which representational strategies are distinctive to one medium or common to different media. I discuss Roman building inscriptions and their stylized representation of the building process as well as visual representations of building in Roman relief sculpture, and explore how both draw attention to the 'madeness' of the structures they adorn or frame. I relate the representational strategies of both media to those of literary accounts of construction, which will be explored further in the following chapters.

---

[27] However, Thomas (2007), in his rich investigation of monumentality in the Antonine Age, discusses some ecphrastic texts which depict construction (see esp. 200 on the tomb of the Flavii, with 260–2 for the full text). Webb (1999, 2001) discusses ecphrases of the construction of church buildings in late antiquity. For literary representations of processes of manufacture in other media, cf. De Jong (2015) on forging the shield of Achilles, and Stover (2010) on shipbuilding. Roby's (2016) investigation of 'technical ecphrasis' (which includes construction of various types) introduces the helpful notion of 'generativity', which characterizes ecphrastic texts in which 'the artifact is described through instructions that show it coming together before the reader's eyes' (199): see also further 200–9 on generativity and 230–1 on the relationship between competent production and competent description.

[28] On madeness, see further p. 16.

INTRODUCTION 9

In Chapter 2, I turn from urban and suburban monuments to large-scale engineering projects. I discuss not only representations designed to enhance the reader's appreciation of a particular structure, but also those designed to diminish it, and I consider how the two types interact. Against the background of Roman discourse on large-scale construction projects, especially those manipulating the boundaries between land and water, I focus on one particular engineering project of which we possess several literary accounts: the emperor Claudius's attempted draining of the Fucine Lake in Central Italy. I argue that in depicting this project, authors participate in a larger contemporary debate concerning the legitimacy of human interventions in nature. The strategies which they use in negotiating the minefield of (un)ethical engineering are the subject of Chapter 2.

In Chapters 3–5, I argue that describing the process of (architectural) construction within a literary text can also be a way of encouraging the reader to consider the (literary) 'madeness' of the text itself. In Chapter 3, I first offer a brief history of architectural metaphor in Greek literature which demonstrates its versatility: it can be employed to comment on the structure, aesthetics, durability, size, or ambition of a literary work. I then concentrate on one particular architectural image for text production which appears to represent an innovation in Roman literature—the construction of a city. I analyse literary city building in the work of Vitruvius, Manilius, Propertius, and Vergil, arguing that the specific form each author gives to city building impacts the way in which the reader is asked to envisage and appreciate the poetic task. The authors' mutual engagement through their competing city foundations also allows them to stake out their literary ambitions in relation to one other. In attempting to understand the potency of the metaphor, as well as the specific forms it takes in the texts discussed, I also consider the political role of city building in the Roman Empire during the late republic and its changing cultural resonances during the early principate.

In Chapter 4, I investigate how the 'madeness' of monuments and texts coincides in Statius's panegyric *Silvae*, where the author attempts to enhance the impact of certain building projects by representing the process of their construction, while simultaneously conveying a particular poetics of construction uniquely suited to the *Silvae*. I argue that Statius develops a provocatively un-Callimachean poetics of construction which both draws on and in turn feeds the panegyric representations of construction in Domitianic Rome and Italy.

10 BUILDING IN WORDS

In Chapter 5, I analyse a mythical version of the construction metaphor: the Greek hero Amphion sang a song which bewitched stones to form themselves into the walls of Thebes. In this myth, poetic composition is not only *like* building, it *is* building. Literary representations of this myth are used by many Greek and Roman authors to illustrate the creative power of poetry. Statius's *Thebaid* itself, however, offers a different perspective: as the poem's nefarious war advances, Amphion's musical magic and his walls are shown gradually to lose their power. Victorious at the end of the *Thebaid* is not the mythical founder-poet but the poetic narrator, who has sung Thebes into destruction. The myth of Amphion thus reveals troubling implications of the construction metaphor for the wholeness and stability of poetic artefacts: what has been built can also be destroyed.

The interplay between representations of construction and destruction is further developed in the Conclusion. Here, I recapitulate and contextualize the results of my study by considering representations of destruction and demolition. I revisit inscriptions and visual representations, and then focus on a scene of physical and literary demolition in Pliny's *Panegyricus*.

Finally, an Epilogue shines a spotlight on one particular moment in the reception of Roman constructions: the staging and representation of construction in Benito Mussolini's Fascist Italy. I argue that turning to a moment of reception can help us better understand how ancient Roman representations of construction have shaped modern conceptions of architecture and 'Romanness'. Conversely, we begin to see how modern receptions of ancient Roman construction have influenced our image of what ancient construction looked like and what it meant.

While the bipartite structure of the book thus broadly distinguishes between 'real' and metaphorical building processes, these are not in fact confined to distinct texts, nor do they exist within the same text independently of each other. I draw attention to their dynamic interaction throughout the book and especially focus on it in Chapters 4 and 6.

I am mainly concerned with representations of construction from the late first century BC to the early second century AD. It is a plausible (though unprovable) supposition that it was the technological advances and logistical changes in construction during this period that put the process of building on the map as a literary theme and encouraged authors to engage with it creatively. Nevertheless, I venture into later periods when there are specific developments to be pursued, and earlier material is introduced where I am concerned with models or predecessors. As a result, despite the overall focus

INTRODUCTION 11

on early imperial Rome, Homer and Ammianus Marcellinus both appear in this study.[29]

I use a capacious definition of 'building' and 'construction', which may seem surprising when viewed from the perspective of the modern building trade. However, ancient definitions of the domain of architecture were both broader and more flexible than ours. Ancient 'architecture' concerned itself with 'building' in the traditional sense, but also with water engineering, mechanics, military engineering, roadworks, and temporary structures.[30] Analogously, written discourses of architecture, construction, and of certain types of engineering function in very similar ways, which should be considered in unison, rather than being assigned to different (anachronistic) domains. A telling example of this are Statius's *Silvae*, treated in Chapter 4, where the construction of a temple (*Silvae* 3.1), the assembly of a monumental bronze sculpture (1.1), and the construction of a road (4.3) are tied together by Statius's 'engineering poetry'. I am broadly concerned with all human processes of monumental creation which involve patrons, architects, contractors, or workmen, and feature the transport and use of raw material, hard physical labour, heavy lifting, or the use of tools. On the other hand, this book cannot offer a compendium of all passages in Roman literature that mention construction. Rather, its chapters serve as different windows onto a literary theme, demonstrating the validity of an approach which reads texts as engaged in shaping the meaning of architecture by depicting its creation.

I hope that my work will be of interest not only to classicists but also to archaeologists and architectural historians interested in the social meanings of architecture in ancient Rome. Where Roman architectural historians have turned to ancient texts, they have often, and justifiably, looked to Vitruvius's treatise *De Architectura* as their main source of information, and have been guided by it in the questions asked of Roman architecture and in prioritizing certain areas of research over others.[31] There is, however, a whole range of other texts, from epic to historiography, from love elegy to didactic poetry, which may not at first glance seem to be particularly concerned with

---

[29] One further reason for not venturing further into the second century is the thorough treatment of the Antonine Age undertaken in Thomas (2007).

[30] Thomas (2010), 838–9.

[31] Cf. the important study of Wilson Jones (2000). Senseney (2011) has 'examine[d] the importance of Greek building and thought for the creation of *architecture as Vitruvius understood it* in a Roman context' (xi, my italics). Taylor (2003), in his investigation of 'architectural process', is critical of this emphasis (4–5). Thomas (2010), 844, calls this 'the Vitruvius problem' of the study of Roman architectural history.

12 BUILDING IN WORDS

architecture, but which in fact do aim to configure perceptions of architecture: for example—as this study shows—by representing its creation.[32] By focusing almost exclusively on non-technical texts, this study seeks somewhat to redress the balance in the study of ancient architecture in Roman literature. I aim to show how diverse literary texts actively engage in the attribution of meaning to architecture and in the debates surrounding built structures.[33]

---

[32] One reason for Vitruvius not playing a major role in this study is that *De Architectura* is much less concerned with describing the process of creating buildings than with the desired result of construction. Taylor (2003) argues that 'Vitruvius shows minimal interest in the sequential logic of design and construction ...' and that 'his book is a series of descriptive or prescriptive snapshots ... without much attention to architecture as a process' (4). Another is that his work was written just before the major developments in construction technology really began to transform building in Rome; Taylor (2003), 7.

[33] This is not to say that technical texts like *De Architectura* do not engage in the complex processes of attributing meaning to Roman architecture—merely that they have hitherto been more 'visible' to students of architecture than other types of texts. For an example of very sophisticated literary analysis of extremely technical texts, see Roby (2016). For recent insights into Vitruvius in his cultural context, see Nichols (2017); Oksanish (2019); or the articles in Cuomo and Formisano (2016).

1

Making Memories

Representing Construction in Rome

Introduction

Architectural structures can commemorate many things: they may initially be intended to preserve the specific memory of individuals or of a significant event, but in their long history, they can also come to fulfil diverse and evolving commemorative functions for the communities which interact with them.[1] But there is one event that *all* man-made monuments commemorate to some extent: the event of their own construction. In the second book of his *Histories*, the Greek historian Herodotus writes about his travels through Egypt. When he turns to the time of Cheops and launches into a discussion of the pyramids, they represent for him, above everything else, a reminder of the inconceivable effort of their construction (Hdt. 2.124.1–3, 5):[2]

κατακλήισαντα γάρ μιν πάντα τὰ ἱρὰ πρῶτα μέν σφεας θυσιέων ἀπέρξαι, μετὰ δὲ ἐργάζεσθαι ἑωυτῷ κελεύειν πάντας Αἰγυπτίους. τοῖσι μὲν δὴ ἀποδεδέχθαι ἐκ τῶν λιθοτομιέων τῶν ἐν τῷ Ἀραβίῳ ὄρεϊ, ἐκ τουτέων ἕλκειν λίθους μέχρι τοῦ Νείλου· διαπεραιωθέντας δὲ τὸν ποταμὸν πλοίοισι τοὺς λίθους ἑτέροισι ἔταξε ἐκδέκεσθαι καὶ πρὸς τὸ Λιβυκὸν καλεύμενον ὄρος, πρὸς τοῦτο ἕλκειν. ἐργάζοντο δὲ κατὰ δέκα μυριάδας ἀνθρώπων αἰεὶ τὴν τρίμηνον ἕκαστοι. χρόνον δὲ ἐγγενέσθαι τριβομένῳ τῷ λεῷ δέκα ἔτεα μὲν τῆς ὁδοῦ κατ᾽ ἣν εἷλκον τοὺς λίθους, τὴν ἔδειμαν ἔργον ἐὸν οὐ πολλῷ τεῳ ἔλασσον τῆς πυραμίδος, ὡς ἐμοὶ δοκέειν. . . . τῇ δὲ πυραμίδι αὐτῇ χρόνον γενέσθαι εἴκοσι ἔτεα ποιευμένη. . .

For by closing all their temples he [Cheops] first kept them from sacrificing, and then he commanded all Egyptians to work for him. To some it had

---

[1] Some elements of this chapter's sections on 'epigraphic memories' and 'visual memories' have been published in a briefer form in Reitz (2012), 317–32.

[2] The text is quoted from Hude (1927).

Building in Words. Bettina Reitz-Joosse, Oxford University Press. © Oxford University Press 2021.
DOI: 10.1093/oso/9780197610688.003.0002

14 BUILDING IN WORDS

been appointed to take stone from the quarries in the Arabian mountain and from there to haul it as far as the Nile; others he commanded to take over the stone, carried across the Nile on boats, and to haul it all the way to the so-called Libyan mountain. They were working in groups of a hundred thousand people, each three months at a time. The people were worn out for a period of ten years through the road over which they hauled the stones, a work that was not much less than the pyramid, it seems to me. . . . For the pyramid itself to be built it took a period of twenty years. . .

What fascinates the historiographer most about the pyramids is the effort which had been made to construct them.[3] This (now invisible) history of the genesis of the structure is at least as relevant as its physical appearance. Therefore, the aesthetically unambitious track leading up to the pyramids is almost as great a work as the pyramids themselves.

Awareness of the history of the making of a monument adds to its impact. If one would like to maximize a monument's effect on its viewers, one might then simply rely on the fact that any built structure will lead at least some viewers to speculate on the history of its making. But there are also certain strategies by which viewers can be encouraged to consider and to imagine this history, and to include it in their appreciation of the monument as a whole. If we continue reading about the pyramids, after a description of the methods used for construction we find Herodotus reporting the following (125.6–7):

σεσήμανται δὲ διὰ γραμμάτων Αἰγυπτίων ἐν τῇ πυραμίδι ὅσα ἔς τε συρμαίην καὶ κρόμμυα καὶ σκόροδα ἀναισιμώθη τοῖσι ἐργαζομένοισι· καὶ ὡς ἐμὲ εὖ μεμνῆσθαι τὰ ὁ ἑρμηνεύς μοι ἐπιλεγόμενος τὰ γράμματα ἔφη, ἑξακόσια καὶ χίλια τάλαντα ἀργυρίου τετελέσθαι. εἰ δ' ἔστι οὕτω ἔχοντα ταῦτα, κόσα οἰκὸς ἄλλα δεδαπανῆσθαί ἐστι ἔς τε σίδηρον τῷ ἐργάζοντο, καὶ σιτία καὶ ἐσθῆτα τοῖσι ἐργαζομένοισι; ὁκότε χρόνον μὲν οἰκοδόμεον τὰ ἔργα τὸν εἰρημένον, ἄλλον δέ, ὡς ἐγὼ δοκέω, ἐν τῷ τοὺς λίθους ἔταμνον καὶ ἦγον καὶ τὸ ὑπὸ γῆν ὄρυγμα ἐργάζοντο, οὐκ ὀλίγον χρόνον.

It was indicated in Egyptian letters on the pyramid how much had been spent on radish and onions and garlic for the workers. And as I well

---

[3] Cf. Thomas (2007), 165–6, who analyses responses to the pyramids through antiquity, diagnosing a 'weakening in the mnemonic power of the pyramids'; and Elsner (1994), 230–44, on the pyramids in Greco-Roman discourse, with 234–5 and 239–40 specifically on this section.

remember the interpreter who read the letters to me saying, sixteen hundred talents of silver were paid. If that is so, how much in addition is likely to have been expended on the iron with which they were working and on the grain and the clothes for the workers? Seeing that the time they took for the work of construction, on the one hand, was the one mentioned [20 years], I think that the time they took for cutting and transporting the stone and for making the underground trench, on the other hand, was not short.

There is no evidence that such inscriptions really did exist, more so since the ancient Egyptians did not have a money economy and no Egyptian inscription could therefore have mentioned talents of silver. However, the principle is important—Herodotus reports, or more likely imagines, how such an inscription, regardless of whether it contains the truth (εἰ δ᾽ ἔστι οὕτως ἔχοντα ταῦτα . . .), stimulates its reader to reflect further on the building-history of the structure. This awareness then becomes part of the appreciation of the finished monument.

Inscriptions are one means of encouraging such reflection, and they will be considered first in this chapter, but other media can also be used to encourage the viewer to consider a building in terms of the achievement of its construction. In this chapter, I also consider visual representations and literary accounts of construction in progress. All three media 're-present' the ephemeral process of construction and thereby encourage a re-enactment of the monument's making in the viewer's mind. The representations thus engender what I call a 'memory' of construction. My use of this term will bear some clarification. I mean by it that from the unique interaction of a specific viewer's own predispositions, knowledge, and earlier recollections, on the one hand, and the representation of construction, on the other hand, a mental image of the monument's construction is either formed or (if the viewer already has a recollection or impression of the process) manipulated in the viewer's mind. No epigraphic, visual, or literary representation of construction simply is able to call forth a historically accurate recollection of the construction process—nor is it designed to do so. Rather, any 'mediation' of the construction process is shaped by its specific context, purpose, and its medial constraints.[4] On the other hand, any particular viewer's image of the construction process is always personally and culturally situated: influenced

---

[4] On mediation and remediation of memory, see Erll and Rigney (2009).

16   BUILDING IN WORDS

by the individual's unique perspective and experience, and by their social relationships.[5]

By engendering 'memories' of construction, such representations activate a quality inherent in any monument. As noted in the Introduction, I call this quality 'madeness': the fact that a monument—or indeed any artefact—was once made, that it was designed, created, and constructed in the course of a process that required creativity, initiative, money, manpower, material, skill, and time. The 'madeness' of an artefact is activated when its audience is prompted to consider this process of creation, for example by means of a representation of it. The subjects of this book are such representations, and more specifically the different strategies they employ. Epigraphy, visual art, and literature all rely on strategies appropriate to their different forms of expression. All three abridge or exaggerate, stylize and adapt, and all three, I shall argue, can in different ways filter out (or indeed highlight) some less immediately appealing aspects of the construction process—the noise or the inconvenience which accompanies construction, or the duration of construction—while evoking and emphasizing those which can be used to bolster the positive impact of the monument. Building inscriptions, visual representations of the construction process, and literary descriptions of building will be considered in turn, in order to investigate and compare their mechanisms and strategies of 'making memories', and to understand the interactions which can take place between them.

Epigraphic Memories

One way of influencing the way in which a building is viewed is to inscribe it. An inscription functions as a 'viewing instruction', designed to impact the

---

[5] Experiments have shown the extent to which an individual's memory of a certain event is really a construction on which language and an external, tendentious representation of events have a considerable influence: cf. the famous experiment of Loftus and Palmer (1974). Students of collective or cultural memory have also long seen memory as 'formed' by cultural processes within social groups over time (see e.g. Assmann (1999), 56, on 'Geformtheit' as a characteristic feature of cultural memory). I focus on memory as a result of the interaction between the representational medium and the *individual* viewer/reader rather than (primarily) larger collective and cultural processes, although I do not in any way attempt to deny that these are also taking place. Wagoner (2017) points out that the difference between memory of individuals and groups is a difference of emphasis, rather than a fundamental distinction (2).

MAKING MEMORIES   17

way a building is evaluated by encouraging its reader to note especially and to appreciate certain aspects of the building it frames.[6]

The typical building inscription contains a minimum of two basic elements: the name of the builder in the nominative, and a verb such as *fecit* or, as the case may be, *refecit* or *restituit*.[7] In addition, it can contain different elements of extra information. Most commonly, such additional information consists of a specification of the building that has been built or restored (in the accusative), or of the individual or community for which the building was constructed (in the dative). However, many inscriptions expand even further on this standard repertoire, providing details of scale, execution, duration, or financing of the work.

It is widely acknowledged that the most important element of a building inscription and the element with the most impact on its viewer and reader would have been the name of the builder, and this is often apparent even from the respective letter sizes used.[8] Nevertheless, a verb is (almost) always part of a building inscription, albeit in a very generic form, and the significance of this should not be underestimated.[9] The verb is usually the final word of the inscription, a position which confers an added visibility, even for a viewer who only cursorily glances over the inscription. Through the verbal expression of making, a building inscription demands from the viewer of a building that he considers not only the monument as it stands, but also its 'madeness': the fact that it was made at all, that it did not simply appear but had to be constructed in a process that required the initiative of a patron, money, manpower, material, and time.

---

[6] This framing function is, for example, noted by Elsner (1996b) ('. . . inscriptions and texts as a crucial framing device', 35) and applied on the largest possible scale. He argues for an interpretation of the *Res Gestae* as framing its readers' view of the entire city of Rome (40). On the interaction of inscriptions with their environment, see generally Corbier (2006). Cf. also Horster (2001), 12–13, on the communicative aspect of building inscriptions.

[7] On the basic elements of a building inscription, see Horster (2001), 31–75. She systematically discusses all imperial building inscriptions outside Rome, but these 'unterscheiden sich in ihrem Aufbau, ihrem Aussehen und ihrer Funktion nicht grundsätzlich von Bauinschriften, die ein oder mehrere Individuen, eine Stadt oder eine Gemeinschaft an einem Gebäude anbringen ließen' (10). Cf. also Saastamoinen (2010) for a detailed investigation of the elements of North African building inscriptions. For more general overviews, see Meyer (1973), 59–61; Almar (1990), 173–92.

[8] Cf. e.g. Alföldy (1991), a seminal article on the Augustan epigraphic culture, which stresses the strategy of inscribing the title Augustus all over the empire. See also Woolf (1996), esp. 28–9, on the way in which inscribing one's name is a way of defining one's identity and place within one's community, city, and society.

[9] DeLaine (2002) stresses that 'the directness of *fecit* can easily be forgotten' (223). See Horster (2001), 49 n. 135, for a list of the few exceptional (and doubtful) imperial building inscriptions without a verb.

18 BUILDING IN WORDS

Even in its most basic form, the manipulative and stylizing effect of building inscriptions in shaping or creating a memory of construction is not difficult to perceive. First, a building inscription, through its basic structure of name of builder in the nominative and a verb, simplifies and disambiguates issues of 'ownership' or 'authorship' of the monument. While the building in question might have been constructed by thousands of workmen, while architects, engineers, and sculptors worked on it together, the inscription can reduce the entire operation to one act of creation on the part of only one person. Furthermore, the representation of the process of construction in this briefest of forms, as *fecit* or *restituit*, effectively elides the fact that construction is not one single act of creation, but a million small ones, which take place over an extended period of time.

The more details of the construction process an inscription provides, the more specific a memory of the construction process it creates for its viewer-reader. I consider here a number of examples of inscriptions which expand on the standard repertoire and provide additional information about the building process. This selection is not intended to be representative of building inscriptions in general, since only a minority of them provide such a wealth of detail and information. The aim is rather to explore what is possible in building inscriptions, and what strategies they employ to create a memory of construction and integrate it into the viewer-reader's experience of the monument itself.

Let us first consider an inscription that recalls the rebuilding of a bath complex in Novara (ancient Novaria, situated on the road from Vercellae to Mediolanum):[10]

C(aius) Valerius C(ai) f(ilius) Claud(ia) Pansa flamen / divorum Vesp[a]siani Traiani Hadrian(i) p(rimus) p(ilus) bis / trib(unus) coh(ortis) VIIII pr(aetoriae) proc(urator) Augusti provinc(iae) Britanniae / [balineum quod vi] consumptum fuerat ampliatis solo / [et operibus intra bie]nnium pecunia sua restituit et dedicavit / [in quod opus legata] quoque rei p(ublicae) testamento Albuciae Candidae / [uxoris suae HS C]C consensu ordinis amplius erogavit

Gaius Valerius Pansa, son of Gaius, of the *tribus* Claudia, *flamen* of the divine Vespasian, Trajan and Hadrian, *primus pilus* and twice tribune of the

---

[10] *CIL* 5.6513 = *EDR* 108483, and Fagan (1999), 257–8 n. 84. The inscription is discussed in DeLaine's (1999) groundbreaking article (72–3).

MAKING MEMORIES   19

ninth praetorian cohort, imperial procurator of the province Britannia, rebuilt this bath building, which had been consumed by force [i.e. of fire], from the ground up and, moreover, with enlargements, within two years, with his own money and dedicated it. For this work he also spent, by the consent of the *ordo*, the bequest made to the state by his wife Albucia Candida, to the amount of 200,000 sesterces, and more.

The inscription provides additional information on a number of features of the rebuilding process, for all of which there are numerous parallels in other building inscriptions. The inscription gives the reason for rebuilding (destruction by fire, *vi* (sc. *ignis*) *consumptum*), an extremely common feature in rebuilding inscriptions.[11] The fact that the complex had to be built up again *solo*, from the earth, i.e. from the foundations, evokes an image of the extent of the work done, as does the claim that the buildings were enlarged in the process (*ampliatis et operibus*).[12] We learn how the restoration was paid for—the donor paid for it *pecunia sua*. Finally, and very importantly, the inscription gives the amount of time it took to accomplish the restoration, namely only two years: *intra biennium*.[13] The last category especially helps us to understand what an inscription can add to a reader-viewer's appreciation. The fast completion of a construction project is an impressive achievement which a builder may well want to ensure is remembered. However, once a building is finished, nothing about the way it looks can still reveal whether it took two, twenty, or two hundred years to build. The achievement of building quickly—indicative of control over a great workforce, efficient organization, and ample means— is therefore particularly well-suited to being recorded in a building inscription in order to augment the impact of the building itself.[14] Other categories

[11] See e.g. Horster (2001), 222–4. Cf. also 52–3, on the different possible elements of additional information that can be combined with the verb *reficere*, which seems to require the specification of a reason for the renovation of the building (*vetustate, terrae motu, vi ignis, vi maris, vi torrentium, vi tempestatis, longa incuria . . . conlapsum*). See also Saastamoinen (2010), e.g. 190–208 (on information about the previous state of a restored building) or 225–34 (on the intended use of a new building).

[12] Saastamoinen (2010), 210–11, on the use of the very common *a solo* and, later, *a fundamentis* (for both new and restored buildings). For participial phrases similar to *ampliatis operibus*, see 216–20.

[13] *[intra bie]nnium* is restored, but even if there were space on the stone for e.g. *triennium* instead of *biennium*, this would not touch the point of my argument.

[14] Thus DeLaine (1999), 72–3: 'The consciousness of the importance of the construction process and the need to keep it in the public eye is perhaps reflected in a mid-second century inscription from Novara, where the benefactor specifically states that the baths destroyed by the fire had been rebuilt and enlarged . . . within two years.' For further examples of the duration of construction in building inscriptions, cf. e.g. *CIL* 5.3329 (rebuilding the city walls of Verona within 9 months), *CIL* 8.2658 (cf.

20   BUILDING IN WORDS

of additional detail, which this particular inscription does not contain, but which are regularly found in ancient building inscriptions, are: the people employed in construction,[15] the materials used,[16] the thoroughness of the workmanship,[17] and the different stages of the building activity.[18] However, with all this extra 'information' about the process of construction, there is an important qualification to keep in mind. In an influential article on 'constructing reconstruction', Thomas and Witschel argue that epigraphic claims about the details of rebuilding are often inaccurate and exaggerated, and that they are determined less by the works that were actually executed, than by more complex ideological motives.[19] While this note of caution raises problems for using building inscriptions as a source for archaeological reconstructions, it further supports my argument here: these epigraphic details (whether accurate or not) strategically aim to 'make memories' of construction.[20]

Building inscriptions most commonly stress the 'madeness' of monuments in order to heighten the achievement of the patron responsible for initiating and financing the construction or restoration work. There are also other (less common) types of inscriptions which aim to encourage their readers to envisage the process of creating a monument while highlighting a different individual's role in this process of creation. For example, architects' signatures were sometimes inscribed into or affixed to completed buildings, and reported the name of the architect responsible for supervising the execution of the building.[21] A specific type

---

p. 954 and *AE* 1973, 645) (building a 39-km aqueduct within 8 months), on which see Horster (2001), 244 n. 40. See Saastamoinen (2010), 213 n. 1200 for North African examples (including *CIL* 8.2658).

[15] Military forces are frequently cited as having been involved in building projects, especially those under imperial control (often in such cases the projects were improvements to the infrastructure, such as bridge building, road building, or the renewal of milestones). See MacMullen (1959); Horster (2001), ch. 4 and 443–5; and Saastamoinen (2010), 285–8, who also cites some instances of civilian building projects.

[16] For examples and a short discussion, see Horster (2001), 214–18, with e.g. number Ib 1 (*CIL* 10.4574, *cum cubulterinis marmoribus*) from her own catalogue, and Saastamoinen (2010), 181–5. A good example is *IRT2009* 467 (Constantinian rebuilding of a basilica with columns of Troad granite: *magnitudine . . . Troadensium columna[r]um adornata*) with Ward Perkins (1992), 68 and 72.

[17] Saastamoinen (2010), 211–13, e.g. *summa cum diligentia* (n. 1190) or *labore incredibili* (n. 1194).

[18] Saastamoinen (2010), 214–25.

[19] Thomas and Witschel (1992). Fagan (1996) raises important objections and justly stresses the formulaic character of building inscriptions, but the core argument about the dangers of using building inscriptions for the reconstruction of archaeological phases remains important.

[20] Cf. Saastamoinen (2010), 23, who summarizes his findings: 'In a word, Roman building inscriptions are not . . . either comprehensive, or exact, or technical, or objective descriptions of building processes. The limited information they contain is selected to produce a positive but vague idea of the quality of the commemorated building activity.'

[21] See Donderer (1996) 24–34 and *passim*. Such signatures are comparatively rare and not (with one exception) found in Rome, where a law apparently forbade inscribing any name other than that of the emperor or patron (Donderer (1996), 30–1). See also Thomas (2007), ch. 5, on Roman architects of the Antonine period and their epigraphic record.

Figure 1.1. Cippus of Nonius Datus, reconstructed at Béjaïa (Algeria).
Photo: wikinm, CC BY-SA 2.0, https://commons.wikimedia.org/wiki/File:B%C3%A9ja%C3%AFa_-_Cippe_romain.jpg.

of surveyor (a *librator*) takes centre stage in a famous monument set up in Lambaesis to commemorate the construction of an aqueduct. In an inscription on a *cippus*, now reconstructed in the city of Béjaïa on the north coast of Algeria (Figure 1.1), the surveyor Nonius Datus proudly records his contribution to the construction of an aqueduct which required tunnelling through a mountain.[22] The inscription offers a vivid narrative

---

[22] *CIL* 8.2728, 18122 = *ILS* 5795, also edited with a linguistic commentary by Adams (2016), 293–306. On the different facets of the monument, see most extensively Cuomo (2011). On the colonial and postcolonial history of the monument and the reasons for its re-erection in Béjaïa (ancient Saldae, the original destination of the aqueduct), see Cuomo (2011), esp. 156–8.

22 BUILDING IN WORDS

of the surveyor's journey and arrival, analysis of the situation (the tunnelling from both sides of the mountain had apparently gone awry so that both sides had not met in the middle as planned), and the problem's solution by his own competent actions. He also cites a number of letters which further underscore his contribution (*ut lucidius labor meus circa duc(tum) hoc Saldense pareret, aliquas epistulas subieci* (31–3)). In terms of representational strategies, the inscription combines uses of literary language and devices, such as the creation of 'narrative rapidity' in the early section of the text by the use of an asyndetic 'staccato' style, and the poetic transitive use of *fleo* (10–11),[23] with a surplus of technical information and terminology (e.g. *fossuras* (14), *rigorem* (15), *depalatus erat* (19)), probably not readily comprehensible to all of his readers but nonetheless (or precisely for this reason) impressive to its audience.[24]

What Mountain? The Inscription on the Column of Trajan

One of the best-known inscriptions of the ancient world is also an excellent example of an inscription that creates such a fictional memory of construction: the inscription on the base of the Column of Trajan (Figure 1.2):[25]

Senatus populusque Romanus / Imp(eratori) Caesari divi Nervae f(ilio) Nervae / Traiano Aug(usto) Germ(anico) Dacico pontif(ici) / maximo trib(unicia) pot(estate) XVII imp(eratori) VI co(n)s(uli) VI p(atri)

---

[23] Adams (2016), 296 *ad loc.* and 305–6. Thomas (2007), 92, even argues that the inscription 'recalls Herodotus' account of the architect Eupalinus' design for a water conduit for Polycrates in Samos' (Hdt. 3.60).

[24] Adams (2016), *ad loc.* and 305–6. However, Cuomo (2001) rightly points out that the audience would have been the inhabitants of Lambaesis, many of whom were members of the military, and therefore some of the technical terminology, and certainly Nonius Datus's specific function, would have been readily comprehensible to a proportion of the readership (160–1). On technical 'surplus' as a device in representations of construction, see pp. 48–51 on Caesar's Rhine bridge.

[25] *CIL* 6.960 (cf. p. 3070, 3777, 4310) = *ILS* 294. Technically, this inscription should not be classified as a building inscription, but as a dedicatory inscription. On the accepted classifications of Latin inscriptions, see e.g. the overview in Meyer (1973), ch. 4. On the definition of the building inscription and the differences between building and honorary inscriptions, see Saastamoinen (2010), 18–23.

Figure 1.2. Base of the Column of Trajan.
Photo: author.

p(atriae) / ad declarandum quantae altitudinis / mons et locus tant[is oper]ibus sit egestus

The Senate and the People of Rome to the Emperor Caesar Nerva Trajan Augustus, son of the deified Nerva, conqueror in Germania and Dacia, Pontifex Maximus, vested with the tribunician power for the seventeenth

24 BUILDING IN WORDS

time, acclaimed as imperator six times, consul six times, Father of the Nation, to declare how high a mountain had been dug away and the site for such great works.

The exact meaning of the inscription has been much debated, but in any case, it desired the viewer to admire how the site of the forum had been cleared and adapted to its purpose.[26] Here, it is not only the inscription which performs this function of commemoration: through the inscription, the column as a whole becomes a marker of the engineering feat accomplished in reshaping the landscape and building the forum. It has been argued that the inscription's claim must be untruthful, that the mountain mentioned as dug away must have been much smaller than the height of the column suggests.[27] Again, the exact truth of this matter is less relevant here than the fact that this inscription actively creates memories of construction, designed to achieve maximum impact for the monument, rather than (exclusively) record historical fact.

Victory over Stone: The Obelisk in Constantinople

My final example, an excursion into late antiquity, concerns the inscriptions on the base of the Obelisk of Theodosius in Constantinople.[28] Obelisks lend themselves particularly well to the illustration of my argument. The impact of obelisks, in particular, derives to a large extent from their 'madeness'. Transporting and raising them was both immensely difficult and visually spectacular.[29] Therefore, those who had erected obelisks often made a special effort to ask the viewer to imagine the effort involved in transporting

---

[26] On the possible reconstructions of the final line and the different interpretations of the inscription, see e.g. Frere and Lepper (1988), 203–7, with an overview of earlier scholarship, and Settis (1988), 49–56; *tantis operibus* was also read in the eighth or ninth century by the Anonymus Einsiedlensis.

[27] Lancaster (1999), 421. See Meneghini (2009), 117, on the (in any case) massive clearing operation, arguing that 300,000 m³ of material had to be removed for building the forum. One ancient viewer-reader was in any case convinced by the claim of the column's inscription: cf. Cass. Dio 68.16.3 with Settis (1988), 52–3. For the inscription's rhetoric of monumentality, see also Thomas (2014), 60–2.

[28] The inscriptions discussed here, as well as the obelisk relief discussed in the next section and the passage of Ammianus discussed in the subsequent section, reach beyond the chronological scope of the rest of this book. This allows for the extended reflection on obelisks as a prime case of 'madeness', and shows that this Roman rhetoric of making remains powerful in centuries to come.

[29] Cf. DeLaine (2002), 214: 'The erection of an obelisk or of a giant column could provide a public display as entertaining as any show in the arena or circus, and just as indicative of imperial power.' On the difficulties of transportation, see van Tilburg (2007), 83, and Wirsching (2013), 75–129.

MAKING MEMORIES   25

and erecting the obelisk and to include this 'memory' of erection in his appreciation of it.[30]

The Renaissance architect Domenico Fontana's detailed documentation of the transport of an obelisk (originally brought to Rome by Caligula) from the Circus of Nero to the square in front of St Peter's basilica allows us to estimate the spectacular scale of the operations that must have taken place.[31] The raising of the obelisk required 907 men and 75 horses, working 40 cranes.[32] The technical challenges attendant on lifting such a load were considerable. Application of force on all these cranes had to be perfectly coordinated to avoid accidents and successfully raise the obelisk. From Fontana's accounts we gather that a large crowd of spectators gathered to see the obelisk raised, but that complete silence was required on the building site (and enforced by the police) so that communication between the workmen was assured, signals could be heard, and force applied in coordination.[33]

The Obelisk of Theodosius was raised by the emperor Theodosius I in the Hippodrome of Constantinople.[34] The base of the obelisk features a set of reliefs including a depiction of the raising of the obelisk, which will be discussed below, and two inscriptions, one Greek and one Latin, referring to the erection.[35] The Greek inscription runs as follows:

Κίονα τετράπλευρον, ἀεὶ χθονὶ κείμενον ἄχθος / μοῦνος ἀναστῆσαι Θευδόσιος βασιλεὺς / τολμήσας <<Πρόκλος>> (!) ἐπεκέκλετο καὶ τόσος ἔστη / κίων ἠελίοις ἐν τριάκοντα δύο

It was only the Emperor Theodosius who dared to raise the four-sided column, which always lay as a burden on the earth. He called upon Proclus,[36] and so great a column stood erect in thirty-two suns.

---

[30] Biermann (2013) makes a comparable argument for the movement of the Vatican obelisk in 1586 and Fontana's documentation of the process as a 'Rezeptionsanleitung'. On Fontana, see n. 31.

[31] Fontana (1590), most easily accessible in the facsimile edition of Conrad (1987). See Iversen (1968), 19–46, on the provenance, history, and inscriptions of the obelisk. Iversen establishes that the obelisk was transported to Rome by Caligula, *pace* Byvanck (1960), 311. For further details on the obelisk's different inscriptions, see Alföldy (1990).

[32] Fontana (1590), fol. 14r.

[33] Fontana (1590), fol. 13r. Biermann (2013) analyses Fontana's rhetorical strategies in this passage (124).

[34] Thorough archaeological studies of the obelisk are Bruns (1935) and Kiilerich (1998).

[35] Greek: *CIG* 4.8612 also transmitted as *Anth. Gr.* 9.682; Latin: *CIL* 3.737 (cf. p. 990) = *CLE* 286 = *ILS* 821. For the position of the inscriptions, see Figure 1.4.

[36] Proculus-Proclus-Proklos was the urban prefect of Constantinople (AD 389–392). The name in the inscription must originally have read Πρόκλῳ (or possibly Πρόκλον), but the name was erased after the fall and execution of Proculus in AD 392, and re-entered incorrectly after his rehabilitation through Arcadius in AD 396. Πρόκλος is grammatically impossible and does not fit into the metre. See Rebenich (1989), 154 n. 8. In the Latin inscription, too, *Proclo* was first erased and then re-entered.

Figure 1.3. Latin inscription on the base of the Obelisk of Theodosius.
Photo: Prioryman, CC BY-SA 3.0, https://commons.wikimedia.org/w/index.php?curid=12067146.

The Latin inscription, on the opposite side of the obelisk base (Figure 1.3), runs:

> Difficilis quondam dominis parere serenis / iussus et extinctis palmam portare tyrannis / omnia Theodosio cedunt subolique perenni / ter denis sic victus ego domitusque diebus / iudice sub <<Proclo>> su[pera]s elatus ad auras

> Though once troublesome, I was ordered to obey the Serene Masters and to bear the palm of victory over the extinguished tyrants. All things yield to Theodosius and his everlasting offspring. I was conquered and subdued in three times ten days, and under the prefecture of Proclus I was lifted high into the heavens.

Both of these verse inscriptions ask the viewer-reader to admire not the obelisk itself but the achievement of raising it. The Latin inscription explicitly states that there were earlier difficulties: *difficilis quondam*. This expression may refer to earlier, abandoned plans of Constantius to transport the obelisk to Constantinople. He died before the obelisk could be transported from

MAKING MEMORIES 27

Alexandria, and thus it lay uselessly on the shores of Alexandria for a long time before it could finally be transported to Constantinople.[37] This situation is also referred to by ἀεὶ χθονὶ κείμενον ἄχθος.[38]

Both inscriptions, Latin and Greek, cite the short amount of time necessary for raising the obelisk as a particular achievement (even though they disagree on the exact number of days).[39] The Greek inscription also makes no mention of the *tyranni*, focusing instead exclusively on the daring of Theodosius and the efficiency of Proculus in raising the long-neglected obelisk within thirty-two days.

According to the Latin inscription, the intention was that the obelisk should serve as some kind of victory monument over the *extincti tyranni*. Most scholars have read this as a reference to recent events, namely Theodosius's victory over the usurpers Maximus and Victor.[40] The inscription thus frames the eventual raising of the obelisk under Theodosius, executed under the supervision of Proculus, as a double victory: while the obelisk now commemorates the victory over the *exctincti tyranni*, its raising itself is also depicted as a victory, not over enemies, but over the heavy block of granite, which used to be defiant but has now been subdued (*cedunt . . . victus . . . domitus*). That the obelisk itself is made to speak in the first person about its raising and the imperial victory is a powerful gesture of control.

There is a model for the deployment of an obelisk as a monument of imperial victory. In the Circus Maximus in Rome, Constantius II had erected an

---

[37] Wrede (1966), esp. 191, who argues convincingly that *difficilis quondam* does not refer to earlier, failed attempts at *raising* the obelisk. We do know that the obelisk was broken, possibly at some point between its selection in Egypt and its raising in Constantinople (about two-fifths of the original height are now missing), cf. Iversen (1972), 9–10. It is also just possible that the inscription is alluding to this accident.

[38] Also in a letter of the emperor Julian (AD 361–363) to the Alexandrians: Julian. *Ep.* 58 (Hertlein). He writes of the obelisk lying abandoned by the sea, and suggests bringing it to Constantinople as Constantius had originally intended. Whether the transport took place in his reign or only under Theodosius, as Wrede (1966), 191, suggests, remains unclear. Cf. Parker (2014), 281–2.

[39] Cameron (1966), 34, has speculated that *domitusque* is a mistake of the stone-cutter, and should originally have read *duobusque*.

[40] They had been vanquished by Theodosius in AD 388. Iversen (1972), in a suggestion that has not generally been accepted, identifies the *tyranni* as Maxentius and Decentius (which would make the *domini sereni* Constantinus II and possibly Constantine). This requires a different punctuation and interpretation of the Latin text, taking *iussus* as a participle (and not a finite verb, with an unexpressed *sum*, as I have done) with the first line. He translates (12): 'I was formerly reluctant to obey the serene masters, even when ordered to proclaim the victory after the extinction of the tyrants.' On the difficulties of the syntax of the Latin inscription, see Cameron (1966), esp. 35–6.

28 BUILDING IN WORDS

obelisk in 357, as a monument of the victory over the usurper Magnentius.[41] The inscription of this obelisk, which was more than six times as long as the inscription of the obelisk in Constantinople, is now lost, but has been preserved in a Renaissance transcription.[42] Since the obelisk in Constantinople is likewise set up in a circus, also functions as a triumphal monument, and also celebrates a victory over usurpers, it is a sound assumption that the later obelisk follows the model of the earlier one.[43] A comparison of the two inscriptions supports such an assumption:[44] thematically, the Latin inscription of the Theodosian obelisk covers the same points as the Roman inscription, condensed into only four lines: the enormous difficulties of transportation and raising (Theodosius: 1; Constantius 7–9, 17–18), the triumph of mastering the obelisk (Theodosius 4–5; Constantius 3–4, 10–13) and the link between this triumph and that over the usurper(s) (Theodosius 2–3; Constantius 1–4, 20–4). The closest direct parallel is *sed quod non crederet ullus / tantae molis opus superas consurgere in auras* (17–18) on the obelisk of Constantius, and *iudice sub Proclo superas elatus ad auras* (5) on the Theodosian obelisk.[45] By means of the inscription, the raising of the obelisk in Constantinople is tied to that in Rome more than thirty years earlier, and the triumphal monument in Constantinople is positioned as an achievement matching the earlier one in Rome.[46]

Even to those readers of the Roman obelisk inscription who were not highly educated, the allusion to the opening of Vergil's *Aeneid* in line 18 must have been obvious: *tantae molis opus* recalls, of course, *tantae molis erat Romanam condere gentem* (Verg. *Aen.* 1.33), one of the most famous lines of the *Aeneid*, which summarizes the entire poem's theme in one phrase. The raising of the obelisk is set up as an achievement comparable

[41] A description of the transportation and raising of the obelisk is provided by Ammianus Marcellinus, 17.4.1–15, discussed later in this chapter (pp. 53–61).

[42] *CIL* 6.1163 = *CLE* 279 (cf. *CLE* 268 = *CIL* 10.1863 for a preserved fragment). The inscription, consisting of twenty-five Latin hexameter lines, was recorded in 1589, when the obelisk was moved to the Lateran: Mercati (1589), 290–311.

[43] Kiilerich (1998), 22–3, on the multiple obelisk-circus ensembles which spring up in imitation of the Circus Maximus model in the fourth century.

[44] See also Wrede (1966), 189–90; Kiilerich (1998), 28.

[45] For other parallels, see Kiilerich (1988), 28. Note also especially the use of *cedere* in lines 10–11 (Constantius) and 3 (Theodosius). Cameron (1966), 35, calls the phrases 'conventional to inscriptions on obelisks'—overlooking, in my view, that obelisks and the inscriptions on them were in no way conventional; rather, they were exceptional, high-profile imperial monuments.

[46] For intertextuality in inscriptions, cf. Saastamoinen (2010), 222–3, on North African building inscriptions which seem to refer to the Column of Trajan inscription (on which see pp. 21–4): '... famous inscriptions were imitated; in other words, building inscriptions too can be intertextually complex texts' (223).

MAKING MEMORIES 29

to that of Aeneas. The second half of the line, which is also taken over by the Theodosian obelisk, recalls Latin epic poetry, too. Rather than a specific reference to a particular line, this phrase generally 'sounds' Vergilian or at least epic (the line-ending *ad auras* is found sixteen times in Vergil alone, the phrase *superas . . . ad auras* is found twice in the *Aeneid* and once in Statius's *Thebaid*).[47] The same effect is achieved by the phrase *iudice sub Proclo* (5), which is perhaps loosely inspired by Ov. *Met.* 11.156 (*iudice sub Tmolo*). Such epic 'tags' are not, in my opinion, a sign that an incompetent poet wrote the inscription.[48] Rather, drawing on the language of Roman epic is a means of invoking the authority of these texts while pushing the boundaries of the epigraphic medium.

To summarize: when building inscriptions create memories of construction, their particular challenge is to do so within very limited space, and their representations of the process are necessarily very condensed. A basic building inscription stylizes and simplifies heavily. By providing information in one or more additional categories (such as speed, money, extent of restoration, workmanship) the memory of construction it produces becomes increasingly specific. But the freedom of the epigraphic medium can be expanded even further. When boundaries between literature and epigraphy are elided, strategies which we would expect to find primarily in other media appear: dramatic representations of engineering as a victory in war and the use of intertextuality in a competition between monuments and for claiming poetic authority.

Visual Memories

Inscribing a building is one way of reminding a viewer of the process of making it, but this can also be achieved by means of images of construction. Depictions of building in progress, displayed on monuments, also encourage viewers to consider the process that has led to their construction.[49]

---

[47] *superas ad auras*: Verg. *Georg.* 4.486; *Aen.* 6.128; Stat. *Theb.* 1.295.

[48] *pace* Cameron (1966), 35–6. On the use of Vergilian phrases in Latin verse inscriptions, see the study of Hoogma (1959).

[49] Representations of technical processes in different artistic media were common both in Greece and Rome (for an overview with bibliography, see Ulrich (2008) and Sapirstein (2018)). Significantly, however, depictions of the process of *construction* are limited to the Roman sphere (Ulrich (2008), 47–8). For a diachronic survey of artistic depictions of construction, see Tutton (2021).

30 BUILDING IN WORDS

Figure 1.4. Base of the Obelisk of Theodosius.
Photo: Dennis Jarvis from Halifax, Canada - Turkey-03233, CC BY-SA 2.0, https://commons.wikimedia.org/w/index.php?curid=66987705.

Seeing It Happen: The Theodosian Obelisk Again

The base of the Theodosian obelisk, the inscriptions on which I discussed previously, also featured a series of reliefs on all four sides of its base, on two levels (Figure 1.4).[50] The reliefs, like the inscriptions, encourage the viewer

---

[50] See Bruns (1935), Abb. 36.

MAKING MEMORIES   31

to consider the raising of the obelisk, while emphasizing a different aspect of this achievement: the visual spectacle of the erection. The top level shows four different scenes on the four sides. All are divided horizontally into two tiers through the depiction of a balustrade, and feature in the centre of the top level a booth where members of the imperial family stand. Around them on the top tier stand nobles and dignitaries; in the bottom tier of the reliefs, lower-ranking personages. The lower part of the base is decorated on the south-east and north-west sides with the two inscriptions discussed earlier. The south-west and north-east sides are decorated with relief panels.[51]

The top part of the base on the south-east side shows the imperial family watching a dance performance (depicted in the bottom tier of the same panel) in the Hippodrome.[52] The north-west side shows the reception of different groups of barbarians (including Germans, Africans, and Persians), who come bearing presents for the emperor.[53] They are shown kneeling in the bottom half of the relief, with the imperial family and nobles pictured above them. The inscriptions discussed earlier are found below both of these scenes.

The top-level reliefs on the south-west and north-east sides are closely connected with the relief panels on the block below. On the south-west side, the relief on the top part of the base shows the imperial court watching a circus performance,[54] which is depicted on the block below.[55] Several phases of the race are shown in the one panel: in the bottom half, a carriage-race; in the top half, two phases in a horse-race and a presentation ceremony. The obelisk is depicted several times in its position on the spina of the circus.[56]

On the north-east side (Figure 1.5), the top-level relief, too, shows the imperial court in the role of spectators.[57] The spectacle they are watching is again shown on the block below. This time, however, it is the raising of the

---

[51] For a new interpretation of the imperial reliefs, see Rebenich (1991), who suggests new identifications for some of the members of the imperial family depicted and reads the base in the context of Theodosian propaganda: Theodosius and his family are shown to rule the entire empire, while Valentinian II (the Augustus in the west) is shown to be dependent and subordinate.

[52] The respective dating of the different relief panels has been a source of debate. Byvanck (1960), 16, for example argues that the relief has been altered and the dancers added later. See Rebenich (1991), 452–3 for an overview of different suggestions. He himself makes a good case for the unity of the ensemble.

[53] Bruns (1935), Abb. 37–43, description 36–43.

[54] Bruns (1935), Abb. 62–9, description 53–8.

[55] Bruns (1935), Abb. 70–6, description 59–61.

[56] For the placing of the obelisk in the middle of the spina, see Wrede (1966), 187–8.

[57] Bruns (1935), Abb. 44–50, description 43–7.

Figure 1.5. Obelisk of Theodosius, north-east side.
Photo: Diego Delso, CC BY-SA 4.0, https://commons.wikimedia.org/w/index.php?curid=8538566.

obelisk itself that they are following (Figure 1.6).[58] The panel showing the raising is unfortunately badly damaged, since a fountain was attached to this

---

[58] Bruns (1935), Abb. 51–61, description 47–53. Kiilerich (1998), 69 interprets the scene not as the raising but as the transport of the obelisk into the arena, which does not sit easily with her own conclusion that '(t)his composition is like an accompanying illustration to the texts of the inscription, a pictorial narrative of the work procedure' (69), since the inscriptions only mention the raising, but not the transport of the obelisk.

Figure 1.6. Obelisk of Theodosius, obelisk-raising scene.
Photo: Derzsi Elekes Andor, CC BY-SA 4.0, https://commons.wikimedia.org/w/index.php?curid=36978670.

side of the obelisk not long after construction, which required a pipe to run vertically through the surface of the relief.[59] It is horizontally divided into two tiers.

On the right-hand side in the top tier, the obelisk is lying on the ground, in the process of being raised. From the obelisk, thick ropes run to the left-hand side, to the pulleys depicted in the top and bottom tier of the relief. Four men are engaged in turning each of the pulleys to raise the obelisk (Figure 1.7). In the centre of the bottom tier, the relief shows a group of musicians. Bruns argues that the gap left by the pipe leading to the fountain would originally have been filled by a flute-player.[60] To the right in the bottom tier, a group of men is shown perhaps freeing the now erect obelisk from the ropes and coverings necessary for raising it, or engaged in a celebration in connection with the recent erection of the obelisk.[61]

The ensemble of inscriptions and reliefs on the base of the obelisk in several ways focuses the viewer's attention on the act of raising the obelisk. While the inscriptions ask the viewer to recall how quickly the obelisk was subdued and raised, the visual depiction adds the element of the spectacular to the representation.[62] The erection of the obelisk is inserted into an ensemble of state occasions, and it is viewed by the imperial court with the same attention as a

---

[59] Bruns (1935), 16–18, 75, 85–6.
[60] Bruns (1935), 50.
[61] The first is suggested by Bruns (1935), 51, the second by Kiilerich (1998), 71–2.
[62] Cf. Carey (2003), 87–8, although she seems to confuse the different sides of the base, claiming that the figures shown above the obelisk are in fact watching a horse race.

Figure 1.7. Obelisk of Theodosius, detail of capstan in obelisk-raising scene.
Photo: Dosseman, CC BY-SA 4.0, https://commons.wikimedia.org/w/index.php?curid=76721423.

games display, or a state reception of foreign emissaries.[63] Raising an obelisk thus becomes no less a display of imperial power than the public humbling of barbarian peoples. The relief shows different stages of the erection, actively encouraging viewers to picture the impressive spectacle and to identify their own act of viewing the relief with that of the depicted viewers gazing at the spectacle of the obelisk.

The Tomb of the Haterii

Visual representations of construction in progress are found not only on such pioneering, high-profile, spectacular edifices. They can also be found on the walls of private tombs, such as the tomb of the Haterii and the tomb of Trebius Iustus. Such building scenes on tomb interiors are usually classified with other scenes of craftsmanship in tomb art and are interpreted as relating

---

[63] Technically, Theodosius was not in Constantinople to oversee the erection of the obelisk (Rebenich (1991), 451–2), but he is nevertheless represented as viewing the process in the relief: Iversen (1972), 16, with n. 5, and Rebenich (1991), 470–1.

to the lives and achievements of the tombs' owners.[64] While this is their most important function, I hope to show that the depiction of construction in funerary contexts, too, can participate in the process of 'making memories'. They allow a finished edifice to speak about the process of its creation, and the memory of this creation becomes part of the viewer's experience of the completed building.[65]

The so-called Haterii relief (Figure 1.8) was found in the context of a Roman tomb building on the Via Labicana.[66] It was discovered during an excavation in 1848, along with other sculptural decoration.[67] The documentation of the excavation does not allow us to establish the exact location of the relief within the tomb building or precinct.[68]

The relief shows a tomb building to the right side of the panel. The tomb is richly decorated in figural and ornamental relief. Its interior is depicted in a separate scene on the roof of the building. To the left stands a large crane, which rises taller than the building to the right. It is operated by five men on a treadmill and two more holding ropes. Two workmen have climbed up the arm of the crane, the top of which is decorated with a basket.

The crucial question which faces interpreters of this relief is that of the relation between the crane on the one hand and the tomb on the other, since it cannot be argued that the crane is actually engaged in constructing the tomb (the tomb is finished and already houses the deceased Hateria, while the crane is not lifting any visible load). Some have interpreted the crane and tomb as a unified composition, generally relating both of them to the afterlife of the owner of the tomb. In such interpretations, the crane becomes part of a ritual connected with the tomb or the deceased.[69] In

---

[64] On representations of the deceased's profession in tomb art, see Zimmer (1982).

[65] I am confining my analysis to the tomb of the Haterii, but the same approach might also fruitfully be applied to the tomb of Trebius Iustus. Rea (2004) is a full publication of the tomb. See esp. Bisconti (2004), 133–48, on the decorative programme.

[66] Museo Gregorio Profano, Rome, inv. nb. 9998. Sinn and Freyberger (1996), nb. 6 (51–9) and Tafel 11–16.

[67] For a catalogue of all items associated with the Tomb of the Haterii, see Sinn and Freyberger (1996), ch. 6. An attempt at a holistic interpretation of the sculptural decoration is Leach (2006).

[68] On the excavation of the tomb and the available documentation, see Sinn and Freyberger (1996), 11–21. For details of a brief re-excavation in 1970, see Coarelli (1979). On placement cf. Leach (2006), esp. 5, 11.

[69] For example, Jensen (1978) has interpreted the basket on top of the crane as 'two *likna* . . . joined together into a conical whole for the obvious reason of containing an erect phallus' (182), with the crane corresponding to *machina* mentioned in Livy's description of the Bacchanalia as carrying worshippers away to secret caves (Livy 39.13.13) The crane becomes 'the means of transportation into the next world'. Ambrosetti (1960), too, relates the crane to the afterlife, interpreting the basket at the top of the crane as containing an eagle of apotheosis, about to be released.

36 BUILDING IN WORDS

Figure 1.8. Tomb-crane relief from the tomb of the Haterii, Vatican (Museo Gregoriano Profano), Rome (cat. 9997).
© 2021. Photo Werner Forman Archive/Scala, Florence.

my view, the most likely explanation for the decoration of the crane is that it relates to a ritual or celebration associated with the completion of a building project.[70]

[70] Adam (1984), 49.

MAKING MEMORIES   37

Others read the crane as virtually unrelated to the tomb building.[71] They argue that, while the representation of the tomb refers to the death and afterlife of the deceased Hateria and her children, the crane relates only to the professional achievement of the owner of the tomb. It seems probable that the *pater familias* of the family buried in this tomb actually worked in the building industry—we know that he was called Haterius, and an inscription has been found elsewhere which mentions a *redemptor* (a building contractor) by the name of Q. Haterius Tychicus.[72] It is therefore a plausible assumption that the crane relates to the professional life and achievement of Haterius. Ownership of sophisticated building equipment like a crane was crucial for the economic success of a builder, and the detailed depiction of the crane shows how seriously the artist must have taken its technical function.[73] While I agree that the crane relates to Haterius's trade, I do not believe that the representations, directly juxtaposed, of an instrument necessary for construction and a completed building should be regarded as unrelated. Instead, I argue that the crane relief is involved in a sophisticated creation of memories of construction. The construction scene functions on several levels, and the ensemble of relief sculpture and surrounding tomb architecture opens up more general questions about the workings of commemoration.

On one level, the crane in action represents and commemorates the effort involved in creating the tomb, depicted next to it in its finished state. The conflation of construction and constructed in a single image represents the monumental achievement in its entirety.[74] On a second level, the crane relief should also be considered in the context of the remaining tomb decoration. Besides two portrait busts, one of Haterius and one of his wife, the tomb also contained the extremely famous panel relief which depicts five

[71] Sinn and Freyberger (1996), 56, argue that 'der Kran steht . . . völlig isoliert neben dem fertigen Grabbau', and deny an 'inhaltliche Verbindung von Kran und Bau' (58 n. 63). Cf. Ulrich (2008), 37: 'Yet, despite the plethora of details, the image of the crane is incidental to the overall composition.'

[72] *CIL* 6.607, cf. 30801b. On the identification of the owner of the tomb with this Haterius, see Coarelli (1979), 266–8. Further corroboration is provided by the parallel of a Capuan relief panel, decorated with a crane employed to raise a column of a *proscaenium*, and bearing the following inscription (*CIL* 10.3821 = *ILS* 3662): *Lucceius Peculiaris redemptor proscaeni / ex biso fecit.* On the Capuan relief, see De Nuccio and Ungaro (2002), 515–17 with select bibliography.

[73] See DeLaine (2006), 248 on builders' technical equipment. The detailed depiction of the crane with its system of pulleys corresponds in almost every respect to Vitruvius's description of a crane in *De arch.* 10.2.5–7. On the correspondences and differences, see Benndorf and Schöne (1867), 216–19.

[74] Cf. Thomas (2007), 184–5, who considers the relief in the context of his investigation of 'monumentality': 'Although apparently already complete, the building is also shown still under construction, with cranes operated by small putti, to emphasise the role of architecture in creating a monument'.

Figure 1.9. Relief of buildings in Rome from the tomb of the Haterii, Vatican (Museo Gregoriano Profano), Rome (cat. 9998).
© 2021. Photo Scala, Florence.

buildings in Flavian Rome (Figure 1.9). They may well be building projects in which Haterius was professionally involved.[75] The juxtaposition of two ways of commemorating a monument which is present within the crane relief—showing its finished state and creating an awareness of its construction—returns in the juxtaposition of the crane relief and the Rome panel.[76] The depiction of the finished buildings emphasizes their perpetuity and lasting achievement, while the crane asks the viewer to remember or envisage the spectacular achievement of erecting these buildings in the first place.

On a third level, the crane in action also impacts the way in which a potential visitor to the tomb might consider not only the depicted, but also

---

[75] This is the most widely accepted interpretation of the relief: Sinn and Freyberger (1996), 71. For a different view, see e.g. Leach (2006), 11.

[76] Unfortunately, we do not know how the two reliefs were placed in relation to each other inside or outside the tomb building. The fact that they were found on different dates might indicate that they were found in different areas during the excavation, but this remains mere speculation. Cf. Sinn and Freyberger (1993), 22.

the *actual* tomb complex. The tomb depicted on the crane relief is generally considered to be a model, or at least an idealized version, of the two-storey tomb itself with its surrounding gardens.[77] Coarelli has argued that Haterius, as a *redemptor*, erected his family tomb himself, with his own workforce.[78] He commemorates his own achievement in constructing it, not only to celebrate his technical proficiency in his profession, but also to represent his own participation in the process of monumentalizing memory. The tomb itself is a memorial for Haterius and his family. Through the addition of the self-referential crane relief, it also becomes a memorial of Haterius's achievements as a builder, both of important public buildings in Rome, and of his own family tomb. It thus becomes a monument to Haterius's *making* of a monument, a commemoration of commemoration.

Roman Foundations: The Basilica Aemilia Frieze

In the case of the Constantinople obelisk and the Haterii relief, the connection between the image of construction and the monument itself is beyond doubt. In both cases, the building projects represented were those which the reliefs adorned in their finished state. I now turn to two examples where the relation between the construction scene and its built context is, at first sight, less clear.

The so-called Basilica Aemilia stood on the north side of the Forum Romanum, between the curia and the site later occupied by the temple of Antoninus Pius and Faustina.[79] During their excavations of the basilica, Boni and Bartoli discovered 280 fragments of a frieze, sculpted in Pentelic marble, which together make up 22 metres in length.[80]

---

[77] See Sinn and Freyberger (1993), 33, and Wrede (1981), 90–1. The original layout and architecture of the tomb are difficult to reconstruct on the basis of the excavations so far conducted. As far as we know, the tomb might have had a less symmetrical layout than the representation suggests, but it did correspond to the type of the two-storey tomb temple which inspired the relief carver. Other tombs provide parallels for this sort of visual documentation of the building on or within the tomb: e.g. detailed descriptions of the tomb in inscriptions (cf. *CIL* 6.15593 from the tomb of Claudia Semne, on which see Wrede (1971) and (1981), 83–5, or even maps of the tomb layout on marble slabs (Gregori (1987/1988), esp. 181–3; Toynbee (1971), 98–9; and Meneghini and Santangeli Valenzani (2006), 30–4).

[78] Coarelli (1979), 268–9.

[79] The results of the major project of the German Archaeological Institute on the Basilica Aemilia have been published in Ertel, Freyberger, Lipps, and Bitterer (2007); Ertel and Freyberger (2007); Lipps (2011); and Freyberger and Ertel (2016).

[80] On the excavation of the Basilica Aemilia and the discovery of the fragments, see Bartoli (1950), 289–94. Major works on the frieze with detailed descriptions are Carettoni (1961); Furuhagen (1961); Simon (1966); Kränzle (1991); Ertel and Freyberger (2007), 118–29; and Freyberger and

Figure 1.10. Building scene from the Basilica Aemilia frieze, Curia Iulia, Rome.

Photo: author. Courtesy of the Ministero per i beni e le attività culturali e per il turismo, Parco Archeologico del Colosseo.

The frieze depicts scenes related to the early history of Rome, among them the foundation of a city, which has been interpreted as Rome or Lavinium (Figure 1.10).[81] The scene shows a half-built ashlar masonry wall and three workmen who are engaged in constructing it. The figure of one of these, on the far left, is badly damaged, only his legs remaining. Another one, to his right, is standing behind the wall, only visible from the arms upwards. He is turned towards the right and towards another workman, who is standing in front of the wall and facing left. The workman on the right is carrying a stone on his shoulders, which he appears to be passing to his colleague behind the wall, who is extending his right arm to receive it. On the far left, a

---

Ertel (2016). The frieze is currently housed in the Curia Iulia. It is possible that the frieze continued around the entire nave along a length of 184 metres, in which case our fragments only make up one-eighth of the original length, but it has also been argued that the 'frieze' actually consisted of separate relief panels: Ertel and Freyberger (2007), 118–21, with figs. 11 and 12; Freyberger and Ertel (2016), 70–74.

[81] In the Curia Iulia, Rome. Capelli (1993) fig. 1; Carettoni (1961), 16–21. Simon (1966), 834–43, connects all scenes with the legendary foundation of the city of Rome and the reign of Romulus. Others have argued for a broader scope, connecting some of the scenes with the saga of Aeneas (Carettoni (1961); Furuhagen (1961)). Albertson (1990) argues for a relation between each scene and an event of the Roman calendar commemorating the early history of Rome, making the frieze a figured calendar.

Figure 1.11. Building scene from the Esquiline frieze, Museo Nazionale Romano, Rome.

Photo: author. Courtesy of the Ministero per i beni e le attività culturali e per il turismo, Museo Nazionale Romano.

female figure is supervising the building process—most likely a divinity who is favourably disposed towards the foundation process, or the personified city herself, as may be suggested by the mural crown she wears.

In terms of the general layout of the scene, the postures of the persons depicted, and their arrangement, the image closely resembles the depictions of two city foundations on the so-called Esquiline frieze (Figure 1.11), most likely the foundations of Lavinium and Alba Longa.[82] The construction scene on the frieze, then, seems to fit within a conventional repertoire of mythohistorical scenes of early Rome. But one interesting feature should give us pause. The man standing behind the wall and receiving a block of stone seems to have been given portrait features. It has been suggested that the features are those of a member of the Aemilian *gens* under whose auspices the Basilica was restored in the first century BC.[83] If we accept this interpretation,

---

[82] In the Museo Nazionale Romano, Rome. Capelli (1998).
[83] Different dates have been suggested for the frieze and different identifications for the member of the *gens Aemilia* depicted: Gaggiotti (1996), 17–18, suggests a restoration in 80/79 BC and argues for

42 BUILDING IN WORDS

then the insertion of the portrait into the scene of city building allows the builder of the basilica to insert himself into the early history of Rome, and to stress the ancient origins of the family of the Aemilii and their relation to Aeneas himself.[84]

Furthermore, the patron's involvement in the process of construction in the decoration also relates directly to his responsibility for the construction of the building which bears the frieze. The image shows the man responsible for the reconstruction of the basilica personally engaged in the act of construction, and thereby asks the viewer to consider his involvement in the erection of the building bearing the frieze. This link between the depicted mythical construction and contemporary construction, apart from the portrait features of the builder, might also have been supported by other, now lost building scenes.[85] A fragment of one of the lost scenes shows a mechanical lifting device for heavy stone blocks.[86] Such devices were usually only depicted in representations of contemporary construction, and only very rarely in scenes depicting the mythical past.[87] This contemporary touch in one of the other construction scenes thus supports the connection between the depicted construction and the contemporary rebuilding of the Basilica.

The image manipulates the viewer's memory of construction in several ways. Showing the noble patron himself engaged in hands-on construction work uncomplicates questions of agency and ownership between patron, architect, and financier (who, depending on the phase of restoration, may have been Augustus), visually communicating the direct involvement of Aemilius in the process of restoring the basilica. In this respect, the representation is comparable to the shorthand *fecit* of building descriptions. Second, inserting the construction scene into a narrative of the early history of Rome raises the status of the foundation and reconstruction of the basilica.

---

an identification of the figure with M. Aemilius Lepidus, under whose censorship the original basilica may have been built in the second century BC. Capelli (1993) dates the frieze to the 50s BC, and identifies the builder, and hence the portrait, with either L. Aemilius Paulus or P. Aemilius Lepidus (69). Ertel and Freyberger (2007), 121–9, and Freyberger and Ertel (2016), 74–6, argue for an Augustan dating of the frieze, connecting it to a reconstruction of the basilica after it had been destroyed by a fire in 14 BC: see Ertel, Freyberger, Lipps, and Bitterer (2007), 493–524, on the dating and history of the basilica. The validity of my observations does not depend on dating the frieze to a particular phase of the building's history.

[84] Capelli (1993).

[85] Kränzle (1991), 115, argues that the fragments of building scenes have to belong to at least four different city foundations.

[86] In the Museo Nazionale Romano, Rome, inv. nb. 3174. Carettoni (1961), 19–20 with figs. 15–17; Kränzle (1991), 43.

[87] Kränzle (1991), 43.

MAKING MEMORIES 43

The Aemilian act of (re-)foundation is to be ranked with the most important moments in Roman history, and becomes part of the foundation story of Rome.[88]

Getting Construction Organized:
The Column of Trajan Again

For my final example in this section, I return to the Column of Trajan (the inscription of which I discussed earlier) and its famous spiral frieze depicting Trajan's two campaigns against Dacia. Any viewer looking at the column and its reliefs from any vantage point very soon comes across a depiction of construction in progress. Lehmann-Hartleben has calculated that one in ten figures on the column is engaged in construction (of camps, walls, boats, etc.),[89] and the frieze shows as many scenes of unfinished camps under construction as of completed camps in use.[90] Even taking into account the much-discussed problems of visibility, several scenes of construction would have been visible to any viewer.[91]

The standard explanation for the frequency of scenes of construction in progress is that they draw the viewer's attention to the engineering prowess and technical superiority of Roman soldiers, and are part of the column's representation of war as an ordered operation of efficiency[92]—a convincing interpretation, especially since the column strategically juxtaposes the construction of Roman camps and the destruction of Dacian buildings, using the interplay between them to stress Roman superiority. Dacians may be shown fighting, but not engaged in construction: building is the victor's prerogative.[93]

---

[88] Cf. DeLaine (2002), who argues that this scene, especially in a basilica that 'embodied the civilizing role of law in Roman society' symbolizes 'the foundation of a civilised, urban community; . . . the building of the walls, the symbolic barriers between the savage uncontrolled wilderness and the settled, orderly life of the citizen . . .' (220).

[89] Lehmann-Hartleben (1926), 39.

[90] Coulston (1990), 40–1.

[91] I assume that a viewer of the column can make out what is happening in the scenes in the lowest spirals, while the continuation of similarly detailed relief all the way up the column mainly creates the impression of 'surplus': see Brilliant (1984), 96. Some sections of the frieze could also be viewed from the galleries of the buildings flanking the column, usually called 'libraries' but in fact of unclear function: Meneghini (2009), 146–51; Claridge (2007), 82–4, who considers them 'auditoria-cum-honorary statue galleries'. On the difficulties of viewing, see Veyne (1988); Settis (1991); Huet (1996). On strategies of arrangement, storytelling and visual 'reading' extensively, see Settis (1989), 107–241.

[92] See e.g. Rossi (1978); Davies (2004), 132–3; and Wolfram Thill (2010), who further develops this interpretation.

[93] For a further exploration of the effect of this juxtaposition see pp. 201–212. The only exception (scene LXVII) is a scene of Dacians cutting down timber for a fortification: Coarelli (2000), 119,

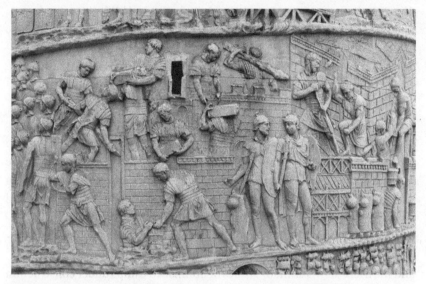

Figure 1.12. Scenes XI–XIII, spiral relief of the Column of Trajan.
Photo: Anger, Neg. D-DAI-Rom 91.155.

However, the construction scenes on the Column of Trajan also have another purpose. They visually evoke the process of the creation of the very monument the viewer is contemplating, as well as of the architectural complex in its entirety. The prominence of construction in the scheme of the relief prompts the viewer to envisage the engineering achievement and the amount of manual labour that lies behind the carving of the relief, the erection of the column, and of course the entire Trajanic forum complex.

The reliefs do not, of course, afford the viewer an adequate record of what the construction of the forum really looked like. They are representations of camp-building, not forum- and column-building. However, they manage visually to link themselves to the construction of the forum, and thus also impact on the viewer's 'memory' of the construction of the complex. This will become clear if we consider one of the many construction scenes in detail. Scenes XI–XIII in the numbering of Cichorius (Figure 1.12) are particularly well suited to such a close analysis, since they are located in the second spiral from the base, and can therefore easily be viewed in significant detail from

pl. 75; Frere and Lepper (1988), 105–8; Wolfram Thill (2010), 38. However, the Dacians are there represented in twisted, tortuous poses, without any appearance of working in coordination—in clear contrast to the much calmer, more restrained poses of Romans engaged in construction or timber-working all over the column.

the ground.[94] Furthermore, the discussion is relevant to most construction scenes, since despite variations in layout and details, they have many typical elements in common.[95]

A group of legionaries is represented in the process of building a fortification. In the foreground, one soldier is standing up to his waist in a trench that he is digging, while another is taking from him a basket filled with earth. The scene of digging is foregrounded in the representation here and elsewhere, and we might connect this prominent representation of digging as an important part and prerequisite of engineering work with the inscription of the column and its emphasis on the clearing of the site for the construction of the forum.[96] Furthermore, Coulston argues that the type of basket used by the diggers on the column (see Figure 1.13) is not inspired, as might be expected, by specialized military equipment, but by the baskets used by labourers on the Trajanic building sites in Rome.[97] We may add that the earth baskets are also very similar to those employed on the Esquiline frieze (Figure 1.11) and in the tomb of Trebius Iustus.[98] The allusion is thus both to building as it looked in Rome, and to its appearance in familiar images of civilian construction.[99]

Behind the diggers, a group of soldiers is engaged in carrying and piling up squared blocks of what might represent either stones or *caespites*, blocks of turf.[100] The fact that there is debate over this point is interesting in itself. It seems logical that *opus quadratum* buildings would have been highly impracticable in the Dacian forests, and that these blocks must therefore represent turf. But if that is so, why do the sculptors choose to depict blocks of

[94] Coarelli (2000), 55, pl. 11; Frere and Lepper (1988), 60–3. I had the opportunity personally to confirm the visibility of the details discussed here from a viewing point directly next to the column base.

[95] Lehmann-Hartleben (1926), 44–6, discusses the correspondence of all construction scenes to similar types, the use of stock figure poses, and the limited number of activities depicted.

[96] The importance of spectacular rock-cutting for imperial display is confirmed by the so-called Pisco Montano at Terracina, where Trajanic engineers cut back a headland to clear a pass for the Via Appia. The process of digging down was marked with Roman numerals, carved into the rock every ten feet, down to the new ground level (*CIL* 10.6849, cf. p. 991, 1019). See Coarelli (1996), fig. 219; Frere and Lepper (1988), 20; Ventre (2004), 126–9. Cf. also DeLaine (2002), 210–11, on the importance of landscaping as a source of wonder in Roman construction.

[97] Coulston (1990), 42.

[98] Rea (2004), 142 and fig. 82.

[99] DeLaine (2002), 220, points out that the depictions allude to mythological wall-building scenes (like those from the Esquiline and the Basilica Aemilia) with their message of civilization through construction.

[100] In favour of stone, see e.g. Lehmann-Hartleben (1926), 42; Coulston (1990), esp. 43–6; and most extensively Wolfram Thill (2010), esp. 29–32. In favour of turf, see e.g. Richmond (1935), 18–21; Frere and Lepper (1988), 62.

Figure 1.13. Digger's basket (detail of Figure 1.12).

turf in a way which corresponds closely to representations of stone construction in comparable images? On the Esquiline frieze (Figure 1.11) and on the Basilica Aemilia frieze (Figure 1.10), men are engaged in erecting city walls from blocks which look very similar, and which are most definitely supposed to represent stones.[101] From the ground, a viewer would only have been able to make out squared blocks being put together. The visual representation of the turf-fortifications is deliberately similar to that of a Roman *opus quadratum* building, and, incidentally, similar also to the high ashlar wall which separated the forum from the Markets of Trajan.[102]

The depiction of construction techniques and processes, especially when the forum and column were recent additions to the cityscape, may have

---

[101] Cf. also the Terracina relief, showing an emperor or high magistrate supervising the construction of a harbour building with marble blocks: see e.g. Coarelli (1996), figs. 210–11, with discussion and bibliography, 434–54. Wolfram Thill (2010) also stresses the 'symbolic importance' (29) of representing fortifications as stone constructions and argues that this presents 'technical skill, cultural sophistication and the permanence of the Roman army in Dacia' (35).

[102] Coulston (1990), 44, believes that the sculptors were unconsciously influenced by the construction work around them, especially of the forum perimeter wall with dry-laid *peperino* tufa blocks. While he argues that this similarity is accidental, I agree with Wolfram Thill (2010), 35: 'The choice probably had little to do with confusion and much more to do with a conscious desire to harness the evocative power of that method of construction.'

MAKING MEMORIES 47

triggered actual memories of the time when the forum and column were under construction.[103] But they do more than that: the reliefs also actively *construct* a memory of the building process, manipulating and overlaying already existing recollections of the building site of the forum or encouraging viewers to envisage such a building history while viewing the forum.

The reliefs present the building process in a heavily stylized form. Legionaries work together in ordered small groups, their poses repeating themselves in regular intervals. The overwhelming impression of coordination, teamwork, and order carries òver into the viewer's imagination of the building process. The stylization is also visible in the simplifications which the conventions of Roman relief sculpture allow the sculptor. Just as on the Basilica Aemilia frieze and the Esquiline frieze, the builders lift blocks of 'stone' alone and with apparent ease. The less attractive aspects of building, the hard manual labour and the possible danger attached to lifting heavy loads, are glossed over in the representation of effortless wall-building on the column.

The emperor Trajan appears fifty-nine times on the column, and is often shown supervising the building works. As on the Basilica Aemilia frieze, this creates an impression of direct involvement of the emperor in the building process. Furthermore, the emphasis on *viewing* the process of building, similar to the spectating imperial court in the obelisk relief, encourages the viewer to consider the spectacular aspect and visual impact of the process of construction.

Like the Constantinople obelisk, the Column of Trajan thus combines two different media for the representation of construction: an inscription and relief sculpture. The inscription desired the viewer to admire how the site of the forum had been cleared and adapted to its purpose. The reliefs, with the prevalence of scenes of construction in progress, further nuance the viewers' image of constructing, by asking them to visualize the process of construction, to mentally re-enact the coordinated effort of thousands of workmen which so speedily produced the magnificent forum complex.[104]

---

[103] On the construction of the column, see Lancaster (1999); on that of the markets, Lancaster (1998) and Lancaster (2000). According to the Fasti Ostienses, the column was dedicated in AD 113, the forum in AD 112. Even if the reliefs were carved under Hadrian, as Claridge (1993) suggests, the construction of the forum complex would still have been within the living memory of most viewers of the relief. However, Claridge's view has not generally been accepted and is rejected e.g. by Coarelli (2000), 22, on the basis of coin evidence. Cf. Claridge (2007) for a reply to Coarelli's objections.

[104] The combined effect of the inscription and the scenes of engineering on the frieze are also noted by Seelentag (2006) in his analysis of the visual programme of the column: 'Mit der Darstellung des Legionärs als Kulturbringer korrespondiert die Inschrift auf der Basis der Traianssäule. . . . Die Legionäre waren also im Felde bei ebenjenen Arbeiten zu beobachten,

48 BUILDING IN WORDS

To summarize: visual representations of construction often have to work harder than inscriptions to link themselves to the building whose construction they commemorate, and representations are influenced by the need to create visual links. In some cases, visual depictions function in combination with inscriptions, with the two media combining their different powers of memory-making. Visual depictions, like inscriptions, can create the impression of a direct involvement of the patron. The visual context in which a depiction of construction is placed can heighten the status of the act itself— as in the case of the spectating imperial family or mythical foundation scenes. Certain stylizing elements can be used to create the impression of order and ease of the process, while the spectacular element of construction is highlighted by depictions of the viewing of the process itself.

Literary Memories

A literary representation of building offers, encourages, manipulates, and nuances a (re)enactment of this process in the reader's mind. All remaining chapters of this book are dedicated to investigating the different facets of construction in literary texts. In this section, I take a first look at representational strategies specifically available to literary authors, identifying them and analysing them in dialogue with those of the media discussed PREVIOUSLY. These literary strategies will then be investigated further in the following chapters.

High-Tech in Prose: Caesar's Rhine Bridge

Julius Caesar, in the fourth book of his *De Bello Gallico*, famously describes the construction of a bridge across the Rhine.[105] He recounts (4.17.1–2):

> Caesar . . . Rhenum transire decreverat, sed navibus transire neque satis tutum esse arbitrabatur neque suae neque populi Romani dignitatis esse

---

mit denen die zivilen Ingenieurleistungen und Baumaßnahmen in der Hauptstadt korrespondierten. Hier wie dort war die feindselige Natur von Rom besiegt worden . . .' (411).

[105] The Caesarian bridge falls outside the category of urban and suburban monuments which this chapter primarily focuses on. Instead, it points forward to Chapter 2 and its discussion of literary representations of human interventions in nature, especially involving water management.

MAKING MEMORIES 49

statuebat. Itaque etsi summa difficultas faciundi pontis proponebatur propter latitudinem rapiditatem altitudinem que fluminis, tamen id sibi contendendum aut aliter non traducendum exercitum existimabat.

Caesar had decided to cross the Rhine. But neither did he believe that it would be sufficiently safe to cross it in boats, nor did he deem it consistent with his own dignity or that of the Roman people. Even though the difficulty of constructing a bridge that presented itself was huge because of the breadth, fast current and depth of the river, he still thought that he had to attempt it or else not lead his army across.

This opening, which stresses both the difficulty of the task (*summa difficultas*) and the prestige associated with its accomplishment (*dignitas*) for Caesar himself and the Roman people, is followed by a description of the construction of the bridge.[106] Despite the technical and systematic appearance of this passage, Caesar's description of the structure as a whole does not aim to make clear how different parts of the structure fit together. Rather, it depicts the steps of its construction, treating the different components of the bridge in the order in which they were built.[107] Furthermore, the description does not offer a complete or even comprehensible description of the different steps of the construction process.[108] This selective presentation of the procedure may have had different effects, depending on the envisaged readership(s) of the work.

---

[106] For the technical aspects of the bridge, a starting point is Saatmann, Jüngst, and Thielscher (1939), who provide a detailed, phrase-by-phrase discussion of the description of construction (95–158). A rhetorical analysis of all depictions of engineering works in Caesar's work is undertaken by Dodington (1980), esp. 56–62 and 70–7 on the Rhine bridge. For a close reading of the Rhine bridge passage and further bibliography, see Grandazzi (2009).

[107] Dodington (1980), 11–12.

[108] Cf. the frustrated remark of the trained carpenter and classicist Gelbe: 'Die Rekonstruktion der Brücke ist oft versucht worden und wird—leider—noch oft versucht werden; umsonst, denn die Beschreibung Caesars ist einerseits zu laienhaft, andererseits zu lückenhaft', quoted in Saalmann, Jüngst, and Thielscher (1939), 85. In 1999, a team of engineers and archaeologists, with the help of a team of the Territorial Army Royal Engineers, tried, and struggled, to recreate Caesar's feat on the basis of his description for a BBC programme on 'Secrets of the Ancients': see https://www.dailymotion.com/video/x6sd6lx (accessed 24 September 2021). In this respect, the Rhine bridge is by no means unique among Caesar's descriptions of military engineering projects. It is, however, the longest of the technical descriptions in the *De Bello Gallico*, apart from a description of the siege works used in the climactic battle of Alesia (7.72–3). On other descriptions of engineering in the work of Caesar, see e.g. Wimmel (1973) and Erickson (2002).

50 BUILDING IN WORDS

It is beyond question that this description was composed for a public signif-icantly more familiar than the average modern reader with standard military procedure like the construction of wooden bridges, and with Roman wood-working techniques—but how familiar precisely?[109] It is possible that those readers who had in some capacity been involved in military campaigns (i.e. a very significant part of the male upper classes) would have been able to follow the description on the basis of their intimate knowledge of bridge construction technology, needing only those aspects explained to them which were specific to this particular bridge, adapted as it was to withstand the particular force and width of the Rhine.[110] If, on the other hand, the intended readership was less uniformly expert on matters of engineering, the selective and technical repre-sentation of bridge construction (and other engineering work) in the *De Bello Gallico* would have been at best only partly comprehensible to most readers. However, in that case, the technical detail still serves an important purpose. The surplus of challenging and technological details serves to enhance the reader's admiration for the troops' and Caesar's mastery of complicated engineering procedures beyond the reader's own horizon.[111]

Apart from the suggestive selectivity of the description, the specific strate-gies most evident in Caesar's creation of a memory of this feat of construction are already familiar from the two other media studied in this chapter. The speed of building, which featured prominently in building inscriptions, is also stressed by Caesar: *diebus decem, quibus materia coepta erat comportari, omni opere effecto exercitus traducitur*—'The whole work was completed in ten days from that on which the collecting of building material began, and the army was led across' (4.18.1).[112] This description also features the

---

[109] The intended audience of the *De Bello Gallico* is a source of lively scholarly debate: Wiseman (1998) has argued for a popular audience, while most scholars consider the Roman aristocracy or possibly a slightly larger 'elite' group the main readership. Busch (2005) argues that one primary audience of the text was the Caesarian veterans of the Gallic wars themselves. For a summary of the audience debate, see Riggsby (2006), 12–15.

[110] E.g. the special way of securing the timber pilings of the bridge in the riverbed, angling them to withstand the current, or protecting the bridge from flotsam with some separate pilings placed further upstream. Saarmann, Jüngst, and Thielscher (1939) are optimistic about the average Roman's knowledge of bridge construction, assuming that any Roman reader ('jeder römische Leser') knew how the Roman military constructed bridges, and would have been perfectly able to understand Caesar's description (95).

[111] See Kraus (2006), 173: '[T]hese instances of "soldier talk" emphasise our separation from the world of the *BG* at the moment of connecting us closer to it.' See also Scarola (1987) on reading the walls of Avaricum (*BGall.* 7.23) as an ecphrasis, displaying the descriptive powers of the narrator.

[112] Saatmann, Jüngst, and Thielscher (1939), 164–6, consider ten days just possible, but only if a significant number of time-consuming preparations were already completed in advance. This flexible attitude towards reality is already familiar from epigraphic memories. On speed see also Dodington (1980), 13.

MAKING MEMORIES   51

fictional direct involvement of the one ordering and financing a project in the construction process itself. The literary text, even though it has every opportunity of expanding on the compressed *'fecit'* of building inscriptions, does not choose to do so. For example, Caesar takes full credit for developing the ingenious method of construction: *rationem pontis hanc instituit . . .* (4.17.3), and he himself executes the placing and joining of the wooden elements of the bridge (*iungebat . . . defixerat . . . adegerat . . . statuebat*).[113] No mention here of the skilled engineers and the numerous legionaries who actually executed all these operations. This illusion of direct involvement recalls, for example, the active participation of the patron on the Basilica Aemilia frieze. Finally, the text contains an account of the impact of the construction feat on the enemy (4.18–4.19). The Sugambri and Suebi are so impressed by the sudden appearance of the bridge that they sue for peace and flee from Caesar's advance.[114] Just as the obelisk relief provided a spectating audience for the obelisk erection, Caesar depicts an audience for his Rhine bridge construction, but his medium allows for greater specificity in the depiction of the audience's reaction: the German tribes acknowledge the significance of the construction feat by interpreting it as evidence of Caesar's superiority as a military leader.

Caesar's strategies may appear similar or at least comparable to some of those encountered in epigraphic and visual memory-making, but there is one significant difference between this description and other representations of construction discussed in this chapter. This text is not designed to enhance the reader's appreciation of an extant monument. Caesar's Rhine bridge had probably never been seen by many of those who read the *commentarii*,[115] and, more importantly, at the time of writing the bridge was no longer in existence. Caesar reports that after his successful punitive expedition on the other side of the Rhine . . . *(Caesar) se in Galliam recepit pontemque rescidit*—'Caesar returned to Gaul and destroyed the bridge' (4.19.4).[116] The monument, torn down in reality, is reconstructed in the text. The process of building is always ephemeral, but in this case, the bridge itself is, too. All that remains is the written 're-construction'.

---

[113] Riggsby (2006), 231 n. 50 and 104; Dodington (1980), 30; Grandazzi (2009), 548–9.
[114] Dodington (1980), 23–24.
[115] Although note Busch's theory, n. 109.
[116] See Saalmann, Jüngst, and Thielscher (1939), 159, on possible methods of destruction. On destroyed engineering works in Caesar's work, see Dodington (1980), 18–19.

52 BUILDING IN WORDS

Mirabilia and *memoria*: Pliny on Moving the Obelisk

Pliny the Elder's *Naturalis Historia*, a monumental encyclopaedia in thirty-seven books which covers not only the geography, botany, and zoology, but also the art and philosophy of the world Pliny knew, has only recently come into focus as a literary work in its own right. Recent studies have covered various aspects of Pliny's ambitions and the intellectual context of his enquiry into the nature of the world and of humankind.[117] Book 36 of the *Naturalis Historia* deals with the topic of 'stone' in its different manifestations.[118] The first half of the book covers sculpture, followed by a section about architectural marvels, including obelisks, the pyramids, and the Cretan labyrinth. In the second half of the book, building materials and glass are discussed. In a passage about all obelisks in the city of Rome (*HN* 36.70–4), Pliny first deals with obelisks in Egypt and dwells extensively on the technical challenges of cutting, transportation, and erection and the imaginative solutions to these challenges which the pharaohs and their engineers allegedly found. After this build-up, the greatest challenge of all, the transport of obelisks from Egypt to Rome, is discussed last.[119] Pliny describes how the ship that was used under the emperor Augustus to transport the first of a pair of obelisks from Heliopolis to Puteoli was later exhibited to the public (36.69–70):[120]

> Super omnia accessit difficultas mari Romam devehendi, spectatis admodum navibus. Divus Augustus eam, quae priorem advexerat, miraculi gratia Puteolis perpetuis navalibus dicaverat; incendio consumpta ea est.

> The difficulty of transporting obelisks to Rome by sea was greatest of all, with the ships a great attraction for spectators. The deified Augustus dedicated the ship that had transported the first obelisk at Puteoli in a permanent dock on account of the miracle [i.e. of the successful transport]. It has been destroyed by a fire.

---

[117] See Gibson and Morello (2011), vii–viii.

[118] For a literary discussion of book 36 as a whole, see Carey (2003), 79–99.

[119] On the transportation of obelisks from Egypt to Rome, see Wirsching (2010), who argues for the use of three interconnected ships.

[120] Of the two obelisks from Heliopolis, one was placed in the Campus Martius and used as the pointer of the Augustan Meridian (and probably not, after all, a sundial), on which see Heslin (2007), Haselberger (2011) with responses and additions by Heslin, Schütz, Hannah, and Alföldi, and Frischer (2018). The other was placed in the Circus Maximus. They were erected in the same year, 10 BC, and given identical inscriptions (*CIL* 6.701 and *CIL* 6.702). Today they are to be found in front of S. Maria del Popolo and Palazzo Montecitorio. On this passage, see Carey (2003), 87, for an analysis in the context of the *mirabilia* theme. I quote the text of André in André, Bloch, and Rouveret (1981).

MAKING MEMORIES   53

In this short passage, several aspects of 'making memories' are in play. Firstly, Pliny reminds his readers that the obelisks they know as standing in the Circus Maximus and on the Campus Martius were only brought to Rome with considerable difficulty (*super omnia accessit difficultas . . .*).[121] The real *miraculum* is not the obelisk itself, but the feat of its transportation. Mentioning it here is a means of inscribing into the reader's appreciation of this (and any) obelisk the memory of its transportation.[122]

The passage is also concerned with an earlier attempt at preserving a memory of the transport of the obelisk. The dock which housed the ship in Puteoli seems to have been turned into a sort of museum, *perpetuis . . . navalibus*, where the ship remained, dedicated by the emperor himself. The immediate impact of the spectacle of transportation (*spectatis . . . navibus*) was perpetuated, by giving people the opportunity to continue viewing the ship which had been the means of transportation.[123]

However, with the deceptively inconspicuous final four words (*incendio consumpta ea est*), Pliny in fact suggests a contest between methods of memorialization. The Augustan attempt at preservation of the ephemeral moment of spectacular transportation failed: the physical record of it, the ship displayed in a museum, burned down. In contrast to the destruction of this record, Pliny's literary memorialization has, at the moment of reading, succeeded, and it has superseded the physical one. The most important representational strategy of this passage is therefore the way in which it implies a superiority of its own commemorative powers over those of other media.

Obelisks in Ammianus Marcellinus's *Res Gestae*

The work of the Roman historian Ammianus Marcellinus, writing in the last decades of the fourth century AD, likewise contains an excursus on obelisks (*Amm. Marc.* 17.4), which takes as its point of departure the project of Constantius II (originally conceived, according to Ammianus, by

---

[121] Note that *CIL* 6.1163 (the Roman obelisk inscription) also speaks of the *difficultas* of the operation (and cf. Caesar's Rhine bridge, p. 49). On the rhetoric of difficulty in engineering descriptions, see Cuomo (2011), 161–2.

[122] Cf. Parker (2014), who relies on this passage to argue that 'the monumental aspect of Rome's obelisks is closely entwined with their mobility' (278).

[123] The theme of the spectacular ship is continued in the following section on a Claudian obelisk (36.70). The ship used on that occasion is described as *omnibus quae umquam in mari visa sunt mirabiliorem*—'more amazing than all things that had ever been seen at sea'.

54 BUILDING IN WORDS

Constantine) to bring an especially large obelisk from Thebes in Egypt to Rome.[124] In book 16, Ammianus recounts that Constantius II promised an obelisk to Rome during his visit to the city in 357 (16.10.17). The realization of this promise, later in the same year, is described in book 17, where Ammianus first gives a short overview of the history of Egyptian Thebes, then explains the nature of obelisks and of hieroglyphs, narrates the transport and erection of the obelisk, and concludes with the translation of the hieroglyphs of an obelisk in the Circus Maximus.[125]

I will highlight a number of the strategies of Ammianus's representation of obelisk transportation and erection. Firstly, the text involves itself in a debate about the meaning of the monument with which it deals. Describing the history of a monument is one way of influencing the viewer-reader's valuation of it, and this text participates, as we shall see, in a competition of different versions or interpretations of the story. The narrative of transport and erection begins as follows (17.4.12):[126]

> Et quia sufflantes adulatores ex more Constantium id sine modo strepebant, quod, cum Octavianus Augustus obeliscos duo ab Heliupolitana civitate transtulisset Aegyptia, quorum unus in Circo Maximo, alter in Campo locatus est Martio, hunc recens advectum,[127] difficultate magnitudinis territus, nec contrectare ausus est nec movere. . . .

> And because flatterers were, as they usually do, inflating Constantius's ego, and clamouring without moderation that, although Octavianus Augustus had brought over two obelisks from the Egyptian city Heliopolis, of which one was placed in the Circus Maximus, the other in the Campus Martius, this one (that was recently transported) he had neither dared to touch nor move, terrified by the difficulty caused by its size. . . .

---

[124] The inscription of this obelisk is discussed earlier, pp. 27–8.

[125] The identity of the obelisk which bears the hieroglyphs translated by Ammianus is very difficult to establish. A number of scholars have taken the mention of the city of Helios (17.4.19, 21, 23) as evidence that the obelisk came from Heliopolis, and that it is therefore the obelisk brought to the Circus Maximus by Augustus in 10 BC. However, this conclusion is not supported by Erman's analysis of the hieroglyphs (Erman (1914), 235–73; less sceptical is Iversen (1961), 449–50). On Ammianus's obelisk, see further Sabbah (1970), 171 n. 39, and de Jonge (1977), 109 and 118–19.

[126] I cite the text of Seyfarth (1978).

[127] *recens advectum* must refer to Ammianus's own time of writing and is used to draw the distinction between the Augustan obelisks and the one transported by Constantius. The obelisk was not already *advectus* at the time of speaking of the sycophantic advisors. See de Jonge (1977), 118.

The account thus begins with a story within a story—Constantius's advisors tell the emperor that the great Augustus himself did not dare to transport this particular obelisk due to its size. This version of events is subsequently revealed to be incorrect: according to Ammianus, Augustus's motivation was quite different (see later discussion). The text here stages a (real or fictional) competition of different stories told about the past of this obelisk. The advisors' (allegedly) false claims about Augustus's inability to move this obelisk are contradicted by the narrator: *discant, qui ignorant* . . . ('let those who do not know it learn that . . .'), followed by his alternative explanation.[128]

Another kind of debate about the story of the transportation and erection of the obelisk is played out between Ammianus's narrative and a different textual medium. According to the version of events presented by Ammianus, Constantine himself intended the obelisk for Rome. He uprooted it, had it transported up the Nile to Alexandria, and had a ship constructed for the journey across the sea (17.4.13). After Constantine's death the task was, after some delay, completed by Constantius II. However, the official inscription which was placed on the base of the obelisk when it had finally been erected offers a different version of events.[129] According to the inscription, the obelisk was first intended by Constantine for Constantinople, but Constantius changed the destination. Furthermore, the inscription claims that the obelisk had already arrived in Rome before 353 (the end of the usurpation of Magnentius, who is mentioned), but remained on the ground until it could be raised by Constantius II.[130]

Ammianus edits out any suggestion of Constantinople as a competing destination for the obelisk. Kelly explains this striking omission in light of Ammianus's 'Rome-centric' agenda: this is just one of many instances where Ammianus stresses the importance of Rome at the cost of Constantinople.[131] It is striking that Ammianus would so explicitly contradict the official inscription on a high-profile triumphal monument, which would have been

---

[128] On this alternative explanation, see further pp. 60–1. As regards the sycophants' attempt to make Constantius's achievement even greater, Kelly (2008), 229 n. 13, suspects that it stems from a lost panegyric text, but in the absence of any evidence other than this passage, this has to remain (attractive) speculation.

[129] On this inscription (*CIL* 6.1163 = *ILS* 736) see pp. 28–9.

[130] See Kelly (2008), 225–30 for the contradictions between Ammianus's version and *CIL* 6.1163, and 225 n. 8 for further bibliography.

[131] See Kelly (2003), esp. 603–6 and, on the role of Rome in the *Res Gestae* more generally, Stenger (2015).

56   BUILDING IN WORDS

visible to anyone in Rome. His version reads as a reaction to the inscription, a correction of the version of events it represents.[132]

Ammianus acknowledges the existence of different versions of the history of the monument and proceeds to prove one of them right and others wrong. I will return to the idea that the meaning of a monument is subject to debate, and that texts which tell the story of its making participate in and stage this debate, especially in Chapter 2, where moral aspects of engineering are discussed, and in the Conclusion, which deals with one particularly forceful way of attacking previous interpretations of a monument: descriptions of destruction.

The opening of the narrative of the obelisk also points to a further strategy of representation. Ammianus's text engages not only with the contemporary political discussion, but also with its literary context. It has been shown that Ammianus's use of intertextuality is pervasive and of the highest level of sophistication.[133] It is all the more surprising that the relationship between Ammianus's obelisk excursus and the only other extended discussion of obelisks known to us from antiquity, that of Pliny the Elder, of which a section was discussed earlier, has until now gone unnoticed.[134] Only in the context of the writings of his encyclopedic predecessor does Ammianus's narrative gain its full significance.

Pliny first comes into the picture when Ammianus mentions the two obelisks transported to Rome by Augustus from Heliopolis. Ammianus spells out that of the two obelisks *unus in Circo Maximo, alter in Campo locatus est Martio*. He may well be (directly or via another source) drawing on Pliny, who also discusses this pair of obelisks from Heliopolis (*HN* 36.71): *is autem obeliscus quem divus Augustus in circo magno statuit ... is vero, quem in campo Martio....* And indeed, this overlap in theme is quickly confirmed to have been no accident. Ammianus's vivid, rhetorically polished historical narrative has at first sight little in common with Pliny's encyclopedic account

---

[132] Kelly (2008), 227–9, even argues that Ammianus deliberately alludes to the inscription. However, he may be overplaying the significance of some very small textual details (not crucial to the sense). Especially central to his argument, and especially problematic, is the reference to the Tiber in both the inscription and Ammianus, since the Tiber-reference of the inscription is, as Kelly himself acknowledges, restored on the basis of Ammianus.

[133] See above all Kelly (2008), especially ch. 4 for a general discussion of the special nature of Ammianus's intertextuality.

[134] Very possibly, Ammianus also knew and reacted to other accounts of obelisk transportation and raising, but only Pliny and Ammianus have come down to us from antiquity. Parker (2007), esp. 213–14, and (2014), 277–8, briefly discusses Pliny and Ammianus together but does not mention the possibility that the accounts may be related.

MAKING MEMORIES 57

of obelisks, but the frame of Ammianus's narrative section alone is a gesture towards a different genre. The story of Egyptian Thebes, the explanation of the nature of obelisks and account of hieroglyphs which precede it, and the translation of inscriptions which follows it are less inspired by historiographical practice than by an encyclopedic drive towards an all-encompassing account.[135]

The competition between obelisks into which Constantius enters is matched, on a literary level, by a contest between the two accounts of obelisks. The obelisk of Ammianus's account is of course so large that the advisors of Constantius claim that Augustus, *difficultate magnitudinis territus*, did not dare to attempt its transport. This contradicts Pliny, who opens his section on spectacular Augustan obelisk transportation with *super omnia accessit difficultas* ... (*HN* 36.69). When Constantius's advisors urge him to surpass the great Augustus, Ammianus marks this struggle with a reference to the Plinian praise of Augustus.

As we saw earlier, Pliny accorded special emphasis to the spectacularly large ships employed for transportation by Augustus and Claudius (*spectatis admodum navibus ... omnibus quae umquam in mari visa sunt mirabiliorem*, 36.70). Ammianus counters (17.4.13):

quo convecto per alveum Nili proiectoque Alexandriae, navis amplitudinis antehac inusitatae aedificata est sub trecentis remigibus agitanda.

And when it [i.e. the obelisk] had been shipped down the channel of the Nile and had been brought on land at Alexandria, a ship was constructed of previously untried size, which was to be rowed by three hundred oarsmen.

Ammianus, too, comments on the size of the ship, which apparently is (even at this late date, with scores of obelisks already transported to Rome) of an untried or at least very unusual size. Ammianus even adds a precise number of rowers to back up his claim.[136] As regards river transport, Pliny briefly

---

[135] For example, Pliny and Ammianus both offer a definition of obelisks (*HN* 36.64, *Amm. Marc.* 17.4.7) and both explain what hieroglyphs are, though Pliny (36.64) does so much more briefly than Ammianus (17.4.8–11).

[136] Perhaps a ship with 300 rowers was not the biggest Roman ship that had ever been built, but in the case of a cargo vessel such a huge number must have been very remarkable. See de Jonge (1977), 103 *ad loc.* with bibliography. Wirsching (2010), 266, argues that the number of 300 refers to the total number of rowers, who were divided up into three teams of 100 rowers who took turns to increase speed.

58 BUILDING IN WORDS

comments on the difficulties of transporting the obelisk up the Tiber (*HN* 36.70):

> alia ex hoc cura navium, quae Tiberi subvehant, quo experimento patuit non minus aquarum huic amni esse quam Nilo.

> Following on from this there is another problem, that of the ships which are supposed to carry [the obelisks] up the Tiber, from which test it has become clear that the Tiber does not carry less water than the Nile.

Ammianus, too, dwells on the similarity, or rather difference, between Tiber and Nile, but while for Pliny, the Tiber is demonstrably up to the challenge of transporting the obelisk, Ammianus's dramatically anthropomorphic Tiber appears afraid to convey this gift of the strange river Nile to Rome (17.4.14):[137]

> ... per ... fluentaque Thybridis velut paventis, ne, quod paene ignotus miserat Nilus, ipse parum sub emeatus sui discrimine moenibus alumnis inferret...

> ... over ... the waters of the Tiber, who seemed to be afraid that he himself, subject as he was to the danger of his own stream/estuary, might hardly be able to carry into the walls which he nurtures [i.e. those of the city of Rome] that which the almost unknown Nile had sent...

The ambition of Constantine and Constantius to transport and raise the biggest obelisk of all time is matched by the desire of Ammianus to surpass his predecessor with his longer, more detailed excursus on obelisks, in which Pliny's superlative praise is outdone on a number of occasions.

A third strategy often found in descriptions of construction becomes especially apparent when Ammianus turns to the raising of the obelisk. On the obelisk base of Theodosius, considered earlier, the raising of the obelisk was represented as a spectacle viewed and staged by the imperial family. In his description of the raising of the obelisk in the Circus Maximus, Ammianus, too, stages the raising as a feast for the eye (17.4.15):[138]

---

[137] The parallel also noted by Sabbah (1970), 169 *ad loc.*
[138] On the numerous textual problems of this passage De Jonge (1977), 110–15.

MAKING MEMORIES 59

sola post haec restabat erectio, quae vix aut ne vix quidem sperabatur posse
compleri. † idestisque periculum altis trabibus—ut machinarum cerneres
nemus—innectuntur vasti funes et longi, ad speciem multiplicium liciorum,
caelum densitate nimia subtexentes. quibus colligatus mons ipse effigiatus
scriptilibus elementis paulatimque in arduum per inane protentus diu pensilis
hominum milibus multis tamquam molendarias rotantibus metas, cavea
locatur in media eique sphaera superponitur aenea aureis lamminis nitens...

After this only the raising remained, which was hardly—or even not at all—
thought to be possible. . . . danger . . . to tall beams—so that you might
see a grove of scaffoldings—huge and long ropes were tied, which looked
like manifold heddle leashes,[139] screening the sky because there were so
many of them. To these ropes the mountain itself, adorned with written
characters, was attached. Little by little it was pulled upright through the
empty air, and it was suspended for a long time while many thousand men
were turning what looked like millstones. It was placed in the middle of the
circus and a golden orb was put on top of it, shining with gold-leaf.

The text focuses on the notion of the spectacular: it presents an imaginative, highly metaphorical account of how the apparatus employed for
the raising of the obelisk would have appeared to the viewer (*cerneres, ad
speciem*).[140] Some metaphors are drawn from nature: a viewer would see a
grove of beams, while the obelisk appears as a mountain. The ropes, on the
other hand, are described by means of a scaled-up weaving metaphor (they
are compared to heddle leashes, i.e. the loops which tie the warp threads to
the wooden heddle): there are so many of them, running across the air, that

---

[139] The interpretation of the word *licium* is difficult. The word may signify 'thread' (*OLD* 1), in
which case the plural *multiplicia licia* could be interpreted as something like a 'weave' or 'web' ('Netz'
is the translation of Seyfarth (1968), 'web' that of Rolfe (1935); cf. also De Jonge (1977), 111 *ad
loc.*, 'embroidery'). However, *licium* is also a technical weaving term, with *licia* referring to 'heddle
leashes', i.e. the threads which were looped around the individual warp threads in order to attach
them to the heddle-rod (Öhrmann (2017)). As a metaphor for ropes tied to wooden beams, this
specific meaning of *licium* appears extremely apposite in this context. If we assume that Ammianus
is using the term here in its precise technical sense, this has significant consequences for the interpretation of his description. Heddle leashes all run in parallel to one another, while the idea of a web
supposes criss-crossing. Wirsching (2006), taking for granted Seyfarth's interpretation 'Netz', bases
his reconstruction of the method described by Ammianus on the fact that the ropes need to cross
one another, while *licia* certainly allows for a reconstruction with all ropes running in parallel to one
another.

[140] The reliability of Ammianus's account in terms of the actual method of erection has long been
doubted, although see Wirsching (2006), 348–52, for a spirited defence of Ammianus's account and
an attempt at a technical interpretation of its details (but see n. 139 for a methodological difficulty).

60 BUILDING IN WORDS

together, they even obscure the sky. Ammianus here uses his entire literary repertoire to render visible and tangible for his readers how spectacular and overwhelming the raising appeared to those watching it. For example, the language renders the spectators themselves (and the readers who are invited to imagine being spectators) deliberately small: the descriptions of grove, mountain, and ropes viewed from underneath are focalized through the eyes of an ant-like spectator, gazing up at the huge lifting apparatus. Ammianus also evokes the rhetorical category of the sublime, combining metaphors drawn from impressive natural spectacles with 'vertical' language (*altis, caelum, in arduum*) and high-flown diction, bordering on the poetic.[141] In rhetorical convention, the sublime style was traditionally reserved for the description of events suited to its register, such as manifestations of the divine or overwhelming natural spectacles. Its use here implicitly associates the raising of the obelisk with such sublime subjects.

Ammianus's description creates visibility in its very own way, offering suggestive images and stressing the spectacular and overwhelming. The notion of viewing the process of construction, of the spectacular side of building and engineering, is one which we will encounter frequently in this investigation. Analysis of epigraphic, visual, and literary sources in this chapter has brought out the importance of issues of visibility and of spectacle. All three media in a sense try to make visible to the mind's eye what is no longer visible—the process that produced the monument. Literary texts especially often engage self-consciously with the non-visual nature of their medium and the means of still conveying the visible and the spectacular.

Finally, I turn to the moral dimension of the obelisk donation. Ammianus offers a somewhat ambivalent account of the permissibility of removing the obelisk from its original situation. Following the introduction of the obelisk narrative (17.4.12, quoted earlier), the suggestions of the advisors regarding Augustus's alleged motivation for leaving this obelisk behind are corrected (17.4.12–13):

> . . . discant, qui ignorant, veterem principem translatis aliquibus hunc intactum ideo praeterisse, quod deo Soli speciali munere dedicatus fixusque intra ambitiosi templi delubra, quae contingi non poterant, tamquam apex omnium eminebat. verum Constantinus id parvi ducens avulsam hanc

---

[141] See e.g. De Jonge (1977), 112 *ad loc.*, on *caelum subtexentes*. Note also the sound effect of the m-alliteration in the description of the grinding, turning pulleys, which add an auditive element to the vividness of the scene.

molem sedibus suis nihilque committere in religionem recte existimans, si ablatum uno templo miraculum Romae sacraret, id est in templo mundi totius, iacere diu perpessus est, dum translationi pararentur utilia.

. . . let those who do not know it understand that the old emperor [Augustus], although he had already brought over several obelisks, passed this one by and left it untouched, for the reason that it had been dedicated to the Sungod as a special gift, placed in the surrounding temple's sanctuary, which might not be polluted, and stood tall like the summit of all things. But Constantine, considering it of little account that this mass had been torn from its place, and rightly thinking that he was committing no sacrilege, if he were to dedicate the marvel, which he had taken from one temple, in Rome, that is to say in the temple of the entire world, allowed it to lie there for a long time, while the practical preparations for its transportation were being made.

Ammianus is sending mixed messages. On the one hand, Augustus's respect for the holy nature of the obelisk seems to be portrayed in a positive light, and Ammianus presents the religious laws of the Egyptians as a fact: *templi delubra, quae contingi non poterant.* Constantine's removal of the obelisk is described in violent, emotionally evocative language: ***avulsam hanc molem sedibus suis.*** But in the very same sentence, Ammianus changes tack: *nihilque committere in religionem recte existimans.* Rededicating the obelisk in Rome, the *templum mundi totius,* makes it all right. It is hard to judge whether this passage is ironical, or whether the focus on Rome as the religious centre of the entire world is part of Ammianus's larger strategy of talking up Rome, especially at the expense of Constantinople.[142] However we read the passage, it is clear that the removal of the obelisk is an action which was open to moral-religious criticism—and that Ammianus also offers a way in which that criticism could be countered. The question of the moral permissibility (in a broader than 'religious' sense) of large-scale engineering projects is of key importance in the literary accounts we will go on to consider.[143]

---

[142] For the first view see Sabbah (1970), 169 n. 31, for the second, Kelly (2003), 603–6. De Jonge (1977), 98, simply believes Ammianus to have been insensitive to Egyptian religious feelings: '[H]e makes no effort to understand the mentality of this completely different and old civilisation'.

[143] See esp. Chapters 2 and 4 of this volume. For my investigation, the question of the greatest relevance is how the description of the *process,* of the actions of the builder, can have the function of influencing the moral perception of the audience.

Conclusion

From the consideration of construction in three different media, the following chapters will move on to focus almost exclusively on texts. The groundwork laid in this chapter, however, will form the basis for many of the observations made in later chapters. Understanding the strategies of inscriptions and visual depictions is important from more than the purely comparative perspective. For a literary text about architecture, inscriptions and images are partners in a dialogue. They make up the visual and readable world of representation in which literary texts have to be understood and read.

At the same time, my analysis of Pliny and Ammianus has demonstrated that in order to understand the function of a description, we have to understand the literary context in which it is placed—to read the passage within the larger work of which it is part, with its models and intertexts in mind and in the context of intellectual discussion at the time. Descriptions of construction participate in larger literary or social debates.

There is another complication, only just glimpsed in this chapter, which renders literary representations of construction even less straightforward: the complicated relationship between the built monument and the text itself; this will form the subject of the second half of my study. A literary text which commemorates the making of a monument, by doing so, implicitly or explicitly enters into a competition between two different media of commemoration: the architectural versus the textual, already glimpsed in Pliny the Elder's competition between the physical and the textual commemoration of obelisk transportation. The interrelation between text and monument can be extremely complex. Architecture is commonly used as a metaphor or an image for a literary work. In a literary text describing the creation of a physical monument, there is often, explicitly or implicitly, a relation between the achievements of building and of writing. This means that in literary texts, the way in which they represent the creation of the monument is frequently also determined by the way in which they would like to recreate the literary creative process which produced the text itself. This aspect of representations of construction will form the subject of Chapters 3, 4 and 5.

2

Debating the Draining of the Fucine Lake

Introduction

This chapter, like the previous one, deals with the question of how representations of the process of building can be designed to influence the impact of a finished structure. I now turn from urban and suburban monuments to large-scale engineering projects, such as landscaping or water management.[1] At the same time, I broaden the selection of texts I discuss to include not only representations designed to enhance the reader's appreciation of a particular structure, but also those designed to diminish it, and I consider how the two types interact. In this chapter, I also contextualize these descriptions within larger Roman debates about large-scale construction projects—debates about nature and construction, luxury and frugality, victory and defeat, boundaries and excess.

Large-scale engineering projects were no less controversial in Rome than they are today. Ancient texts present us with a bewildering range of reactions: effusive praise for the emperor who constructed a new aqueduct, harsh condemnation of a rich man's landscaped gardens, wonder at the miraculous achievement of a new harbour, moral outrage at a daring canal-building project. What are we to make of these fierce opposites? How can such projects represent the most defining achievements of the Roman people and at the same time be a sign of its advanced corruption and depravity?

It is possible to seek the reason for the different reactions in the individual projects: for example, one might assume that projects which were too expensive or designed to further only private luxury would be condemned, while projects designed to benefit the general public would be worth the expense and welcomed as admirable achievements.[2] Another possibility is

---

[1] See however my earlier discussion of one engineering project, the Caesarian bridge, in Chapter 1, pp. 48–51.

[2] See the clear summary of this aspect of the discussion by DeLaine (2002), 222–6, who quotes (224 n. 90) Cic. *Mur.* 76 as the earliest formulation of the antithesis (*odit populus Romanus privatam luxuriam, publicam magnificentiam diligit*).

Building in Words. Bettina Reitz-Joosse, Oxford University Press. © Oxford University Press 2021.
DOI: 10.1093/oso/9780197610688.003.0003

64   BUILDING IN WORDS

to understand the differences in terms of a development over time: it has been argued that huge interventions in nature were generally viewed with suspicion by the writers of the republic and early principate, while attitudes seem to undergo a change towards the end of the first century AD.[3] Both explanations are important and need to be taken into account, but neither is sufficient by itself.

An exclusive focus on external factors elides the fact that in describing human interventions in nature, authors always have a choice.[4] *Any* such project can theoretically either be praised or condemned. Whether an author activates the positive or negative sides of a project (or type of project) depends not so much on the kind or scale of the activity itself, but rather on the character of his text and the context in which the project is mentioned. Concentrating on descriptions of the *process* of engineering or construction, I shall examine in this chapter the rhetorical strategies that authors employ to address the ambivalence about intervention in nature.

Water Engineering in Rome

Since the corpus of Latin texts praising or condemning engineering achievements is far too large and diverse to be considered as a whole, I base my analysis of the strategies of environmental rhetoric on descriptions of water engineering—a choice motivated by the central importance that water and its management have in the debates surrounding interaction between nature and man.

Fierce condemnations of large-scale human interventions in nature are especially common in 'moralizing' texts, where construction on too grand or too luxurious a scale is criticized as (often socially) inappropriate, hubristic, or sinful.[5] As Edwards argues, the theme of water and of the manipulation

---

[3] See e.g. Pavlovskis (1973), 1–25, on the new enthusiasm for technical advances in the Flavian period expressed by Statius and Martial; and Armstrong (2009), investigating the 'particular constellation of attitudes' (75) towards man-made marvels in the Augustan period.

[4] None of the scholars cited earlier deny that this is the case. Cf. also Hinds's reaction to Fantham's question regarding changing attitudes towards luxury, as evinced by Stat. *Silv.* 2.2, in Hinds (2001), 260–1.

[5] The literature on Roman moralizing and luxury building is vast. Edwards (1993), ch. 4, is an excellent introduction, drawing on a wide range of texts to support a convincing argument. Purcell (1987) establishes the link with the archaeological evidence. A wide-ranging survey of the ideologies of landscape in Rome, with much useful material on the relationship of man and nature and on criticism of luxury, is Spencer (2010).

DEBATING THE DRAINING OF THE FUCINE LAKE   65

of boundaries between water and land takes a central position in such moralizing discourse.[6] She explains moralizing criticism of (especially luxury) construction as a vehicle for the elite's articulation of social hierarchies and social boundaries. The prominence of water engineering in such discussions can be explained by the clear natural boundaries at stake there: land and sea, lake and sea, lake and land, river and land.[7]

But water engineering is not only a favourite theme of moralizing criticism of society. Water management had great ideological and economic significance for Roman culture. As Purcell argues, since the earliest days of the city of Rome, maintaining the city's habitability had involved a struggle to control water and render the marshlands of the Tiber fit to live in. This struggle of man against water is central to how Romans saw themselves and is reflected by a variety of cultural phenomena, from the prominence of water and water deities in foundational mythology to the water games of luxury villas.[8] Grand imperial projects of water management were often locally motivated economic investments, designed to increase production and habitability, but at the same time they offered opportunities for grandiose displays of conquest of nature by way of a 'rhetoric of control over the landscape'.[9]

The language of moral outrage analysed by Edwards and the rhetoric of environmental power that Purcell investigates are not two completely separate ways of talking about water management in Rome. This becomes apparent if, rather than asking which attitude would have been more typical, or how Romans *really* responded to a particular type of project, we turn to the *strategies* of the texts which have transmitted these 'attitudes'. How precisely do authors construct their account of the project in order to activate the desired connotations and control the potentially problematic ones?

Two near-contemporary accounts of large-scale canal-building offer a first test case. One appears in Tacitus's *Annals*, the other in Pliny the Younger's letters

---

[6] Edwards (1993), 147. She may be right in suggesting that the theme is more prominent than a modern reader would expect. Truly harmful exploitation of human or environmental capital remains uncensured, while fishponds, which do not cause anyone (except the owner) the least inconvenience, are treated as a fundamental threat to society and morality.

[7] Edwards (1993), 147: 'The division between land and sea often appears in invective against luxury as one of the most archetypally natural distinctions.'

[8] On the early mythology of Rome and its preoccupation with water, see Purcell (1996), 184–9. On Roman villas, see 198–9: 'The games villa owners played with underground conduits and fountains and ponds were not just whimsies, but allusions to the control of water as it had gone on since Romulus built his city in the water-meadows.'

[9] Purcell (1996), 206. On the martial associations and rhetoric of Roman bridge-building, see Kleiner (1991); on the link between power and rivers in Rome more generally, see Campbell (2012), esp. 369–88.

66 BUILDING IN WORDS

to the emperor Trajan. Within his predominantly negative account of Nero's reign,[10] Tacitus describes Nero's ambitious project of connecting the *lacus Avernus* to Ostia by means of a channel (*Ann.* 15.42.2).[11] He omits any mention of the economic benefits of the project (ships bringing Egyptian grain from Puteoli to Ostia would no longer have had to navigate the dangerous Cape of Misenum)[12] and via its immediate context associates it with the construction of the wasteful Domus Aurea on (allegedly) stolen ground. The architects in charge of Nero's building projects, Severus and Celer, are described as follows: ... *quibus ingenium et audacia erat etiam quae natura denegavisset per artem temptare*— '... who had the genius and the daring to attempt through skill even what nature had denied'. Their work does not respect natural boundaries, such as mountains, which have to be dug through (*per montis adversos*). In terms of the economic side of the project, Tacitus only calls it *intolerandus labor nec satis causae*—'intolerable toil and for an insufficient reason', and Nero an *incredibilium cupitor*— 'a desirer of incredible things'—for attempting the impossible.[13]

Pliny's letter to Trajan (10.41), designed to convince both his immediate reader Trajan and a larger audience of the benefits of a canal-building project in his province of Bithynia, dwells extensively on the economic benefits of the project (10.41.2), but also addresses several of Tacitus's causes for concern in respect of Nero's projects, albeit with the opposite intention.[14] This project, too, is daring and ambitious, but Pliny presents this fact in a very different light (10.41.1):

> Intuenti mihi et fortunae tuae et animi magnitudinem convenientissimum videtur demonstrari opera non minus aeternitate tua quam gloria digna quantumque pulchritudinis tantum utilitatis habitura.

> When I consider the nobility of both your status and your mind, it seems very fitting that I should let you know of projects worthy of eternal fame no less than of your glory and likely to be as splendid as they are useful.

---

[10] On Tacitus's portrayal of Nero, see the introduction by Keitel (2009), with further bibliography there.

[11] On this canal-project, see Griffin (1987), 107–8.

[12] Cf. the catastrophe described at *Ann.* 15.46.2, where a large part of the fleet is lost when attempting to navigate the Cape of Misenum in dangerous weather conditions.

[13] For the construction of Nero as the ruinous builder, see Elsner (1994).

[14] The correspondence between Pliny and Trajan makes up the tenth book of Pliny's *Epistulae*. The letters were written between AD 109 and 112, when Pliny was *legatus pro praetore* in the province of Bithynia and Pontus. For an introduction to this correspondence, see the up-to-date bibliography collected by Gibson and Morello (2011), 295 (item 3) and 305 (item 27).

DEBATING THE DRAINING OF THE FUCINE LAKE 67

Where the *audacia* of Nero's architects was suspect, and he an *incredibilium cupitor*, the *animi magnitudo* of the emperor Trajan is precisely what is praised.[15] The Bithynian project, too, would require huge amounts of manual labour (*hoc opus multas manus poscit*—'this project requires many hands'), but Pliny hastens to add that this manual labour is in fact locally available. The danger of such a great project being left unfinished (exactly what happens to Nero's ambitious plans, called an *inrita spes*, 'a vain hope', by Tacitus), is addressed explicitly by Pliny, but turned by him into an additional source of prestige. A Bithynian king had already attempted the digging of a channel, but had failed, *intercepto rege mortalitate an desperato operis effectu*—'because the king had been stopped by his own death or had despaired of finishing the project' (10.41.4). Pliny turns this earlier failure to account as follows (10.41.5):

> Sed hoc ipso (feres enim me ambitiosum pro tua gloria) incitor et accendor ut cupiam peragi a te quae tantum coeperant reges.

> But this is exactly what spurs me on and incites me to wish that you should accomplish what kings merely had begun (for you will permit me to be ambitious for the sake of your glory).

The juxtaposition of these passages shows that the categories of praise and censure overlap considerably.[16] Cost, labour, risk, size, and ambition can all work either way. These are not two separate discourses—both authors are aware that it is perfectly possible to put the opposite construction on the facts they present. They face a rhetorical challenge: how to activate the desired connotations of the project in question, while silencing the undesired ones.

I now turn to the contribution made to this kind of rhetoric by representations of the process of engineering. I do so by focusing on one particular, high-profile project of water engineering of which several literary accounts have been preserved. It offers a perfect opportunity to experience the 'debate' in action, and to scrutinize the strategies by which literary texts attempt to attribute a particular meaning to the project.

---

[15] On the link between the Trajan's power and his control of water made here and in *Ep.* 8.4 (about Caninius Rufus's poem on the Dacian War), see Campbell (2012), 370.

[16] Cf. Edwards (1993), 142, on rhetoric and luxury building: 'Those who praised luxury used the same categories as those who condemned it'.

68 BUILDING IN WORDS

Debating the Draining of the Fucine Lake

In central Italy, about 86 kilometres east of Rome and 155 kilometres north of Naples, stretches a fertile plain of 150 square kilometres, called 'Il Fucino'. This plain is the result of a gigantic engineering operation, carried out between 1855 and 1876 on the initiative of Count Alessandro di Torlonia: the complete drainage of the largest lake of central Italy, the lago Fucino.[17] Alessandro di Torlonia was not the first to attempt this ambitious project. The draining of the Fucine Lake had already been considered by Julius Caesar and Augustus, before Claudius eventually embarked on the huge operation.[18]

The area around the Fucine Lake was initially populated by the Marsi.[19] For the inhabitants of the area, the lake provided a large quantity of fish, and the soil surrounding it was fertilized by frequent floods. However, the danger of these floods outweighed their beneficial effects. The level of the lake could change rapidly, causing substantial losses to agriculture, while the constantly waterlogged soil offered an ideal breeding ground for malaria.[20]

The Claudian plan involved digging an underground tunnel to connect the lake to a nearby river, the Liris (Figure 2.1). The assumption was that part of the water of the lake would flow into the river, resulting in a partial draining of the lake.[21] The tunnel would form a natural outlet to prevent flooding, and the additional water directed into the river Liris would render this small river more navigable.[22]

The potential agricultural and economic benefits were thus enormous, but the project itself was enormous too: a tunnel of 6 kilometres had to be dug underground, through both earth (under the Campi Palentini) and hard rock (under the Mons Salvianus) (Figure 2.2). The project thus combined

[17] Alexandre Brisse, the last of the engineers to direct the project (from 1869 to its official completion in 1878) published a detailed account of the draining operation: Brisse and de Rotrou (1876). For a more recent account and assessment of the project, see Burri (2011).

[18] See Suet. *Iul.* 44.3 on Julius Caesar, where the Fucine Lake is included in a long list of Caesar's ambitious plans, and *Claud.* 20.1 on Augustus, who denied the Marsians' request for the draining of the lake (for this passage see also p. 91).

[19] On the Marsi in antiquity, see Letta (1972), or, for a briefer introduction, Letta (2001) = Letta (2003). The Roman colony of Alba Fucens was founded in 304 BC to the north-west of the lake.

[20] On the pre-draining situation of the land around the Lacus Fucinus, see Lycoph. *Alex.* 1275–80, Sen. *Q Nat.* 3.3.1, Str. 5.3.13, and *RE* s.v. *Fucinus lacus* (J. Weiss, VII 1, 188–9).

[21] There is absolutely no doubt that Claudius only ever intended a *partial* draining of the lake, a fact not sufficiently acknowledged on most discussions of the literary descriptions of the project, where the fact that the lake was not drained completely is too often seen as proof of its failure (cf. e.g. the dramatic, but in this respect misguided, re-creation of Osgood (2011), 168–9). The evidence for partial draining is presented by Messineo (1979), 140, 165–6; D'Amato (1980), 61–85, 151–3; and Letta (1994), 203.

[22] This last effect is only mentioned in Cass. Dio 60.11.5.

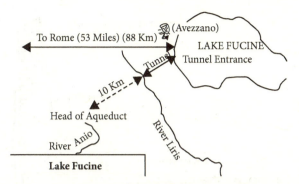

Figure 2.1. Schematized map showing the location of the tunnel.
From Thornton and Thornton (1985), 117 (detail). Courtesy of Ares Publishers, Inc.

potential practical and economic benefits with the chance of demonstrating the emperor's astounding control over nature.[23]

The work was carried out between AD 41 and 52. Our literary sources diverge substantially in their opinions of its degree of completion and success. As far as an accurate assessment is still possible today on the basis of the meagre archaeological remains, the Claudian outlet did function, in that it connected lake and river, stabilized the water level of the lake, and very slowly began a partial draining of the lake. However, construction work on the network of drainage channels was probably not yet quite complete. Therefore the tunnel did not yet accomplish drainage significant enough to gain arable land in large quantities.[24] This could in part account for the seemingly paradoxical nature of the literary sources: the channel did function, but at the same time it was an economic failure, in that the investment was not returned through the gain of land. Until the age of Hadrian, the tunnel appears to have continued to function as it did at the death of Claudius, with considerable improvements made by Hadrian.[25] Sometime between

---

[23] The close connection between the two, for which Purcell (1996) also argues (see p. 65) is expressed in the pointed formulation of Suet. *Claud.* 20.2: *non minus compendii spe quam gloriae*—'no less in the hope of profit than of glory', on which see p. 91.

[24] Letta (1994), 207, argues that the project was not finished by Claudius, and that a well-functioning network of drainage channels would have required further investments by Nero, who, however, was not interested in continuing his predecessor's work. D'Amato (1980), 95–6, suggests that the collecting channel leading from the lake to the tunnel entrance was only finished after the (disastrous) opening ceremonies. Then the drainage began, but Nero's neglect of the project soon led to problems and the blocking of the channel.

[25] D'Amato (1980), 109–48; Letta (1994), 207–10. Hadrian's repair works are mentioned at SHA *Hadr.* 22.12. On Trajanic works on the outlet, see pp. 74–5.

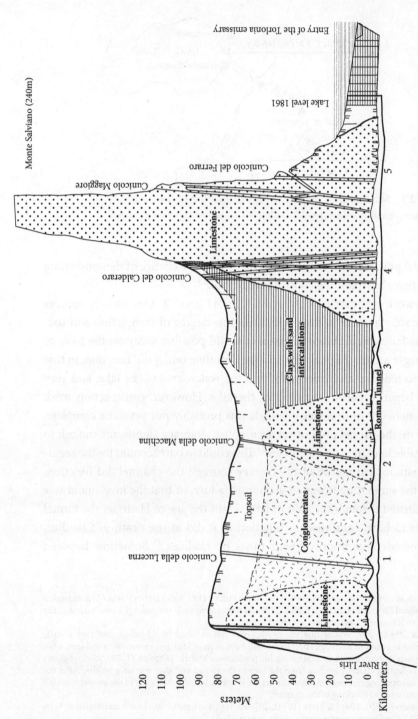

Figure 2.2. Drawing of longitudinal section of the tunnel, indicating vertical shafts ('pozzi') and tunnels ('cunicoli') and types of soil and rock encountered. The ratio between vertical and horizontal scales is 20.

After Brisse and de Rotrou (1872), plate IV, and Thornton and Thornton (1985), 118. Original image courtesy of Ares Publishers, Inc.

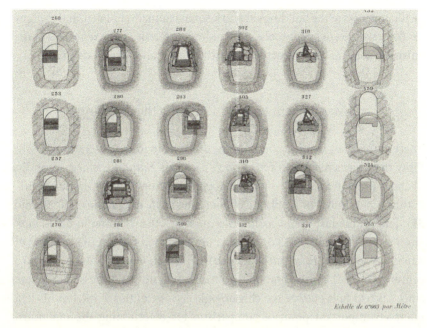

Figure 2.3. Drawing showing the overlapping of the ancient and the nineteenth-century tunnels between 2,400 and 3,600 metres.
Brisse and de Rotrou (1872), Plate V.

AD 362 and 380, the tunnel was damaged by an earthquake and ceased to function.[26]

The drainage works of the nineteenth century almost entirely destroyed the ancient tunnel works, since a larger and wider tunnel was cut through the mountain along the trajectory of the ancient tunnel. Brisse and de Rotrou attempted to document the ancient tunnel before its destruction: their illustrations show how the modern tunnel overlaps with the ancient one for almost the entire length of the conduit (Figure 2.3). The remains still visible today are mostly confined to the shafts ('pozzi') and tunnels ('cunicoli') connecting the ancient channel to the surface. The approximately forty vertical shafts leading from the channel to the surface, the locations of which are indicated in Figure 2.1, were needed to lift water and rock out of the tunnel during the building works, as well as for later maintenance of the conduit.[27] There were also a number of larger tunnels (nine are known to date), designed to

---

[26] Letta (1994), 210.
[27] See Burri (2001) for a brief exposition of the archaeological record of the conduit and the 'pozzi'. On the lifting mechanisms for water and earth used in the shafts, see Giuliani (2003b).

72   BUILDING IN WORDS

facilitate access to the building sites, to keep the tunnel ventilated, and to allow for the transport of larger tools and building materials.[28] The remnants of the entries to some of these structures can still be seen above ground today.[29]

A Magnificent Failure? Debating the Draining

There are four surviving accounts of the draining in Roman literature. Firstly, Pliny the Elder's mention of it in book 36 of his *Natural History*; secondly, Tacitus's dramatic account of the two opening ceremonies in *Annals* 12.56–7; thirdly, a number of mentions in Suetonius's *Life of Claudius* (20, 21, and 31). Finally, the historian Cassius Dio mentions the draining in his *Roman History* (60.11.5, and 60.33.3–5, the latter preserved only in the excerpts of Xiphilinus and the *Excerpta Valesiana*) written in Greek in the early third century AD. Dio's representational strategies will not be discussed in detail, since his text falls outside the chronological scope of this work, but his text offers an important point of comparison for determining the individual authors' contributions.[30] Building on the previous chapter's conclusions about the representational strategies of different media, I shall also briefly consider an epigraphic and a visual source, both concerned not with the initial drainage but with later repair and maintenance works on the outlet (although probably roughly contemporary with the composition of the texts of Tacitus and Suetonius): these sources are an inscribed Trajanic statue base, and a panoramic relief from the Collezione Torlonia. The relief and inscription allow us a glimpse of other kinds of representational strategies, and thus offer an important frame of reference for our literary texts.

The texts of Pliny, Tacitus, and Suetonius all postdate the draining by several decades, and between the publication of Pliny's and of Suetonius's text lie a further forty years.[31] However, the project and the significance attached to it were acutely relevant also at their time of writing: repair and maintenance works on the tunnel were being carried out, and other, comparable

---

[28] Burri (1994b), 235.

[29] On one of the best-preserved sections of the 'cunicoli', see Cairoli, Torrieri, and Agostini (1994).

[30] On the question of Dio's sources see Millar (1964), 34–8; see also 85–7 and 105 on Dio and Suetonius. For the imperial period, it has been argued that Dio draws not so much on Tacitus himself as on older historical sources, some of which were used also by Tacitus (Syme (1958), 271–303). It is likely that one of Dio's primary sources was Pliny's lost historical work: Hurley (2001), 16.

[31] Pliny the Elder's *Natural History* is dedicated (1 *praef* 3) to Titus during his sixth consulate (AD 77–8). Tacitus's *Annals* were probably written after the author's return from his proconsulship in Asia (AD 113), but the precise dates are unknown. The first two (or perhaps first six) books of Suetonius's *Lives* were published before AD 122 (since they are dedicated to the urban prefect Septicius Clarus).

DEBATING THE DRAINING OF THE FUCINE LAKE 73

projects were being set in motion by the emperors under whose rule these texts were composed.[32] The three authors write in different genres, mention the draining within different contexts, and interest themselves in different aspects of it. Although their respective representations of the draining of the Fucine Lake are influenced by these factors and consequently appear (at first sight) to be very different, it is a plausible supposition that Tacitus and Suetonius were familiar with Pliny's earlier treatment of the subject, and I aim to show that acknowledgement of this can actually be detected in their texts.[33] As regards the relation between Tacitus and Suetonius, it is impossible to date the texts securely with respect to each other—all we can safely say is that the authors were contemporaries—but it is likely that they also knew each other's treatment of the event.[34] Quite aside, however, from questions of dating and mutual influence, reading these three texts as a group—and thus staging a 'debate' between the three authors about the Fucine Lake and its significance—reveals a number of patterns and common themes that structure the authors' engagement with the event.[35] These texts participate in the larger, fundamental debate about human intervention in nature, sketched in the previous sections of this chapter. The thematic structure of the debate surrounding the Fucine Lake helps us also to understand better the wider debate about the economic, moral, and political implications of large-scale water engineering. Although I pay some attention to the authors' concrete references to each other, I will therefore concentrate especially on the focal themes of the debate that we can identify by reading the texts as a group.

The debate about the Fucine Lake is characterized by an astonishing discrepancy in the different authors' assessments of the project, ranging from magnificent achievement to complete failure, from major public benefaction to disgraceful waste of money. The first theme or focus of the debate is the most

There are virtually no other reliable clues to the dating of the *Lives* (the change in Suetonius's use of sources in the later books does not have to be due to the loss of his post as imperial secretary).

[32] See pp. 75–8.

[33] On Tacitus's use of Pliny for the Fucine Lake episode, see Koestermann (1967), 206 ('Möglicherweise diente Tacitus für seine Erzählung Plinius als Vorlage'), and Syme (1958), 1.292. Suetonius does not name any literary sources in the *Life of Claudius*, but in the whole of the *Lives* the Elder Pliny (presumably in his lost historical work) is one of only five credited sources (Suet. *Tib.* 73). See Mottershead (1986), xii–xiii and Hurley (2001), 14–16 for possible common sources used by both Suetonius and Tacitus (especially Pliny the Elder and Cluvius Rufus).

[34] That Suetonius knew Tacitus's *Annals* is almost undisputed: Wallace-Hadrill (1983), 2: 'Suetonius was undoubtedly looking over his shoulder at Tacitus'. Woodman (2009b) on 'Tacitus and the contemporary scene' demonstrates how an investigation of Tacitus's interaction with his literary environment can move beyond identifying the 'direction' of influence. See 36 specifically on Tacitus and Suetonius.

[35] The different literary accounts of the draining of the Fucine Lake have been analysed as a group, but so far exclusively to investigate the technical, economic, or archaeological side of the project: see Thornton and Thornton (1985); Leveau (1993); and most extensively Letta (1994), a thorough reconsideration of the literary sources with a view to a better understanding of the archaeological record.

74   BUILDING IN WORDS

obvious and important for the modern reader, though not, as we shall see, for the ancient authors: the actual success of the enterprise, or indeed its failure. Closely related is the question of whether the work was completed, or whether it was abandoned while still unfinished. A second focus of the debate arises from the sheer difficulty of assessing how efficiently the channel actually functioned: Is it even possible, the authors ask, to judge and to express the value of the project? And in particular, to what extent can visual impressions be a guide to one's assessment, especially regarding a project which was almost entirely underground? Finally, the third focus of the debate concerns the relationship between man and nature, and the ways in which they interact in the course of the draining. Is the project, for example, cast in terms of a struggle or a conflict between nature and man—a basic constellation that can be rhetorically exploited in various ways? Who won or lost in this struggle? Who emerged triumphant, who was humiliated? Was there (perhaps excessive) violence?

Keeping Up the Good Work: The Non-Literary Representation of Maintenance Operations

There is only one epigraphic source that mentions the engineering works at the Fucine Lake.[36] It is a statue base, which was discovered reused in a wall of the church of San Bartolomeo in Avezzano and transcribed only twice before disappearing.[37] The inscription runs as follows (*CIL* 9.3915, cf. *AE* 1994.546):

> Imp(eratori) Caesari divi / Nervae fil(io) Nervae / Traiano Optimo / Aug(usto) Germanico / Dacico Parthico / pont(ifici) max(imo) trib(unicia) pot(estate) XX[I imp(eratori) X]III / co(n)s(uli) VI patri patriae / senatus populusq(ue) Rom[anus] / ob reciperatos agros et possess[ores reductos] / quos lacus Fucini violent[ia exturbarat]

> To the emperor, the son of the deified Nerva, Caesar Nerva Trajan Optimus Augustus, conqueror in Germania, Dacia and Parthia, the

[36] There is another epigraphic find connected with the emissary: a number of marble tablets with indications of distance which were placed along the underground tunnel at certain intervals, possibly to facilitate orientation (*CIL* 9.3888–90): Burri (2001), 11.

[37] Its authenticity has been called into question due to an apparent error in the indication of the tribunician year: the transcription preserves *trib pot XXIII*, clearly a mistake, since Trajan was only invested with the *tribunicia potestas* for the twenty-first time in the final year of his reign. Mommsen's explanation for the *CIL* edition is to read *trib(unicia) pot(estate) XXI im[p(eratori) XII]*. Letta (1994), 208, argues for reading *trib(unicia) pot(estate) XX[I imp(eratori) X]III*, which would date the completion of the repairs into the final year of Trajan's reign, AD 117, and I have taken over his reading here. See also Catalli (2011) for a thorough discussion of the inscription.

Pontifex Maximus, invested with the tribunician power twenty-one times, proclaimed imperator thirteen times, consul six times, Father of the Fatherland, the senate and people of Rome (dedicated this statue) because he had reclaimed the acres and reinstated the landowners whom the violence of the Fucine Lake had driven away.

The inscription refers to Trajanic restoration works of the tunnel, which needed regular technical maintenance to remain functional. It has been argued that a major collapse in the tunnel had rendered it completely incapacitated, a problem these engineering works apparently rectified.[38] In return, the *Senatus Populusque Romanus* set up a statue of the emperor with this inscription, commemorating the achievement. The inscription personifies the lake, endowing it with *violentia* and the power to rob rightful owners of their land and drive them away. Trajan is set up as overcoming this *violentia* and restoring the order that the misbehaving lake had threatened.[39]

During the construction works for the nineteenth-century tunnel, a number of fragments of a large limestone panel relief were discovered.[40] At least some of the relief panels had already been part of an earlier ancient monument before being recycled for the panel relief discussed here.[41] In the Middle Ages, the panels were apparently used as building material for medieval restorations of the ancient tunnel.[42] The five fragments turned out to have been part of a large panoramic scene. Of the largest two fragments, one shows a settlement with orthogonal streets and a theatre in the top left-hand corner (Figure 2.4). To the right of the walled settlement, the surrounding countryside is depicted, featuring a road, a river, and a bridge.

The second large fragment (Figure 2.5) is mostly covered by the representation of waves, very probably indicating the Fucine Lake. In the top right-hand corner, the shoreline is marked by trees. Two disproportionally large capstans are visible along the shore, each worked by two men. Further, smaller fragments of the relief also show parts of buildings and settlements. Giuliani has proposed a reconstruction of the entire composition, measuring

---

[38] Letta (1994). There was a regular maintenance crew for the conduit (a *statio classiarii* from Ravenna) installed there by Claudius, but the work required in this case seems to have been beyond their capacities: see Letta (1994), 208. However, considering the unreliability of rebuilding inscriptions for questions of detail and especially scale of restoration (Thomas and Witschel (1992) and p. 20 in this volume), I do not consider the inscription conclusive proof that the conduit had actually completely ceased to function at any point.

[39] For comparable rhetoric of victory over water in Trajanic inscriptions, see the examples quoted by Purcell (1996), 203 n. 2.

[40] On the archaeological discoveries during the nineteenth-century draining, see Segenni (2003).

[41] Facenna (2003), 72–5.

[42] Segenni (2003), 56–7.

Figure 2.4. Torlonia relief, panel 2 (city and landscape). Castello Piccolomini: Collezione Torlonia e Museo d'Arte Sacra della Marsica, Celano.

Courtesy of the Ministero per i beni e le attività culturali e per il turismo, direzione regionale Musei Abruzzo.

Figure 2.5. Torlonia relief, panel 1 (lake, ships and capstans). Castello Piccolomini: Collezione Torlonia e Museo d'Arte Sacra della Marsica, Celano.

Courtesy of the Ministero per i beni e le attività culturali e per il turismo, direzione regionale Musei Abruzzo.

a stunning 2 by 3.5 metres (Figure 2.6).[43] Taking into account the few specific topographic details provided in the representations, he divides the scene into three levels. On his reconstruction, the relief presents the view from the mountains on the east side of the lake. The lowest level shows the eastern

[43] Giuliani (2003a).

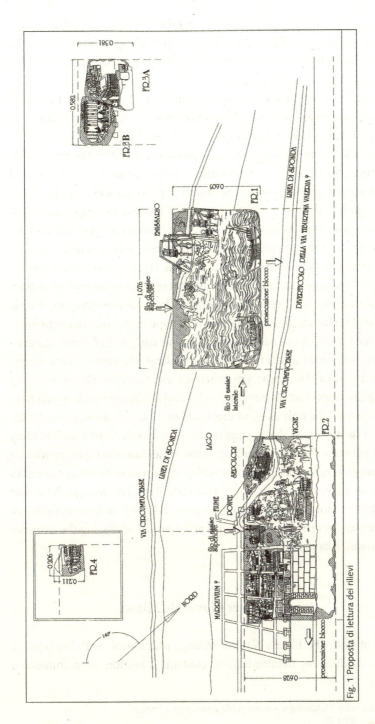

Figure 2.6. Possible reconstruction of the Fucine Lake relief, with the positions of known fragments, including panel 2 (Marruvium?) at the bottom left, and panel 1 (lake) in the centre.
From Giuliani (2003), fig. 70. Reproduced courtesy of Prof. Cairoli Fulvio Giuliani.

78 BUILDING IN WORDS

shore of the lake, featuring Marruvium and the river Iuvencus. The middle level is taken up by the lake itself, while the top level represents the opposite (western) shore of the lake, where the smaller fragments show part of further settlements on that side of the lake.

The context of this relief is completely unclear. It could have been part of a public monument or a private funerary one.[44] It is tentatively dated on stylistic grounds (of the relief proper as well as of the earlier carvings on the reused blocks) to the mid- to late second century AD.[45] For the present investigation, the prominent representation of the capstans, centrally placed within the composition, is most relevant. It appears unlikely that the scene is a straightforward representation of the Claudian drainage, since the reliefs were probably produced at least a century after the completion of the Claudian works. One possibility is that the representation shows a specific instance of maintenance work, for example the Hadrianic improvements of the tunnel.[46] However, I favour a more abstract reading of the representation.

The theme of the relief is the flourishing landscape surrounding the Fucine Lake. The entire work shows a civilized landscape of production, with boats crossing the lake, bridges, roads, sanctuaries, and safely walled cities. The conduit which prevented the lake from flooding the land surrounding it was simply an integral part of this landscape—albeit an invisible one. The only way of rendering this important element of the civilized landscape visible would have been to represent the only element that could ever be seen above ground—the capstans at the top of the shafts, employed to convey water, earth, and building materials between tunnel and surface. At the same time, the representation of work in progress functions in a similar way to the representations considered in the previous chapter. Just as the crane in the Haterii relief encourages the viewer to consider the effort and skill necessary for constructing the tomb building, so do the capstans here evoke the technical achievement of digging the emissary and maintaining its functionality.

Pliny the Elder's Invisible Miracle

Book 36 of Pliny the Elder's *Natural History*, which deals with the topic of 'stone' in its different manifestations, contains a section on architectural

---

[44] Facenna (2003), 75, leaning towards a public monumental context.
[45] Facenna (2003), 76.
[46] Facenna (2003), 76–7, cf. Giuliani (2003a), 82 n. 1.

DEBATING THE DRAINING OF THE FUCINE LAKE   79

marvels.[47] The passage describing the draining of the Fucine Lake forms part of the climax of this section, dedicated to aqueducts and other forms of large-scale (mostly water) engineering. After a passionate encomium of Roman aqueducts in general (*vera aestimatione invicta miracula*—'miracles unsurpassed in their genuine value', *HN* 36.121) and the Aqua Claudia in particular,[48] Pliny turns to another admirable project of the emperor Claudius (36.124):[49]

> Eiusdem Claudi inter maxime memoranda equidem duxerim, quamvis destitutum successoris odio, montem perfossum ad lacum Fucinum emittendum inenarrabili profecto impendio et operarum multitudine per tot annos, cum aut conrivatio aquarum, qua terrenus mons erat, egereretur in verticem machinis aut silex caederetur quantaque intus in tenebris fierent, quae neque concipi animo nisi ab iis qui videre neque enarrari humano sermone possunt!

> Among the most memorable [deeds] of this same Claudius, I at least venture to count, even though [the project] was abandoned because of the jealousy of his successor, the mountain that has been dug through to drain the Fucine Lake, with indeed indescribable expense and a multitude of workmen over so many years, because, either, where earth formed the interior of the mountain, water that collected in the tunnel had to be transported to the top [of the shaft] by hoists, or [where the mountain was made of rock] the rock had to be cut out, and operations of such magnitude executed underground in the darkness, as can neither be understood (except by those who have seen them) nor described in human language.

The word *equidem* in the first sentence already serves to acknowledge that Pliny's assessment of the Fucine Lake project has a place within a debate, and that there may be others who have expressed different opinions.[50] In terms

---

[47] On Pliny's *Natural History* and its 36th book, see p. 52.

[48] *HN* 36.123: *quod si quis diligentius aestumaverit abundantiam aquarum in publico, balineis, piscinis, euripis, domibus, hortis, suburbanis villis, spatia aquae venientis, exstructos arcus, montes perfossos, convalles aequatas, fatebitur nil magis mirandum fuisse in toto orbe terrarum.*—'But if someone were to assess quite carefully the abundance of water in public places, in baths, fish ponds, channels, houses, gardens, country estates near the city, and if someone were to assess the distances traversed by the water, the arches that have been erected, the mountains that have been dug through, the valleys that have been levelled, he would admit that there has been nothing more worthy of admiration in the whole world.'

[49] I quote the text of André (1981).

[50] For this common function of *equidem*, see *OLD* 1b.

80 BUILDING IN WORDS

of the first theme which we identified as a focus of the debate, Pliny is brief and to the point. The channel was not finished, the project was abandoned after Claudius's death: *quamvis destitutum successoris odio*. The remark looks innocuous, but it is of considerable interest. There is no other source that mentions the work having been left incomplete at Claudius's death. As we shall see, Tacitus, Suetonius, and Dio all assume that the work was completed in Claudius's lifetime, albeit with technical problems. By saying nothing of work that was inadequate or of technical failures, but instead pointing to its unfinished nature, any flaws and imperfections that may have been known to readers are by implication attributed solely to Claudius's untimely death. By linking the abandonment and hence failure of the project to the proverbially 'bad' emperor Nero (whose aqueducts are also unceremoniously left out of the list of aqueducts which precedes this passage), the eventual result of the drainage, evidently thought unsatisfactory, is associated only with Claudius's supposedly jealous and incapable successor and entirely separate from the magnificent Claudian undertaking. Besides deviously reapportioning responsibility, Pliny also strongly downplays the importance of the function-ality of the outlet. This project is *maxime memorandum* and indescribably great, and the criteria that render it so are discussed at length. Whether the tunnel actually *worked*, Pliny suggests, is not a measure of its greatness.

In dealing with the value of the project and the possibilities of determining and describing it, Pliny combines two different strategies. On the one hand, he claims that words cannot capture the magnitude of the cost or the labour needed for the endeavour (*inenarrabili profecto impendio* and *quae . . . neque enarrari humano sermone possunt*). Inexpressibility is a well-known rhetorical *topos*,[51] and Pliny here increases its effect by combining this language of impressive vagueness with a number of categories that one might encounter in, for example, a building inscription, and in respect of which it would be perfectly possible to be more specific (the scale of works carried out, the time needed, the expense).[52] Leaving all these elements unspecified suggests that they are too large to *be* specified. The Fucine Lake therefore surpasses in greatness even the Aqua Claudia, called the most admirable thing of the entire world only a few sentences earlier, since the cost of the aqueduct was still specifiable (36.122). As the reason for this immeasurability, Pliny points

---

[51] Pliny also uses it at *HN* 2.6, 8.21, 8.159, 10.3, 12.38, 12.86, 12.110, 17.35, 21.1, 32.1, 35.158, 37.57, 37.80, 37.90. For the innumerable as a *topos* in imperial praise, see Men. Rhet. 368.21–369.2.

[52] On these categories in building inscriptions, see pp. 17–21. They are taken up by Suetonius; see pp. 92–3.

to the special difficulty of the work:[53] the challenge of digging through earth, requiring constant removal of water, and cutting through hard rock.[54]

There would be only one way, Pliny suggests, of actually grasping the magnitude of the project, namely to see the work in progress for one-self: *quae neque concipi animo nisi ab iis qui videre (. . .) possunt*. For Pliny, the greatness of the project lies in the execution of a near-impossible feat. Unfortunately, both the building work and the finished result of the Fucine Lake project were completely invisible, hidden underground. The artist of the Torlonia relief addressed the problem of invisibility by representing the only element of the entire mechanism that *was* visible above ground, the capstan-mechanisms, in action, in extra-large size, and in a prominent position near the centre of the relief.[55] Pliny, on the other hand, turns precisely the invisibility of the works to account. The claim that one would appreciate the greatness of the works if one could see them creates a suggestion of accountability. At the same time, the fact that no one will ever be able to do so adds to this greatness, since all the work was carried out *in tenebris*.

As a third focus of the debate, I identified the interaction between man and nature during the execution of the draining. However, any reference to this relationship is conspicuously absent from Pliny's description of the draining. It is characterized neither as harmonious nor as confrontational. This absence is 'conspicuous' because of the relation between this passage and the wider context of the *Natural History* and the views on the relationship between man and nature expressed there.[56] As a general principle, Pliny approves of human use and deployment of resources that nature readily provides, but not of major human interventions in the 'natural state' of things, which are often driven by the desire for more than an appropriate share.[57] For example, book 33 opens with a forceful condemnation of mining. Digging up precious stones and metals is morally wrong, since it involves taking from nature by force something that she has withheld from us for our own good (33.1–2):

---

[53] Cf. the *difficultas* invoked as a category of praise by Caesar in *BGall.* 4.17.2 and Pliny in *HN* 36.69; see pp. 49 and 53.

[54] The Torlonia relief helps us to understand how the mechanism for the removal of water and earth functioned; see Giuliani (2003a).

[55] See pp. 76–8 and Figure 2.5.

[56] On attitudes to nature in Pliny, see generally Beagon (1992) and (1996), Wallace-Hadrill (1990), and Sallmann (1986).

[57] This ideal of the 'natural' is never clearly defined, but in general, as Wallace-Hadrill (1990), 88, phrases it, 'the idea of the natural is . . . intimately linked with simplicity, cheapness, and accessibility. . . . Luxury, by contrast, is characterised by superfluity. It is always excess to requirements. It is wasteful and destructive.' Cf. also Beagon (1996), 306: 'Indeed, it is Pliny's careful evaluation of what man's needs really are, both material and moral, that often leads him to place restrictions on man's activities in nature.' On the 'natural' as a moral category, see also Edwards (1993), 144–5.

82   BUILDING IN WORDS

persequimur omnes eius fibras vivimusque super excavatam, mirantes
dehiscere aliquando aut intremescere illam, ceu vero non hoc indignatione
sacrae parentis exprimi possit. imus in viscera et in sede manium opes
quaerimus, tamquam parum benigna fertilique qua calcatur . . .

We go in pursuit of all her [i.e. the earth's] bowels, and live above [the earth]
that we have hollowed out, marvelling that occasionally she splits open or
begins to tremble—as if this could not indeed be elicited by the indignation
of our holy parent. We penetrate her innermost parts and seek for riches in
the dwelling-place of the spirits of the dead, as though [the part] where we
tread upon her were not sufficiently beneficent and fertile.

The digging up of precious metals and stones is described in terms of
harming the physical body of the earth and causing her to tremble in pain—
unnecessarily, since what she provides for us above ground is generous
enough (*tamquam parum benigna fertilique qua calcatur*). Greed drives
humans even to disturb the most inviolable and sacred of natural boundaries, that between the living and the dead: *in sede manium opes quaerimus*.[58]
Book 36, which ends shortly after the Fucine Lake passage, opens with an
extensive diatribe against human violation of mountains (36.1–2):

montes natura sibi fecerat ut quasdam compages telluris visceribus
densandis, simul ad fluminum impetus domandos fluctusque frangendos ac
minime quietas partes coercendas durissima sui materia. . . . (2) promunturia
aperiuntur mari, et rerum natura agitur in planum; evehimus ea, quae
separandis gentibus pro terminis constituta erant. . . .

Mountains nature had made for herself to serve as a kind of structure for
holding firmly together the innards of the earth and at the same time to
subdue the violence of the rivers, to break the force of the sea, and so to
restrain her least restful elements with her hardest material. . . .
(2) Headlands are opened up to the sea [by us], and nature is flattened out.
We remove the features that are set as boundaries to separate nations. . . .

Again, nature is strongly and emotively personified, as possessing a body
(*telluris viscera*) and as having provided well for mankind. Her mountains

---

[58] On the importance of boundaries and their violation as a measure of moral depravity, see
Edwards (1993), ch. 4 *passim*, esp. 143–9, and pp. 64–5 in this volume.

DEBATING THE DRAINING OF THE FUCINE LAKE 83

function as natural boundaries which humans have a moral obligation to accept (*pro terminis constituta erant*), and they are essential for keeping the larger order of the world intact.[59]

Against this background, it becomes clear that Pliny's praise of the Fucine Lake tunnel presents him with a challenge. He has to contend not only with the potential moral criticism of other authors, but also with his own, strongly expressed moralizing strictures. Having first criticized the manipulation of mountains as essentially sinful and transgressive, and having stressed their essential function for keeping apart different bodies of water, he now extols digging through a mountain to disperse large quantities of water from a lake into a river, with the object of turning water into land. In this context, the absence of any hint at opposition between man and nature should be understood as a deliberate strategy to dissociate Claudius's act of engineering from such human acts of transgressive violence.[60] 'Packaged' between a number of successful projects of unassailable *utilitas* (the aqueducts, the harbour at Ostia), this massive, though flawed, engineering project is carefully protected from any association with human disrespect for natural boundaries.[61]

Tacitus's *Annals* 12.56–7

Tacitus treats the Fucine Lake project towards the end of his account of the reign of Claudius.[62] In the Claudian books of the *Annals*, the princeps's central characteristics are his passivity and his lack of control. Agents other than Claudius often take centre-stage, especially Messalina and Agrippina. Towards the end of *Annals* 12, Agrippina's grip on Claudius is at its strongest, and she uses it ruthlessly to manoeuvre her son Nero into position as the future princeps. Tacitus's depiction of the Fucine Lake has to be understood in this context. Although its focus is completely different, it can nevertheless be read as reacting to Pliny's earlier version of events and participating in the struggle over the interpretation of the Fucine Lake project. Tacitus chooses to describe not the execution of the engineering work but the two opening

[59] For the philosophical background of Pliny's views on nature, see Beagon (1992), ch. 1.

[60] Cf. Reitz (2013) on another Plinian strategy for achieving this end: his use of the *topos* of cooperation between nature and builder.

[61] On *utilitas* in Pliny, see Citroni Marchetti (1982). For an overview of Claudius's 'useful' engineering projects, see e.g. Levick (1990), 108–12, and Osgood (2011), 168–89.

[62] The first Claudian books are lost; the narrative only picks up halfway through Claudius's reign, in AD 47. Malloch (2009) offers a good introduction to the treatment of the Claudian reign in the *Annals*. See also Vessey (1971); Seif (1973); Mehl (1974) (on events at court); Martin (1981), 144–61; Griffin (1990); Hausmann (2009), 149–439.

84   BUILDING IN WORDS

ceremonies for the channel, both of them spectacular public displays (*Ann.* 12.56–7):[63]

(56.1) Sub idem tempus inter lacum Fucinum amnemque Lirim perrupto monte, quo magnificentia operis a pluribus viseretur, lacu in ipso navale proelium adornatur, ut quondam Augustus structo cir<ca> Tiberim stagno, sed levibus navigiis et minore copia ediderat. (2) Claudius triremes quadriremesque et undeviginti hominum milia armavit, cincto ratibus ambitu, ne vaga effugia forent, ac tamen spatium amplexus ad vim remigii, gubernantium artes, impetus navium et proelio solita. in ratibus praetoriarum cohortium manipuli turmaeque adstiterant, antepositis propugnaculis, ex quis catapultae ballistaeque tenderentur. reliqua lacus classiarii tectis navibus obtinebant. (3) ripas et colles montiumque edita in modum theatri multitudo innumera complevit, proximis e municipiis et alii urbe ex ipsa, visendi cupidine aut officio in principem. ipse insigni paludamento neque procul Agrippina chlamyde aurata praesedere. pugnatum quamquam inter sontes fortium virorum animo, ac post multum vulnerum occidioni exempti sunt. (57.1) Sed perfecto spectaculo <cum> apertum aquarum iter, incuria operis manifesta fuit, haud satis depressi ad lacus ima vel media.[64] eoque tempore interiecto altius effossi specus, et contrahendae rursum multitudini gladiatorum spectaculum editur, inditis pontibus pedestrem ad pugnam. (2) quin et convivium effluvio lacus adpositum magna formidine cunctos adfecit, quia vis aquarum

---

[63] The description comes at the end of the year AD 52. However, since two opening ceremonies are described, with some time, possibly even years, between them (*tempore interiecto*), it seems most likely that the second of the two openings took place in AD 52, while the first one dates to an unspecified earlier year. Cf. Koestermann (1967), 204, *ad* 56.1. The text quoted is Heubner (1994).

[64] On the text here, see Hausmann (2009), 392 n. 1228, who convincingly defends *vel media*, deleted by, among others, Heubner (1994). Letta (1994), 204, adduces archaeological arguments for deletion, perhaps assuming a rather more detailed understanding of the design of the mouth of the emissary than Tacitus may have possessed. Cf. also Koestermann (1967), who suggests emending to *vel medii*. In fact, *vel* here has the force of *saltem* (*KSt* 2.109): 'not to the depths or even just to the middle levels'. What precisely Tacitus's understanding of the improvements was remains a difficult question, since we cannot say precisely what part of the work *specus* represents. He may have thought that the actual tunnel was dug out more deeply, a possibility excluded by the archaeological evidence (Letta (1994), 204). Various attempts have been made to explain the failure that Tacitus mentions. Considering the lack of archaeological evidence, I see no way of deciding between them. D'Amato (1980), 240–4, argues that there may have been a collapse in the tunnel at the last moment before the opening, which blocked the channel. Letta (1994), posits a protective dam-like structure designed to regulate the flow of water into the outlet (important especially in case of high water levels) and argues that in some way the ducts (*specus*, a solution that explains the plural) leading through this dam to admit the water to the tunnel in a controlled way had not been constructed at a low enough level, and the water in fact could not drain away through them. A number of further explanations are summarized by D'Amato (1980), 234–8.

prorumpens proxima trahebat, convulsis ulterioribus aut fragore et sonitu exterriti<s>. simul Agrippina trepidatione principis usa ministrum operis Narcissum incusat cupidinis ac praedarum, nec ille reticet, impotentiam muliebrem nimiasque spes eius arguens.

(56.1) At around the same time, after the mountain between the Fucine Lake and the river Liris had been broken through, a naval battle was arranged on the lake itself, in order that the magnificence of the project might be seen by a greater number of people—just as Augustus had once produced one, having constructed a pool near the Tiber, though his battle featured light vessels and a smaller force. (2) Claudius armed triremes, quadriremes and nineteen thousand men. He lined the perimeter with rafts, so that there would not be any unrestrained escapes, nevertheless enclosing enough space for the violence of the rowers, the skills of the steersmen, the attacks of the ships and usual utensils for battle. On the rafts maniples and squadrons of praetorian cohorts stood by. Outworks had been put in front of them, from which catapults and ballists might be directed. Marines controlled the rest of the lake on covered ships. (3) An innumerable crowd filled the banks, hills and mountain heights like a theatre, [some] from the nearest cities and others from Rome itself, out of their desire to view or out of duty towards the princeps. He himself, wearing a remarkable military cloak, and not far from him Agrippina in a golden chlamys presided. Although the battle was fought between criminals, it was fought with the courage of brave men, and after a lot of wounding, they were exempted from killing each other. (57.1) But when on completion of the spectacle the channel for the water was opened, the carelessness of the work was brought to light, since it had not been dug out sufficiently to the lowest or even the middle levels of the lake. And for this reason, after some time had elapsed, the cavities were excavated more deeply, and to assemble a crowd again, a gladiatorial spectacle was put on, for which planks were placed on the water so they could fight on foot. (2) There was even a banquet which was laid out near the outlet of the lake and terrified everyone, because the force of the waters in breaking forth tore with it everything that was close by, while what was further away was made to totter or was terrified by the crashing and thundering. At the same time Agrippina, taking advantage of the shock of the princeps, accused Narcissus, who had been in charge of the work, of greed and embezzlement, and he did not hold back either, criticizing her female weakness and her excessive ambitions.

86 BUILDING IN WORDS

Did the draining of the Fucine Lake succeed? A reader of Tacitus's account is hardly in a position to judge, since Tacitus does not offer the slightest indication of what the project was supposed to achieve: *inter lacum Fucinum amnemque Lirim perrupto monte* is all he provides as a description of the project itself. In terms of the effectiveness of the tunnel, Tacitus claims that the first attempt at draining failed because of careless workmanship. At the second opening of the channel, the force of the water gushing through is much stronger than expected, and it frightens and endangers the spectators and even the imperial family, but the actual result of the improvements is left open.[65] Although there is a general suggestion that the work was carried out badly, Tacitus, like Pliny, does not dwell on the question of the functionality of the tunnel.

Considering the lack of information on this crucial point, how, then, is a viewer of the spectacle (or a Tacitean reader) supposed to judge the project? In terms of the second focus of the debate, the differences between Tacitus's and Pliny's accounts are especially instructive. As far as the categories invoked by Pliny in his praise of the project are concerned, Tacitus is silent on the *multitudo operarum* and the number of years of hard work. The expense, which for Pliny served as one of the indescribable assets of the project (*inenarrabili profecto impendio*), is taken up by Tacitus only in his suggestion of corruption and embezzlement, an accusation levelled by Agrippina against Narcissus, the *minister operis* (12.57.2).[66] The great difficulty of the work, too, is turned into criticism rather than praise by Tacitus, since it was evidently too great for Claudius's engineers, and the opening of the channel therefore resulted in the emperor's public humiliation. Pliny's categories of praise are thus either ignored or invoked to discredit the project.

As we saw earlier, Pliny points to the importance of actual *vision*, as opposed to mere description, for the appreciation of the magnificence of the project. Only those who had seen the work with their own eyes could really comprehend how difficult and impressive it was—a neat strategy for using the invisibility of the structure to his advantage. Tacitus, on the other hand, depicts *only* happenings visible above ground, i.e. the opening spectacles, but uses the contrast between the impressive display and the failure of the

---

[65] Again, different reconstructions have been attempted of what could have caused the alarming flooding, among them another collapse, causing obstruction in the channel and therefore a forceful resurgence of the water at the lake-end of the tunnel (D'Amato (1980), 244–52; Letta (1994), 206); or a collapse of the protective dam-structure mentioned in n. 64 of this chapter (Letta (1994), 206–7).

[66] Narcissus's embezzlement is also mentioned (as a rumour) in Cass. Dio 60.33.5.

DEBATING THE DRAINING OF THE FUCINE LAKE 87

opening proper to illustrate precisely the *unreliability* of visual impressions. The theme of viewing is introduced in the first sentence of the section (. . . *quo magnificentia operis a pluribus viseretur*), but the focus in this passage is on the conscious orchestration of viewing and view: staging, spectacle, theatrical performance. The opening of the tunnel is on both occasions preceded by large displays of gladiatorial fighting, and the passage shows throughout a sustained use of the vocabulary of spectacle and stage: *visendi cupidine . . . perfecto spectaculo . . . spectaculum editur.*[67] The draining of the lake is, more than anything else, a huge spectacle in its own right, and even the natural situation of the lake becomes part of the theatrical display of the emperor: *ripas et collis montiumque edita in modum theatri multitudo innumera complevit.* The viewing public is not supposed to judge the work objectively: they are being manipulated by Claudius's and Agrippina's dazzling show.

The theme of discrepancy between appearance and reality also offers the key to the two-part structure of the Fucine Lake passage.[68] The first round of spectacles initially seems impressive and successful, but this positive impression is deceptive: the project itself turns out to be a failure. Claudius would like to show off the *magnificentia operis* (56.1), but instead, the *incuria operis* emerges (57.1).[69] He would like to appear as another Augustus (*ut quondam Augustus structo cir<ca> Tiberim stagno*, 56.1), but fails to live up to his model.[70] In order to sharpen the contrast between attempted *magnificentia* and evident *incuria*, Tacitus even suggests that the failure was apparent immediately (*manifesta fuit*), a version of events that cannot be reconciled with the technical facts.[71] Understanding the passage in terms of the contrast between first, deceptive, appearance and its unmasking also allows for an

---

[67] Santoro L'Hoir (2006), 240.

[68] On the contrast between the two parts of the description, see Seif (1973), 222–3, and Hausmann (2009), 389–95. On the contrast between appearance and reality more generally in the work of Tacitus, see Pearcy (1973), a study on the words *species, imago, effigies,* and *simulacrum* in Tacitus.

[69] Seif (1973), 222; Hausmann (2009), 392. On Tacitus's use of the word *magnificentia*, see Koestermann (1967), 27, *ad* 11.1.1.

[70] Keitel (1977), 199, and Hausmann (2009), 392, on this contrast. Hausmann especially points to the importance of the revelation for the characterization of the emperor (393): 'Es wird deutlich, daß Tacitus durch seinen auffallend gleißenden Bericht in ann. 12,56 lediglich eine Fallhöhe für Claudius aufbauen wollte, von der aus er den unliebsamen Kaiser anschließend ins nahezu Bodenlose hinabstoßen konnte.' On Claudius's (failed) attempts of setting himself up as another Augustus in the *Annals*, see O'Gorman (2000), 107–9. On Augustus's *navalia* that Claudius intends to outdo, see Coleman (1993), *passim*; see Berlan-Bajard (2006), 346–8, on Claudius's *navalia* as *imitatio Augusti*.

[71] Even with the highly functional draining channel constructed in the nineteenth century, the draining of the lake took sixteen years. With the less ambitious Claudian channel, where even slower drainage would have been expected, the *incuria* could hardly have been obvious immediately. See Cozzo (1928), 303.

88 BUILDING IN WORDS

improved understanding of the theme of the relationship between man and nature, the third focus of the debate, to which I now turn.

From Tacitus's (and, as we shall see, Suetonius's) accounts, it appears that Claudius intended his achievement to be seen in terms of his triumph and domination over nature.[72] On both occasions, the opening is preceded by a display of fighting, which could suggest that Claudius wanted his project to be understood as another sort of fight—one between human ingenuity and the waters of the lake. The unusual costumes of Claudius and Agrippina, which both Pliny and Tacitus comment on, also suggest this:[73] Claudius's coat, the *paludamentum*, is a general's cloak, while the gold *chlamys* worn by Agrippina in Tacitus's version is also a (Greek) military cloak, and is even worn by triumphant generals.[74] The emperor attempts to cast himself as the victor in a struggle with nature, in the same way that Trajan, in the inscription discussed earlier, is set up as subduing the violent lake and thus restoring natural order.

Tacitus thus at first sight appears to follow and reproduce Claudius's ideological display, but he quickly turns the significance of this staged confrontation on its head. I argued earlier that the rhetoric of environmental control and that of moral transgression employ the same *topoi* and lie perilously close to one another. Tacitus uses this circumstance to his advantage when he subtly activates the paradigm of the Persian king Xerxes and his reckless and fatal disrespect for natural (and national) boundaries in his description of the second gladiatorial display: *gladiatorum spectaculum editur, inditis pontibus pedestrem ad pugnam.* The fighting takes place, Tacitus claims, on planks laid across the water.[75] Even though water is naturally available, and

---

[72] For comparable Claudian displays of victory over water, see Osgood (2011), 180–5, on the Porta Maggiore as a monument of triumph over water, a whale hunt in the harbour of Ostia (described in Pliny, *HN* 9.14–15), canal-building at Ostia, and measures against the flooding of the Tiber in Rome. Berlan-Bajard (2006) sketches the gradual loss, during the early empire, of the direct association between staged sea battles and naval military victories (348–50), and analyses the different ways in which aquatic spectacles served as a 'célébration d'une maîtrise surnaturelle des éléments marins' (350–61).

[73] Pliny has Agrippina wear a golden *paludamentum* (*HN* 33.63): *nos vidimus Agrippinam Claudi principis, edente eo navalis proelii spectaculum, adsidentem et indutam* **paludamento** *aureo textili sine alia materia.*—'I saw Agrippina the wife of Claudius, when he was putting on the spectacle of a naval battle, sitting next to him and clad in a *paludamentum* made of golden cloth without any other material.' Pliny does not explicitly connect this description to the Fucine Lake, simply referring to a sea fight as the occasion.

[74] Suetonius also has Caligula wear a *chlamys* on the occasion of a triumph over water, the inauguration of the bridge between Puteoli and Baiae: Suet. *Cal.* 19.2. For the parallel, see also Koestermann (1967), 206 *ad* 12.56.3.

[75] It remains unclear precisely what kind of construction we are to imagine: a wooden platform, or boats that have been interconnected by means of wooden planks; *pons* is used of planks employed for entering the enemies' boats during naval battles (*TLL* 10.1.2669.33–49) and for planking which

DEBATING THE DRAINING OF THE FUCINE LAKE 89

was used for a sea battle at the first opening, the emperor now chooses to demonstrate, yet again, human dominance over the boundaries between land and water by laying planks across the water, which allow for fighting on foot—on water. Through the juxtaposition of *pontibus* and *pedestrem*, Tacitus stresses the perverse nature of this display, and through using the word *pontibus* in a context where a powerful ruler turns water into land on a grand scale, Tacitus evokes Xerxes's bridge over the Hellespont, one of the best-known paradigms of the immoral and hubristic crossing of the boundaries between land and sea.[76]

Finally, Tacitus combines the theme of the contrast between appearance and reality with that of the struggle between man and nature through the way in which nature's reaction to Claudius's use of violence is phrased. In the first sentence of the Tacitean passage, the digging of the tunnel is described by the word *perrumpere* (56). The Tacitean *perrupto monte* (perhaps even a deliberate reaction to Pliny's more neutral *montem perfossum*), suggests a powerful, possibly even violent action.[77] The danger inherent in using this kind of force against nature is demonstrated towards the end of the passage, when the water behaves in an unexpectedly violent fashion itself: it bursts forth with such violence that it sweeps away everything in its reach. The *perrupto monte* of the first sentence is here taken up by *vis aquarum prorumpens*. To violence, nature responds with violence, and its counterattack spreads terror among spectators and the imperial family. Similarly, the use of *vis* here may also recall the *vim remigii* which Claudius *could* (still) control and contain during his initial spectacle. This revelation of Claudius's lack of control over nature and her forces fits with Tacitus's larger theme of the emperor's weakness. Not only his wife, but even nature herself refuses to take the emperor seriously.

The contrast between the initially positive description of the spectacle and the revelation of its complete emptiness illustrates the unreliability of

connects boats into a temporary bridge (*TLL* 10.1.2669.59–69). On the use of *pontes* during sea battles, see *TLL* 10.1.2670.4–9 and especially Plin. *HN* 16.190, which refers to a *pons naumachiarius* (the sense of which is also obscure).

[76] See also Plin. *HN* 4.75. For the use of the Xerxes paradigm in a similar context, cf. Suet. *Calig.* 19.3. On Xerxes as a paradigm of transgressive manipulation of nature, see also Edwards (1993), 146, on Plutarch; and Traina (1988), 320–32 on Vitruvius.

[77] Pliny uses this expression twice in quick succession, once in 36.123 concerning the Aqua Claudia, and then again in 36.124 with reference to the Fucine Lake; *perfodere* suggests continuous labour, while *perrumpere* evokes a single, violent action. The word *perrumpere*, for example, is also used in *Ann.* 15.42 (. . . *si perrumpi possent, intolerandus labor nec satis causae*), discussed earlier, p. 66.

90 BUILDING IN WORDS

visual impressions, but on another level, it also reveals the unreliability of narrative itself. Just as the emperor is able to dazzle his subjects with empty spectacles, so can the writer, if he chooses to do so, lead his readers astray in their evaluation of events, as Tacitus does in the first half of the Fucine Lake episode. In this context, the confrontation between Agrippina and Narcissus that concludes the episode may be suggestive. Both try to use the terror and impressionability of the nearly drowned Claudius to pitch their interpretation of events to the princeps. Agrippina would like him to understand the disaster as an illustration of the greed and corruption of Narcissus. Narcissus, on the other hand, urges the princeps to see the events as revealing Agrippina's lack of self-control and moderation. Tacitus here displays his awareness of the manipulability of the event's meaning. He shows Agrippina and Narcissus attempting to control the significance of this powerful confrontation between man and nature through their use of rhetoric (*arguens*). This may also be a nod towards the magisterial controlling act that he has just performed for *his* audience.

Suetonius's *Life of Claudius*

In Suetonius's *Life of Claudius*, the draining of the Fucine Lake is mentioned not once, but three times. This is due to the nature of Suetonius's work: the individual emperors' biographies are not presented as chronological narratives, but are organized according to thematic categories (*per species, Aug.* 9), covering the public aspects of the emperor's reign (such as generosity to the populace, military achievements, or administration) as well as his private life and personality (for example, personal appearance or habits).[78] Accordingly, the engineering works appear in chapter 20, which treats Claudius's public building projects, while the spectacles held to celebrate the opening of the tunnel are discussed separately, in the subsequent section on the spectacles that Claudius produced for the populace during his reign (21). Finally, in chapter 32, the dinner party of the royal family on the occasion of the (second) opening of the channel is mentioned briefly in the context of Claudius's *convivia*. Being able to deal with different aspects of

[78] On the structure of Suetonius's *Lives*, and the provenance and function of the rubrics he uses, see Wallace-Hadrill (1983), ch. 7. See also Hurley (2001), 17–19, on the structure and design of the *Life of Claudius*. Roughly, *Claud*. 10–25 pertain to Claudius's public works and administration, *Claud*. 26–42 to his personality. On the 'building' rubric in the *Life of Claudius*, see Osgood (2011), 172.

DEBATING THE DRAINING OF THE FUCINE LAKE   91

the draining of the Fucine Lake under different biographical rubrics allows Suetonius to exploit the ambivalent potential of the project most effectively. He can construct one image of the draining and subsequently modify it by throwing light on the project from a different angle—a technique that can be observed regarding all three areas of the debate identified earlier.[79]

The Fucine Lake is first introduced at the opening of the section on public building (20.1), where Suetonius offers an overview of the projects to be treated subsequently:[80]

> . . . ductum aquarum a Gaio incohatum, item emissarium Fucini lacus portumque Ostiensem, quamquam sciret ex iis alterum ab Augusto precantibus assidue Marsis negatum, alterum a Divo Iulio saepius destinatum ac propter difficultatem omissum.

> . . . an aqueduct that Gaius had begun, likewise the outlet of the Fucine Lake and the harbour at Ostia, although he knew that of those last two one had been denied to the Marsians by Augustus although they begged him most fervently, and that the other had quite often been considered by the deified Julius and been abandoned due to its difficulty.

After a short (and approving) assessment of the Claudian aqueducts, Suetonius turns to the Fucine Lake:

> Fucinum adgressus est non minus conpendii spe quam gloriae, cum quidam privato sumptu emissuros se repromitterent, si sibi siccati agri concederentur. per tria autem passuum milia partim effosso monte partim exciso canalem absolvit aegre et post undecim annos, quamvis continuis XXX hominum milibus sine intermissione operantibus.

> He took on the Fucine Lake driven by a hope for profit no less than for glory, since there were those who contracted themselves to drain the lake at their private expense, if the drained farmland were given to them. But the channel, which was three thousand feet in length, he finished, partly

---

[79] I structure my discussion of Suetonius's account according to the different sections of the *Life*, in order to facilitate understanding of the modification of earlier impressions. For each section, I consider the relevant themes of the debate in turn.

[80] Suetonius regularly introduces a new category with such a *partitio*, a structuring sentence summarizing the content of the following section, designed to help the reader in following the movement from one category to the next. See Hurley (2001), 19.

92 BUILDING IN WORDS

by digging and partly by cutting through the mountain, with great difficulty and only after eleven years, although thirty thousand men worked on
it continuously without interruption.

The mention of Augustus's rejection of the project in the introduction might
hint at insurmountable difficulties or suggest that Claudius was rash to take
on such a difficult project.[81] In what follows, however, Suetonius is no more
expansive than his predecessors on the subject of the success or failure of
the project. Precisely two words are accorded to the question of whether the
canal was completed (and none to whether it worked): in flat contradiction
of Pliny's report, Suetonius makes it clear that Claudius *canalem absolvit*—
'finished the canal' (20.2).[82]

Suetonius also engages Pliny on what I have identified as the second
focal point of the debate. His introduction of the Fucine Lake within
exactly the same context as Pliny (preceded by the aqueducts, followed by
the harbour at Ostia) activates the model (as well as creating a general aura
of *utilitas* for the project), and Suetonius subsequently takes his cue from
Pliny for the categories by which to measure the emperor's achievement: the
expense, the time that the project required, the amount of work to be carried
out, and the extreme difficulty of execution, involving both digging and
rock-cutting. However, while Pliny uses the unquantifiability of these categories as an indication of the project's greatness, Suetonius gives us an exact
number of workmen as well as the time required for building (the cost of
the enterprise is not specified, although it is pointed out that it was borne
by external investors). Much suggests that Suetonius's 'exact' numbers are
not particularly closely related to reality,[83] but the number of 30,000 men
is a solid, factual(-seeming) response to Pliny's vagueness and to his claim
that the magnificence of the project cannot be expressed in words (*neque
enarrari humano sermone possunt*, 36.124).[84] The figures Suetonius quotes

[81] The *difficultas* of constructing a harbour at Ostia did not in fact turn out to be insurmountable: cf. *Claud.* 20.3.

[82] On *absolvit* meaning 'finished', see Hurley (2001), 146 *ad. loc.*

[83] In a quantitative analysis of the draining of the Fucine Lake, it has been calculated that
restrictions of space in the tunnel would have made it impossible for more than 3,000 workmen to
have been employed there at any one time, even according to the most generous estimates: Thornton
and Thornton (1985), 107–12. While their calculation of workforce, cost, and time needed has some
methodological flaws (cf. Wiseman (1991)), their calculation of the workforce employed in the
tunnel, drawing partly on Brisse's detailed account of his own tunnel-building works, appears convincing to me. On managing the work forces of several Claudian projects, including the Fucine Lake,
see also Thornton (1986), 37–9.

[84] Multiples of three are elsewhere used for almost magical impressiveness. Cf. e.g. 3, 30, and 300 as
a prelude to *sine fine* in Jupiter's speech to Venus at *Aen.* 1.265–79.

DEBATING THE DRAINING OF THE FUCINE LAKE   93

are so overwhelmingly high that they are, after all, a means of expressing the achievement.[85]

The passage offers little in terms of the third focus of the debate. The slightly military ring of *Fucinum adgressus est* possibly hints at a 'confrontation' between Claudius and the lake, as does the *gloria* the emperor hopes to gain from the project, but the general tone of the passage is neutral and technical.[86]

The reader's first image of the draining is a positive one. Suetonius seems to refer to, and agree with, Pliny's favourable and admiring assessment of the project. He even goes further than Pliny's praise when he has Claudius finish the project and provides the numbers to back up Pliny's claims of magnitude. However, the emerging picture of the project receives substantial modification in the subsequent section, concerned with the emperor's public spectacles (*Claud.* 21.6):

quin et emissurus Fucinum lacum naumachiam ante commisit. sed cum proclamantibus naumachiariis: 'have imperator, morituri te salutant!' respondisset: 'aut non', neque post hanc vocem quasi venia data quisquam dimicare vellet, diu cunctatus an omnes igni ferroque absumeret, tandem e sede sua prosiluit ac per ambitum lacus non sine foeda vacillatione discurrens partim minando partim adhortando ad pugnam compulit. hoc spectaculo c

lassis Sicula et Rhodia concurrerunt, duodenarum triremium singulae, exciente bucina Tritone argenteo, qui e medio lacu per machinam emerserat.

Even when he was about to drain the Fucine Lake, he arranged a sea battle first. But when the fighters cried: 'Hail emperor, those who are about to die salute you!' and he replied: 'or not', and when after he said this no one wanted to fight any longer, since they thought that they had been pardoned, he long hesitated about destroying them all with fire and sword, but finally jumped up from his throne, ran to and fro along the perimeter of the lake with his ugly tottering gait, and forced them to fight partly by threats and partly by encouragements. In this spectacle, a Sicilian and a Rhodian fleet engaged, each consisting of twelve triremes, with a silver Triton calling on

---

[85] Suetonius's rhetorical use of numbers has its origins in a historiographical tradition of citing 'exact' figures; a tradition which Lucian parodies at *Hist. conscr.* 20 as a transparent trick for creating narrative authority.

[86] On the sense of attack in *adgredior*, see Hurley (2001), 145, *ad loc.*

94 BUILDING IN WORDS

his horn, who had emerged from the middle of the lake by means of a lifting device.

The Fucine Lake spectacle is the last in a long list of *beneficia*, but what is set up to be the climax of Claudius's lavish entertainments for the people turns out to be a farce. In the Tacitean account, the *naumachia* was a splendid, well-organized display for an admiring public—unfortunately in stark contrast with the badly engineered draining operation that they were supposed to celebrate. Splendid appearances there contrasted with a grim reality of overreaching and failure. Suetonius reacts to this Tacitean reversal with a reversal of his own. His first, positive account of the draining proper is juxtaposed with a disastrous failure of precisely the *visual* part of the project.

How precisely does Suetonius deviate from the Tacitean version? According to Tacitus, 19,000 men were involved, an incredible number, and they fought so bravely that the survivors were eventually exempted from fighting each other to the death. While Suetonius gives an inordinately high estimate for the men working at the Fucine Lake, the number of ships in his account is significantly lower than that quoted by Tacitus.[87] The bravery of the men that Tacitus stresses is now absent—instead, the convicts initially refuse to fight and have to be forced to do so. The main focus of the episode lies on the grotesque behaviour of Claudius himself, which turns the entire display into a comic spectacle.[88] Realism is left aside in Suetonius's description of the accidental farce enacted by the emperor. There is nothing surprising about the convicts' initial refusal to fight,[89] but in Suetonius's comedy, it is the two joking words (*aut non*) uttered by the emperor from the side of the lake that cause the fiasco—they are apparently heard by hundreds (or thousands) of fighters on a very large lake, who then in a concerted action refuse to fight.[90]

---

[87] Suetonius's modest number of twelve triremes would never fit Tacitus's 19,000 fighters. Cass. Dio 60.33.3 accords fifty ships to each side, while Tacitus, unlike Suetonius, speaks of both triremes and quadriremes. See Kierdorf (1992), 114 *ad loc.*; Hurley (2001), 158 *ad loc.*

[88] The section on public displays contains another example of a spectacle which accidentally descended into comedy: the announcement of the secular games (21.2). Claudius wanted to hold them again, believing that the Augustan calculations had been incorrect, but the herald's announcement that the games would be such as 'no one had ever seen before' caused general ridicule, since many of those present would have seen the Augustan games, and even some of the actors had already appeared under Augustus.

[89] The *naumachiae* were simply a form of public execution, hence the anti-escape measures described by Tacitus. In Dio's account, the convicts also refuse to fight and have to be forced to do so (60.33.4). There is no mention of Claudius's joke. See also Seif (1973), 220.

[90] Presumably, Claudius meant to point out that not all of those greeting him were in fact *morituri*, since some survivors might be pardoned. However, the fighters understood (or pretended to understand) *aut non* as an imperial pardon.

DEBATING THE DRAINING OF THE FUCINE LAKE   95

No more realistic, and no less farcical, is the image of Claudius running along the perimeter of the lake (which would have been about 50 km), upbraiding the fighters. A reference to Claudius's handicap, a well-known source of comedy for contemporary audiences, completes the humorous sketch.[91]

For Tacitus, the impressive spectacle served as a foil for the ensuing disaster. Suetonius's account of the spectacles is as disastrous as Tacitus's account of the draining, but the treatment of different aspects of the same incident under different rubrics means that the fiasco of the sea battle does not explicitly detract from the earlier, positive assessment of the value of the enterprise.

One detail at the end of this passage is highly relevant for the third focus of debate. Only Suetonius reports that the spectacle included a silver statue of Triton, rising from the middle of the lake by means of a mechanical device and blowing on his horn. Public spectacles frequently included mythological re-enactments, and while Suetonius's account suggests that one of the functions of this Triton was to call the fleets to battle, the actual significance of the call seems to lie in a different mythological association.[92] In the first book of Ovid's *Metamorphoses* a terrible flood extinguishes almost all human life. When finally only Deucalion and Pyrrha survive, Jupiter calms the skies, and Neptune embarks on the task of restoring the sea to its original state (Ov. *Met.* 1.330–9, 341–7):[93]

> nec maris ira manet, positoque tricuspide telo   330
> mulcet aquas rector pelagi, supraque profundum
> exstantem atque umeros innato murice tectum
> caeruleum Tritona vocat, conchaeque sonanti
> inspirare iubet fluctusque et flumina signo
> iam revocare dato. cava bucina sumitur illi,   335
> tortilis in latum quae turbine crescit ab imo,

---

[91] The comic effect is strengthened through the use of the unusual word *vacillatio*, only attested here and once in Quintilian's *Institutio Oratoria* in a discussion of ridiculous mannerisms of speakers (Quint. 11.3.128). On Claudius's gait, see also *Claud.* 30; for an exploitation of its comic potential, see most famously Sen. *Apocol.* 1.2, 5.3. For Claudius as a comic figure in Suetonius, cf. also *Claud.* 41 (a recitation turned farce) and *Claud.* 45 (his death kept secret by bringing in comic actors). Santoro L'Hoir (2006) detects a comic side to the proceedings also in the Tacitean version of the Fucine Lake episode (240). See also Dickison (1977) on Claudius and comedy in Tacitus.

[92] On mechanical devices (such as the rising Triton) as part of Roman spectacles, see Hammer (2010).

[93] The reference to *Met.* 1 is pointed out by Hurley (2001), 158, *ad loc.* For a different type of re-enactment of mythical episodes staged by the emperor, see Coleman (1990) on public executions.

96 BUILDING IN WORDS

bucina quae, medio concepit ubi aera ponto,
litora voce replet sub utroque iacentia Phoebo.
tum quoque . . .
. . .
omnibus audita est telluris et aequoris undis,   341
et quibus est undis audita coercuit omnes.
iam mare litus habet, plenos capit alveus amnes,
flumina subsidunt collesque exire videntur,
surgit humus, crescunt sola decrescentibus undis;   345
postque diem longam nudata cacumina silvae
ostendunt, limumque tenent in fronde relictum.

And the anger of the sea does not last. Laying aside his three-pronged fork, the god of the sea soothes the waters, and he calls dark-blue Triton, who shows himself above the sea, his shoulders covered with live murex. He orders him to blow on his resounding shell and by giving this signal now to recall the floods and rivers. He takes up the hollow twisted horn, which grows in width from the bottom of the spiral, the horn which, as soon as it has been blown in the middle of the sea, fills the shores which lie beneath the rising and the setting sun with its sound. Then, too, . . . it was heard by all the waters of the earth and of the sea and it restrained all the waters by which it had been heard. Already the sea has a shore, their riverbed confines the full streams, rivers fall and hills are seen to emerge. The land rises, the ground increases as the waves decrease. After a long day the woods show uncovered tree-tops, and they retain the mud which has been left behind in their leaves.

In Ovid's depiction, Triton rises from the sea (*supraque profundum exstantem*), just as he does from the lake in Suetonius due to a mechanical device. Triton's horn (likewise called a *bucina*, likewise sounded from the middle of the water (337)) orders the waters to recede, and as the waters obey, more and more ground emerges. The appearance of just such a Triton from the waters of the Fucine Lake must have been designed to turn the draining of the lake into a mythological re-enactment of this event, and thus to render this project a divine act of cosmic significance, with Claudius implicitly in the role of the divinity (Jupiter and/or Neptune) who orders the Triton's appearance. In terms of the theme of the relation between man and

DEBATING THE DRAINING OF THE FUCINE LAKE   97

nature, Suetonius thus hints at Claudius's ambitions of ruling over the elements as the gods do and effecting an almost cosmic change by making a lake disappear.[94]

This is the impression the reader is left with at the end of the section on public spectacles: a positive assessment of the economic and engineering aspect of the project, but a spectacle that accidentally deteriorates into a farce and deflates Claudius's claims to divine control of the floods. But a final modification of the reader's image of the Fucine Lake project is still in store. In a section on Claudius's *convivia*, the following brief episode occurs (*Claud.* 32):

> convivatus est et super emissarium Fucini lacus ac paene summersus, cum emissa impetu aqua redundasset.

> He also feasted above the outlet of the Fucine Lake and was almost submerged when the water was let out in such a rush that it overflowed.

The word *summersus* here may recall the final word of the previous section on the Fucine Lake, where the Triton majestically emerged (*emerserat*) from the waters of the lake at Claudius's desire. While Claudius through this action attempted to show his divine control of the waters, this final spotlight that Suetonius throws on the Fucine Lake project shows the princeps as completely incapable of controlling the floods, since he is almost drowned himself. In a final twist, comparable to that at the end of Tacitus's account, the water here regains control and responds to Claudius's interference with violence (*impetu*). We also learn only now that Claudius was feasting while the *naumachia* and the opening of the channel took place. Eating at the wrong time and in the wrong place is a *topos* in descriptions of a bad ruler or leader, and Claudius's dinner during this less-than-perfect performance adds another morally doubtful note.[95]

In three separate episodes, Suetonius has encouraged us to look at the Fucine Lake differently each time. A positive assessment of the useful, economically sound, and extremely difficult engineering project appears in a

[94] Although Suetonius does not spell out the significance of the Triton's appearance, most of his readers would presumably have been familiar with the myth and/or the opening of Ovid's *Metamorphoses*.

[95] On the *topos* of rulers eating at inappropriate times (especially times connected with death, killing, or mourning), see Malloch (2009), 118 and n. 12 (specifically on Tacitus), and (more generally) Paul (1991), 164–6. For Claudius's constant, often ill-timed, and inappropriate desire for food, see also *Claud.* 33.1: *cibi vinique quocumque et tempore et loco appetentissimus . . .* —'most desirous of food and wine, at whatever time and place . . .'. Cf. also Tac. *Ann.* 12.64.2, Sen. *Apocol.* 8.2, Cass. Dio 60.2.5–7.

98 BUILDING IN WORDS

different light when the associated spectacles reveal Claudius as a laughing-stock. A final, short mention sets Claudius's pretensions at divine control over water and land into a different light again—he is not only a comic figure, but dangerously negligent, and rather than mastering the lake, the lake almost masters him. For a reader who encounters the three episodes in the correct order when reading the text in its entirety, the final modification may remain as the strongest impression, but no effort is made within the *Life of Claudius* to reconcile the different aspects of the project. Suetonius's thematic approach does not necessarily aim at creating one coherent image of Claudius's reign and personality. Different aspects appear as more or less positive, and the whole presents the image of an emperor who was neither good nor bad. Suetonius can use three different perspectives on the Fucine Lake project to illustrate completely different aspects of Claudius's life, and this threefold use of the project demonstrates *in nuce* the extreme flexibility of the associations of large-scale engineering projects for which I argued earlier in this chapter.

Conclusion

We do not know what really happened at the Fucine Lake. On the basis of the literary evidence available, it is impossible to establish whether the project was completed by Claudius or not, whether the channel functioned or not, whether the surrounding land was partially drained or not. However, the literary texts allow us to understand something potentially even more interesting: How was the draining of the Fucine Lake *talked about*? How was its significance debated? It emerges that to tell the story of the tunnel's creation, to represent the process of construction and of the opening of the outlet, allows the authors to manipulate their readers' assessment of it.

A number of parallels in phrasing and theme perhaps point to some direct connections between the versions of Pliny, Tacitus, and Suetonius. More importantly, however, the authors' versions of the events of the Fucine Lake reveal significant overlap in respect of the criteria according to which the event is represented and assessed. These criteria emerge as three thematic areas around which the debate of the Fucine Lake is structured.

The first focus of the debate turned out to be of minor importance only. Whether the channel was finished, and whether it worked, is usually not accorded more than a few words, and appears a near-irrelevant criterion for assessing the project. Secondly, the debate focuses on how the value of the project can be assessed and quantified. The invisibility of the project is an obstacle to a viewer's appreciation. Claudius's opening spectacle and staging of the draining are themselves an attempt to render the invisible visible. The Torlonia relief has to rely on the visual clue of capstans to suggest work under ground, only intelligible to those already aware of the existence of the tunnel. While Pliny claims that viewing the work in progress guarantees appropriate appreciation, Tacitus attacks this notion: viewing gives no guarantee of true perception, nor does narrative, as his own piece demonstrates. Suetonius first offers reassuring specifications in Pliny's measurable categories of time, workforce, and difficulty, but his subsequent, confusing spotlights leave us with a general sense of disorientation as to how the project may be judged. Thirdly, Claudius intended the draining as an imperial triumph over nature and a spectacle of god-like control over the elements, and the rhetoric of a comparable attitude informs the Trajanic restoration inscription. Pliny is unable to extract a positive message from Claudius's struggle with nature because of associations of this theme that he wants to and has to avoid. Tacitus and Suetonius activate precisely those negative aspects that Pliny seeks to evade. In the *Annals*, nature responds to Claudius's transgressive behaviour with equal violence, while Suetonius comically deflates the emperor's pretence to divine control over the elements.

The Fucine Lake thus turns out to be a battleground of rhetoric. Each writer tells his own story of the lake, and in doing so values or devalues the project according to the requirements of his narrative. The themes that recur in their versions can partly be linked to the positive features of the building process activated in the representations discussed in Chapter 1 (speed, manpower, cost). But the Fucine Lake debate reveals that there is also an ethical dimension to descriptions of construction. In their literary versions of construction the authors problematize the possibilities of 'staging' engineering and the resulting difficulty of seeing through such displays and shows. They also use descriptions of engineering to tap into a moral discourse about humans and natural boundaries, selecting and activating different elements of this debate to manipulate the impact of the project they describe. In terms of the flexible valuations attached to it, the Fucine Lake is no exception but the rule. To a Roman writer, any large-scale engineering project could be a Fucine Lake, and to tell the story of a project's execution was one way of turning it into a marvel and a victory, or deceit and failure.

3

Writing Cities, Founding Texts

The City as a Poetological Metaphor

Introduction

The previous two chapters focused on the possible relations between descriptions of construction and actual buildings and monuments in the physical world. I considered how telling the story of a structure's creation can be a means of influencing the viewer-reader's response to or evaluation of that structure. In the second part of this study, I turn to a more text-immanent question. I ask how descriptions of the construction process impact on the reader's evaluation not only of something *outside* the text, but also of *the text itself*. I argue that describing construction can be a means of encouraging readers to consider and appreciate the 'madeness' of the text itself. The reader can be invited to do so explicitly, for example when the processes of building and composition are compared, but also subtly and implicitly.

Architecture is one of the most common images for text.[1] We may immediately think of such prominent examples as Horace's claim to have erected a *monumentum aere perennius*, a 'monument more permanent than bronze' (*Carm.* 3.30.1), or of Vergil's poetic temple at the beginning of the third book of his *Georgics*, but much less elaborate architectural images, often used unconsciously, permeate human discourse about text—everyday speech and prose of all kinds, just as much as artful poetry. In the previous chapter, I unconsciously used a number of architectural metaphors, which most readers would not notice as such.[2] Talking about text in terms of architecture

---

[1] In fact, the word *text* derives from an Indo-Iranian root found in Avestian and Vedic (*taks-*), meaning 'to put together' in the context of building with wood or stone (the Latin *texere*—'to weave'—represents a narrowing of the original, broader meaning); Darmesteter (1968), 28–9.

[2] E.g. '**on the basis** of the meagre archaeological remains . . .' (p. 69); '[b]**uilding on** the previous chapter's conclusions about the representational strategies of different media . . .' (p. 72); 'the two-part **structure** of the Fucine Lake passage' (p. 87); 'drawing on a wide range of texts to **support** a convincing argument' (p. 64).

Building in Words. Bettina Reitz-Joosse, Oxford University Press. © Oxford University Press 2021.
DOI: 10.1093/oso/9780197610688.003.0004

WRITING CITIES, FOUNDING TEXTS 101

is not exceptional but entirely normal.[3] However, this does not mean that such 'standard' instances and unconscious uses of metaphor are meaningless. Far from it: since the groundbreaking work of Lakoff and Johnson on 'conceptual metaphors', it has been recognized that such uses of metaphor are highly meaningful, through what they reveal about the way we conceptualize and mentally structure the world around us.[4] By talking of texts in terms of buildings, even if we do so unconsciously, we conceptualize them as possessing certain qualities, while lacking others.[5] For example, talking about a text as a building suggests that it is an ordered whole, made up of smaller parts such as words or sentences, and that it is produced following a 'plan', with an intended result (a built structure) in mind. If I were to call a text a 'river', on the other hand, I would be conceptualizing it as something natural, externally inspired, ever-changing, or forceful and potentially uncontrollable.[6]

Although these features of human language and thinking are by no means irrelevant to my investigation, I address a different set of questions. This book deals with representational strategies, and in the chapters that comprise its second part, I will specifically be concerned with the literary strategies that motivate and inform the use of architectural imagery. I therefore focus on instances of conscious, often elaborate, and (usually) highly marked use of architectural metaphor in literary texts.[7] I analyse in what way the link

[3] Construction as a metaphor for the putting together of words and sentences is already well attested in the earliest Indo-Iranian languages: Darmesteter (1968) and Schmitt (1967), 296–8, find in Avestan and in Vedic Sanskrit close parallels for the early Greek phrase ἐπέων τέκτων. See also Nünlist (1998), 99, and the more extensive list of Asper (1997), 191 n. 254. The metaphor is, however, also found in the earliest texts from entirely different language families (e.g. in Egyptian and Hebrew: Nünlist (1998), 103, quoting the Old Testament (1 *Kings* 2.4), and Lichtheim (1976), 153 and 185 n. 1). This seems to confirm that thinking, and thus talking, about human utterances, spoken and written, in terms of architecture is a form of expression deeply embedded in our languages and our imagination.

[4] Lakoff and Johnson first introduced their influential theory of 'Metaphors we live by' in Lakoff and Johnson (1980), republished in 2003 with a new afterword by the authors. A clear and up-to-date introduction to conceptual metaphor theory is now Kövecses (2010). See also Steen (2011), who argues for a broader approach to metaphor theory that expands on this cognitive linguistic approach to include the study of metaphor in communication. Sjöblad (2009) applies a cognitive linguistic approach to an ancient text in his investigation of '*Metaphors Cicero Lived By*', analysing the role of metaphor and simile in Cicero's *De senectute*.

[5] See Lakoff and Johnson (1980), ch. 3, on the notions of 'highlighting' and 'hiding'.

[6] Cf. the term 'stream of consciousness' for a particular type of writing.

[7] However, a clear-cut division between fully 'conscious' and definitely 'unconscious' uses of a metaphor is impossible, especially since we are dealing with a small literary corpus in a dead language. See further n. 12 in this chapter. The metaphor of construction as an image for literary production has been the object of several large-scale studies. Hamon (1988) presents a broad and imaginative reflection on the connections between architecture and text. For more specific investigations of the building-as-text metaphor, see e.g. Cowling (1998), ch. 5, on French medieval and early modern literature. Cf. also Eriksen (2001), who proposes an architectural reading of Renaissance literature.

102 BUILDING IN WORDS

between construction and text production is achieved, why construction is used as an image for writing in a particular text, and how exactly the author represents construction to achieve a certain effect.[8]

After a short introduction to the history of the building metaphor from archaic to hellenistic Greek literature, I devote this and two subsequent chapters to considering construction as a poetological metaphor in Roman literature from a number of perspectives.[9] In this chapter I analyse a selection of texts in which city-building and text-production are linked to each other, focusing on this particular image to explore in depth the mechanisms and implications of its usage. In Chapter 4, I concentrate on a single author and set of texts, analysing the specific aesthetic of construction which Statius develops in his *Silvae*. Finally, in Chapter 5, I examine the literary functions of the myth of Amphion, the Greek hero who built the walls of Thebes, moving the stones by playing his lyre.

Architectural Poetics in Greece: A Short History

The language of craftsmanship (often not specific enough to be clearly attributable to a *particular* profession, such as construction) is already, if rarely, applied to the poet's activity in the very earliest Greek poetry.[10] For example, the making of song is described by the word τεύχειν in Hom. *Od.* 24.197 (Achilles's ghost predicts the gods' fashioning of a song in praise of Penelope).[11] From the beginning of the fifth century, however, the language of craft and specifically of building and construction abounds in self-reflexive poetic

[8] The use of metaphors in poetic texts can be exceptional in a number of ways: see Lakoff and Turner (1989); Kövecses (2010), ch. 4. Metaphorical expressions there tend to be less clear, though richer in meaning, than metaphors used in speech or non-fiction (Kövecses (2010), 49–52). Kövecses (2010), 53–5, identifies and explains the strategies by which metaphors tend to be manipulated in literary texts (extending, elaboration, questioning, and combining).

[9] I shall continue to use the term 'metaphor' in its broad sense to refer to all linguistic expressions that articulate an idea drawn from one domain (target domain) in terms of one drawn from a different domain (source domain), rather than to a specific type of imagery distinct from, say, metonymy or comparison (except where I specifically draw attention to such distinctions in my discussion).

[10] See Ford (2002), 93–157, on the development of the language of craftsmanship in early Greek poetry; cf. also the compilation of poetological metaphors in early Greek poetry in Nünlist (1998), with 85–125 on craftsmanship and 98–107 specifically on building. While Nünlist gathers examples from the eighth to the end of the fifth century and orders them thematically, Ford attempts to chart developments and innovations in literary-critical discourse over time, arguing that 'the major difference between archaic and early classical criticism [lies] in the development, during the early fifth century, of an approach to song as verbal craftsmanship' (93).

[11] Cf. also the uses of ἐντύνω in Hom. *Od.* 12.183 and Hom. *Hymn* 6.20. Ford (2002), 115 n. 5, argues that these are exceptional cases since the fashioner in each case is a divinity.

WRITING CITIES, FOUNDING TEXTS   103

utterance.[12] The works of Bacchylides and Pindar show a highly developed use of construction metaphor.[13] Very influential for later poets is the opening of Pindar's 6th *Olympian* (1–5):[14]

Χρυσέας ὑποστάσαντες εὐ-
  τειχεῖ προθύρῳ θαλάμου
κίονας ὡς ὅτε θαητὸν μέγαρον
πάξομεν· ἀρχομένου δ' ἔργου πρόσωπον
χρὴ θέμεν τηλαυγές.

We shall set up golden columns to support the well-walled porch of the chamber, as when we construct a wondrous palace; for when a work begins, it is necessary to make its front shine from afar.

In this self-conscious opening, Pindar boldly extends the building metaphor to its stretching point. The poem first appears to be a chamber (θάλαμος). The proem is its well-walled porch (εὐτειχεῖ προθύρῳ) supported by golden columns; it is also a far-shining façade of the building (πρόσωπον). The poet's activity is to set up (πάξομεν) these columns, an activity compared to the setting up of an admirable palace or hall (θαητὸν μέγαρον).[15] The metaphor is suggestive in two different ways. It primarily relates to the aesthetics of the poem, linked to those of a palatial building, the impact of which largely rests on a strong first impression. But at the same time, it is suggested that such poetic architecture should also be solidly constructed, with one element securely based on another: the columns have to be able to support the porch that rests on them. All these desirable assets of a good poem are expressed in terms of the process of its construction—it is in the placing of the golden

---

[12] Ford (2002) speaks of an 'explosion' (114), although he admits that the evidence for the period between the Homeric poems and the fifth century is too lacunose to date this development with any certainty (113). As mentioned earlier, we cannot always be sure that the metaphor was felt as such, especially where it consists of only one word. Cf. for example the two uses of ὀρθῶν of a poem, in Pind. *Ol.* 3.3 and Pind. *Isthm.* 4.38, with Nünlist (1998), 105. See also Nünlist's remarks in his introduction, 7–10, on 'lebende' and 'tote' metaphors, which cannot be distinguished when working with such a limited corpus of poetic texts from a period where we have almost no access at all to comparable 'everyday' use of language.

[13] Ford (2002), ch. 5; Nünlist (1998), 98–107.

[14] On the architectural imagery in this passage, see e.g. Bowra (1964), 20–1; Steiner (1986), 55; Bonifazi (2001), 104–12; and Morgan (2015), 402–5.

[15] Because of the apparent shift between different types of architecture within the metaphor (in *Ol.* 6.27, a 'gate of hymns' further complicates the picture), it seems best to conclude, as Morgan (2015) does, that 'the architectural metaphor is not specific' but rather combines associations of treasury, palatial building, and even temple (403, agreeing with Bonifazi (2001), 105).

104 BUILDING IN WORDS

columns, in making the front shine, that the poem's opening comes into existence.[16]

There are numerous further instances of architectural metaphor in Pindaric poems.[17] For example, in *Pyth.* 6.10–18, the song is called a treasure house of hymns (ὕμνων θησαυρός, 7–8), which will withstand the onslaughts of wind and weather (10–14) and, like the palace of *Ol.* 6, present a shining πρόσωπον (14) to the world. The architectural metaphor is employed to combine aesthetic impact with endurance, an important feature of Pindaric self-presentation, and a striking image that has influenced one of Horace's most famous poems.[18]

Of the tragedians, Euripides is particularly engaged in using language and images drawn from the sphere of architecture, but from a recent thorough investigation of his use of architectural imagery, it appears that architecture is not regularly used as an image for poetic production.[19] In old comedy, on the other hand, architecture is regularly used as a poetological image. For example, Aristophanes says of himself in *Pax* 749–50:

ἐποίησε τέχνην μεγάλην ἡμῖν κἀπύργωσ' οἰκοδομήσας
ἔπεσιν μεγάλοις καὶ διανοίαις καὶ σκώμμασιν οὐκ ἀγοραίοις

He has created a great art for us, and built it up and raised it to towering heights with mighty words and ideas and with jokes that are not vulgar.

The metaphor, apparently already conventional enough at this stage to be parodied by Aristophanes, allows for not only positive but also negative

---

[16] It may also be significant that the porch of a building would not be the first, but one of the last elements of the construction process. Perhaps the implication is also that a shining porch, i.e. proem, is added to an already advanced poetic composition as a fitting and impressive entrance into it. For ἄρχομαι in a proem cf. Aratus, *Phaen.* 1: ἐκ Διὸς ἀρχώμεσθα.

[17] Nünlist (1998) cites a number of passages in the works of Pindar (101–5): poets are called τέκτονες (builders) in *Pyth.* 3.113 (although in *Nem.* 3.3–5 apparently performers of the song are called the τέκτονες); a poem or speech has a κρηπίς, a foundation, in *Pyth.* 7.1–4, *Pyth.* 4.138, fr. 194.1–3. A treasury of songs (ὕμνων θησαυρός) features in *Pyth.* 6.5–9. A song is erected (ὀρθῶν) in *Ol.* 3.3, *Isthm.* 3/4.38.

[18] Bowra (1964), 21–2. The idea of the endurance of a building is famously taken up by Horace, who compares his work to a physical monument immune to erosion by wind and rain (*Carm.* 3.30). On the other hand, *Carm.* 3.1.45–6 may be interpreted as a more critical reaction, in defence of Horace's moral and aesthetic choices, to the opening of Pind. *Ol.* 6: *cur invidendis postibus et novo / sublime ritu moliar atrium?*—'Why should I toil at a sublime atrium with enviable pillars and in a new style?'

[19] Stieber (2011) in ch. 1 examines the language of architecture in Euripidean tragedy. She argues that Euripides's use of the 'language of craft' is a feature of his realism and interest in the visual arts, but she does not devote as much space to the question of whether Euripides conceived of (his own) poetic activities as a 'craft' (though see 415–26 on the craftsman's σοφία). Cf. also a Sophoclean fragment, possibly from a *Daidalos* (a satyr-play?): *TrGF* 159: τεκτόναρχος μοῦσα.

WRITING CITIES, FOUNDING TEXTS   105

value judgements.[20] It is used, for example, by the Hellenistic poet Theocritus in criticizing excessive ambition in a poet. In his *Thalysia*, the mysterious poet-figure Lykidas praises Simichidas's modesty with the following simile (*Id.* 7.45–8):[21]

ὥς μοι καὶ τέκτων μέγ' ἀπέχθεται ὅστις ἐρευνῇ   45
ἴσον ὄρευς κορυφᾷ τελέσαι δόμον Ὠρομέδοντος,
καὶ Μοισᾶν ὄρνιχες ὅσοι ποτὶ Χῖον ἀοιδόν
ἀντία κοκκύζοντες ἐτώσια μοχθίζοντι.

How much I hate the craftsman who seeks to accomplish a house equal to the top of the Oromedon, and the cockerels of the Muses who toil in vain, crowing against the bard from Chios.

The meaning of the first part of the simile is explained in the second part, introduced by καί: inferior poets (cockerels who only crow, not sing) should not attempt to rival the great Homer. This injunction is expressed through the image of the construction of a house that equals the height of the (unknown) mountain Oromedon.[22] Building a structure of excessive height serves as an illustration of the *hybris* of the over-ambitious poet.[23]

Sophisticated architectural metaphors thus have a long tradition in Greek poetry. A matching sophistication can be observed when a vocabulary of rhetoric and literary criticism begins to develop in technical prose texts. This terminology, too, is frequently derived from architecture,[24] as is, for example, apparent from technical terms of composition such as κανών

---

[20] Cf. also Ar. *Ran.* 1004, referring to Aeschylus, and Ar. fr. 657 *PCG* (φθέγξαι σὺ τὴν φωνὴν ἀνατείχισας ἄνω). Pherecrates too uses an architectural metaphor in connection with Aeschylus (*Krapataloi* fr. 100 *PCG*: ὅστις <γ'> αὐτοῖς παρέδωκα τέχνην μεγάλην ἐξοικοδομήσας). On architectural metaphor in Old Comedy more generally, see Müller (1974b), 33–6.

[21] On this simile in the context of Hellenistic poetological metaphor, see Asper (1997), 191.

[22] On the significance of this particular mountain, see Krevans (1983), 208–9.

[23] Metaphors expressing poetic aesthetics also abound in the poetry of Theocritus's contemporary, the poet Callimachus: see Asper (1997). For example, the crowing cockerels are reminiscent of the braying donkeys of the *Aetia* prologue (fr. 1 Harder 30–2). Architectural metaphor, however, is not (clearly) attested in the works of Callimachus that have come down to us. Thomas (1983) argues attractively, in spite of little textual evidence, for a metapoetic reading of a list of temples in an unplaced fragment of the *Aetia* (which he suspects stood at the beginning of the third book): see further pp. 151–2.

[24] That is not to say that it does not make use of many other source domains, such as the body, or the universe. On these metaphors, and their combination with architectural metaphor, see also further pp. 109–13.

106 BUILDING IN WORDS

or ὕλη.[25] However, ancient theorists of language and composition also show their awareness of the details and implications of the use of this terminology to conceptualize language, and they employ it for argumentative and rhetorical purposes:[26] consider, for example, the detailed comparison between the builder of a house (οἰκόδομος) and someone who composes a text, used by Dionysius of Halicarnassus to illustrate his theory of σύνθεσις.[27]

This short overview shows the versatility of the metaphor in Greek literature: architectural imagery is employed in order to comment on the structure, the aesthetics, the durability, the size, or the ambition of the literary work. Although the metaphor is so versatile, its crucial, overarching strength—and one that Roman authors will be keen to exploit to the full—lies in the fact that it activates a reader's sense of the 'madeness' of the text and, as a result, brings about an increased appreciation of the achievement of the poet or writer who produced it.

The metaphor has a similar breadth of application in Roman literature—ranging from the fleeting use of construction vocabulary to extended similes and sustained, sophisticated imagery.[28] The specific images for literary constructs also differ widely in scale, from house-construction through temples and cities to the entire cosmos. The remainder of this chapter concentrates on one image at the upper end of this scale: the analogy between the building of a *city* and the making of a poetic text.[29] There are no known examples of this particular form of the building metaphor in the Greek literature before our period. Although the sheer amount of text that we have lost prevents us from drawing any definite conclusions, I consider it likely that this form of the metaphor represents an innovative modification of the already well-developed construction metaphor by the Roman authors I discuss.

---

[25] κανών: literally *the mason's rule* or *measure*; metaphorically *rule, standard* (e.g. of grammar). ὕλη: literally *timber*, or more generally *building material*; metaphorically *subject matter*. See van Hook (1905), 41, for these and further examples, and further pp. 116, 164-5, and 168 in this volume on ὕλη.

[26] For useful collections of examples of architectural metaphor in rhetorical treatises, see van Hook (1905), 40-1, and de Jonge (2008), 188 n. 63.

[27] This comparison is analysed by de Jonge (2008), 188-90.

[28] I do not attempt to provide a complete list of such instances (the compilation of which would in any case be enormously impeded by the fuzzy division between 'living' and 'dead' metaphors: see n. 12 in this chapter). Instead, I undertake detailed analyses of the literary and cultural strategies of a number of authors and texts. A history of the text-as-building metaphor in Greek and Latin poetry (62-76), as well as some moments in its reception (76-94), can be found, however, in Lieberg (1985).

[29] For a short introduction to this trope, see Edwards (1996), 6-8.

The City and the Text

The poetic metaphor of city-construction first seems to appear in Roman literature during the transitional period between republic and principate. Arguably, Vitruvius's treatise on architecture, *De Architectura*, is the earliest text which suggests and exploits a sustained identification between the composition of a literary work and the foundation and construction of a city.[30] The order of arrangement of the material corresponds to the building of a city, from choosing a site and procuring building materials, to the construction of public and private buildings, decoration, a water supply, and finally, the means of defending the city in case of war. As we read *De Architectura*, the matrix of an ideal city comes into being: an 'Everycity', adaptable to different conditions of terrain, climate, supply, and habitation. Through the arrangement of his material, Vitruvius renders *De Architectura* a city of words and himself both its founder and its builder. In doing so, he stands at the beginning of a trend. In the space of a few decades, the text-city metaphor begins to appear in a range of texts and genres which, unlike his own work, do not focus on architecture as their main theme: in historiography and epic, love elegy, and didactic poetry.

In attempting to understand the potency of the metaphor, as well as the specific forms it takes in the texts discussed, we must take into account the key political role of city-building in the Roman Empire during the late republic and its changing cultural resonances during the early principate.[31] From the beginning of Rome's expansion, cities formed the basis of Roman control and administration of the empire's growing territory. City-foundation, or the reconstruction of an existing or destroyed city, served to impose administrative orderliness upon an otherwise ungovernable territory.[32] Already in the third century BC, the characteristically schematic Roman city, laid out on a grid, began to develop.[33] The reason for its universal success over hundreds of years and a vast empire was the Romans'

---

[30] As I have argued in Reitz-Joosse (2016), where I focus on Vitruvius, but draw for comparison on the Propertian and Manilian passages discussed more extensively in this chapter. Others who have noted the significance of Vitruvius's arrangement of material include Gall (2006); 103, Fritz (1995), 132–3; and McEwen (2003), 282–4.

[31] Cf. Reitz-Joosse (2016), 195–7.

[32] Owens (1991), 121: 'Cities were the primary level of the administration of the empire, upon which the central government devolved a heavy burden of responsibility for the administration of both local affairs and certain imperial duties.' See also Kolb (1984), 169–203, and Edmondson (2006), 253–5.

[33] Lorenz (1987), 72, 99–124.

108   BUILDING IN WORDS

'highly standardized, but nevertheless flexible, approach to town planning.'[34] This 'combination of adaptability within a standardized arrangement', which guaranteed the successful urbanization of the Roman empire,[35] is neatly reflected in Vitruvius's adaptable Everycity in *De Architectura*.[36] During the period of Rome's civil wars, city-foundation also becomes, more than ever, an instrument of power for individual military leaders. The settlement of veterans and the reorganization of conquered territories require the foundation of cities on an ever-larger scale. When Vitruvius wrote *De Architectura*, city-foundation and city-building would have been a mark of fundamental political power and control, and he co-opts this potential as the creator of the ideal text-city, whose principles all would-be city founders must follow if they want to succeed.

Vitruvius's vision of the ideal Everycity distinguishes him from those authors writing only a few years later, and to whose works we now turn: Vergil's *Aeneid*, Propertius's fourth book of *Elegies*, and Manilius's *Astronomica*. As a representative of a 'culture of transition', Vitruvius had still predominantly drawn on the symbolic and political significance of city-foundation in the late republic.[37] For those authors who develop the metaphor in the years following, the powerful Augustan rhetoric of Rome's re-foundation, as well as the visual and cultural emphasis on the mythical founders of Rome, Aeneas and Romulus—and their present-day successor—brings about a realignment of the metaphor. As we shall see, all three authors 'Romanize' the text-city, modifying the Vitruvian model from the universal to the specific. The text-cities founded in the works of the Augustan and post-Augustan poets are, they suggest, to be identified with the city of Rome. They use the text-city analogy to suggest a parallel between their own textual foundations and the ancient foundation and contemporary re-foundation of the city of Rome, casting themselves as part of the Augustan project of restoration.

My analysis will proceed in reverse chronological order, from Manilius's *Astronomica* to Propertius's fourth book of *Elegies* to Vergil's *Aeneid*. The latest author, Manilius, offers the most explicit connection between

---

[34] Owens (1991), 120. For an extended case study of Roman urbanization in Gaul, see Woolf (1998), ch. 5; cf. McEwen (2003), 282–4.

[35] Owens (1991), 120.

[36] Cf. Fritz (1995), 131. However, Fritz underestimates the flexibility of Roman city planning, as well as focusing exclusively on Roman colonies as a model for *De Architectura* (133).

[37] For understanding Vitruvius's work as emerging from the intellectual climate of the 40s and 30s, see most recently Nichols (2017), e.g. 21–22; and on Vitruvius as representative of a 'culture of transition', see Romano (2016). On the dating of *De Architectura*'s production and publication, see Nichols (2017), 2–3 with n. 9 for further bibliography.

WRITING CITIES, FOUNDING TEXTS   109

city-building and poetry. By tracing our way backwards through the tradition, we are able to use his and Propertius's reading of the earlier *Aeneid* as a guideline for our own approach to the more implicit connections to be found there. Incidentally, this reverse chronological process also takes us through the different stages of the building process in the correct order: from the gathering of the building materials in Manilius, to the construction of walls in Propertius, to the construction of the entire city in the *Aeneid*.

School, City, Body, Universe: Manilius's Mixed Metaphors

The poet Manilius, writing around the second decade of the first century AD, presents in the five books of his *Astronomica* descriptions of the universe, the constellations that surround the earth, and their influences on human beings.[38] In book 2, when discussing the complicated phenomenon of the *dodecatemoria* of the planets, the poet breaks off, announcing that in order to understand the whole, *totum corpus*, one first needs to understand its individual *membra* (2.752–3), and since the planets have not yet been treated, the discussion of this combination of zodiacal and planetary influence is postponed (and never resumed).[39] The poet's method of first presenting different aspects of the universe individually, before connecting them into a complex explanation of the whole, is then justified by a methodological double simile.[40] The didactic strategy is compared first to the way in which children are taught to read and write, and then to the way in which a city is built. The schoolteaching simile (2.755–71) prepares for the city-building simile and will therefore be considered first:[41]

---

[38] About Manilius himself we know nothing besides what we can infer from the *Astronomica*, which is very little. See Volk (2009), ch. 1, for a discussion of the (lack of) evidence, and an attempt to render this biographical blank productive for interpretation.

[39] On the *dodecatemoria*, see Volk (2009), 87–8. The *dodecatemoria* are subdivisions of each sign of the zodiac into twelve sections of 2.5°, which are again assigned to the twelve signs of the zodiac (so that, for example, Aries has an Aries section, followed by a Taurus section, etc.). These tiny sections can then be further subdivided into five parts (of 0.5° each), which in turn are assigned to the five planets (Saturn, Jupiter, Mars, Venus, and Mercury). Here Manilius breaks off, since the planets have not yet been treated in any detail, and in fact, they will not be, in the extant *Astronomica*. On this puzzle, see most extensively Volk (2009), esp. 48–57 and 116–26, and Goold (1983), who posits a large lacuna after 5.709 that, according to him, dealt with the planets.

[40] It is also the 'ausgedehnteste Gleichnispartie antiker Lehrdichtung'; Schindler (2000), 253. For a thorough discussion of the double simile in the context of similes on Latin didactic poetry, see Schindler (2000), 252–72.

[41] The text of Manilius is taken from Goold (1998[2]) unless otherwise indicated. Translations are adapted from Goold (1977).

110   BUILDING IN WORDS

> ut rudibus pueris monstratur littera primum　　　　　　755
> per faciem nomenque suum, tum ponitur usus,
> tum coniuncta suis formatur syllaba nodis,
> hinc verbi structura venit per membra legendi,
> tunc rerum vires atque artis traditur usus
> perque pedes proprios nascentia carmina surgunt,　　760
> singulaque in summam prodest didicisse priora
> (quae nisi constiterint primis fundata elementis,
> effluat in vanum rerum praeposterus ordo　　　　　　764
> versaque quae propere dederint praecepta magistri),　763
> sic mihi per totum volitanti carmine mundum　　　　　765
> erutaque abstrusa penitus caligine fata,
> Pieridum numeris etiam modulata, canenti
> quoque deus regnat revocanti numen in artem,
> per partes ducenda fides et singula rerum
> sunt gradibus tradenda suis, ut, cum omnia certa　　770
> notitia steterint, proprios revocentur ad usus.

Just as children who have not yet begun their lessons are first shown the shape and name of a letter, and then its value is explained; then a syllable is formed by the conjoining of its linkable elements; followed by the building up of the reading of a word by way of its component syllables; then the meaning of expressions and the rules of grammar are taught, and then verses come into being and rise up on feet of their own, and it benefits the final outcome that [the student] has mastered each of the earlier steps (for unless these are firmly founded on first principles, the badly ordered material will vanish into nothing, and the instructions that teachers have hurriedly given will be overturned)—so, as I wing my way in song throughout the whole universe, sing of fates drawn from deep-seated darkness, even tuning them to the Muses' rhythm, and summon to my art the power by which God rules, I too must by degrees win credence and assign each matter to its correct step, so that, when all the individual parts are grasped with sure understanding, they may be called upon for their proper uses.

The comparison is between the way children are taught, step by step, from recognizing individual letters to the composition of whole poems, and the way in which the poet presents his material, bit by bit in the

WRITING CITIES, FOUNDING TEXTS   111

correct order, before the whole can be deployed and all elements taken together to work out a horoscope (a stage which Manilius does not actually reach).[42]

One feature of this simile is of special importance with regard to the city-building simile to follow. Although it seems to draw a straightforward parallel between two forms of didactic (poetry and schoolteaching), a closer look reveals that it contains a whole range of images drawn from completely different areas, which cross-fertilize each other.[43] Within the 'dominant' teaching simile, the poet draws a number of metaphors from the language of the human body. Apart from the introductory remark about the *corpus* and the *membra* of the poem, which immediately precedes the simile,[44] the subjects of the lessons also take on a biological quality: syllables have *nodi*,[45] a word has *membra*, poems are born (*nascentia*) and rise up on their feet (*per pedes proprios . . . surgunt*). At the same time, another layer of metaphorical language is already prefiguring the next simile, taken from the realm of architecture: the building up of the reading of a word, the *structura verbi . . . legendi*, introduces architectural metaphor of language and text, continued by the argument being founded upon (*fundata*) first principles and the teachings being overturned (*versa*) if they were too hasty.[46] The rising of the poem could even be seen to combine anatomical and architectural metaphor, since *surgere* is regularly used of nascent building projects in Latin poetry, especially where a metapoetic dimension is involved (as in the following city-building simile: *surgunt . . . urbes*, 772, matched by *consurgit opus* in 782).[47] Finally, underpinning this simile and the entirety of Manilius's

---

[42] For a reading of the absence of the horoscopes from the *Astronomica*, see now Green (2009).

[43] Cf. also Schindler (2000), 256: 'Es fällt auf, daß Manilius die Verbindungen zwischen Buchstaben, Silben, und Wörtern, die im Elementarunterricht sukzessive erarbeitet werden, mit Metaphern aus verschiedenen Bereichen charakterisiert.'

[44] Man. 2.751–4: *nunc satis est docuisse suos ignota per usus, / ut, cum* **perceptis** *steterit fiducia* **membris** */ sic* **totum corpus** *facili ratione notetur / et bene de summa veniat post singula carmen*—'now it is enough to teach new principles by demonstrating their uses, so that, when you have acquired confidence in your grasp of the elements (lit. *body parts*), you will be thus able by simple reasoning to mark the complete pattern (lit. *the whole body*), and my poem can fittingly pass on from details to deal with the whole'.

[45] The *OLD* s.v. *nodus* classes the usage of the word in this passage under 6a as 'something which binds things together, a bond, tie', but the meaning abutting this one (6b) is the application of meaning 6a to the body ('joint, tendon,' etc.), and this also is possibly evoked here.

[46] Schindler (2000), 257, who also sees a possible reference to the house-building simile in Lucr. 4.513–21, where the house collapses because the foundations are not level. For a systematic analysis of the meaning of *structura*, see Lieberg (1956).

[47] For *surgere* of the coming into being of a literary work, cf. Ov. *Fast*. 5.111 and *Tr*. 2.559–60 (and cf. Ov. *Am*. 1.1.17, a play on the elegiac metre); cf. also Stat. *Theb*. 10.445–6 *mea carmina surgant / inferiore lyra*. Instances where *surgit opus* is used of an architectural structure, but with a plausibly metapoetic significance: Ov. *Fast*. 4.830 with Barchiesi (1997), 69, and Fantham (1998), 247 *ad*

112 BUILDING IN WORDS

poem is the 'megametaphor' of Manilius's text as a small universe to match the large one he describes.[48] As Volk has argued, 'Manilius . . . throughout the *Astronomica* stresses the parallel between his song and his subject matter, beginning with his simultaneous worship at the altars of *carmen* and *res* in 1.21–2'.[49] By means of his learning-to-read simile, Manilius recalls the famous and recurring Lucretian simile of the atoms as letters.[50] He thereby suggests that the universe is, like the Lucretian cosmos, made up of the 'letters' he describes (atoms in the case of Lucretius, the individual elements of the universe for Manilius).[51] In the language of the learning-to-read simile, this 'megametaphor' flashes past in the phrase *primis fundata elementis*, the 'first principles' on which the *singula priora* have to be based: *elementa* can mean both the letters which schoolboys have to learn as a first step and the elements which make up the universe.

The remarkable density of metaphorical language from three distinct areas (anatomy, architecture, nature of the universe), in a simile drawn from schoolteaching, achieves a number of different purposes. Firstly, it combines different images that occur frequently throughout the entire work (the text as a body, the text as universe, and, more indirectly, the universe as a body).[52]

---

loc.; Luc. 2.679 with Masters (1992), 34. Cf. also the metapoetic *surgit opus* in Man. 1.113, on which phrase see also Cowan (2002), 194, esp. n. 244, Masters (1992), 33. *surgere* with an exclusively architectural reference can refer both to the rising of ongoing construction (*OLD* 6a) and to the towering of a finished one (*OLD* 7). Volk (2002), 233–4, points to a more literal dimension of *surgere* in the *Astronomica*: stars and planets also 'rise' in the heavens (*OLD* 4a). See further p. 122 on Propertius's exploration of the polyvalence of *surgere*.

[48] 'Megametaphors' are metaphors that run through an entire literary text or large portions of it. They do not necessarily 'surface' explicitly in the text except in the shape of 'micrometaphors' which, taken together, reveal the presence of the megametaphor as an undercurrent. See Kövecses (2010), 57–9, and Werth (1994), who calls them 'extended metaphors'.

[49] Volk (2009), 195–6, partly summarizing her more detailed argument at Volk (2002), 234–45, on the significance of Man. 1.20–2 for the whole of the *Astronomica*: *bina mihi positis lucent altaria flammis / ad duo templa precor duplici circumdatus aestu / carminis et rerum*—'Two altars with flame kindled upon them shine before me; at two shrines I make my prayer, beset with a twofold passion, for my song and for its theme'.

[50] Schindler (2000), 259–60. On this simile, see e.g. Snyder (1980), 31–51; Gale (2004), 57–61.

[51] Schindler (2000), 259–60, and Volk (2002), 239–40, show how Manilius hints at the fact that the letter-analogy actually makes more sense within a Stoic world view of an ordered cosmos, where the letters are deliberately arranged, than within the Epicurean parameters of random atomic collisions.

[52] The text as a body and the text as a *kosmos* are also well-known metaphors in rhetorical theory. For the metaphorical domain of the human body in rhetorical texts, see the list of van Hook (1905), 18–23. Cf. also de Jonge (2008), 188–9, on Dionysius's strategic use of organic versus architectural metaphor for organization of subject-matter as opposed to stylistic composition (σύνθεσις). The idea of the text as a *kosmos* is first found in Democritus fr. 21 Diels-Kranz (but see Nünlist (1998), 90–1, on Hom. *Od.* 8.489 and 8.492–3). For further instances of the song or the poem as a *kosmos* (in the basic meaning of something that is well-ordered) in early Greek poetry, see Nünlist (1988), 91–4. On the further development in poetic theory of the text as a universe made up of the elements (στοιχεῖα),

WRITING CITIES, FOUNDING TEXTS 113

The simile thereby creates internal coherence, tying together the different metaphorical spheres of the work in one overarching image. At the same time, this combination of several megametaphors from the entire didactic poem marks out this passage as a crucial point in the poet's self-reflection.

Secondly, the use of architectural metaphor in the didactic simile, combined with the extension of this image in the second simile, allows Manilius to explore in depth the implications of applying architectural metaphor to literary composition. Architectural terminology is, as we saw earlier, a standard way of presenting theory of language.[53] The subtle, easily missed presence of the metaphor in the first simile is deepened and reflected on when the poet proceeds actually to compare the writing of his poem to city-building, making the implicit, conventional metaphor of architecture explicit (2.772–87):[54]

> ac, velut, in nudis cum surgunt montibus urbes,
> conditor et vacuos muris circumdare colles
> destinat, ante manus quam temptet scindere fossas,
> fervit opus: ruit ecce nemus, saltusque vetusti   775
> procumbunt solemque novum, nova sidera cernunt,
> pellitur omne loco volucrum genus atque ferarum,
> antiquasque domos et nota cubilia linquunt;
> ast alii silicem in muros et marmora templis
> rimantur, ferrique rigor per pignora nota   780
> quaeritur, hinc artes, hinc omnis convenit usus;
> tum demum consurgit opus, cum cuncta supersunt,
> ne medios rumpat cursus praepostera cura.
> sic mihi conanti tantae succedere moli
> materies primum rerum, ratione remota,   785
> tradenda est, ratio sit ne post irrita neve
> argumenta novis stupeant nascentia rebus.

And as, when cities are being built on bare mountainsides, and the founder plans to encompass the empty hills with walls, before his team attempt to

---

see de Jonge (2008), 52, and Armstrong (1995), 212–13. On the idea of the universe as a living organism in Manilius (possibly rooted in Stoic philosophy), see Volk (2009), *passim*, esp. ch. 6.

[53] See p. 106.

[54] On the 'Verklammerung' between the first and the second simile by means of close lexical parallels, see Schindler (2000), 262.

114   BUILDING IN WORDS

cut trenches, work proceeds briskly; and see, a forest tumbles and ancient
woodlands fall, beholding sun and stars unseen before; all tribes of bird
and beast are banished from the spot, leaving the immemorial homes and
lairs they knew so well; others, meanwhile, seek stone for walls and marble
for temples and by means of sure clues search for sources of unbending
iron; from their different sides skill and experience of every kind combine
to help; and only when all materials are available in plenty does construction proceed, lest premature effort cause the project to break down in mid-
course. In the same way, as I strive to perform a mighty undertaking, must
I first tell of the matter of my theme, withholding explanation, lest hereafter
explanation prove ineffectual and my arguments be silenced at the outset
before some unanticipated fact.

In this second simile, the mixing of metaphors has all but disappeared.
While the first simile drew together strands of imagery from throughout the
poem, the 'dominant' image of the second simile seems to stand alone. The
building of a city is compared to the composition of the poem, or more precisely, the preparations necessary for the construction of a city are compared
to the preparations necessary before explanation (*ratio*) can be attempted,
namely to first present to the reader the bare facts, the *materies rerum*.
Interestingly, the gathering of building materials corresponds to the *setting
out* of the material in poetry, and not to its *gathering*: in the second half of
the simile (the antapodosis) the *materies*, the (building) material, has to be
presented, *tradenda*, as a first step.[55] In contrast to the first simile, the first
part (the parabole) of the second simile becomes more independent from the
argument. The city-foundation takes on a life of its own, and the poet vividly
sketches the bustling building site.[56]

The simile's representation of the gathering of building materials activates
as a model the literary giant of the previous generation, Vergil, with important implications for the author's self-presentation. One of the simile's most
noticeable features is the density of intertextual references to the *Georgics* and
the *Aeneid*, and especially the multiple references to passages which form

[55] Cf. *OLD* s.v. *tradere* 10a. I therefore disagree with Schindler (2000), who sees the second simile
as representing the process of *inventio*, and the first simile the *dispositio*. The subject of the second
simile is still (as we learn in the antapodosis) the *presentation* of the material, although the focus has
shifted away slightly from the ordering in logical steps. On *disponere* as an architectural and poetic
activity, see further n. 63 in this chapter.

[56] Cf. Schindler (2000), 263, who compares this effect of 'Verselbständigung' of the parabole's subject to that of Homeric similes.

WRITING CITIES, FOUNDING TEXTS   115

a point of contact between both works.[57] Both the *Aeneid* and the *Georgics* are initially activated as intertexts by pointed references to programmatic passages at the beginning of each work. The clearest reference to the *Aeneid* comes in the antapodosis: *sic mihi conanti tantae succedere moli*, referring to *Aen.* 1.33: *tantae molis erat Romanam condere gentem*—'so vast was the effort to found the Roman people'.[58] Vergil's earlier didactic poem, the *Georgics*, is evoked in line 781 (*hinc artes, hinc omnis convenit usus*, recalling *Georg.* 1.133: *ut varias usus meditando extunderet artes*—'so that practice, by taking thought, might hammer out different arts'), and in line 780 (*ferrique rigor*, recalling *Georg.* 1.143: *ferri rigor*).

Thus sensitized to the presence of the Vergilian intertexts, it becomes apparent that the simile especially evokes passages which link the *Aeneid* and the *Georgics*, alluding to both poems simultaneously. Most significantly, at the opening of the simile (*ac, velut, in nudis cum surgunt montibus urbes, / conditor et vacuos* **muris circumdare colles** */ destinat*), the surrounding of hills with a wall suggests the foundation of Rome (*Aen.* 6.781–3: *Roma . . . animos aequabit Olympo / septemque una sibi* **muro circumdabit arces**—'Rome . . . shall let her pride equal Olympus, and with a single city's wall shall enclose her seven hills') in the prophecy of Anchises, with the epic *conditor* Aeneas (also alluded to in Man. 2.784) lurking in the background (*Aen.* 1.33 . . . *Romanam condere gentem*). Anchises's prophecy also already refers back to *Georg.* 2.534–5: *et rerum facta est pulcherrima Roma / septemque una sibi muro circumdedit arces*.[59] The connection that Manilius constructs between city-building in the *Aeneid* and the making of his own poem suggests that we are to read his own poetic effort as rivalling that of Aeneas in founding the *Romana gens*, and of Vergil in 'founding' his epic.[60]

The mention of the cutting down of the forest refers to *Aen.* 6.179–80 (the cutting down of the forest for the funeral pyre of Misenus): Manilius's *ruit ecce nemus, saltusque vetusti procumbunt* picks up Vergil's *itur in antiquam silvam, stabula alta ferarum; / procumbunt piceae*. Vergil's depiction of

---

[57] Many of the intertextual links discussed here (both with the *Georgics* and the *Aeneid*) are identified in Feraboli, Flores, and Scarcia (1996), 350–3, although they do not note the special importance of passages which connect both works. Schindler (2000), 264–6, discusses Manilius's allusions to the *Georgics* as a means of expressing differences between his and his predecessor's teachings. *Non vidi* Landolfi (1990).

[58] See also pp. 28–9 for a reference to this famous line in the inscription of the Constantinian obelisk in Rome (*CIL* 6.1163).

[59] Norden (1957), 320–1 *ad Aen.* 6.782 and 6.784.

[60] Cowan (2002), 193. See also Lieberg (1982), 30–4, on the poetological dimension of the words *condere* and *conditor*.

116 BUILDING IN WORDS

the wood as the former home of wild beasts (*stabula alta ferarum*) is also taken up by Manilius: *pellitur omne loco volucrum* **genus atque ferarum,** / **antiquasque domos** *et nota cubilia linquunt.* However, this passage in the *Aeneid* also recalls the uncomfortable description of the *iratus arator* and his tree-felling in the second book of the *Georgics*, and Manilius's choice of words likewise activates this earlier passage (*Georg.* 2.207–10):

> aut unde iratus silvam devexit arator
> et nemora evertit multos ignava per annos,
> **antiquasque domos** avium cum stirpibus imis
> eruit

> ... or [the sort of land] from which the angry ploughman has carried off the wood, and has felled groves that had been useless for many years, and torn up the ancient homes of birds together with their deepest roots....

This combined allusion to the *Georgics* and the *Aeneid* carries special significance, for, as Hinds has famously argued, the tree-felling passage in the *Aeneid* not only recalls an Ennian description of tree-felling, but actually performs the poet's use of the raw material (*silva/ὕλη*) of his epic predecessor Ennius.[61] Cutting down trees thus becomes a context for epic poets' reflection of their (re-)use of ancient poetic 'wood'. Manilius introduction of his simile with this epic marker of poetic forestry is entirely topical. Also evocative of the *Aeneid* and the *Georgics* together is Manilius's mention of *marmora templis*: it reminds the reader of the temple of marble described at the opening of *Georgics* 3 (3.13: *templum de marmore ponam*), and through it also of the future *Aeneid* that this temple represents.[62] A final striking instance of simultaneous reference to the *Aeneid* and the *Georgics* is the result of seductive conjecture: *fervit opus* in line 775 for the difficult *vertit opus* of the MSS produces a reference to *Georg.* 4.169 (*fervit opus*) and Vergil's description there of the hard work of the bees.[63] There is an allusion to this

---

[61] Hinds (1998), 11–14, on Enn. *Ann.* fr. 175 (Skutsch), and Leeman (1982). It is, however, surprising that the key word *silva* does not occur in Manilius's text.

[62] On this poetic temple, see further pp. 123–4 and 151–2.

[63] Housman (1912), 86 *ad loc.*, prints Woltjer's *fervit*, dismissing *vertit* as 'sine sensu' and pointing to the double allusion to the *Georgics. Fervit* is also accepted by Goold (1977) and (1998). Flores retains *vertit*, and Feraboli and Scarcia argue for *vertere* as a ploughing metaphor ('the *conditor* ploughs/prepares the work) despite the 'apprezzabile durezza metaforica': see Feraboli, Flores, and Scarcia (1996) 352 *ad loc.*, and Schindler (2000), 253 n. 124.

WRITING CITIES, FOUNDING TEXTS   117

passage in the *Aeneid*, where the Carthaginians building their city are compared to bees (*Aen.* 1.436: *fervet opus*).

Why these references to Vergilian epic and didactic poetry, and especially to epic reworkings of didactic poetry? In a simile that deals with building materials, the *Georgics* and the *Aeneid* are evoked as different kinds of building material for the *Astronomica*: the *Georgics* in terms of genre and didactic technique, and the *Aeneid* in terms of literary ambition.[64] But the reference to epic via didactic also has a further significance. It is well known that Vergil's epic similes in the *Aeneid* often draw on (his own) didactic poetry in terms of sphere and subjects, subsuming the spheres of farming and cultivation into the larger epic cosmos of the *Aeneid*.[65] Manilius's reference to the *Aeneid*, and the *Georgics* within the *Aeneid*, in a didactic simile may therefore be read as an attempt to reclaim for didactic the quintessentially epic subject of city-foundation. This theme of city-foundation drives the plot of the *Aeneid* through twelve books. Manilius's single simile here encapsulates it together with the didactic poetry which had already served as material for Vergil's own epic similes. Manilius thus uses this 'Chinese-box' simile as a statement of his own poetic confidence, and the scope and inclusiveness of his poem about the universe.

Walls of Milk and Verse: Propertius 4.1

Propertius's fourth book of elegies, published in or shortly after 16 BC, opens with a pair of introductory poems.[66] This double introduction sets out the tensions which underlie the 'hybrid' fourth book. The whole of book 4 oscillates between the traditional themes of Roman love elegy and the early history of Rome, thus redefining the scope of elegy in Rome. While the elegiac genre as it had emerged in Rome during the previous decades was dominated by erotic themes, Propertius's fourth book combines such poems with

---

[64] On Vergil as a model for Manilius, see Volk (2009), 185–8, on the *Georgics* and the *Aeneid*, with more bibliography cited in 185 n. 21.

[65] See Briggs (1980) generally on the transferral of narrative from the *Georgics* to similes in the *Aeneid*, and 71–3 on the bee simile in *Aeneid* 1, mentioned earlier.

[66] For a summary of arguments in favour of dividing 4.1, see Heyworth (2007), 424–5. Riesenweber (2007), 373–8, judiciously weighs different positions and favours division. Against division argue e.g. Macleod (1983); Hutchinson (2006), 61. I favour division, especially on the grounds of overall book design (on which see Günther (2006), 354–5). On poem-divisions in Propertius generally, see Heyworth (1995). Since my investigation mainly deals with lines 1–70 ('4.1A'), the question of division has little bearing on my argument.

118   BUILDING IN WORDS

others about historical and aetiological themes, in a sense reverting, thematically, to the Callimachean, aetiological elegy which the Roman love elegists
had always avowed as their aesthetic model.[67]

In what is transmitted as lines 1–70, hereafter referred to as 4.1A, the speaker,
guiding an unnamed *hospes* (1) around Rome, points to sites of modern (i.e.
Augustan) Rome, using them to draw a contrast between the undeveloped site
of the future city and Rome as it is at his time of speaking. The gap constructed
between the then and the now opens up the question of how all of these changes
came about: a question addressed from line 39 onwards, where the speaker
turns to the Trojan past, to omens and prophecies regarding Troy's resurrection
as mighty Rome, and to the heroes of two Roman families (39–54).

I am here concerned with only one aspect of this complex poem: Propertius's
strategic use of the metaphor of city-building for the writing of poetry.[68] Just
after the prophecy of Cassandra, which concluded the section 39–54, the
metaphor makes its first appearance (4.1.55–8):[69]

optima nutricum nostris lupa Martia rebus,   55
    qualia creverunt moenia lacte tuo!
moenia namque pio coner disponere versu:
    ei mihi, quod nostro est parvus in ore sonus!

She-wolf of Mars, best of nurses for our community, what walls have
grown up from your milk! For walls are what I would try to lay out in pious
verse: poor me, that the sound from my mouth is so feeble!

In line 56, the walls are said to have grown, *creverunt*, because of the milk of
the she-wolf, the nurse of Rome. This bold metaphorical phrase combines
two separate images from earlier in the poem. First, the idea of the *growth* of

---

[67] Hutchinson (2006), 7–16, offers a concise introduction to the redefinition of elegy in book 4, its
preparation in book 3, and the activation of Callimachus's *Aetia* as not only an aesthetic but also a
thematic model. Günther (2006) interprets 4.1A and 4.1B with special attention to their function for
the book as a whole.

[68] Propertius's shifts between (often unusual) metaphors frequently render his texts extremely dense. The problematic transmission of his text makes interpretation even more difficult.
Riesenweber (2007) tackles the daunting task of a thorough investigation of metaphor and other
forms of 'uneigentliches Sprechen' in the work of Propertius.

[69] I quote the text of Fedeli (2006), except where otherwise indicated. The translations are my own,
but are partly inspired by Goold (1999) and Heyworth (2007). I am convinced by Heyworth (2007),
420–3, who argues that the order of lines is confused here and elsewhere in the poem. However, any
kind of reordering involves considerable speculation: see Hutchinson (2006), 22–3. I will treat the
lines in the order in which they are transmitted.

WRITING CITIES, FOUNDING TEXTS   119

built structures was already introduced in line 5, where the guide pointed out to the *hospes* the temples to the gods, first rustic as the gods themselves, now golden (4.1.5–6):

> fictilibus crevere deis haec aurea templa,
>   nec fuit opprobrio facta sine arte casa;

> These golden temples have grown up for gods of clay, and a hut made without skill was no cause of shame.

The temples have grown like a living being—a plant, or an animal—a metaphor which elides specific human involvement, conveys the notion of organic development in accordance with nature, and of a small beginning and a steady (and one-directional) movement towards greatness.

The she-wolf and her nurslings, too, are referred to earlier in the poem, in lines 37–8:

> nil patrium nisi nomen habet Romanus alumnus:
>   sanguinis altricem non putet esse lupam.[70]

> The Roman nursling (i.e. the Roman of today) has nothing from his forefathers except his name: he would never believe that the nurse of his blood was a she-wolf.

The modern Roman is an *alumnus* of the she-wolf in the sense that she was the nurse, the *altrix*, of his blood, i.e. his race. In the myth, the she-wolf was the nurse of Romulus and Remus, the ancestors of the Roman race. Here, the twins are called the *sanguis* of the Roman—his blood, his origin. The wolf has thus fostered not only the twins but the whole people of Rome—every Roman is her *alumnus*, her nursling.

In neither of these passages is the imagery straightforward, but in 55–6, the expression becomes even bolder, as elements of both earlier images are united:

---

[70] The text of line 38 is difficult: I retain *putet*, transmitted in the majority of MSS, but plausible arguments can be made for the (likewise attested) *putat* (Heyworth) or *pudet* (the last is retained by Fedeli, but produces better sense if *nunc* is read instead of *non*: see Heyworth (2007), 419 *ad loc.*). Hutchinson (1984), 101 n. 25, tentatively suggests retaining *putet*, but reads *quis* for *non*; *quis* would solve the problem of the *Romanus alumnus* as an awkward subject for *putet*, as well as producing good sense: 'who would believe that a she-wolf was the nurse of his blood?'

120 BUILDING IN WORDS

> optima nutricum nostris lupa Martia rebus,
>> qualia creverunt moenia lacte tuo!

> She-wolf of Mars, best of nurses for our community, what walls have grown
> up from your milk!

As in Manilius's first simile, the combination of different images familiar from elsewhere in the poem is used to create internal coherence.[71] The walls have grown from the milk of the she-wolf. The milk of the she-wolf stands as a metonymy for the nurslings who enjoyed that milk, i.e. Romulus and Remus: without this milk, they would never have survived infancy and grown up to become the founders of Rome. *creverunt* is a metaphorical expression for 'were built', and even the walls may perhaps stand as *pars pro toto* for the entire city of Rome.

In the following couplet, however, we encounter a completely different conceptualization of the making of a city 'wall' (57–8):[72]

> moenia namque pio coner disponere versu:
>> ei mihi, quod nostro est parvus in ore sonus!

> For walls are what I would try to lay out in pious verse: poor me, that the
> sound from my mouth is so feeble!

This phrase could be explained through reading *moenia* as a metonymy for the history of the walls: The speaker would like to construct in verse the history of the walls (i.e. the city) of Rome. The verb *disponere* straddles the domains of architecture and writing, encompassing both the idea of architectural construction and that of literary composition.[73] Unlike *crescere*,

---

[71] This analogy between the growth of Rome and the growth of poetry is even already prepared in 3.9.49–52; Macleod (1983), 144.

[72] See Heyworth (2007), 422 *ad loc.*, on the problems of the transition marked by *namque*. Hutchinson (2006), 71 *ad loc.*, explains *namque* as linking the two instances of *moenia*, thereby providing a transition which allows the poet to 'at last gingerly steal . . . onto his plan'.

[73] *[D]isponere* can refer both to an architectural and a poetic activity (building the walls, and setting them out in verse); Shackleton Bailey (1949), 28. It can be used in a rhetorical context, specifically as the action of executing the *dispositio*, one of the five *membra eloquentiae*, TLL 5.1.1424.75–1425.24. *[D]isponere* in architectual contexts (cf. TLL 5.1.1422.44–56) implies putting individual moveable elements into different places, separately, and in some kind of order. The two domains touch each other frequently: Vitruvius uses the term *dispositio* as a part of the discipline of architecture in a passage heavily influenced by the terminology of rhetorical theory (see de Jonge (2008), 191), while Quintilian compares the rhetorical *dispositio* to the putting together of building material (Quint. 7 pr. 1). See also n. 46 in this chapter.

WRITING CITIES, FOUNDING TEXTS   121

disponere suggests human agency and deliberate design. The word also implies that there are already separate pre-existing pieces (stones/words) which need to be fitted together or arranged in a systematic way.[74]

But this analysis does not yet capture the complete extent of the metaphor's significance. In Propertius's formulation, the verse of the poet is, by power of metaphor, turned into more than just lines on papyrus: if this verse can build *walls*, the poem really *is* the equivalent of a city.[75] The poetic *disponere* of the walls of Rome is hence a re-enactment of their original, mythical foundation, referred to in the preceding line.[76] The poet inserts himself into a tradition of the founders of Rome and its walls. Aeneas, who is present in the poem from the very beginning (*Phrygem Aenean*, 2) and constantly in the background because of the strong echoes of his tour of the site of Rome with Evander in *Aeneid* 8, is activated as a founder-predecessor for the poet by the use of the word *pio*, recalling the *pietas* of his mission of founding a new Troy.[77] The walls of Rome themselves were built by Romulus, and the Rome that the *hospes* in the poem is shown is the one changed and remodelled by Augustus, the second Romulus. All these founders are the models which the poet emulates in founding these walls yet once more, in song.[78]

Propertius again uses an architectural image to describe his poetry in the closing lines of 4.1A. Returning to the poetry-city metaphor, he turns himself into a re-founder of the city (67–8):

> Roma, fave, tibi surgit opus: date candida, cives,
>   omina et inceptis dextera cantet avis!

> Rome, smile on me; my work rises for you: citizens, give me fair omens, and may a bird sing on the right for the work that I have begun.

---

[74] See also Fantham (1997), 129: 'Propertius makes [the] walls a symbol of his own ordering and constructive powers . . .'.

[75] Cf. Welch (2005), 27: 'There is a Rome of stone, and a Rome of words.'

[76] On the broader trope (sometimes called '*poeta creator*') of the poet actually, through his poetry, doing the very thing that he describes as being done, see exhaustively Lieberg (1982); and specifically on this passage, Lieberg (1982), 92; Lieberg (1985); Macleod (1983), 144; Gale (2004), 59–61.

[77] The refoundation of Troy is also the theme of lines 39–54.

[78] On Aeneas, cf. Hutchinson (2006), *ad loc.*: 'The poet is another Aeneas . . . founding the imitation Rome of his book.' He also points to the fact that *versus*, which can also mean furrow, plays on the dragging of a furrow with a plough as part of the foundation ritual. For the sequence of founders, cf. Welch (2005), 26: '. . . the repetition of *moenia* . . . makes clear the parallel between Rome's first founder, its refounder, Augustus, and its latest founder, Propertius, each an architect of the city in his own way and with his own tools.' Fantham (1997), 124, sees in this line an allusion to yet another founder figure, arguing that Propertius 'sees himself as another Amphion', who is mentioned already in Prop. 1.9.9–10 and 3.2.5–6. On Amphion in Propertius, see further pp. 178–9.

122 BUILDING IN WORDS

The phrase *surgit opus* here recalls also two earlier uses of the word *resurgere* in the poem, both related to the city of Troy which rises again in the shape of Rome: *arma **resurgentis** portans victricia Troiae!*—'[Venus] carrying the victorious weapons of Troy rising again!' (47)—and, in the prophecy of Cassandra: *Troia, cades et Troica Roma **resurges***—'Troy, you will fall and rise again as Trojan Rome' (87). While *resurgere* is there applied to the city of Troy, which (in a latent personification) rises up again when she has fallen, *surgit opus* refers to the new, Propertian city of verse. *surgere* is another word which, denoting originally 'getting up', 'getting to one's feet', is used regularly both of the architectural and the literary construct,[79] and an *opus* can of course be a building as well as a text.[80] However, the positive omens for which the speaker asks (silence from the people, the bird on the right-hand side) confirm that what is described is a foundational ritual. The poem is a foundation to match the city of Rome. The earlier analogy of poem with city, poet with founder, writing with founding is thus continued.[81]

If we follow the sequence of metaphors of foundation and poetry throughout the poem, we follow a movement through different kinds of source domain. While the foundation of Rome is first framed in anatomical or biological terms, and strongly associated with natural growth and nurture (*crescere*, *lac*), the poet's activity is conceptualized in terms of architecture and structure (*disponere*). The final image of the poem, of the rise of the new foundation (*surgit opus*), connects these two domains: *surgere* spans the anatomical (getting up) and biological (growth of plants) as well as the architectural sphere. The rise of the poetic *opus* thus appears both the result of a natural movement towards greatness, and of conscious poetic design—the best of two worlds.[82]

The city-building metaphor impacts on the reader's understanding of Propertius's manipulation of the elegiac genre in book 4 as well as of the poetic ambition of the book more generally. The vertical movement

---

[79] See pp. 111–2, especially n. 47.

[80] See *TLL* 9.2.849.67–850.20.

[81] Cf. Hutchinson (2006), 73 *ad loc.*: 'The book is also an imitation Rome'. Hutchinson also explains the *candida . . . omina* as silence. He compares Dion. Hal. *Ant. Rom.* 1.88 (Romulus's foundation) for the foundation rituals. The auspicious bird omen is taken up again from 40. See also Macleod (1983), 143.

[82] For a combination of *crescere* and *exsurgere* in a description of city-building, see Livy 4.6. In Reitz-Joosse (2016) I consider the relationship between anatomical and architectural metaphors applied to the city in Vitruvius's *De Architectura* (see 191 on similarities between Vitruvius and Propertius). For a different interpretation of the combination of the metaphors of construction and growth in Propertius's fourth book, see DeBrohun (2003), esp. ch. 2.

of the architectural metaphor has a poetological significance, in that it represents the generic ascent, the rise above the 'humble' love-themed elegy that has gone before and the climb towards more ambitious themes and greater poetic fame. The choice of not just architecture, but city-building specifically, also relates to poetic ambition, just as in Manilius's simile. Propertius's and Manilius's use of the image of the city look very different at first sight: Manilius presents a clear, methodical comparison, Propertius a sequence of bold metaphors. But the two descriptions of city-building have an important element in common: both Propertius and Manilius tie their task to city-foundation as a means of staking out their ambition and the size of their project, and both link their task to city foundation in the *Aeneid*. In different ways, the poets thus suggest that their task is equivalent in ambition and in prestige to that of the city-founder *par excellence*, Aeneas—but also to that of the great poem-founder Vergil. The classically epic subject of city-foundation is reclaimed for their particular genre of choice.

However, an important difference between the two poets is that Propertius's subject matter *is*, in fact, (partly) the foundation of the city of Rome, while Manilius takes a larger conceptual step in using foundation (and foundation in and of the *Aeneid*) as an image for his own poetic activity, even though his poem's subject matter is far removed from the history of Rome. Considering that Manilius's poem postdates Propertius's by about a generation, it seems plausible that Manilius's use of the foundation *topos* was building on earlier uses of the *topos*, such as that of Propertius.

Both Propertius and Manilius forged the link between their poetry and city-foundation via the *Aeneid* and the foundational *telos* of Vergil's epic. Manilius and Propertius thus read back into the *Aeneid* a poetic dimension to city-foundation and city-building. What does this mean for the *Aeneid* itself? There is no *explicit* connection in the epic between the foundation of Rome and the making of the poem. But when we attempt to read the *Aeneid* with the eyes of Manilius and Propertius, an implicit connection between city and text appears possible.

Vergil's Epic Cities

In the *Georgics*, Vergil famously used the construction of a temple as an image for the composition of the future *Aeneid* (or, at any rate, a full-scale

124   BUILDING IN WORDS

epic on a Roman national theme).[83] It is hardly surprising that any explicit use of the composition-as-building metaphor is absent from the epic itself, since the generic conventions of epic do not allow the narrator much leeway, beyond the proems, for explicitly commenting on his literary efforts.[84] Nevertheless, I argue that it is possible to read implicit connections between city and epic in the *Aeneid*, as do Manilius and Propertius, and that reading the *Aeneid* in such a way allows us a deeper understanding of Vergil's own poetic ambitions, as well as those of Propertius and Manilius.

Kraus has interpreted Livy's *Ab Urbe Condita* as 'the gradual, often experimental construction of a written Rome. . . . As such, . . . the historian's project parallels/rivals Augustus's own building of a new Rome via (re)construction of its past.'[85] 'The "real" Rome grows as Livy's text does.'[86] Kraus argues not for an explicit metaphorical link between city and text, but rather reads the physical city of Rome (which grows and is built up in Livy's work) and Livy's work itself, the *Ab Urbe Condita*, as coincident, and is able to show on a textual level the ways in which Livy suggests and explores this analogy.[87] Would a similar reading also be possible for the *Aeneid*, which likewise deals with the foundation story of Rome?[88] Do textual and physical city coincide in Vergil's epic as they do in Livy's work?

In the *Aeneid*, such a connection between city and text, if it exists, cannot be straightforward, since the foundation of Rome, which is initially suggested as the *telos* of the epic (*dum conderet urbem*, 1.5), is not accomplished, or even so much as approached, within the main narrative. Instead of telling of the foundation of Rome, the *Aeneid* is full of other cities and foundations, all related in some way to the larger project of Rome, but none of them the

---

[83] *Georg.* 3.12–16. On this poem, see further pp. 116 and 151–2. See also especially Meban (2008) on connections between temple-building in republican Rome and Vergil's poem, and on the use of the temple metaphor as a means of conveying the poet's literary ambitions.

[84] On the proem (1.1–11), see e.g. Austin (1971) 25–34; Anderson (1969), ch. 1; Buchheit (1963), 13–58. On the 'proem in the middle' (7.37–45), see Kyriakidis (1998), 166–77.

[85] Kraus (1994a), 8.

[86] Kraus (1994a), 111 *ad* 4.6.

[87] See Kraus (1994a) *ad* 1.2, 1.11, and 4.6. Cf. also Kraus (1994b): 'Throughout the *Ab Urbe Condita* the historian draws attention to the overlap of the content of his city (the Urbs he is writing about) and its form (the *Urbs* he is writing)' (268). Cf. Jaeger (1997), esp. ch. 1, who argues for parallels between the physical *monumenta* of the city of Rome and the textual memorials within the *Ab Urbe Condita*. See also Edwards (1996), 6–8.

[88] This is suggested (in passing) by Deremetz (2001), 161: 'Tout se passe comme si Énée effectuait pour fonder Rome ce que le poète effectue dans le présent de l'œuvre pour fonder son épopée romaine.' I argue that while this more direct connection holds true for Propertius's poems, there is a more complex connection in the *Aeneid*.

WRITING CITIES, FOUNDING TEXTS 125

'real thing'.[89] I propose that it is rather the construction of *these* cities and their connection with the ever-visible project 'Rome' that relate to the poetic endeavour of the *Aeneid* itself.

In the course of the epic, Aeneas founds a number of settlements (with varying degrees of success) at the successive stages of his journey towards Italy and the foundation of Rome. But before I turn to analyse this sequence of foundations of would-be Romes, I first consider a different sort of Aenean foundation. The Carthage episode shows Aeneas actively participating in the foundation of the wrong city. I suggest that this deviant Aenean foundation can be read as a reflection of the entire epic's derailment in the Carthaginian books.

In book 1, just cast ashore in Carthage after a storm, Aeneas climbs a hill and from above views the bustling building site of Dido's Carthage (1.421–9):[90]

miratur molem Aeneas, magalia quondam,	421
miratur portas strepitumque et strata viarum.	
instant ardentes Tyrii: pars ducere muros	
molirique arcem et manibus subvolvere saxa,	
pars optare locum tecto et concludere sulco;	425
iura magistratusque legunt sanctumque senatum.	
hic portus alii effodiunt; hic alta theatris	
fundamenta locant alii, immanisque columnas	
rupibus excidunt, scaenis decora apta futuris ...	

Aeneas is amazed by the size of it [i.e. the city], that had once consisted of mere huts; he is amazed by the gates, the noise, and the paved roads. The Tyrians are working eagerly: some of them are setting out the line of walls, toiling at the citadel and rolling up stones by hand, some are choosing the site for a house and enclosing it with a furrow. They draw up laws and elect

---

[89] Others have traced the motif of cities and city foundation through the epic. Morwood (1991) provides an overview of the role of cities in the epic (cities sacked, foundations aborted, misguided, or doomed) as what he calls a *Leitmotiv* (216) in the poem (see esp. 212–16). He then argues that the 'vacuum suggested by the city theme' (221) is filled by the present Rome (re-)founded by Augustus. Carney's (1986) investigation has a similar scope. Unlike Morwood, he offers a 'pessimistic' reading of the absence of the foundation of Rome from the narrative and concludes that 'the cities would seem to represent possibilities lost or not realised but nonetheless regretted' (429). Nelis (2015) concludes that 'Rome is always tantalizingly out of reach' in the *Aeneid* (41) and leaves open the extent to which the Augustan re-foundation of Rome can fill this 'gap'. Fletcher (2014), esp. 80–141 on book 3, analyses the 'colonization narrative' in the context of Aeneas's gradual attachment to the idea of Italy.

[90] The text quoted is Mynors (1969).

126 BUILDING IN WORDS

magistrates and a holy senate. Here some are excavating harbours, there others are laying the deep foundations for their theatre and quarrying vast columns out of the rocks, suitable decorations for the stage to be.

When Aeneas first looks down on Carthage, *miratur molem*. The city of Carthage is called a *moles*, and the Carthaginians are working hard (*moliri*) to bring it about. To Aeneas, it looks exactly like the kind of heroic venture that he has to accomplish, the foundation of a city and a people: *tantae molis erat Romanam condere gentem* (1.33). This impression leads him to exclaim (1.437): *o fortunati, quorum iam moenia surgunt*—'Happy ones, whose walls are already rising!'—recalling the proem and the ultimate aim of the *altae moenia Romae* (1.7).[91]

At this point, Aeneas is still observing and comparing from the outside (only the Carthaginians are *fortunati*, they have already accomplished their mission). Once he has descended to the building site of Carthage, however, he begins to be drawn into the wrong city as he (and the reader) loses sight of the epic *telos*.[92] Aeneas becomes increasingly confused, thinking about Carthage more and more as *his* city and the destination of his mission. This is an understandable mistake to make, Vergil suggests, since the reader is at one point invited to make the same mistake: when the narrative proper of the epic begins, after the proem, with the words *urbs antiqua fuit* (1.12), a first-time reader would expect the words to refer perhaps to Troy, perhaps even to Rome—but the ancient city turns out to be Carthage, the 'wrong turning' on Aeneas's epic journey.

Gradually, the Trojans continue to slip into the wrong epic. Ilioneus's words to Dido suggest that the queen's founding mission is somehow parallel to that of Aeneas (1.522–3):

o regina, novam cui condere Iuppiter urbem
iustitiaque dedit gentis frenare superbas . . .

O queen, to whom Jupiter has granted it to found a new city and to control proud tribes through justice . . .

---

[91] See Nelis (2015), 30–1, on the intratextual resonances of this exclamation.

[92] Bruck (1993), 26, suggests that the parallel between the foundation of Carthage and of Rome is already suggested through the use of *labor* in the bee-simile (1.430–6, *labor* in 431): 'Wie die Stadtgründung des Aeneas im Prooemium als *labor* angekündigt worden war, so bestimmt dieses Phänomen auch die Stadtgründung der Karthager.'

WRITING CITIES, FOUNDING TEXTS 127

On the one hand, these words recall Jupiter's prophecy to Venus earlier in book 1: *populosque feroces / contundet moresque viris et moenia ponet*—'and he [i.e. Aeneas] shall crush wild peoples and lay down laws and build city-walls for his men' (1.263–4). At the same time, they point forward to Anchises's formulation of Rome's mission, *debellare superbos*—'to subdue those who are proud' (6.853).[93] Dido is introduced as a possible role model for Aeneas, but she quickly becomes more than that. When she tells the Trojans that *urbem quam statuo vestra est*—'the city that I am building is yours' (1.573)—she is actively drawing them into *her* ktistic epic.

In book 4, after a joint walk through the city and a temporary disruption of the construction works,[94] the epic's derailment becomes more and more obvious.[95] Hermes, sent by a justly worried Jupiter, comes upon Aeneas fully engaged in building the wrong city (4.259–61):

Ut primum alatis tetigit magalia plantis,
Aenean fundantem arces ac tecta novantem
conspicit.

So soon as with winged feet he touched the roofs of the huts, he catches sight of Aeneas founding fortifications and building new houses.

The unusual word *magalia* recalls Aeneas's first view of the city, *magalia quondam* (1.421). But while he was then watching and admiring from outside, he has made Carthage his project now.[96] Hermes's accusations again highlight that Aeneas is engaged on the wrong epic mission (4.265–7):

tu nunc Karthaginis altae
fundamenta locas pulchramque uxorius urbem
exstruis? heu! regni rerumque oblite tuarum!

---

[93] Carney (1986), 428, also stresses the latter connection.

[94] See *Aen.* 4.74–5 (walking through the city together) and *Aen.* 4.86–9: *non coeptae adsurgunt turres, non arma iuventus / exercet portusve aut propugnacula bello / tuta parant; pendent opera interrupta minaeque / murorum ingentes aequataque machina caelo*—'The towers that she had begun do not rise, the young men do not exercise in arms, or prepare harbours or safe bulwarks for war; the works are broken off and stand idle—the huge merlons of the walls and the crane soaring to the sky.' This interruption of the building works shows Dido's failings as a leader, in contrast to the proper epic hero who does not let himself be distracted (for long) from his aim of founding and building a city. On the meaning of *machina*, see p. 189 and n. 55 in Chapter 5.

[95] Cf. Fletcher (2014), 145–8.

[96] In striking contrast to the earlier scene (1.421–9) in which Aeneas observed the building activity, he is now himself being observed at his construction work (*conspicit*, 4.261).

128 BUILDING IN WORDS

So now you are laying the foundations of high Carthage and building up a splendid city, wife-besotted as your are? Alas, you have forgotten your kingdom and your mission!

Jupiter's question about Aeneas (*quid struit?*—'What is he planning?'), repeated by Hermes when he scolds Aeneas (*quid struis?*), also takes on the meaning 'what are you building?' (especially since the word *exstruis* is used in the sense 'to build' only four lines earlier), stressing once more the parallel between Aeneas's mission and city-building.[97]

When Aeneas has left Carthage and the unhappy Dido has committed suicide, the city's grief is suggestively likened, in a famous simile, to that attending the fall of the city (4.667–71):

> lamentis gemituque et femineo ululatu   667
> tecta fremunt, resonat magnis plangoribus aether,
> non aliter quam si immissis ruat hostibus omnis
> Karthago aut antiqua Tyros, flammaeque furentes   670
> culmina perque hominum volvantur perque deorum.

> The palace rings with lamentation and groaning and women's wailing, and heaven echoes with loud wails. It is as though all Carthage or ancient Tyre has been invaded by enemies and is falling, and raging flames are rolling over the roofs of men and of gods.

The building and then abandonment and suggested destruction of the city of Carthage can thus be read as analogous to the course the epic takes in the first four books. When Aeneas builds the wrong city, the *Aeneid* threatens to turn into the wrong sort of epic. In terms of subject matter, protagonists, and generic influences, the Carthaginian episode strains the limits of epic.[98] While Aeneas is engaged in building Carthage, the epic also seems well on the way to becoming an epic for the wrong nation.[99] The (envisaged) destruction

---

[97] Morwood (1991), 214.

[98] On the various generic influences in the Dido episode, see Hardie (1998), 59–63, with a helpful selection of bibliography. Book 3 of Apollonius's *Argonautica* is a crucial intertext (cf. Servius's famous hyperbole that 'from there [i.e. the *Argonautica*] this entire book is taken over, from the third book of Apollonius's (*in Aen.* 4 *praef* 2–4 Harv.)). Apart from Hellenistic (love-themed) epic, other prominent presences are Catullus 64 and Ariadne's lament, but also entirely non-epic genres, especially tragedy and love elegy: 'One way of viewing the situation in *Aeneid* 4 is as the interference of the values of the world of love elegy in the Roman (and epic) mission of Aeneas' (Hardie (1998), 61–2).

[99] Hardie (1986), 272–3; Nelis (2001), 65–6.

WRITING CITIES, FOUNDING TEXTS   129

of Carthage ends this particular interlude, leaving Aeneas free to return to his mission of founding quite a different city.

Aside from the Carthaginian detour, the *Aeneid* features a sequence of city-foundations by Aeneas, which mark successive stages of his journey towards Italy and the foundation of Rome. The first of these four cities is founded in Thrace, the Trojans' first stop after their flight from their native shores. Aeneas's foundation here is only just begun before it is interrupted by a terrible omen. He begins on the city walls and gives the city a name (*Aen.* 3.16–18):

> feror huc et litore curvo
> moenia prima loco, fatis ingressus iniquis,
> Aeneadasque meo nomen de nomine fingo.

> To this place I sail, and lay out my first walls on the curved shore, beginning the task with fate against us. From my own name I fashion the name 'Aeneadae'.

Aeneas stresses that the walls of the city were the first, *prima*, in a whole sequence of his wall-foundations.[100] The city-foundation gets no further than walls and a name: when Aeneas begins the sacrifices accompanying the foundation, a terrible omen forces the Trojans to abandon the place where their compatriot Polydorus had been brutally murdered. However, a kernel of the later foundation of Rome is already hidden even in this aborted attempt. Aeneas is drawn unconsciously (*feror*) towards Thrace,[101] which he calls a *terra . . . Mavortia* (3.13), and he uses his own name as a basis for the city's name. Both aspects are significant, since Jupiter in his prophecy in book 1 has predicted Romulus's foundation of Rome in the following terms (1.276–7): *Romulus . . . Mavortia condet / moenia Romanosque suo de nomine dicet*—'Romulus shall found the walls of Mars and call the people Romans after his own name.' Aeneas unwittingly fashions himself as a less successful proto-Romulus.

---

[100] Horsfall (2006), 56, *ad loc.*, suggests that *prima* refers to Aeneas's constructions being the foundations of Aenus's future *moenia*. On the identification of this foundation and the location of Polydorus's grave as Aenus, and not Aeneia, see Horsfall (2006), 50–2 *ad* 13–68.

[101] On *feror* and its connotations of passivity, as opposed to deliberate choice of destination, see Horsfall (2006), 47, *ad* 3.11. Cf. also *Aen.* 3.78.

130   BUILDING IN WORDS

The Trojans' second attempt at foundation, this time in Crete (where they sail due to a misinterpreted prophecy), at first shows more promise and advances considerably further (3.132–7):

ergo avidus muros optatae molior urbis   132
Pergameamque voco, et laetam cognomine gentem
hortor amare focos arcemque attollere tectis.
iamque fere sicco subductae litore puppes,   135
conubiis arvisque novis operata iuventus,
iura domosque dabam . . .

Therefore, I eagerly toil at the walls of the longed-for city, call it Pergamum, and urge my people, who rejoice at the name, to love their hearths and to raise a citadel with roofs. And now the ships were just about drawn up on dry land, our young men were busy with marriages and new tillage, and I was giving them laws and houses . . .

The city already has a number of essential features: it has walls, a name, a citadel, and houses.[102] The people are working the soil, marrying, and obeying laws. The word *moliri* appears again, linking this city to the great *moles* that Aeneas has to accomplish, and stressing the element of hard work necessary for success. On the other hand, its name, welcomed by its future inhabitants, expresses the reluctance of Aeneas and the Trojans to let go of the past and begin again.[103] The love they are to feel for their hearths and homes (*amare*) is rooted in nostalgia. This foundation, too, is cut short by expressions of divine displeasure: a plague breaks out among the Trojans, and a drought settles on the fields. Again, the city foundation is abandoned.

After the Carthaginian interlude, considered earlier, two more cities are founded. In Sicily, Aeneas takes aged Nautes's advice to found a city for the aged, weary, and fearful, and to leave them there under the rule of Acestes. This time, a functioning city is founded, and the founder's duties are shared

---

[102] Horsfall (1989), 26–7, provides a list of the different elements of city-founding and their occurrences in the *Aeneid*, including wall-building, the naming of the settlement, and other elements such as houses, foundations, laws, etc.

[103] Aeneas's nostalgic foundations can be compared to another city-foundation that remains caught up in the past: Andromache and Helenus, unable to let go of their Trojan past, have built a mini-Troy in Epirus, a barren enterprise, where the new 'Xanthus' runs dry (*arentem Xanthi cognomine rivum*, 3.350), and the tomb of Hector is empty. See Morwood (1991), 213 with n. 8, and Nelis (2015), 37.

WRITING CITIES, FOUNDING TEXTS 131

by Aeneas and Acestes, perhaps with a nod towards the joint foundation of Romulus and Remus (5.755–8):

> interea Aeneas urbem designat aratro
> sortiturque domos; hoc Ilium et haec loca Troiam
> esse iubet. gaudet regno Troianus Acestes
> indicitque forum et patribus dat iura vocatis.

> Meanwhile Aeneas draws the outline of the city with a plough and allots homes; this part he says should be Ilium and this area Troy. Trojan Acestes delights in his kingdom, appoints a site for the forum and lays down laws to the senate that he has summoned.

The joint foundation is concluded by setting up a shrine of Venus and decreeing rituals for Anchises's tomb. This city-foundation is successful, but despite the fact that it contains even more specific, obviously 'Roman', elements (the digging of the *primigenius sulcus*, the *forum*, and even senators), it is once more a sidetrack. Iris, disguised as Beroë (the maddened Trojan matron who instigated the burning of the ships), had demanded: *nullane iam Troiae dicentur moenia?*—'Shall no walls ever again be called Troy?' (5.633). In accordance with this demand, the city now founded is a surrogate Troy in name and nature. It is an ideal home for those who are afraid of the future. Leaving Acesta behind means that Aeneas must once again let go of his epic (Trojan) past and sail on towards his new mission, a different city in a different land.

Aeneas's final city-foundation within the *Aeneid* occurs when the Trojans have reached their destination. While envoys are sent to King Latinus, Aeneas sets about founding a settlement for the Trojans (7.157–9):

> ipse humili designat moenia fossa
> moliturque locum, primasque in litore sedes
> castrorum in morem pinnis atque aggere cingit.

> Aeneas himself marks out the line of his walls with a shallow ditch and toils at the site and surrounds his first settlement on the shore, after the fashion of a camp, with battlements and a rampart.

The Trojans know that they have arrived at the place that is destined to be their new home, but in spite of Aeneas's renewed toil (*molitur*), this settlement

132 BUILDING IN WORDS

has little permanence about it. The trench that Aeneas again draws to mark out the walls is shallow (*humili . . . fossa*), and the foundation has the characteristic features not of a city, as Acesta did, but of a military camp (*castrorum in morem*): a rampart (*agger*) and battlements (*pinnae*).[104] The foundation is thus suited to the second, 'Iliadic', half of the epic and its martial theme. The temporary status of Aeneas's construction is emphasized further by a direct juxtaposition with the ancient city of King Latinus, where the Trojan emissaries are headed (7.160–1):

> iamque iter emensi turris ac tecta Latinorum
> ardua cernebant iuvenes muroque subibant.

> The young men, meanwhile, had made their way there, and were in sight of the towers and high roofs of the Latins and drawing near to the city wall.

That city has houses and walls—it is an established city full of (Roman-sounding) traditions.[105] The Trojans' foundation, by contrast, is once more preliminary, imperfect, and still only a pale reflection of *the* foundation that the *Aeneid* ultimately purports to be about.

This series of imperfect and problematic city-foundations presents us with a suggestive contrast. On the one hand, Manilius and Propertius set themselves up as following Vergil in founding the city of Rome in verse (Propertius) or comparing their 'foundation' of a poem favourably to Vergil's poetic foundation of Rome (Manilius). Within Vergil's epic, on the other hand, the foundation of Rome, while tantalizingly present as the goal of Aeneas's quest and the fulfilment of history, is never realized. There are numerous stories of foundations in which there is always something of Rome, but they are never the 'real thing'. How then can we (along with Manilius and Propertius), read Aeneas's city-foundations as related to the construction of Vergil's poem?

---

[104] For another description of the construction of a camp with these features (also set up in contrast to an old city), see Stat. *Theb.* 7.441–51, discussed on pp. 190–3. Nisbet (1990), 384, sees in the passage an allusion to modern camp-building, which he interprets in the context of his reading of Aeneas as a Roman general.

[105] See *Enc. Virg.* 3 s.v. *Latini*, 129–30, on this city, its (lack of a) name, and its 'Roman' features. The description of Latinus's palace/temple in 7.169–91 bears a striking resemblance to Roman monuments such as those on the Palatine or the temple of Jupiter Capitolinus: see the detailed analysis of Horsfall (1999), 146–159, with literature quoted on 146, and Harrison (2006), 176–8. Cf. also the formulation in 7.61: *primas cum conderet arces*, said of Latinus: he, too, is a city founder (cf. Horsfall (1999) 86, *ad loc.*). Rossi (2000), 577, also emphasizes that the camp-city opposition here represents an inversion of the plot of the *Iliad*: the Trojans' foundation resembles the *Iliad*'s Greek camp, while Latinus's city reprises the besieged city of Troy.

WRITING CITIES, FOUNDING TEXTS   133

I propose that it is possible to read an analogy between the small city-foundations and Vergil's epic itself, since all these small cities, though imperfect, contain some features of the future city of Rome. The series of foundations charts a journey towards a remote final destination, a development from floundering first attempts to the fulfilment of a divine plan. Rome itself is never founded in the epic—except through the glimpses of what Rome will be that we receive through those smaller foundations.[106] Precisely in this respect, the city-foundations can be read as analogous to the epic itself. Foundation upon foundation is connected with hard work, *moliri*, making it clear that these imperfect, toilsome foundations are precisely what Aeneas's project consists of: *tantae molis erat Romanam condere gentem*.[107] The *Aeneid* emphasizes the difficult journey rather than the happy ending.[108] On the surface the *Aeneid* is neither an epic about the contemporary city of Rome nor an epic about Augustus (although at a deeper level it is, of course, a poem about both). We have reason to believe that an epic about Augustus and the present glory of the Roman Empire was what precisely was expected of Vergil, and he himself had even suggested in the *Georgics*, perhaps inadvertently, that this was what he would be attempting: *in medio mihi Caesar erit* (*Georg.* 3.16).[109] Although there are glimpses of Augustus and his re-founded city at key points in the poem, the *Aeneid* escapes being a straightforward triumphalist epic of contemporary Rome. In that sense, the series of small and imperfect city-foundations reflects what the epic as a whole is trying to achieve, and what it does not: Vergil shows the thorny, difficult, laborious path to glory, the *moles* of the would-be founder, rather than the triumphant arrival, and he refrains from fully satisfying the demands for a full-scale epic of national praise for Rome and its leader in depicting within the main narrative not the foundation of Rome, but some of the many foundations that prepared the way to the final goal.[110] This megametaphor of foundation, if

---

[106] Cf. the glimpses of Rome's future monuments through indirect references throughout the epic; see Harrison (2006).

[107] Besides the passages already noted, see also 4.233 (Jupiter is angry at Aeneas for not fulfilling his mission), 7.127 (Aeneas attributing to Anchises Celaeno's prophecy and rephrasing it to include the word *moliri*), and 7.290 (Juno justly worried about the promising foundational activities of the Trojans).

[108] Reed (2010) similarly interprets the formation of national identity in the *Aeneid*: 'We are never there, we are never done with this poem' (78).

[109] On the expectations raised by the prologue to *Georgics* 3, and the reflection of these expectations by contemporary poets, see Robinson (2006).

[110] That Rome *is* this goal is also affirmed in the great passages of prophecy, where the foundation of Rome as well as the culmination of its power under Augustus is foretold: see 1.125–96, 6.756–886, 8.626–728. See Morwood (1991) on the presence of the Augustan city of Rome in the *Aeneid*.

134 BUILDING IN WORDS

it is one, is never made explicit.[111] However, taking seriously Vergil's near-contemporary readers Propertius and Manilius opens up the possibility of a richer reading of city-foundation in the *Aeneid*, which can enhance understanding of the *Aeneid* as a whole, its ambitions, and its self-imposed limits.

The responses of Propertius and Manilius to Vergilian city-foundation, too, appear in a different light when we consider how elusive the foundation of Rome really is in the *Aeneid*. When they announce that they will found Rome in verse, they claim to be completing what Vergil tantalizingly holds before us but never quite carries through.[112] Both align their poetic achievements with the foundation of Rome, and they cast this double foundation in terms that recall foundation in the *Aeneid*. By reading back into the *Aeneid* a poetic dimension to city-foundation, they found Vergilian poetic cities that are, in a sense, more 'Roman' than the original.

Conclusion

While thinking of text in terms of architecture is a normal feature of human language and thought, the texts studied in this chapter make strategic and innovative use of this core metaphorical concept. An analysis of three authors' use of the metaphor of city-building has shown not only how diverse and complex their techniques of linking architecture to text are, but also that there are a number of features of the text-city analogy which unite the three works. Its primary impact lies not in aesthetic or structural correspondences between text and city. Instead, comparing one's literary endeavour to the foundation of an entire city creates an impression of taking on a task on a grand scale, emphasizing the poet's daring and readiness for heroically hard work, on a par with that of the heroes of ktistic epic. The metaphor also conveys a sense of overarching, organizational skills, relating the logistical mastery of a huge building site to the poet's organization of a large body of initially unordered, chaotic material—a potential of the metaphor exploited most fully by Manilius, while Propertius tempers it with an emphasis on his city's organic growth. Finally, and most importantly, the city-text metaphor activates the huge contemporary cultural prestige of city-construction and city-foundation. The poetic intricacies and the literary mediation of the

---

[111] On megametaphors, which can underlie an entire narrative, see n. 48 in this chapter.

[112] On Propertius's use of the building metaphor as a means of staging a competition between his poetry and Vergil's, see also Robinson (2006), 205–6.

foundation-*topos* should not blind us to the fact that city-building was deeply relevant to Roman global politics in general, as well as to the powerful contemporary Augustan discourse of re-foundation and *renovatio*. The sudden emergence and development of the city-text metaphor has to be understood within an environment where city-building was a particularly powerful physical as well as intellectual presence.

4

Engineering Poetry

The Aesthetics of Construction in Statius's *Silvae*

Introduction

In Chapters 1 and 2, I considered how representations of the making of a monument alter the impact of the completed edifice.[1] I then turned to the literary-metaphorical potential of descriptions of construction: in Chapter 3, I began to investigate how descriptions of construction aim to alter the reader's assessment of the finished text. In this chapter I argue that descriptions of the building process in Statius's *Silvae* are designed to combine both effects—to influence the reader's assessment of the architectural as well as the textual construct.

The *Silvae* are a collection of short poems initially written for specific occasions but later combined into books by the poet. The first three books of the *Silvae* appeared (either all at the same time or in quick succession) between AD 92 and 94, a fourth book followed in AD 95, and the final book was published posthumously.[2] The themes, metres, length, and addressees of the individual poems are extremely varied, and only a small proportion of the poems concern the process of building and construction. These poems, *Silvae* 1.1, 3.1, and 4.3, will be the focus of this chapter. All three commemorate the construction of specific monuments. In *Silvae* 1.1, Statius describes a recently dedicated honorific equestrian statue of the emperor Domitian and its erection in the Forum. *Silvae* 3.1 concerns the construction of a temple in the grounds of Statius's patron Pollius Felix, and *Silvae* 4.3 deals with the building of the Via Domitiana, a road leading from Sinuessa to Puteoli. The

---

[1] The fourth section of this chapter, 'Engineering Aesthetics', has been published in a briefer form in Reitz (2012), 332–41.

[2] Arguing for a joint publication of the first three books (analogous to Horace's *Odes*) are e.g. Vollmer (1898), 3–13 (on the basis of a 'Gesamtkonzeption'); Newmyer (1979) 46–9; Bright (1980), 53–4; and Coleman (1988), xvi–xvii, who deftly summarizes earlier arguments and argues for a date no earlier than January 93. Successive publication in yearly intervals (between 92 and 94) is defended by van Dam (1984), 3; Nauta (2002), 287–9.

Building in Words. Bettina Reitz-Joosse, Oxford University Press. © Oxford University Press 2021.
DOI: 10.1093/oso/9780197610688.003.0005

ENGINEERING POETRY   137

individual poems praise the achievement of construction in different ways, and they recreate (a version of) the building process to heighten the reader's esteem for the completed work, using strategies familiar from Chapters 1 and 2. In the *Silvae*, these strategies are combined with a sustained metapoetic dimension. Statius describes the process of construction as a means of commenting on and justifying a specific aesthetic appropriate to the collection. He also exploits the coexistence of these two levels of meaning and the interaction between them.

Memories of Construction

The texts under consideration in this chapter represent construction in order to heighten the impact of built structures. Each of the poems was written for the occasion of a monument's dedication and was presented or performed in connection with it.[3] They all offer their readers an exemplary interpretation of the monument and render the process of construction, or rather the 'memory' of it that they produce, part of that interpretation. In this section, I give an overview of how the texts represent the monuments and, especially, their construction process. The resulting picture will then be modified in the fourth section, 'Engineering Aesthetics', where I reconsider these descriptions on a metapoetic level and point out how the two levels interact.

The very structure of *Silvae* 1.1 guides the reader towards the desired reception. The poem begins with a series of questions about the provenance and possible makers of the equestrian statue (Stat. *Silv.* 1.1.1–7):[4]

> Quae superimposito moles geminata colosso   1
> stat Latium complexa forum? caelone peractum
> fluxit opus? Siculis an conformata caminis
> effigies lassum Steropen Brontenque reliquit?
> an te Palladiae talem, Germanice, nobis   5

[3] *Silvae* 1.1 was presented to the emperor on the occasion of the dedication of the equestrian statue (see Stat. *Silv.* 1.ep.17–20): see Nauta (2002), 422 with n. 141 for the dating of the poem, 361–2 on the unlikelihood of oral presentation, and 365–74 more generally on the practice of presenting poems in writing. *Silvae* 3.1 was most likely performed for or presented to Pollius Felix in connection with the dedication of the temple of Hercules (cf. *Silv.* 3.ep.10–11). The context of presentation or performance for *Silvae* 4.3 is unclear. Coleman (1988), 105, tentatively suggests that the poem may have formed part of (hypothetical) celebrations for opening the Via Domitiana, while Nauta (2002), 359–60, stresses that the *deixis* of the poem only establishes a *fictional* context.

[4] I cite Courtney's (1990) text of the *Silvae* unless otherwise indicated.

138   BUILDING IN WORDS

> effinxere manus, qualem modo frena tenentem
> Rhenus et attoniti vidit domus ardua Daci?

What massive structure stands there, extending over the Latian Forum, doubled by a colossal statue on top of it? Did this work flow down from heaven completely finished? Or was the statue moulded in Sicilian foundries, and did it leave Steropes and Brontes exhausted? Or did the hands of Pallas portray you in such a way, Germanicus, as the Rhine and the high house of the impressed Dacian saw you not long ago, holding the reins?

These opening lines immediately draw attention not only to the size of the work of art itself, but also to its 'madeness': they ask *what it took* to get the statue there. The list of possible mythical builders encourages reflection on the superhuman achievement of constructing the huge equestrian statue. These lines are followed by a detailed description of the work of art, full of ecphrastic markers: the author describes how the emperor on his horse surveys and controls the forum with his gaze, while being viewed himself,[5] and he admires the fact that the representation is so lifelike that you might expect the statue to breathe, and the horse to gallop off.[6] This first section of the poem creates a static impression, but in line 61, in a moment of 'flashback', the poem shifts from the description of the horse and rider as they stand in the forum and away also from its overall time frame (1.1.61–70):

> Nec longae traxere morae. iuvat ipsa labores   61
> forma dei praesens, operique intenta iuventus
> miratur plus posse manus. strepit ardua pulsu
> machina; continuus septem per culmina Martis[7]

---

[5] *discit et e vultu* (25), *tuentur* (29), *videt* (31), *prospectare videris* (32), *visum* (52), *aspiciens* (55), *viso* (73), *tueri* (77), *lumine fesso* (87), *despectus* (88), *videre* (89), *videas* (107). The statue renders the monuments of the forum spectators of its own beauty (lines 29–31) and also exerts control over its surroundings by gazing out over the forum, over the other monuments, and up towards the Palatine (lines 32–6). The precise location of the statue in the forum is unclear; see Thomas (2004) for a suggestion. For a broader consideration of Domitianic architecture in terms of 'surveillance', cf. Fredrick (2003), esp. 214–20 on *Silv.* 4.2 and *Silv.* 1.1.

[6] A type of observation often made in connection with viewing or judging art in antiquity: the best art strains the boundaries of its own medium by appearing completely lifelike. In line 57, this liveliness of the statue even communicates itself to the physical surroundings: the earth 'pants' under the great weight of the horse: *insessaque pondere tanto / subter anhelat humus* (cf. also 3.1.54: *anhelantes agros*).

[7] Proposed by Gronovius and adopted by e.g. Shackleton Bailey (2003) for the transmitted (and impossible) *montis*, which seems to derive from 59.

ENGINEERING POETRY 139

it fragor et magnae vincit vaga murmura Romae. 65
Ipse loci custos, cuius sacrata vorago
famosique lacus nomen memorabile servant,
innumeros aeris sonitus et verbere crudo
ut sensit mugire forum, movet horrida sancto
ora situ meritaque caput venerabile quercu ... 70

No long delays dragged on. The very likeness of the god is present and renders the work easy, and the men who are working hard are amazed that their hands have become stronger. The high crane rumbles as it is set in motion.[8] Through the seven hills of Mars sounds a continuous din and surpasses the shifting noises of great Rome. The guardian of the place himself, whose name the holy chasm and the famous lake commemorate, hearing the countless clashes of bronze and the Forum bellowing from a brutal blow, raises his face, which is rough from hallowed old age, and his head, venerable because of its well-deserved oak wreath ...

All at once, the statue is no longer finished, standing in the forum being admired and itself looking out over the space. We have stepped back in time, and it is only in the process of being constructed. The description of the erection of the statue picks up the questions asked at the very beginning of the poem about the supposedly divine origins of the statue. In effect, questions and answers about the construction of the horse frame the description of its visual impact. The connection between the first lines and lines 61–5 is emphasized by verbal echoes.[9] *Operi* (62) recalls *opus* (3); the *manus* (63) of the workmen

[8] *machina* (64) can mean both 'crane' (*TLL* 8.12.70–13.7) and scaffolding (*TLL* 8.13.11–22). The first meaning is the more probable in this case. A scaffolding (supported by Shackleton Bailey (2003), 36 n. 19) would certainly have been required, since the assembling of the elements of a bronze statue involves the joining together of different pieces at considerable height. On the other hand, a crane (supported by Vollmer (1898), 226 *ad loc.*) is associated with noise also in Sen. *Phoen.* 468 (*stridente tardum machina ducens onus*, on which see also pp. 182–3), and the high *machina* in Vergil's description of the building works at Carthage (*Aen.* 4.89) is also generally thought to refer to a crane (see n. 55 in this chapter). If *machina* is taken as 'crane', *pulsus* may here mean 'the action of setting in motion' (*OLD* s.v. *pulsus* 3, a meaning similar to that of *impulsus*): the crane is moved by means of workmen walking in a wooden treadmill (see Vitr. 10.2.7: *calcantes homines*), undoubtedly a noisy activity. The Haterii relief (Figure 1.8) shows such a Roman crane and its treadmill in which several workmen are busy moving the crane. The noise and the need for a crane (or scaffolding) in any case suggest that the statue was not completely finished in the workshop, but transported to the forum in parts, and only combined and finished there. This is a strong argument in favour of those who argue that the statue was a *colossus*, or at least significantly larger than a 'normal' equestrian statue, since a normal-sized statue would have been completed in the workshop. On the colossal size of the statue, see Nauta (2002), 422 n. 142, and Dewar (2008), 78–80, refuting Geyssen (1996), 24–7. On the technology of ancient large bronzes, see Bol (1985), 118–72.

[9] Geyssen (1996), 103.

140 BUILDING IN WORDS

recall mention of Minerva's hands (6). The theme of divine involvement in the manufacturing of the statue (2–7) is taken up by *forma dei praesens* (62).

By dwelling not only on its finished state but framing the contemplation of its appearance with passages about its production, the poem inscribes admiration of the achievement of the statue's manufacture into the canon of appropriate reactions to it. The representation of construction specifically stresses certain elements of the construction, such as speed, the noise of construction, and the divine presence and assistance that facilitate the great work.[10] It engineers a 'memory' of construction which influences how the statue is viewed and evaluated.

Comparable framing strategies can also be observed in the other two construction poems. In *Silvae* 3.1, which deals with the temple of Hercules in the grounds of Pollius Felix's villa at Surrentum, reflections on the process of construction likewise frame the central section of the poem (the description of the picnic and thunderstorm which led Pollius Felix to initiate construction). *Silvae* 3.1 opens with a series of amazed comments on the differences between the humble old shrine and the splendid new temple (3.1.1–15).[11] Stressing above all the speed of the alterations, the passage opposes the earlier uncultivated state of nature to the domesticated landscape, enriched through the building of the temple.[12] The juxtapositions of the 'then' and the 'now' subsequently merge into a series of questions recalling those that open *Silvae* 1.1 (3.1.10–11, 15–17):[13]

> unde haec aula recens fulgorque inopinus agresti   10
> Alcidae? . . .
>
>   quaenam subito fortuna rigentes   15
> ditavit scopulos? Tyrione haec moenia plectro
> an Getica venere lyra?

---

[10] The speed of construction is expressed in the phrase *nec longae traxere morae* (61), which introduces the description of the manufacturing; *fluxit opus* (3) and *plus posse manus* (63) also dwell on the same theme. On speed as part of the memory of construction created in building inscriptions, see p. 19 with n. 14 in Chapter 1 of this work, and DeLaine (2002), 222–3, on speed of construction as a 'virtue in itself'. Noise is especially emphasized in lines 63–9, the divine presence of the likeness of the emperor in lines 61–2.

[11] Attributes associated with the old temple (and its patron deity) in 1–15: *pauper* (3), *vagis habitabile nautis* (4), *reclusum limen* (8–9), *parva ara* (9), *inglorius custos* (9), *steriles harenae* (12), *sparsum pelago montis latus* (13), *hirta dumis saxa* (13–14). Associated with the new temple: *maior tholos* (3), *nitidi postes* (5), *Grais effulta metallis culmina* (5), *aula* (10), *fulgor inopinus* (10).

[12] References to speed in the opening lines: *recens* (10), *velox, nuper* (12), *subito* (15), *annus, angusti bis seno limite menses* (18).

[13] On Statius's use of questions as an opening device in the *Silvae*, see Geyssen (1996), 38–40.

ENGINEERING POETRY   141

Where did the new hall come from and this splendour, which rustic Hercules did not expect? . . . What fortune has suddenly endowed the stark rocks with riches? Did these walls arrive due to a Tyrian plectrum or a Getic lyre?

While 1.1 names as potential makers of the equestrian statue Vulcan and the Cyclopes or Pallas Athena (1–6), the rhetorical question here already hints at the close connection between construction and poetry by suggesting Amphion and Orpheus as possible builders.[14]

The stress on the speed of building (*aula recens, subito*) continues when we learn that the building was completed within only one year, and the lines which immediately follow give the poet's explanation for the astonishingly fast execution of construction: the god himself must have participated in this Herculean labour (*labores*, 3.1.17) to render such a miracle possible (3.1.19–22):[15]

> deus attulit arces
> erexitque suas, atque obluctantia saxa   20
> summovit nitens et magno pectore montem
> reppulit: immitem credas iussisse novercam.

The god has brought and raised his own walls. By exerting himself he has moved aside reluctant boulders, and with his great chest has pushed back the mountain. You might think that his implacable stepmother had ordered him to do so.

Compared to the presence of the emperor's divine *genius* as an inspiration for the workmen in 1.1, the element of divine presence is developed much further here. The god takes an active role in the heavy physical work. He helps to overcome resistant nature (*obluctantia saxa*, 20) by physical force (*magno pectore*, 21).[16]

---

[14] On the myth of Amphion, see Chapter 5, especially pp. 183–5 on Amphion in the *Silvae*. On Orpheus in the *Silvae*, see e.g. Lovatt (2007); Morzadec (2009), 275–7.

[15] See Laguna (1992), 133 *ad* 17b on Herculean *labores* in 3.1.

[16] The expression *magno pectore* recalls a description of Pollius Felix's Epicurean mindset in companion-poem *Silvae* 2.2.124–5: . . . *qui pectore magno / spemque metumque domas*. The *pectus magnum*, the brave spirit, of Pollius Felix helps him to tame the forces of *spes* and *metus*, while Hercules uses his more 'physical' *pectus* for the taming of nature (*domare* is also used of Pollius's taming of nature at 2.2.56, and of Hercules's at 3.1.168). On the phrase *magno pectore*, see also further n. 75 in this chapter.

142 BUILDING IN WORDS

Towards the end of the poem, the motifs of these first lines recur, in an even more extensive reflection on the process of construction (3.1.117–38), already prepared for by the god's own appeal to Pollius Felix (91–116) and his promise to lend a hand himself. The divine involvement leads to astonishingly fast progress overnight (134–5) and to the short construction time of only a year; the speed of the works is picked up in 135–8. The theme of taming resistant nature returns in 110–13 and 123–4.[17] A rich description of the sound of construction (128–33) picks up another theme already familiar from *Silvae* 1.1. *Silvae* 3.1 thus develops further the motifs of the noise and speed of construction and divine involvement in it, combining them with the contrast between 'then' and 'now' and the human struggle against resistant nature.

Silvae 4.3 praises the newly built Via Domitiana. Unlike a temple or a statue, a road can hardly be praised for its beauty or other aspects of its appearance: its main asset is its utility. Yet again Statius combines praise of the construction process and its (useful) end result by means of time-shifts.[18] *Silvae* 4.3 opens with a question about origins, recalling its companion-poems 1.1 and 3.1. However, in this case the question immediately makes clear that the building is currently underway (4.3.1–3):

> Quis duri silicis gravisque ferri
> immanis sonus aequori propinquum
> saxosae latus Appiae replevit?

> What monstrous sound of hard flint and heavy iron has filled the sea-facing side of the paved Via Appia?

---

[17] In 110–13, Hercules announces that he will help with removing a mountain that stands in the way: *nec te, quod solidus contra riget umbo maligni / montis et immenso non umquam exesus ab aevo, / terreat. ipse adero et conamina tanta iuvabo / asperaque invitae perfringam viscera terrae.*—'And be not daunted [Pollius] because a solid hump of unfriendly mountain that measureless time has never consumed stands stark in the way. I myself shall be there to assist so great an enterprise, breaking through the rugged bowels of the reluctant earth.' Removing or breaking through a mountain is a sublime achievement, which for example Trajan draws attention to in connection with the construction of his forum (see pp. 21–4 in Chapter 1); cf. also Plin. *Pan.* 16.5. Contrast with this forceful rhetoric Pliny's emotive appeal to respect the natural boundaries of the earth, where he describes the function of mountains as *compages telluris visceribus densandis*—'a structure for holding firmly together the innards of the earth' (36.1). Since in Statius's poem it is the god himself who is speaking, the action is (to some extent) protected from appearing hybristic or transgressive.

[18] On time-shifts in 4.3, see Nauta (2002), 359–60.

ENGINEERING POETRY   143

Several explanations for the loud noise are rejected (Hannibal's troops, Nero's canal-building activity), before it is revealed that it is the sound of the emperor Domitian's road-building activity (9–26).[19] Time-shifts occur in lines 27–39, where the road appears completed and its utility is praised (it has reduced a travel time of one day to only two hours) and again in line 40, where we return to the construction in progress. The labour of laying the road is described in detail, and the precise wording of the description links 4.3 to 1.1 and 3.1.[20]

While 1.1 and 3.1 both contain the speech of a divinity who reacts to the new monument, 4.3 contains *two* speeches in praise of the new road. One is pronounced by the river god Volturnus, who seems to be raised from his riverbed by the noise of construction (like Curtius from the Lacus Curtius in 1.1) and praises the work as it is nearing completion. As the climactic conclusion of the poem, the Sybil of Cumae then prophesies a glorious future for the emperor.[21]

The theme of human struggle against and victory over nature, already present in 3.1, is developed at much greater length in 4.3. The description is a challenge for the poet. Representing large-scale human intervention in nature brings with it all the difficulties discussed in Chapter 2. In praising the emperor Domitian's achievement, Statius stretches the very limits of panegyric, while walking a fine line between imperial triumph and dangerous *hybris*.[22] Statius's poem displays the typical features of the triumphal rhetoric of control over nature. He represents the emperor's actions as a war against nature, and his victory as a triumph over a vanquished foe.[23] The

---

[19] On Nero's abortive attempt at building a canal between Lake Avernus and Ostia, see p. 66.

[20] For example, the description begins with *hic primus labor* (4.3.40) recalling the theme of the Herculean *labores* in 3.1. Coleman (1988), 116, notes that the 'declamatory use of pronouns' in lines 4.3.50–60 (*hi ... hi ... illi ... hi ... hae ... his*) recalls 3.1.118–29. The busy *manus* of the workmen appear in 4.3.49 as well as 1.1.63 and 3.1.118 (*innumerae coiere manus*); 4.3.62 picks up 1.1.65 (*it fragor* is repeated).

[21] Volturnus: 72–94; Sybil: 124–63. The description of the noise and its echoes (62–5) just before the appearance of Volturnus makes the situation recall the appearance of Curtius. The description of the river god also evokes Vergil's Tiber in *Aeneid* 8: Smolenaars (2006), 229.

[22] See Chapter 2, especially pp. 88–9.

[23] See Kleiner (1991) on Roman bridge-building as victory over the river, esp. 184–6 on *Silvae* 4.3. The strongest (and, for the modern reader, most uncomfortable) concentration of such language is found in the speech of the river god Volturnus (*Silv.* 4.3.72–84). The river has been forced to submit, as the martial metaphors show, only after a struggle in which man has triumphed over river. The river god now speaks of himself in the language of a slave taken in war: he is bound (*ligasti*) and suffers servitude (*servitus*), while the builder is in command and gives orders (*te duce, te iubente*)—at the same time, however, he professes himself glad with his slavish new role and enjoys being trampled by those crossing the bridge (*iam pontem fero perviusque calcor*), since he is happy to have submitted to the illustrious emperor. This kind of martial language is also employed in *Silvae* 2.2 (esp 52–9) and 3.1 (20: *obluctantia saxa,* and 12–16). Newlands (2002) analyses this aspect of 2.2; see esp. 134–5. See also Pavlovskis (1973), 2–21.

144   BUILDING IN WORDS

emperor's military triumph over nature is also connected to a sense of universal, cosmic control over nature. Not only can the emperor apparently (metaphorically) move Baiae closer to Rome (25–6),[24] but he would even be able to bring about beneficial global climate change (135–7).[25]

Statius's means of dealing with the potentially undesirable connotations of his description is so unusual that it has led some commentators to suppose that he may be conveying a much more critical or at least 'anxious' attitude towards the emperor by means of his ostensible praise.[26] For example, he explicitly mentions the negative *exempla* with which the activity might be connected. In the opening lines of the poem the *sonus immanis* of the road-building is at first (falsely, as it turns out) associated with two classic examples of hybris, Hannibal and Nero (4–8)—an implicit acknowledgement that the building activity of Nero would have sounded no different from that of Domitian, but at the same time also a means of tackling undesirable connotations head-on.[27] Similarly, the classic *exempla* of Xerxes's projected canal through Mount Athos and his bridge of ships over the Hellespont, both a byword for a tyrant's *hybris* and sinful interventions in nature, are brought up in the description of road construction, as are the failed attempts of several rulers to break a canal through the Isthmus of Corinth (4.3.56–60):[28]

---

[24] The arresting phrase (*aestuantes / septem montibus admovere Baiae*) is paralleled in an inscription from Puteoli, in which the inhabitants of Puteoli officially express their thanks for Domitian having moved their town closer to Rome (*AE* 1973, 137): *colonia Flavia Aug(usta) Puteolana . . . urbi eius admota*. On the wording of the inscription, see Coleman (1988), 110 *ad loc.*; on the monument and the inscription's reuse, see Flower (2001); on its erasure after Domitian's *damnatio memoriae*, Flower (2006), 256–8 and fig. 72. *[L]egere* (84) also has a double significance: Domitian 'shall be read of' in an inscription on the bridge against which Volturnus is leaning, as well as in Statius's poetry: Smolenaars (2006), 231, and Coleman (2008), 39–42.

[25] *Natura melior potentiorque, / hic si flammigeros teneret axes / largis, India, nubibus maderes / undaret Libye, teperet Haemus*—'If he [i.e. Domitian] had the flaming chariot in his keeping, better and mightier than Nature, India would be damp with generous clouds, Libya watered, Haemus warm.' Following the arguments of Coleman (1988), 132, *ad loc.*, I retain the original line order. Shackleton Bailey (2003) transposes 135 after 136. For *axes* as 'chariot' not 'sky', see Smolenaars (2006), 239; Nauta (2010), 262 n. 85.

[26] Ahl (1984b), 92, in his analysis of *Silvae* 1.1, argues that Statius's ostensible rejection of a possible negative interpretation serves only to draw the reader's attention to it. Newlands (2002) suggests that Statius's panegyrical poems do not so much voice criticism as reveal the poet's 'anxiety' as to the nature of Domitian's autocratic rule by means of 'faultlines' (23–6): for her interpretation of the negative *exempla* in 4.3 in terms of 'anxiety', see 290–3.

[27] The relationship between Neronian and Domitianic construction is crucial, as the Via Domitiana actually served as the replacement of the aborted Neronian canal project; Laurence (1999), 47. On the role of Nero in the poem cf. also the chapter in Meijer (2021) on 'De(Legitimising Rulership and (De)Stabilising Empire in Statius, *Silvae* 4.3'.

[28] A canal through the Isthmus was allegedly attempted by Caesar, Gaius, and Nero: see e.g. Suet. *Iul.* 44.3, *Cal.* 21, *Nero* 19.2, 37.3.

ENGINEERING POETRY 145

hae possent et Athon cavare dextrae   56
et maestum pelagus gementis Helles
intercludere ponte non natanti.
his parens, nisi di viam vetarent,[29]
Inous freta miscuisset Isthmos.   60

These hands might have been able to hollow out Mount Athos and to separate the gloomy sea of mourning Helle with a bridge that did not float.
Obeying these hands, Ino's Isthmus might have mingled its waters, if the
gods had not forbidden the passage.

Naturally, Domitian is cast as a completely different kind of ruler from Nero
and Xerxes, religiously observant and committed to restoring and guarding
Roman laws and morals (9–19), but at the same time his achievements are
placed in competition with those of overreaching tyrants. I am not persuaded
by the view that Statius's panegyric poetry is intended as criticism in disguise.[30]
Rather, as I argued in Chapter 2, the discourses of triumph and *hybris* deal in
the same themes and categories, and their extremes lie uncomfortably close to
one another. Statius's strategy for preventing his praise from eliciting undesirable connotations is to make them explicit and then to dismiss them, by clearly
stating the 'preferred reading' of any potentially dangerous allusion.[31]

The three poems all offer their audience an exemplary way of viewing
and interpreting the respective construction projects. By means of time-
shifts, Statius frames reflections on the finished state of the monuments

[29] This line presents several difficulties. Like Shackleton Bailey (2003), I cautiously adopt Postgate's
parens for the transmitted *parvus*, which Courtney (1990) and Coleman (1988) retain, the latter
tentatively explaining it (119 *ad loc.*) as 'an easy task for these', i.e. the labourers. Courtney and
Shackleton Bailey also accept Barth's conjecture *di viam* for the transmitted *deviae*.

[30] Statius's *Silvae* have often been read as clever, ironic expressions of criticism of the emperor, see
e.g. Ahl (1984a and 1984b) or Klodt (1998 and 2001), further bibliography in Leberl (2004), 15 n. 35.
This view has also been variously attacked, e.g. by Römer (1994), esp. 100–13; Dewar (1994); Geyssen
(1996); Nauta (2002). It is just as impossible to exclude either alternative as an 'incorrect' reading as
it is to reconstruct the author's personal convictions. Panegyric by its very nature has to touch and
extend the boundaries of the 'sayable', and irony is always a possible reading of any hyperbole or comparison; Nauta (2002), 424–6. The effectiveness of panegyric is a function of its clearly defined context, as Nauta (2002) argues (426): '... panegyric is only possible on the basis of a contract between the
poet and his audience which defines the context of utterance as, precisely, panegyric.' Cordes (2017)
shows how the meaning of panegyric texts is already unstable in antiquity, and explores mechanisms
of the 'Umkodierung' of Neronian and Domitianic panegyric after their deaths.

[31] Cordes (2014) analyses the strategy of 'preferred readings' at work in *Silvae* 1.1: Statius
disambiguates praise that may possibly be interpreted ironically by adding explicitly which reading
is to be 'preferred'. Cf. also Nauta (2002), 426, on 'disclaimers' in the speech of the Sibyl in *Silvae* 4.3.
Another example is the comparison with Phaeton (135–7, quoted in n. 25 of this chapter), analysed
by Nauta (2010), 262–4. See also more generally Cordes (2017, *passim*) on 'safe praise' in the *Silvae*.

146   BUILDING IN WORDS

with descriptions of their construction process. He thereby encourages his readers to admire their 'madeness' and to focus on the achievement of their manufacture or construction. In Statius's poetic representations of construction, a number of themes turn out to be especially prominent. One of them, the speed of construction, is readily explicable and familiar from the representations of construction studied in Chapter 1. Other recurring themes are more difficult to understand, such as the intense focus on the sound and noise of construction: noise is hardly a 'positive' element of construction that one would commonly choose to stress as a means of praise. In the following section I argue that some of these specific choices are (additionally) motivated on a metapoetic level.

The Making of the *Silvae*

Before I reconsider the descriptions of construction in this metaphorical light, I briefly turn to one special feature of the collection. When the individual poems were republished in book form under the title *Silvae*, the poet composed a prose preface for each book in the form of a short epistle addressed to the book's dedicatee. Johannsen has argued that these dedicatory texts are designed to 'frame' the poetry book and steer the reception of the poems.[32] In reading the prefaces, it immediately becomes apparent that this framing predominantly consists of creating an image of the *composition* of the poems by describing the circumstances and, especially, the speed at which this composition was achieved. The *praefatio* to the first book of poems begins (1–5):

> Diu multumque dubitavi, Stella . . . an hos libellos, qui mihi subito calore et quadam festinandi voluptate fluxerunt, cum singuli de sinu meo pro< . . . >[33], congregatos ipse dimitterem.

> For a long time I have hesitated a lot, Stella, about whether I should myself collect and publish these little texts, which came to me in a flow, in the heat

---

[32] Johannsen (2006) offers a thorough investigation of function and design of the prose prefaces in Martial and Statius. On the prefaces as 'rezeptionssteuernde Rahmung' (framing), see 45–7. On the prose prefaces as paratexts, see 38–45. For her detailed analysis of the prose prefaces of the *Silvae*, see 241–370.

[33] Many ways of filling this *lacuna* of thirteen letters have been proposed; see the critical commentary of Liberman (2010), 59 *ad loc.* for an overview.

ENGINEERING POETRY 147

of the moment and in a kind of pleasurable rush, when they < . . . > from my bosom individually.

The poet then wonders whether his poems, initially written for particular occasions and patrons, will in this new format meet with a cool reception from the general public (11–15):

> Sed apud ceteros necesse est multum illis pereat ex venia, cum amiserint quam solam habuerunt gratiam celeritatis. nullum enim ex illis biduo longius tractum, quaedam et in singulis diebus effusa. quam timeo ne verum istuc versus quoque ipsi de se probent!

But among the other readers[34] the poems will necessarily meet with much less goodwill, since they will have lost the only charm they had: that of speed. For in no case was the time I worked on a poem drawn out for longer than two days, and some were even poured out in a single day. How much I fear that the verses themselves will also testify about themselves that this is true!

In what follows the speaker invokes the addressees of the individual poems as witnesses for the truth of his claims about near-miraculous *celeritas*. For each poem, he indicates briefly the content and the addressee and pays special attention to the time required for composition (usually only one or two days). For example, the third poem of the first book, a description of the Villa of Manlius Vopiscus at Tibur, is introduced as follows (1.ep.24–7):

> Manilius certe Vopiscus . . . solet ultro quoque nomine meo gloriari villam Tiburtinam suam descriptam a nobis uno die.

> To be sure, Manilius Vopiscus . . . regularly boasts on his own initiative and on my behalf that I described his villa at Tibur in a single day.

In the prefaces to the second and third book, the theme of fast composition returns, while the indications of time required for composition diminish even further.[35] The veracity of these claims has been doubted,

---

[34] I.e. not the original dedicatees of the poems.
[35] Johannsen (2006), 317.

148 BUILDING IN WORDS

but it is not an issue here. Whether fictional or not—the 'memory' of composition created in these prefaces is a means of steering their reception, analogous to the memories of construction steering the reception of monuments.

How do these *praefationes* interact with the metapoetic dimension of the descriptions of building and construction that I am about to analyse? On the most basic level, the *praefationes* sensitize the reader for the aesthetic reflections to follow. They fix the process of composition in the mind of the reader at an early stage as a crucial context of reception and so prepare for further reflections on the making of poetry. In the following section, I analyse how the aesthetic and poetological pronouncements of the prefaces are strengthened, supplemented, and modified through Statius's representation of construction.

Engineering Aesthetics

The themes that receive special emphasis in the construction poems, such as speed, sound, and the manipulation of rivers or trees, are not only part of the 'memory' of the physical construction process, but also specifically appropriate to the special aesthetics of the *Silvae* that Statius is seeking to justify. The way in which the process of construction is figured shapes the reader's perception of the *Silvae*.[36] The aim of the descriptions of construction is to influence not only the way in which readers regard the construction projects, but also the way in which they read the poetry that praises them. The metaphorical relation between construction and poetry is a flexible tool in the *Silvae*, and building and poetics are linked in a variety of ways. 'Building' is by no means always a straightforward metaphor for 'writing poetry': different aspects of the construction process are exploited for their particular associations, while the 'literal' and the 'metaphorical' levels of construction interact in different ways. The positive associations of one particular feature in one sphere can be exploited for the other.

---

[36] Since both *Silv.* 1.1 and *Silv.* 3.1 are placed at the opening of their respective books, they are particularly suited to establishing a poetic programme for the *Silvae* and formulating their aesthetic categories; see Geyssen (1996) on 1.1, esp. 122; Egelhaaf-Gaiser (2007) and Newlands (1991) on 3.1; and Newlands (2002), esp. 49–50 and 69–73. On the metapoetics of *Silv.* 4.3, see Newlands (2002), ch. 9; Smolenaars (2006).

Speed

Statius's emphasis on the speedy progress and completion of the work highlights one of the features by which high-budget building projects were meant to impress.[37] However, the emphasis placed on fast construction also recalls the strong focus on fast composition in the *praefationes*, where Statius describes his poetry as composed at impressive speed for specific occasions. While fast construction is a conventional element of praise for a builder, fast writing is a very unusual, perhaps even (for Statius's contemporaries) perverse, poetic boast. With these claims Statius violates one of the most widely accepted principles of Latin poetic aesthetics, which Latin poets ultimately (claim to) derive from the influential pronouncements of the Hellenistic poet Callimachus.[38] Latin poets regularly pride themselves on slaving over their work for decades, working through the night and polishing every single word. The accusation of hasty production is a standard element in attacks on 'bad' poets.[39] Statius's claim to have composed 300 hexameters in only two days (1.ep.22–3) reads like a deliberate reaction to Catullus's and Horace's criticism of inferior colleagues who write too many lines too quickly.[40] Statius's challenge to 'mainstream' aesthetics (or rather the mainstream *articulation* of aesthetics) is communicated and justified in a number of ways. One of them is the metaphor of construction for poetic composition. It helps to formulate speed as a new category of poetic achievement, by allowing the

---

[37] See e.g. p. 19, n. 14 and pp. 27 and 50.

[38] Nauta (2006), 35: 'we see in Statius not just a neutralization, but even an inversion of the Callimachean apologetic scheme'. For a recent treatment of Latin poets' engagement with Callimachus, and an overview of earlier literature, see Hunter (2006). Cf. also Fantuzzi and Hunter (2004), 444–85, on 'Callimacheanism' in the Greek world and in Rome. The manifold Roman adaptations of the initially very specific Callimachean aesthetic principles turned them into an extremely flexible tool of literary self-reflection, open to Roman poets working in any genre. This flexibility made it unnecessary, and indeed virtually impossible, for Roman poets to disagree with the 'Callimachean' aesthetic principles.

[39] Callimachus himself does not explicitly mention the fast production of poetry. He condemns poetry that is not carefully made, is too long, or not sufficiently original. In the *Aetia* prologue (Callim. *Aet.* fr. 1 Harder), he rejects poems of many thousand lines (Callim. *Aet.* fr. 1.3–4 Harder) and recommends judging poetic merit by the standards of art, and not the Persian 'chain', a land-measure (Callim. *Aet.* fr. 1.17–18 Harder). However, Roman 'Callimachean' poets as a rule do condemn fast composition, and praise poetry that is the product of years of laborious execution: cf. Catull. 95.1–3, Hor. *Sat.* 1.4.9–10, Hor. *Ars. P.* 291–4, 386–90. Statius himself makes the common poetic claim to careful polish achieved during long years of composition for the *Thebaid*, both in the poem itself (Stat. *Theb.* 12.810–12) and in the *Silvae* (Stat. *Silv.* 3.5.35–6; 4.7.26), for which cf. also Callim. *Epigr.* 27 Pf on Aratus's work during the night.

[40] Catullus in 95.1–3 praises Cinna's *Zmyrna*, carefully composed over the course of nine years, and favourably contrasts this with Hortensius's production of 500,000 lines in the same time. Horace in *Sat.* 1.4 and 1.10 likewise condemns Lucilius for composing too many lines too quickly: *in hora saepe ducentos, / ut magnum, versus dictabat stans pede in uno* (*Sat.* 1.4.9–10).

150 BUILDING IN WORDS

poet to harness the positive connotations of fast construction in real building for the production of his own poetic work.

The link between poetic and architectural production is forged at the very beginning of *Silvae* 1.1 through a direct reference to the immediately preceding dedicatory *epistula*. In the *praefatio*, Statius claims that the poems *mihi subito calore et quadam festinandi voluptate fluxerunt*—'came to me in a flow, in the heat of the moment and in a kind of pleasurable rush' (1.ep.3–4). Lines 2–3 of poem 1.1 on the erection of the Domitianic statue pick up the vocabulary of a miraculous 'flow' in production: *caelone peractum / fluxit opus?*—'Did this work flow down from heaven completely finished?'[41] Apart from the opening questions about miraculously sudden appearance, the theme also opens the description of the construction proper, which begins in 61 with the words *nec longae traxere morae*—'no long delays drew out the time', picking up on 1.ep.13–14: *nullum enim ex illis biduo longius tractum*—'for (the time spent on) none of them was drawn out for longer than two days'.[42]

The other two construction poems further explore the aesthetics of speed. In *Silvae* 3.1, the poet combines the celebration of impressive speed of building with the theme of divine help with construction.[43] The idea is already present in 1.1, where the *forma dei praesens* (62) inspires the workmen, but in 3.1 the theme is developed at much greater length. Earlier in this chapter, we saw that the involvement of Hercules himself is celebrated (especially in 3.1.19–22) as the reason for the astonishing speed at which construction is completed.[44] Divine inspiration of the poet and his work is

[41] The parallel is noted by Geyssen (1996), 43–4. In the context of a bronze statue, the vocabulary of 'flow' is translated from the purely mental-metaphorical to the material, since the bronze for the statue is indeed liquid and 'flows' at some point during the casting process.

[42] Here, the rejection of *mora* is also a hint at the interruption of the narrative 'delay' of ecphrasis. Cf. also 3.1.117, where an ecphrasis of the temple is succeeded by a description of the process of construction, yet again marked by the words *nec mora* (117). The description of the forging of the shield of Aeneas in the *Aeneid* is introduced by an exhortation of Vulcan to the Cyclopes: *praecipitate moras* (*Aen.* 8.443). Statius's play on *mora* at the opening of two anti-ecphrastic passages interprets Vergil's *praecipitate moras* likewise as anti-ecphrastic signposting. Vulcan's work produces the shield, an ecphrastic object (8.626–738). Hercules's activity in *Silvae* 3.1 recalls Vulcan's creative activity (see p. 141), when he likewise creates an object for a (much less privileged) ecphrastic description. However, in *Silvae* 3.1 as in 1.1, the ecphrastic description is displaced, occurring before, rather than after, the description of the object's production.

[43] Newlands (1991) explores the metapoetic layer of *Silv.* 3.1: see esp. 449–50, where she notes the connection between speed of building and fast poetic production.

[44] These lines are quoted on p. 141. The importance of divine intervention for the speed of construction and the miraculous transformation is also strengthened by links between *Silv.* 3.1 and the Ovidian episode of Philemon and Baucis (Ov. *Met.* 8.626–720). A pious elderly couple offers humble shelter to a god (see esp. *Silv.* 3.1.32–3: *felix simplexque domus fraudumque malarum / inscia et hospitibus superis dignissima sedes*), and subsequently divine intervention turns a lowly hut (*Silv.* 3.1.82: *tenuis casa*) into a gleaming temple at incredible speed. The connection between *Silv.* 3.1 and

also a stock feature in ancient poetic texts. Here, it is responsible for speedy building as well as rapid poetic production. Hercules's helpful intervention thus helps to formulate a new, valid aesthetic for the *Silvae* that suits quickly produced but also divinely sanctioned and inspired poetry.[45]

Silvae 3.1 offers further opportunities for connecting architectural and poetic production, since it describes the construction of a temple. As mentioned in the previous chapter, temple-building was already an established poetic metaphor, most famously employed at the opening of Vergil's third book of *Georgics*.[46] I suggest (tentatively, considering the nature of the evidence) that Statius here adapts another well-known and possibly Callimachean *topos* for a sharper definition of his poetic ideal. A fragment from Callimachus's *Aetia* (fr. 118 Harder), in a very bad state of preservation and unplaceable,[47] has been suggested by Thomas as a common model for *Georgics* and *Silvae* 3.1:[48]

].φ.ορειϲ οἵ τε μάλιϲ[τα   1
]ν. [λ]ειαίνουσι· τὸ δ᾽ ἱερ[ὸν
ἐξ αὐ]τοσχεδίης κεῖνο τεκ.[
]..ύ..ι σταφύλη.[.]ο.[
].........ν λειαμε.[5
].......ιησι μελιχροτ[
]ἀκριβὲς καὶ τότε Λητο[ΐδ
]..τό δ᾽ ἔμελλεν εσ[
]..ἀμφιπερικ[
]ωη.αν..ε.[10
].[

Philemon and Baucis is explored in detail by Newlands (2013) and already touched on by Thomas (1983), 104, who mentions it as another theoxeny-episode also related to the Callimachean *Victoria Berenices* and its Hercules-episode, in which the hero stays in the simple hut of Molorchus before his fight against the Nemean lion (cf. *Silv.* 3.1.29–30). On the Molorchus-episode and *Silv.* 3.1, see also Egelhaaf-Gaiser (2007).

[45] The preface to book 3, addressed to Pollius Felix, the builder of the temple, already suggests that we should read the poem as divinely inspired. There, the poet characterizes his poem as a spontaneous expression of piety in response to the divine presence: *nam primum limen eius Hercules Surrentinus aperit, quem in litore tuo consecratum, statim ut videram, his versibus adoravi*—'For its threshold is opened by Hercules of Surrentum; as soon as I saw him consecrated on your shore, I paid him homage with these verses.'

[46] *Georg.* 3.12–16: see pp. 116 and 123–4.

[47] Harder (2012), 908–9.

[48] Thomas (1983). He himself stresses the speculative nature of his arguments.

152 BUILDING IN WORDS

Although the passage is so fragmentary as to be untranslatable, the vocabulary suggests that Callimachus focusses on the workmanship of a number of temples, quite possibly different (phases of) temples of Apollo at Delphi (Λητο[ῖδ, 7).[49] Apparently one of the temples was 'improvised' on the spot (ἐξ αὐτοσχεδίης, 3), there are workmen (or do they not yet exist, as Harder thinks?) who smooth (λειαίνουσι, 2) stone (?), and something, possibly one of the temples, is described by the adjectives μελιχρός (6, in the comparative or superlative) and ἀκριβές (7). Although there is certainly no clear indication of a poetic temple-metaphor in the text as it stands, the expressions used here by Callimachus to describe architecture are also attested in literary-theoretical or poetological contexts, and μελιχρός is in fact used only twice more in the extant œuvre of Callimachus, both times in passages setting out Callimachus's aesthetic programme.[50] The passage is even more appropriate as a potential model for *Silvae* 3.1 than Thomas suggests, since Callimachus and Statius both deal with earlier and later phases of temples and the contrasting workmanship of these phases. As far as we can tell, Callimachus distinguishes between an earlier temple built ἐξ αὐτοσχεδίης, and a later temple (or temples) described as more accomplished and artistically pleasing. I tentatively suggest, in the light of the fragmentary evidence, that *if* Statius is indeed referring to the Callimachean (possibly metapoetic) temples in fr. 118, his reason for doing so may well be to show that his own work unites un-Callimachean, fast, *ex tempore* composition with artistically satisfying result. Statius's poems can be *both* μελιχρός *and* composed ἐξ αὐτοσχεδίης.[51]

---

[49] Pfeiffer (1949), *ad loc.*, Asper (2004), 187, and Harder (2012), 906–7, all connect the fragment with the temple of Apollo in Delphi (cf. Paus. 10.5.9–13, Str. 9.3.9): Harder (2012), 907. Pfeiffer (1949), *ad loc.*, argues that Callimachus is comparing *two* temples: 'Fort. de templo quodam, vel potius de duobus templis, narratur, priore "ex tempore" facto, altero ab architectis arte peritis aedificato.' Harder (2012), 907, argues for *three* temples.

[50] *Aet.* fr. 1.16 Harder and *Epigr.* 27.2–4 Pf. Thomas (1983), 98 and n. 38. The occurrence of μελιχρός in this passage appears to be the strongest argument for a metapoetic reading. Harder (2012), who rejects a metaphorical reading, admits that 'it is not easy to see what this word must refer to in a context of building' (910 *ad* 118.6).

[51] The link between *Silvae* 3.1 and the *Aetia* appears particularly strong. Laguna (2002), 129 *ad* 2, interprets the reference to *causas* (3.1.2) and *exordia* (3.1.49) as generic markers of aetiological poetry, but the use of the word *causa* can also recall the title of Callimachus's *Aetia* more specifically: cf. Ov. *Fast.* 1.1 and Green (2004), 27–8. Statius may be inviting us to read the poem as a response to the *Aetia*: the close thematic links (on which see also Egelhaaf-Gaiser (2007) and Thomas (1983), 104–5; note especially the mention of Molorchus in *Silv.* 3.1.29) are offset by a contrasting poetic aesthetic.

ENGINEERING POETRY   153

The theme of speed is most pervasive in *Silvae* 4.3, the poem praising the construction of the *Via Domitiana*. The theme there is no longer exclusively linked to construction—it has spread to different areas and elements of the poem. The stress on the fast construction of the road links this poem to 1.1 and 3.1. The description of the physical construction suggests feverish activity: *o quantae pariter manus laborant* (49) is followed by *hi ... hi ... illi ... hi* (50–5), indicating that work is progressing in many different places at the same time. The theme of divine inspiration as the reason for faster construction (and poetic production) is recalled during the appearance of the river god Volturnus: his divine presence possibly facilitates the completion of a stretch of the road, which is hyperbolically described as *marmoratus* (95–6).[52] However, the main theme of the poem is the speed of travel which the newly constructed road allows. The contrast between the slow and laborious progress on the old road and the freshly gained travelling speed on the new one is stressed throughout the poem.[53] Not only construction, but also travel along a road is an extremely well-established poetic metaphor—there may be a connection between the fast travel and fast poetic composition.[54] Finally, the fast-moving hendecasyllabic metre commonly indicates fast movement, and could here mimic poetically the speed of travel and/or the speed of construction.[55] In 4.3, the speed of construction, transport, and poetic composition are thus bound together in a nexus of imagery. The fast movement on the road functions as a metaphor for rapid poetic composition, and is also itself metaphorically indicated by the fast-moving metre and the speed of construction. Speed forms the centre around which poetic praise for road, emperor, and poet revolves.

[52] For the idea that divine presence facilitates construction, see Vollmer (1898), 458 *ad loc.* Coleman (1988), 126–7 *ad loc.*, points out that there is no direct expression of Volturnus's influence in the text. The interpretation of the passage (*se levarat / ingenti plaga marmorata dorso*) is contested. Coleman (1988) takes *plaga* as a stretch of road, *marmoratus* as hyperbole for 'paved'.

[53] For example, before the new road was built, *nec cursus agiles, sed impeditum / tardabant iter orbitae tenaces ...* (32–3), and the change in speed achieved by the building project is elaborated in the contrast of *hic quondam* (27) and *at nunc* (36). Words indicating speed abound (see e.g. *citus* in 101 and 110; *velox* in 39 and 103).

[54] For travelling along a road as a poetic process in Callimachus, see Wimmel (1960), 'Die Symbolgruppen des Weges', 103–11, and Asper (1997), 21–107, extensively on Callimachus and his predecessors. In Latin poetry cf. e.g. Hor. *Epist.* 1.19.20–1, Lucr. 1.925–6, where the point of the metaphor is walking on previously untrodden ground. The common charioteer image also implies that the chariot is travelling along a poetic road; cf. e.g. Verg. *Georg.* 2.541–2, Prop. 2.10.2, Ov. *Ars am.* 3.467–8.

[55] Coleman (1988), 105; Morgan (2000), 114–19; Newlands (2002), 309.

154 BUILDING IN WORDS

Sound

The second prominent theme of Statius's descriptions of constructions is the noise that accompanies building. Unlike speed, noise seems a surprising choice for a panegyric poem. It is an undeniably realistic feature, but must surely have been one of the side effects of construction that annoyed and irritated people, and that one would rather not want them to think about when viewing the finished product.[56] I suggest that one reason for the prominence of sound and noise in all three poems is the metapoetic potential of the theme, which Statius exploits in two different ways to reflect on the poetics of the *Silvae*.

Firstly, the sound of building and the 'sound' produced by poetry are related to each other in terms of their range of impact, especially in poems 1.1 and 4.3.[57] In *Silvae* 1.1, the shift from the contemplation of the statue to its production brings with it a switch from one sense-perception to another. In the ecphrastic description of the equestrian statue's position and appearance in the first sixty lines, the pertinent experience is the visual. When the focus shifts to the statue's manufacture, a different sense-experience takes over (1.1.63–70):

> strepit ardua pulsu
> machina; continuus septem per culmina Martis
> it fragor et magnae vincit vaga murmura Romae.   65
> Ipse loci custos, cuius sacrata vorago
> famosique lacus nomen memorabile servant,
> innumeros aeris sonitus et verbere crudo
> ut sensit mugire forum, movet horrida sancto
> ora situ meritaque caput venerabile quercu...   70

The high crane rumbles as it is set in motion. Through the seven hills of Mars sounds a continuous din and surpasses the shifting noises of great Rome. The guardian of the place himself, whose name the holy chasm and the famous lake commemorate, hearing the countless clashes of bronze

---

[56] Conversely, if one were trying to discredit the monument or building activities, one might stress noise: see especially Pliny's criticism of the din caused by Domitianic building activities (Plin. *Pan.* 51). Tib. 2.3.43–4 also refers to the *tumultus* of transporting building materials in a passage on the corrupting influence of *praeda*. Juvenal complains about the noise of wagons and the dangers of transportation to the building sites of Rome; Juv. 3.236–8, 254–61; cf. also Hor. *Epist.* 2.2.72–3.

[57] See Morzadec (2009), 308–11, on sound, and especially the motif of the echo, in the *Silvae*. She stresses the importance of the Statian soundscapes ('paysages sonores', 311) as a way of emphasizing the impact of the construction works on the wider area: 309–10.

ENGINEERING POETRY   155

and the Forum bellowing from a brutal blow, raises his face, which is rough
from hallowed old age, and his head, venerable because of its well-deserved
oak wreath . . .

The reference to the loud sounds of construction offers the poet a way of
reflecting on the potential impact of his own poetry. The sound of the building
site, travelling far and wide through the city, metaphorically suggests Statius's
own poetry. The sound announces the presence of construction works long
before they come into view. The impact of the monument is communicated
far beyond its immediate surroundings, not only through the sound of the
construction works, but also through its poetic re-creation by Statius. This
interpretation is supported by the fact that Curtius, raised by the sounds
of construction, greets the statue as follows (74–5): *salve, magnorum proles
genitorque deorum, / auditum longe numen mihi.*—'Hail, offspring and be-
getter of great gods, deity that I have heard (of) *longe*.' *Auditum longe mihi*
can be understood, with Shackleton-Bailey, as 'known to me by distant
report'[58] but following directly upon a passage which dwells quite literally on
sensations of hearing, it might also be a play on the way in which the sounds
of construction/the poem announce the fame of the ruler before one even lays
eye on the statue ('heard from afar', i.e. from deep under water). The statue is
visible only in the forum, but its 'sound' (both real and poetic) can be heard
throughout and even underneath the city.[59] The poet further encourages
such a reading by recalling the building noise that resounds through the hills
of Rome in the opening of the following poem, *Silvae* 1.2: *Unde sacro Latii
sonuerunt carmine montes?*—'Why did the hills of Latium resound with sacred song?' (1.2.1). There, the sound filling the hills of Latium *is* indeed the

---

[58] Shackleton Bailey (2003), 37.

[59] This interpretation of the sound of construction is also supported by the fact that Statius regularly
speaks of his poetry as 'sound' in the sense of poetry presented orally or as song: see e.g. the transition
between his song and that of the Sibyl in 4.3.119–20 and 141–4. On the emphasis on oral culture in
the *Silvae*, see Coleman (2008), 30; on Statius as *vates*, see Lovatt (2007), 146–8. Contrasting passages
where the reference is clearly to *written* poetry are rarer (cf. *Silv.* 2.1.17–8; see Coleman (2008), 30,
on the scarcity of references to writing in the *Silvae*). Nauta (2008), 171, discusses 4.8.35–41, where
the illusion of singing and lyre-playing simply coexists with the realities of commissioned writing.
Since the *Silvae* refer to themselves both as song and as text, these references are difficult to interpret
in establishing whether a particular poem was performed, presented in writing, or both. Some of
Statius's poems appear to have been presented orally (at least in a preliminary version) before being
published in writing, while others were immediately offered in writing (see in detail Nauta (2002),
256–77 and 356–64 on oral presentation, 277–90 and 365–74 on presentation in writing). In any
case, the oral performance and recitation, as well as the poetic illusion of song, lyre-playing, and vatic
utterance, create a strong sense of the *Silvae* as poetry that can be *heard*, and this concept may also lie
behind Statius's use of the metaphor of the sound of construction.

156 BUILDING IN WORDS

wedding song for Stella and Violentilla, sung by Apollo, the Muses, and (the poet suggests) himself.[60]

In *Silvae* 3.1.128–9, the sound of Hercules's night-time digging activities also travels far, carrying all the way to the island of Capri: *ditesque Caprae viridesque resultant / Taurubulae et terris ingens redit aequoris echo*—'rich Capri and verdant Taurubulae reverberate and the sea's mighty echo returns to the land.'[61] Again, sound travels further than sight, since despite the spectacular panoramic views from Pollius's estate across the bay, the island of Capri, which lies further west, appears not to have been visible from the villa.[62] The connection between real and poetic sound is hinted at by the use of the word *echo*, which emphasizes the far-reaching effect of the poet's imitation of the construction, as well as alerting the reader to the intertextual 'echoing' of Vergilian sound-effects in the passage immediately following.[63]

In 4.3, sound is established as a key theme of the poem in the opening lines (cited earlier, p. 142). The impact of the sound clearly surpasses that described in 1.1. The reach of the sound described in 1.1.64–5 (*continuus septem per culmina Martis / it fragor*) is picked up and outdone by 4.3.62 (*it longus medias fragor per urbes*). While in 1.1 the *fragor* filled the seven hills, now it fills the cities along the road. The fame of the builder and his poet spread simultaneously. The single (divine) listener of 1.1 (Curtius) is multiplied in 4.3.62–71 (Gaurus, Massicus, Cyme, the Liternian marsh, Savo, Volturnus). The mention of sound itself is multiplied as well: the *innumeros sonitus* (68–9) in 1.1 are matched by *immanis sonus* (2), *sonant* (4), and *miratur sonitum* (65) in 4.3.[64] Again, the poet marshals the fame of the builder also for his poetic achievement: just as the audience of the construction achievement is no longer confined to the city of Rome but extends to all cities along the road, so the audience of this poetry, too, will be enlarged, and his poetic fame will travel not only through all of Rome but far beyond.[65] The

---

[60] See also 1.2.222–4 on the travelling sound and its echo (*resultant*, 223); Taisne (1994), 26–8.

[61] We do not know precisely what may be meant by *Taurubulae*; see Laguna (1992), 171–2, *ad loc.*

[62] The views from the villa are laid out in 2.2.72–84. Cf. also 3.1.147–53, cited on p. 165.

[63] See p. 160. On the role of echo in the *Silvae*, see Morzadec (2009), 308–9, and Taisne (1994), 25–8, and generally on echo as an intertextual marker, e.g. Heerink (2015), 8 with n. 35, and *passim*.

[64] Perhaps the phrase *miratur sonitum* also hints at a competition, already implied in 1.1, between the visual impact of a physical monument and the auditory impact of its construction, as well as the poetry about it. The verb *mirari* is usually applied to visual sensation (when used in the meaning 'to look at in wonder and awe' (*OLD* 3)), but here, it is the sound rather than the appearance of the road that is marvelled at. Cf. also Newlands (2002), 296, on *miratur* 'as an expression of the aural rather than the visual imagination'.

[65] Cf. Morzadec (2009), 310–11: 'Le pouvoir de Domitien, les talents poétiques et les prouesses techniques des hommes et des dieux s'inscrivent aussi dans le paysage sonore'.

ENGINEERING POETRY   157

theme of the echo, reprised from 3.1, again emphasizes the role of the text in reworking, multiplying, and disseminating the physical construction works: *atque echo simul hinc et inde fractam / Gauro Massicus uvifer remittit*, 63–4—'and grape-bearing Massicus sends the echo back to Gaurus, broken up from both directions at the same time'. These readings of 1.1, 3.1, and 4.3 suggest that the sound produced by construction can metaphorically be related to the poetry produced by the poet. Statius uses this relation to reflect on the difference in range of influence between visual and aural sensations and to stress the ability of his poetry to reach a larger audience than the finished monument alone.

The second way in which Statius exploits the connection between construction noise and poetic sound is related not to the range of impact but rather to aesthetics. This may surprise, since the sound-descriptions chosen by the poet appear deliberately unpleasant. Expressions such as *strepere*, *fragor*, *mugire*, and *immanis sonus* suggest sounds that are violent and disruptive, sounds one would not enjoy hearing. How might this tally with a metapoetic dimension of the sound of construction? In the *Aetia* prologue, Callimachus repeatedly refers to the desired sound of poetry. Bad poetry is indicated by sounds that are loud and unpleasant to the ear. The braying of asses (θόρυβον... ὄνων, 30) or thundering (βροντᾶν, 20) metaphorically represent the bloated and bombastic poetry that he rejects in favour of the well-crafted. The metaphor is subsequently modified and adapted by a host of later writers. In the poetological pronouncements of Latin texts, loud and ugly sounds also often function as an image for undesirable poetry, though not necessarily (as for Callimachus) 'bad' poetry. Instead, loudness often comes to be connected with the kind of poetry that a poet is excusing himself from writing at this point: usually epic, often in a panegyric mould.[66] These (mock-)modest refusals of too-large or too-difficult poetic tasks become formalized in Latin poetry as so-called *recusationes*.[67]

I suggest that Statius, in the face of convention and Roman 'Callimacheanism', tries to justify—with a judicious dose of humour—a rhetoric of loud, powerful, and overwhelming sound. Loud sound, like fast

[66] For example, Calliope in Prop. 3.3.40–2 uses the sound of horses and the blaring of the trumpet as an illustration of the poetry Propertius is not supposed to write. The loud, ugly sound is there presented as a violation of aesthetic principles, but also made more specifically appropriate to the rejection of epic on warlike themes.

[67] The authoritative treatment on the Augustan poets is still Wimmel (1960), although his brief discussion of Statius's use of *recusatio* (316–19) as 'biedere Gesten' (319) does not do justice to the complexities of Statian aesthetics. On Flavian *recusationes*, see Nauta (2006).

158 BUILDING IN WORDS

poetic production, is part of his formulation of a bold poetic aesthetics for the *Silvae*. Just as the greatness of the building projects he describes causes them to be particularly noisy, so the greatness of Statius's poetic subjects justifies loud and thundering poetry.[68] A link between the noise of construction and the sound of Statian poetry is hinted at through the connections noted earlier in terms of the range of its impact. But in *Silvae* 3.1, Statius also makes the link more explicit with regard to the aesthetics of sound. In 3.1, Hercules appears not only as a temple-builder (who makes a large amount of noise) but also as a poet. In lines 91–102, trying to convince Pollius Felix of the wisdom of building him a new temple, he delivers an abbreviated version of Statius's earlier poem for Pollius Felix, *Silvae* 2.2. Hercules's tendentious version of this poem especially stresses that Pollius's house proves his prowess as a builder, and that there can be no reason for him to neglect the god's abode in comparison.[69] Hercules as poetic figure is brought into the poet's traditional invocation of the Muse that introduces the aetiology of the new temple (3.1.49–51):

> Sed quaenam subiti veneranda[70] exordia templi
> dic age, Calliope; socius tibi grande sonabit   50
> Alcides tensoque modos imitabitur arcu.

> But come, Calliope, tell the venerable origins of this temple which suddenly appeared. Hercules will accompany you with grand sound and imitate your rhythm with his taut bowstring.

Hercules, companion and accompanist of the Muse Calliope,[71] is thus humorously made to intervene in matters of poetic aesthetics. While standard *recusationes* reject loud sound, this one is inverted to offer a justification for

---

[68] In *Aet.* fr. 1.29–30 Harder, Callimachus says of himself that he sings among those who love the sound of the cicada. The sound of the cicada is invoked for its special acoustic quality (called λιγύς, 29), but it is also a quieter sound than the braying of asses or the thundering of Zeus. Perhaps Callimachus also implies that the sound of the cicada is more 'exclusive', since only a few select people can hear it at the same time. In that case, Statius also differs from Callimachus in that respect, approving of sound (and poetry) with the largest possible reach.

[69] For the verbal and thematic parallels between 2.2 and 3.1, see Laguna (1992), 161–3 *ad* 97b–102a. For example, Statius's own pronouncement *non … innumeras valeam species cultusque locorum / Pieriis aequare modis* (2.2.36–42) is shortened by Hercules to *vix opera enumerem* in 3.3.102.

[70] Following Laguna (1992), 146 *ad loc.*, I omit Courtney's commas bracketing *veneranda*. I take the adjective with *exordia* rather than *Calliope*.

[71] On the association of Hercules with the Muses and literary testimonies for the *Aedes Herculis Musarum*, see Laguna (1992), 147 *ad* 50b–1.

ENGINEERING POETRY   159

loudness. Hercules himself intervenes, and being Hercules and using his bow as a musical instrument, the sound he produces is not small and subtle but *grandis:* both loud and lofty.[72] In *recusationes*, deities usually intervene to suggest to the poet a smaller genre or a more refined sound, but Hercules's intervention does the opposite: it calls the poet to create something larger and louder.[73] And Hercules sounds *grande* not only in a poetic sense, but also as a builder. The inverted *recusatio* is recalled during the most extensive description of Hercules's construction activity and the noise it causes: *non tam grande sonat . . .* (130).[74] Hercules's activities as a builder and as a poet explicitly link the loud sound of construction to Statius's poetics of loudness.[75]

In *Silvae* 3.1, an important intertext for Statius's sound-descriptions also comes into sharper focus, indicative of the ambition connected to the aesthetics of loud sound. Already in *Silvae* 1.1.3–4, the speaker asked (of the statue of Domitian): *Siculis an conformata caminis / effigies lassum Steropen Brontenque reliquit?*—'Or was the statue moulded in Sicilian foundries, and did it leave Steropes and Brontes exhausted?'[76] Brontes and Steropes are the names of two of the Cyclopes, who are usually said to work in Vulcan's Sicilian workshop. Their most prominent literary appearance in Latin is in *Aeneid* 8, where they help the god to forge the shield of Aeneas (*Aen.* 8.424–53).[77] In *Silvae* 3.1, the Cyclopes feature in the cluster of sound-descriptions that accompany Hercules's construction activities (3.1.125–34):

hic pater ipse loci . . .   125

ipse fodit, ditesque Caprae viridesque resultant   128

---

[72] As noted by Laguna (1992), 147 *ad loc.*, *grande* here has a double meaning: both 'elevated' (of speech) and 'loud': cf. *OLD* s.v. *grandis* 4b and 6a.

[73] For a similarly humorous divine intervention as part of a *recusatio*, cf. Ov. *Am.* 1.1, which features Cupid stealing a foot and offers this as an excuse for the avoidance of epic. Hercules's music on his bowstring justifies the 'loud' rhetoric of the *Silvae* in the same humorous way in which Cupid in the *Amores* justifies the writing of elegiacs about matters of love.

[74] Laguna (1992), 172 *ad* 130, van Dam (2006), 204.

[75] A similar link is perhaps suggested through the expression *magno pectore* in 3.1.21: ostensibly, Hercules there moves boulders by pushing against them with his broad chest, but the expression may also be suggestive of (un-Callimachean) sound: contrast Propertius 2.1.40: *intonet angusto pectore Callimachus.* Laguna (1992), 147 *ad* 50b–1, also links both *grande sonabit* and *magno pectore* to the loud voice of Hercules. Volturnus is another god who imports into the poem his own (un-Callimachean) sound. His speech is introduced by the phrase *raucis talia faucibus redundat* (4.3.71): the river comically features a hoarse throat (*fauces* can refer to both throat and river-mouth; Coleman (1988), 122 *ad loc.*); while Smolenaars (2006), 229, suggests that *redundat* is a play on excessiveness.

[76] See Vollmer (1898), 216; Geyssen (1996), 44–5; Newlands (2002), 53; and Dufallo (2013), 215–16 on 1.1.3–4 and the epic significance of the Cyclopes there.

[77] On this scene, see Egelhaaf-Gaiser (2008). They are referred to as *Brontes Steropesque* in *Aen.* 8.425.

160   BUILDING IN WORDS

Taurubulae, et terris ingens redit aequoris echo.
non tam grande sonat motis incudibus Aetne   130
cum Brontes Steropesque ferit, nec maior ab antris
Lemniacis fragor est ubi flammeus aegida caelat
Mulciber et castis exornat Pallada donis.

Here, the patron of the place in person . . . is himself digging, and rich Capri
and green Taurubulae resound, and the mighty echo of the sea returns to the
land. Aetna does not sound so loudly with shuddering anvils, when Brontes
and Steropes strike them, and the noise that comes from the Lemnian caves
is no greater, where flaming Mulciber embosses the aegis and equips Pallas
with chaste gifts.

The parallels between this passage and *Aeneid* 8 are evident (and further
marked by the use of the words *resultant* and *echo*).[78] The phrase *Brontesque
Steropesque* is repeated exactly from 8.425, the epithet *Lemniacis* as referring
to Vulcan recalls *Aen.* 8.454 (*pater . . . Lemnius*), and the forging of weapons
for Pallas in *Aen.* 8.435–8 is recalled by *castis exornat Pallada donis*.[79]

However, the sound produced by Hercules is said to outdo even the thundering of the Cyclopes, and by analogy, the sound produced by Statius in
relating it is louder than the 'thundering' of Vergil's famous epic scene of
forging. Phrases such as *non tam grande sonat* or *nec maior . . . fragor* make
it clear that Statius's temple poem is claiming not to imitate, but to trump the
epic Cyclopes' sound.[80] The word *maior* in particular often carries overtones
of generic ascent, and emphasizes the play on epic ambitions in this passage.[81]

The comically 'super-epic' acoustics of the small-scale poem are also,
in themselves, a Callimachean trope. One major intertext for Vergil's
forging scene (besides the obvious Iliadic model of Achilles's shield) is
Callimachus's *Hymn to Artemis*—a fact that is not lost on the author of the
Silvae. In the early part of Callimachus's hymn, the young goddess visits

---

[78] On *echo* see earlier, p. 156. On these parallels and their interpretation, see e.g. Egelhaaf-Gaiser
(2007), esp.76–8.

[79] The passage in *Aeneid* 8 is also itself reminiscent of a simile from Verg. *Georg.* 4.170–5, and the
close of *Silv.* 3.1.130 recalls Verg. *Georg.* 4.173 (*gemit impositis incudibus Aetna*); Laguna (1992), 172.
Brontes might also evoke the Callimachean βροντᾶν (*Aet.* fr. 1.20 Harder).

[80] Laguna (1992), 172 *ad* 130 ('el tono épico'); and van Dam (2006), 204: Statius 'surpass(es) the
Aeneid in one of its most thundering passages'. Van Dam discusses imitation of epic models in the
Silvae; on epic and the *Silvae*, see also Taisne (1996); Gibson (2006a).

[81] For *maior* with overtones of generic or literary ascent, cf. *Silv.* 4.4.96 (and e.g. *Aen.* 7.44–5, *Ecl.*
4.1). For *minor* and generic descent, cf. 4.4.3.

ENGINEERING POETRY   161

the workshop of the Cyclopes to request from them a bow and arrows (46–86).[82] In this scene, the sound-effects of the forge are described in playful detail: the hammering, the sound of the bellows, and even the snorting of the uncouth Cyclopes themselves (54–6). The sound echoes between various geographic locations around Sicily and the Italian mainland (55–61): a motif that Statius, as we have seen, richly exploits in the *Silvae*, himself 'echoing' the Callimachean scene.

The Callimachean forging scene has been read as be a playful assertion of the poet's stance towards epic.[83] As Artemis arrives, the Cyclopes are noisily engaged in a μέγα ἔργον ('great work'), which they have to abandon to turn to Artemis's more refined weapons. This μέγα ἔργον turns out to be very mundane indeed: a gigantic horse trough. Turning the snorting, thundering Cyclopes away from their large but unrefined project and towards the equipment of the young, sophisticated goddess is a programmatic choice, expressed in a scene that deliberately recalls but then undercuts a hugely famous epic model, and to be understood in line with Callimachean poetic ideals expressed elsewhere in his work.

Statius signals the relationship between the Callimachean forging scene and his own description of noisy creation through the fact that the Cyclopes in *Silvae* 3.1 are depicted as engaged in creating *dona* for Artemis's Latin equivalent Minerva. But while Callimachus's scene seems to resolve the incongruity between loud, brutal sound and sophisticated poetry when Artemis interrupts the creation of the μέγα ἔργον (while the creation of her own commission is described in only two words and without any sound description: οἱ δ᾽ ἐτέλεσσαν), Hercules in *Silvae* 3.1 is precisely praised for producing Cyclopean sound himself.[84] In the ostensibly 'small-scale' *Silvae*, Hercules's construction activity is depicted as not only equal, but actually superior to the sound of Vergilian epic, contributing to Statius's 'forging' of a new aesthetics of loudness.[85]

---

[82] McCarter (2012); Casali (2006).

[83] Casali (2006), esp. 197–200; Dufallo (2013), 216 with n. 33.

[84] In the earlier *Thebaid*, the Cyclopes also appear, having forged (together with the Telchines and Vulcan himself) Harmonia's fateful necklace (*Theb.* 2.273–4). However, the Cyclopes are there said to forge the necklace *docti quamquam maiora* (*Theb.* 2.273)—'although they were trained for bigger projects'. In his epic, Statius's stance of self-disparagement and inferiority compared to the *maiores* of epic, Homer and Vergil, is visualized through the smallness of the necklace, demeaning to the Cyclopes who forged the shields of Achilles and Aeneas: Feeney (1991), 363–4.

[85] Note that Hercules also plays a role in Callimachus's hymn, with a humorous take on his apotheosis: Effe (2003), 35–6.

162 BUILDING IN WORDS

In conclusion, the sound that accompanies building contributes, like the speed at which construction is executed, to the configuration of a new poetics suited to the panegyric of the *Silvae*. Statius humorously responds to Callimachean strictures against loud, noisy poetry: in the *Silvae*, 'thundering', the daring use of fulsome rhetoric and unrestrained hyperbole, is an integral feature, and one that can be expressed, defined, and justified through the use of the construction metaphor.

Managing the Poetic River

Descriptions of engineering and interventions in nature, too, can offer the poet a way of influencing the reader's view of the finished poem. This becomes especially clear in poem 4.3, where the manipulation of the river Volturnus not only conveys the emperor's victory over nature, but also contributes to Statius's reflections on the aesthetics of the *Silvae*.

The river's transformation as a result of Domitian's construction works activates the famous and influential Callimachean comparison of bad poetry to a dirty river (Callim. *Hymn* 2.108–12). It has so far been argued that Volturnus's transformation, as it is described in 4.3.73–94, turns the river into an image of Callimachean poetics.[86] However, Volturnus is not turned from a muddy river into the fresh and untouched fountain of Callim. *Hymn* 2.110–12 or *Epigr.* 28 Pf. Instead, the river which was previously *pulvereus* and *gravis caeno* (88) and *turbidus minaxque* (76) is turned into a channelled, proper stream (*amnis esse coepi*, 80), which can proudly claim (4.3.92–4):

> sed talis ferar ut nitente cursu
> tranquillum mare proximumque possim
> puro gurgite provocare Lirim.

> ... but I shall flow in such a way that I can challenge the calm sea with my sparkling course, and with my pure stream the Liris that flows close by.

The river has been cleared of the debris it was carrying, and it has been tamed, but nowhere does the text claim that the river is now narrow.[87] In fact, Statius

---

[86] Newlands (2002), 306–9; Smolenaars (2006), 231–3; Gibson (2006b), xxvi.
[87] *pace* Newlands (2002), 306: 'Volturnus . . . has become a safe, narrow stream'.

makes it explicit that the river is *not* narrow: *limite me colis beato* (85).[88] Earlier in the poem, it was precisely small ponds that were unwelcome (54) and lesser streams (*fluvii minores*) that were diverted in the course of the road construction.[89] Volturnus even invites comparison between himself and the sea, another metaphor for bad poetry in Callimachus (*Hymn* 2.106). The river, then, is a consciously Callimachean expression of an un-Callimachean aesthetic, representing exactly the kind of poetry that Statius is creating in the *Silvae*: poetry that deliberately *departs* from some basic Callimachean stylistic ideals, although it still proudly claims for itself stylistic purity and brilliance (*nitente*, 92; *puro*, 94).[90]

The Wood for the Trees: *silvae* in the *Silvae*

The domination and manipulation of nature is a key theme of the *Silvae*, and one intimately connected with narratives of construction, as already discussed in the second section of this chapter.[91] To conclude my investigation of poetic construction in the *Silvae*, I shall focus on one specific aspect of this manipulation of nature: the manipulation of trees and woods, *silvae*, and the special relevance of this theme in a collection of poems entitled *Silvae*.[92] Newlands notes: 'It is not surprising, perhaps, that in a collection entitled

---

[88] For *beatus* here and elsewhere in the *Silvae* meaning *locuples*, see *TLL* 2.1918.20–24.

[89] Perhaps *minores* also hints at the generic inferiority of the Callimachean 'clean little spring-poetry' compared to the strong and broad river of the *Silvae*? Cf. the *maior*-rhetoric of sound in 3.1.131–2 (pp. 160–2 and n. 81 in this chapter).

[90] A similar reinterpretation of 'Callimachean' water metaphors is found several times in the *Silvae*: see e.g. *Silv.* 1.5.23–29 (water of the Roman aqueducts as poetic fount) with Newlands (2002), 215–16, and 4.7.11–12 with Johannsen (2006), 312–13. Wimmel (1960), 318, scornfully talks of Statius's 'kritiklose und ungehemmte Vermischung von Zügen des Großen und des Reduzierten', rejecting a poetic design behind it. The taming of the Volturnus seems to have its counterpart in *Theb.* 4.823–30, where a previously clear stream is muddied by the Argive soldiers, a scene linked by Parkes (2012) to the 'narrative's return to traditional martial epic' (xxiii, see also 323 *ad* 824–7; and McNelis (2007), 87). This reinterpretation of stylistic excellence in 4.3 is also further developed through the adaptation of another Callimachean poetic-polemic metaphor, that of the busy highway (Callim. *Aet.* fr. 1.25–8 Harder; see Cameron (1995), 358). The point of 4.3 is praise of a busy highway, and Statius encourages reflection on the metapoetic relevance of the topic and on the aesthetic differences between Callimachean and his own poetics. He alludes to the highway metaphor in 78, where Volturnus proudly claims: *iam pontem fero perviusque calcor*, recalling the use of στείβειν in Callim. *Aet.* fr. 1.26 Harder. It will be clear that I take a different view to Smolenaars (2006), who argues for an 'obvious clash between subject matter and poetics in the "Via Domitiana"' (233).

[91] See pp. 143–5. Pavlovskis (1973) analyses the *Silvae* (and Pliny's *Letters*) as expressions of enthusiasm for man's skill in domesticating nature.

[92] The title is first used in the *praefatio* of the third book (3.ep.7: *tertius . . . Silvarum nostrarum liber*), but its use there suggests that readers are expected already to be familiar with it: *Silvarum libri* may have been the *titulus* of the book rolls of books 1 and 2; Johannsen (2006), 305; Bright (1980), 20–1.

164   BUILDING IN WORDS

Silvae, "Woods", the domination of nature should be an important theme.'[93] There is an even more specific connection to be detected between poetic and physical *silvae*. Considering how self-consciously other aspects of the construction process are shaped to relate to poetic aesthetics, those stages of the process which actually involve a manipulation of *silvae* deserve the reader's special attention.[94]

The precise meaning of the title *Silvae* has been the subject of some debate.[95] Two different basic meanings of the word *silva* lead to two substantially different interpretations of the title. On the one hand, the singular *silva* can function as the Latin equivalent of the Greek ὕλη, meaning 'raw material' or 'subject matter'.[96] This basic meaning probably also lies behind the use of *silva* as a technical term for an orator's rough or rapidly improvised draft, attested in Quint. 10.3.17. On the basis of this first meaning, the title *Silvae* may be understood to refer to the improvised character and rapid execution of the poems.[97] On the other hand, *silva* can mean a 'forest' or a 'wood', a large group of trees.[98] If this idea of 'woods' lies behind the title, then *Silvae* may also be understood as a collection of many different trees, i.e. a miscellaneous collection of single poems—appropriate, too, since the *Silvae* are made up of different occasional poems, only combined into books at a later stage.[99] It has plausibly been suggested that both meanings coexist in the title.[100] I would even argue that the slippage between *silva* as 'material' and as 'tree' is

---

[93] Newlands (2002), 197, and cf. 100 for a specific analysis of the word *silvis* at 1.2.154.

[94] The construction poems 3.1 and 4.3 contain a particular cluster of occurrences of the word: *silvae* feature three times in 3.1 and twice in 4.3—a further indication of the special status and importance of the construction poems for Statius's poetic self-fashioning. There is only one further occurrence each of *silvae* in book 3 and book 4 (3.3.98, 4.4.90; see also 5.1.24, 5.1.154, 5.2.70, 5.2.139).

[95] Johannsen (2006), 305–6 judiciously sets out the debate. Wray (2007) offers another recent discussion of the semantics and significance of '*Silvae*', relating the title to the Statian 'poetics of genius'. I largely draw on Johannsen's discussion of the title in what follows. See also the clear explanation of the semantic range of *silvae* in Coleman (1988), xxii–xxiv. For a selection of the (extensive) bibliography on the significance of the title, see Nauta (2002), 252 n. 7, and Johannsen (2006), 305 n. 171.

[96] *OLD* s.v. *silva* 5(b). See esp. Cic. *Orat.* 3.12 (*silva* as the raw material of the orator), and further Hinds (1998) 12.

[97] For a defence of this interpretation of *Silvae*, see Nauta (2002), 252–4.

[98] *OLD* s.v. *silva* 1(a).

[99] In favour of this interpretation, e.g. van Dam (1984), 4 with n. 41–2. On the fashion of naming poetry collections after groupings in the natural world, see Newlands (2002), 36; Bright (1980), 40–2.

[100] Johannsen (2006), 305 with n. 173; Coleman (1988), xxii–iv, although for Coleman the aspect of miscellany is clearly the stronger; Newlands (2011), 6–7, and Newlands (2002), 36–7, who also interprets the ambiguity of *silvae* in light of the echo of Verg. *Ecl.* 4.3, where Vergil uses *silvae* to designate his pastoral poetry: 'The title *Silvae* thus in fact conflates two of the major meanings of *silva / silvae*: Virgilian pastoral seen from the perspective of the late first century AD as material to be reworked...' (37).

ENGINEERING POETRY   165

exploited by Statius in his description of the use and manipulation of wood in construction.

Trees (*silvae*) in the *Silvae* form part of a poetic landscape. Even before the process of manipulation and construction begins, *silvae* are imbued with a special poetic significance. This self-consciously poetic and metaphorical relevance of the word *silvae* is established by its use in 2.7, a poem unrelated to construction, but very much concerned with poetry. It is an ode addressed to Lucan's widow on his birthday, and contains an exhortation to the Muses, which eventually merges into an exhortation of nature (12–13): *docti largius evagentur amnes / et plus, Aoniae, virete, silvae* . . . —'let learned rivers stream more copiously, and you, Aonian *silvae*, be greener . . .'. The passage is concerned with poetic inspiration and its expression through nature. In being *docti*, the rivers are clearly marked as the (Heliconian) rivers of poetic inspiration.[101] But the *silvae*, too, are Aonian, they grow in the region of Mount Helicon in Boeotia.[102] The exhortation to the *silvae* may here be understood not only as a reference to the remit of the Muses, but also as an appeal to Statius's own poetry to mourn Lucan appropriately.[103] Furthermore, Lucan himself also composed *Silvae*, of which he completed ten books (now lost),[104] and the word may also serve to acknowledge Lucan as a model for Statius's own *Silvae*.

The double function of *silvae* as elements of a natural and a poetic landscape is also relevant for a passage in *Silvae* 3.1. In 3.1.148, the completion of the temple of Hercules is celebrated with Greek-style athletic games (*fortibus ardens / fumat harena sacris*, 139–40). The entire landscape of the Gulf becomes spectator to the games (3.1.147–53):

spectat et Icario nemorosus palmite Gaurus   147
silvaque quae fixam pelago Nesida coronat
et placidus Limon omenque Euploea carinis
et Lucrina Venus, Phrygioque e vertice Graias   150
addisces, Misene, tubas, ridetque benigna
Parthenope gentile sacrum nudosque virorum
certatus et parva suae simulacra coronae.

---

[101] For *doctus* meaning 'poetical' and the word's frequent appearance in 2.7, a 'poem about poetry as well as about a dead poet', see van Dam (1984), 457 *ad* 2, and 462 *ad* 12–5.

[102] Van Dam (1984), 462 *ad loc.*, points out that the adjective *Aoniae* carries the meaning 'poetical', comparing 4.4.90: *silva Heliconide*.

[103] Johannsen (2006), 306.

[104] We learn this in an ancient *vita* of Lucan by the sixth-century grammarian Vacca: *extant eius et alii complures ut . . . Silvarum X.* The vita can be found in Haskins (1887), xiv–xv.

166   BUILDING IN WORDS

Gaurus also watches, overgrown with Icarian vine, and the wood that crowns the island of Nesis, fixed in the sea, and calm Limon, and Euploea, good omen for ships, and Venus of the Lucrine Lake; and you, Misenus, from your Phrygian promontory, you shall learn to blow Greek trumpets, while generous Parthenope smiles on the rites of her people, the athletic contests of men, and the small likenesses of her own crown.

The *silva* here joins the other features of the Campanian landscape in viewing the athletic contests.[105] The Campanian landscape is traditionally also a literary landscape, already before Statius and especially in the *Silvae*.[106] As Hinds argues, 'anywhere that Statius directs his ecphrastic gaze around the Bay of Naples, he will find himself invoking names charged not just with his own history but with Vergilian literary history, and nowhere more so than *Parthenope* itself'.[107] Statius inserts into this Vergilian literary landscape, which contains the Cape of Misenum as well as Parthenope, a deceptively inconspicuous *silva*—refashioning the literary landscape of Campania to contain his own landmark, and refashioning himself not only as a mere admirer and emulator of Campanian poetic tradition who sits by the tomb of Vergil (*Silv.* 4.4.51–5), but also as an active participant in its literary landscaping.

Trees and woods are not only features of a geographic and literary landscape, however: they are also a commodity which is essential to construction. In both *Silvae* 3.1 and 4.3, trees are felled as part of the works described. In 3.1, *silvae* are cut down when building works are just beginning (3.1.118–20):

> innumerae coiere manus; his caedere silvas
> et levare trabes, illis immergere curae
> fundamenta solo.

> Innumerable hands join together. Some have the task of felling the woods and smoothing the beams, others to sink the foundations into the ground.

The description of road building in 4.3 features a closely related passage (4.3.49–53):

---

[105] Stärk (1995), 138: 'wie überdimensionale Ehrengäste sitzen die Orte im Naturtheater des Golfes'.

[106] See Hinds (2001), 246–54. On Campania as a 'geistige Landschaft', see Stärk (1995), esp. 134–43 on the *Silvae*.

[107] Hinds (2001), 250.

ENGINEERING POETRY   167

o quantae pariter manus laborant!
hi caedunt nemus exuuntque montes,   50
hi ferro scolopas[108] trabesque levant;
illi saxa ligant opusque texunt
cocto pulvere sordidoque tofo ...

How many hands work side by side! Some cut down the forest and strip
mountains; some smooth down stakes and beams with iron; others connect up the stones and weave the work together with baked dust and grimy
tufa ...

Even though this second passage does not contain the word *silvae*, the parallels
between both passages forge a link between them. After a similar introductory marker (*innumerae ... manus* and *quantae manus*), *caedere* and *levare*
occur in both passages to denote the same activities, which both also feature
a distribution of labour between *hi* and *illi*. In both passages, diction that can
relate to poetry as well as construction surrounds the description of wood-
working, signalling to the reader the metapoetic potential of the process: *cura*
(3.1.119), too, can be used in a literary context to refer to poetic care and dili-
gence,[109] while in 4.3.52–3, the fixing together of stones by means of cement,
is described through a weaving metaphor (*opusque texunt*, 52), one of the
most common metapoetic figures.[110] A tree felling itself as a means of gathering construction material is a well-known epic motif, and has, as already
mentioned in Chapter 3, often been read as an indication that the author is
conscious of venturing into poetic territory with a long tradition of using earlier literary works as 'material' for his own poetry.[111] In *Silvae* 3.1 and 4.3, the

---

[108] *scolopas* (a transliterated version of the Greek σκόλοπας, 'stakes') is Nisbet's conjecture for the
transmitted *scopulos*, difficult in a line concerned with timber; Coleman (1988), 116–17, *ad loc.*

[109] *TLL* 4.1462.44–1463.70.

[110] On weaving and poetry, see Scheid and Svenbro (1996). The fitting together of individual elements for the construction of road and poetry is also visualized by the text: 50, 51, and 54 begin with
hi, lines 46–8 all end in dative plural forms (*saxis ... coactis ... gomfis*), and this effect is repeated by
the line endings *laborant ... levant ... texunt* (49–52). The words visualize the alignment of materials
to form the sides of the road. See Morgan (2000), 114–5, on the hendecasyllabic verses looking like a
road on the page.

[111] Cutting down trees to clear a site is an integral part of the construction process, but it can also
function as a metaphor for the manipulation of literary heritage. In his analysis of Vergil's description
of Aeneas's tree-cutting in *Aen.* 6.177–82 and its links with the Ennian model, *Ann.* 175–9, Hinds
(1998), 12–14, demonstrates how the action of felling trees is closely associated with the concept of
carving out for oneself a place in the poetic heritage. Lucan's descriptions of Caesar's desecration of
the grove in 3.432–45 and of the tree-felling in Brundisium (2.261–2) have also been interpreted as
carrying metapoetic significance; Masters (1992), 26–8. See also pp. 115–7.

168 BUILDING IN WORDS

process of tree-felling does not per se reflect a foray into the literary tradition, but it does plausibly relate to the gathering of material (ὕλη) for construction—and composition. In a second step, this woody material is then worked on and refined: both passages use the word *levare* to describe the action of smoothing the raw wood, but *levare* can also be used to refer to the smoothing and cultivation of literary style,[112] while the related adjective *levis* is commonly used to describe polished diction.[113] If this reading of the manipulation of wood is accepted, it can throw new light on the meaning of the title *Silvae* and on Statius's poetic ambitions. The reference to *silvae* as building material activates the interpretation of the title as 'rough drafts', but it is immediately made clear that raw material needs (and receives) smoothing and refining, an action which Statius implies not to have had time for in the prefaces.[114] Again, therefore, we find the poetic 'modesty' evinced in the prefaces substantially undercut by the *Silvae*'s inherent poetics of construction.

A scrutiny of the manipulation of *silvae* also reveals how control over nature and poetic refinement are tied to each other in the *Silvae*. I discussed earlier how the taming of the river Volturnus turns him into an image of Statius's broad-stream poetics. In his speech of thanks, the river claims (4.3.79–80):

> qui terras rapere et rotare silvas
> adsueram (pudet!) amnis esse coepi.
>
> I, who used to rip away earth and spin round[115] woods (shame on me!), have begun to be a river.

The river, tamed and poeticized (though not in the Callimachean mode), now no longer disorders (poetic?) *silvae*. The domestication of nature in the construction process is tied up with literary refinement. This connection between poetry and control over nature is also present in the myths of Orpheus and Amphion, who were able to move trees and stones, respectively, by means of their song.[116] Both are referred to explicitly several times in the

---

[112] *TLL* 7.1237.64–5. Cf. Hor. *Epist.* 2.2.123: *luxuriantia compescet, nimis aspera sano / levabit cultu . . . (poeta).* Morgan (2000), 116, relates *levabit* (4.3.127) to the characteristics of the metre.

[113] For *levis* as applied to literary style, see *TLL* 7.1223.12–42, cf. e.g. Plin. *Ep.* 1.16.5: *inserit . . . mollibus levibusque duriusculos quosdam.*

[114] Statius especially stresses this aspect in the first *praefatio* (1.ep.12–15): see Johannsen (2006), 243–6.

[115] Cf. *OLD* s.v. *roto* 2(a) for *rotare* associated with uncontrolled, chaotic movement and disordered natural forces.

[116] See p. 141. On Amphion and control over nature, see also further Chapter 5.

ENGINEERING POETRY   169

construction poems and possibly also are evoked implicitly in descriptions of the manipulation of trees and stones.[117] The connection forged in the *Silvae* between human intervention in nature and the writing of poetry is doubly efficient. On the one hand, the alignment of engineering with poetic activity is another means of stressing the morally acceptable, non-transgressive nature of the patron's or emperor's intervention in nature.[118] On the other hand, Statius's own poetic activity and his mastery of the material are associated with the human triumphs over nature that his poetry describes.[119]

A final manipulation of *silvae* occurs not in connection with the process of construction but with its ceremonial conclusion. At the close of 3.1, when the building of the temple has been completed, Hercules himself speaks in gratitude of Pollius's restoration of his temple. He praises the construction effort, and promises that the new temple will last forever (*templis numquam statuetur terminus aevi / dum me flammigeri portabit machina caeli*, 180–1)—grandiosely recalling Jupiter's prophecy in *Aeneid* 1, as well as, perhaps, the trope of the immortality of poetic *monumenta*, as we find it, for example, in Horace's *Odes* 3.30.[120] The theme of taming nature, a feat accomplished both by Hercules and Pollius, is also recalled for the last time (*naturae deserta domas et vertis in usum / lustra habitata feris*, 168–9). To confirm his promises, Hercules finally proceeds to swear an oath on his own altar (3.1.184–6):

sic ait, et tangens surgentem altaribus ignem
populeaque movens albentia tempora silva
et Styga et aetherii iuravit fulmina patris.

[117] Explicit mentions in construction poems occur at 3.1.16–17 and 115; see also 2.2.60–2, also about Pollius Felix's building activities: *et tu saxa moves, et te nemora alta sequuntur*, on which see Hinds (2001), 243. An implicit evocation of Orphean/Amphionic miracle-working may be found in 4.3.61: *fervent litora mobilesque silvae*, with Coleman (1988) *ad loc.*: 'perhaps . . . a hint of Domitian as a second Orpheus', and Smolenaars (2006), 228 n. 8.

[118] Tree-felling, especially, can have morally problematic connotations: Thomas (1988) has argued that tree-cutting is generally an ambivalent action, associated with violence and impiety in Vergil's *Georgics* and *Aeneid* and in the work of his epic successors. Cf. *Theb.* 6.84–117, where the cutting down of the grove for Opheltes's funeral is represented as an act of war and violence (110–13). The *Silvae* attempt a 'rehabilitation' of tree-cutting, freeing the process from its martial epic context and its sacrilegious connotations, and inserting it into the positive depiction of construction as a process beneficial to nature and to literary refinement.

[119] Cf. Hinds (2001), 244, on comparable tactics in *Silvae* 2.2: 'Statius uses *his* kind of capital . . . to boost the value of Pollius' kind of capital, and also to increase his own by association'.

[120] Laguna (1992), 188, *ad loc.*, notes the reference to Verg. *Aen.* 1.278–9 (*his ego nec metas rerum nec tempora pono / imperium sine fine dedi*), further interpreted by Egelhaaf-Gaiser (2007), 82–3.

170   BUILDING IN WORDS

Thus he speaks, and touching the fire that rises from his altar and nodding his head white with poplar leaves,[121] he swore both by the Styx and by the thunderbolts of his celestial father.

Hercules is wearing a crown of poplar leaves, a headdress usually worn by his priests. The *silva* here carries double significance. On the one hand, the *silva* has become the equivalent of poetic laurels, recalling familiar passages of poetic crowning as a closural motif of poetic works.[122] Hercules is crowned as a poet, since he earlier intervened in both architectural and poetic construction, plucking on his bowstring (51) and creating epic sound (128–35). Since he himself helped to shape the poetic *silva*, it forms an appropriate crown for him.[123] On the other hand, the crowning of Hercules with the *silva* also metaphorically reflects the fact that he has received *Silvae* 3.1 as a poem of praise. In the *praefatio*, Statius had marked the poem as veneration of the god (*his versibus adoravi*, *Silv.* 3.ep.9–10), and it is now symbolically offered to the god in the shape of the *silva*.

This double interpretation is supported by the allusion of the *populea ... silva* to the songs of the *Salii* in Vergil's *Aeneid* (8.285–8):

> tum Salii ad cantus incensa altaria circum
> populeis adsunt euincti tempora ramis,
> hic iuuenum chorus, ille senum, qui carmine laudes
> Herculeas et facta ferunt ...   285

> Then the Salii are present for their singing around the lit altars, having bound their temples with poplar leaves. Here is the choir of youths, there that of old men, who tell in their song the praise of Hercules and his deeds ...

The Salii adorn themselves with boughs of poplar before they begin praising Hercules's deeds in song. In Statius's *Silvae*, Hercules *himself* is decorated

---

[121] *silva* is here unusually used in the singular to denote 'foliage', 'leaves'; see *OLD* 3a and Johannsen (2006), 306 n. 179.

[122] Cf. e.g. Hor. *Carm.* 3.30.15–6, with Nisbet and Rudd (2004), *ad loc.* for further parallels.

[123] The section immediately preceding the crowning with the *populea silva* is also imagined as spoken by Hercules himself (3.1.166–83). According to Coleman (1988), xxii, Statius does not himself use *Silva* to refer to a single poem. In this case, however, *silva* is used as *totum pro parte*, meaning 'foliage', rather than 'wood'. On a poetic level, *Silva* might by the same token stand for a small part of the larger *Silvae*. On the possible relation between singular *silva* and the plural title *Silvae*, see also Hardie (1983), 76 (who is sceptical), and Newlands (2002), 36–7.

with those poplar branches, because he has been praised and also because he has been the engineer of his own poetic praise.[124]

Conclusion

Descriptions of construction in the *Silvae* impact the reader's assessment of the built monument and at the same time of the poetic construct. The poems function as 'reading instructions', presenting exemplary interpretations of monumental architecture. By means of time-shifts, they insert appreciation of the construction process into the model response to the monument they describe. The prefaces to individual books constitute analogous 'reading instructions' for the poems themselves. They frame the reader's reception of what follows and likewise raise awareness of the process of composing the poems, albeit with an apologetic rhetoric of speed and the resulting lack of polish. However, the inherent 'poetics of construction', expressed on a meta-level through the descriptions of construction in the *Silvae* themselves, substantially modifies the self-disparaging stance of the *praefationes*.[125] Through descriptions of construction, Statius expresses and justifies a new, provocatively un-Callimachean literary aesthetic specifically appropriate to the panegyric *Silvae*.[126] The interaction between the different levels of meaning is deftly exploited by the author: the advantages of a 'realistic' feature of construction are extended to an aspect of literary composition, and conversely, features of the poetic process are used to influence the reader's response to certain human interventions in nature.

How does the 'aesthetics of construction' developed in this group of poems affect the whole of the *Silvae*? On the one hand, the three poems are marked out as a coherent group, ipso facto helping to create a unifying strand in a multi-book collection. They cumulatively present and justify a revolutionary poetic aesthetic tailored to the *Silvae*, especially the panegyric poems. On the other hand, diversity is an inherent aesthetic quality of a collection made up of

---

[124] See Egelhaaf-Gaiser (2007), esp. 80–81 and 92, on *Silv.* 3.1 and the praise of Hercules during the (proto-)Roman Ara Maxima celebrations in *Aeneid* 8.

[125] Cf. Johannsen (2006), a broader study of the overlap in themes between the *praefationes* and the entire poetry collection, which concentrates on explicit comments in the poems on composition and aesthetics (although she takes into account Newlands (1991) on the metapoetics of *Silvae* 3.1).

[126] The articulation of a new aesthetics in the *Silvae* is also discussed in Newlands (2013), who shows how, through its relationship with Ovid's Philemon and Baucis episode, *Silvae* 3.1 'validates a new aesthetics of luxury as a display of virtue' (253) and a 'new encomiastic poetics that calibrates [Statius's] own times . . . in terms of moral and social progress' (258).

172   BUILDING IN WORDS

occasional poems initially composed as separate entities, and the *praefationes* urge us not to lose sight of the incidental origins of the poems. Therefore, it is not surprising that the *Silvae* do not all subscribe to a completely coherent aesthetic. In response to a specific occasion, addressee or subject matter, not only style or metre but also aesthetic principles are pliable—in fact, such flexibility precisely constitutes the virtuoso quality of the *Silvae* as a collection. For example, *Silvae* 4.6, dealing with a small statuette of Hercules belonging to Novius Vindex, has often (and convincingly) been interpreted as a strong statement of Callimachean poetics of smallness and exclusivity, and even as a reversal of the aesthetic values espoused in *Silvae* 1.1.[127] Since *Silvae* 4.6 aims to praise precisely the small size and exclusivity of the expensive gift, the poetic aesthetic playfully follows suit.

Notwithstanding the inherent diversity of the *Silvae* and the corresponding flexibility of poetic ideals, the coherent 'aesthetics of construction' that Statius develops in *Silvae* 1.1, 3.1, and 4.3 takes the exploitation of the construction metaphor to a new level by communicating and justifying aesthetic ideals through descriptions of architectural construction. In the *Silvae*, the analogy between builder and poet is a 'win-win' situation in which the advantages and prestige of one activity are transferred to the other. However, when Statius reappears in the following chapter, we face a surprising reversal: in his *Thebaid*, architectural metaphor instead serves to reflect on the ephemerality and fragility of poetic structures.

---

[127] On the link between the aesthetics of the statuette and the poem, see e.g. Newlands (2002), 73–87, esp. 77–8, and McNelis (2007), 69–70. Newlands (2002) especially brings out the dialogue between *Silvae* 1.1 and 4.6. See also Dufallo (2013), 229–37, on the poem's negotiation of Greek and Roman cultural aesthetics, and Nauta (2002), 321–4, on Statius's competition with Martial.

5

Walls of Song

The Myth of Amphion

Introduction

The myth of the Theban hero Amphion presents a narrative version of the architectural metaphor considered in the previous two chapters. According to the mythical tradition, Amphion erects the walls of the city of Thebes not through physical strength, but by means of his lyre. His song is so powerful that it transports and lifts up the building blocks and forms them into the famous seven-gated city walls of Thebes. The metaphor of the ἐπέων τέκτων is fully realized in the myth of Amphion: in composing and singing a song, he is not only behaving *like* a builder—he really *is* a builder.[1] The numerous versions of the myth are underpinned by a number of unifying themes. Most importantly for our investigation, the myth tells a story about the power of poetry and song to impact reality. At the same time, Amphion's double role as a poet and as the founder of Thebes forges a close connection between the spheres of poetry and of civilization. The ordering and harmonizing power of music and song are linked to the provision of a safe and ordered human existence of city-dwelling. Amphion's counterpart in the myth, his active warrior-brother Zethus, serves to align Amphion more securely with peace, order, and harmony.

The previous two chapters have explored how the building metaphor offers poets a means of shaping their audience's appreciation of their poetry and encouraging reflections on its 'madeness'. The story of the magical construction of Thebes provides similar opportunities: poets' choices and strategies in representing the myth of Amphion can impact the way in which we read their own poetry. The myth allows for reflections on the power, as well as the limitations, of poetry and song, and for probing questions about the durability of poetic works.

---

[1] On this phrase, see p. 101 n. 3. We might see the myth as a narrativized instantiation of the *poeta creator* trope, on which see p. 121.

Building in Words. Bettina Reitz-Joosse, Oxford University Press. © Oxford University Press 2021.
DOI: 10.1093/oso/9780197610688.003.0006

174   BUILDING IN WORDS

Amphion in Greece

The myth of Amphion is first attested in the *Odyssey* and in Hesiod.[2] In both sources, Amphion is mentioned as having built the walls of Thebes together with his brother Zethus.[3] Neither author distinguishes between the contributions of the two brothers, and only Hesiod appears to mention the element of musical magic.[4] Fragments from sixth- and fifth-century authors seem to suggest an increasing distinction between the respective contributions of Amphion and Zethus.[5] The first extensive treatment of the myth preserved in any detail appears in a fragmentary play by Euripides, the *Antiope*.[6] In this play, the brothers are portrayed as exponents of diametrically opposed ways of life. Zethus is a brawny hunter and warrior, a man of action, while Amphion prefers to dedicate his life to song and his lyre, to contemplation and to σοφία.[7] The play contained a famous *agon* in which the brothers argued for their respective positions.[8] We do not know who won the debate,[9] but in any case Amphion's position is given divine sanction at the end of the play. There, Hermes appears as *deus ex machina* and orders

[2] Hom. *Od.* 11.260–5 and Hes. fr. 182 M–W. For other versions of the myth in Greek sources, see Eumelos fr. 13 Bernabé, Minyas fr. 3 Bernabé, Eur. *Antiop.* (for which see also Pl. *Grg.* 485e–486c), Ap. Rhod. *Argon.* 1.735–41, Dio Chrys. *Or.* 32.62, [Apollod.] *Bibl.* 3.5.5, Paus. 9.5.7–8, Lucian *Im.* 14, Philostr. *Imag.* 1.10; see also Lycoph. *Alex.* 604, where Zethus alone is evoked, since he symbolizes building through hard work, as opposed to musical miracles. Hurst (2000) usefully collects much of the material; see also Olivieri (2011), 24–7 on the myth of Amphion and Zethus before Pindar.

[3] Berman (2004) argues that the story of Amphion and Zethus was actually a foundation myth of Thebes which initially coexisted (and competed) with the myth of Cadmus and the earthborn warriors, and that later mythographers attempted to reconcile them by imposing a chronological order: first foundation (Cadmus), then wall building (Amphion and Zethus). Olivieri (2011), ch. 1, analyses Pindar's negotiation of the 'double foundation'.

[4] Hurst (2000), 65–6.

[5] See Eumelos fr. 13 Bernabé, Minyas fr. 3 Bernabé, with Hurst (2000), 66–7.

[6] The fragments of the *Antiope* (ca. 50 in total) are edited by Kambitsis (1972) with a detailed commentary; see also the editions (with translation) of Jouan and van Looy (1998) and Collard, Cropp, and Gilbert (2004), and Snell (1971), ch. 3, for a readable introduction, reconstruction of the plot, and reflection on the main (philosophical) themes of the play. I cite Collard's text in Collard, Cropp, and Gilbert (2004) unless otherwise noted, as well as his line numbers (Kannicht's *TrGF* line numbers are supplied in brackets).

[7] On σοφία in the *Antiope*, see Stieber (2011), 423–5.

[8] See fr. 183–8, 219, 189, 191, 193–4, 196–202, 220 (in Kannicht's *TrGF* numbering used also by Collard, Cropp, and Gilbert (2004)). On the main themes of the debate and possible interpretations of the two positions in the light of contemporary philosophy, see Collard, Cropp, and Gilbert (2004), 266–8, with bibliography. Four passages of this debate are quoted by Callicles in Plato's *Gorgias* when he attempts to argue against excessive philosophizing by adopting the role of Zethus (485e–486a). On Amphion and Zethus in the *Gorgias*, see Dodds (1959), 275–9, and Nightingale (1992).

[9] For the arguments for Zethus's victory (dramatic considerations and Horace's remark at *Epist.* 1.18), see Snell (1971), 97. On Hor. *Epist.* 1.18, see p. 181. Others believe that Amphion won and that Hermes gave divine approval to his victory (see e.g. Collard, 266–7, in Collard, Cropp, and Gilbert (2004)).

Zethus and Amphion to build walls for the city of Thebes (fr. 223.90–7 (119–26 *TrGF*)):[10]

$$\text{δεύτερον δ' Ἀμφίονα} \qquad\qquad 90\,(119)$$
λύραν ἄ[νωγ]α διὰ χερῶν ὡπλισμένον
μέλπειν θεοὺ[ς ᾧ]δαῖσιν· ἕψονται δέ σοι
πέτραι τ' [ἐ]ρυμναὶ μουσικῇ κηλούμεναι
δένδρη τε μητρὸς ἐκλιπόνθ' ἑδώλια,
ὥστ' εὐμ[ά]ρειαν τεκτόνων θήσει χερί. $\qquad\qquad$ 95 (124)
Ζεὺς τήνδε τιμὴν σὺν δ' ἐγὼ δίδωμί σοι,
οὕπερ τόδ' εὕρημ' ἔσχες, Ἀμφίων ἄναξ.

Next [i.e. after instructions intended specifically for Zethus], I command Amphion to arm himself with lyre in hand and sing of the gods in songs; and strong rocks will follow you, bewitched by the music, and trees, abandoning their seats in mother earth, so that they will make light work for the builders' hands.[11] Zeus gives you this honour, and together with him I, from whom you received this invention, lord Amphion.

The power of poetry and song is triumphantly confirmed by Hermes's prediction. The song Amphion sang earlier in the play dealt with heaven and earth, which make up the cosmos (fr. 182a).[12] The honourable task given to him and his lyre confirms the power of music over the subjects of his song, the power to order and civilize and to create things just as useful as what can be made by hand. Where Zethus had urged Amphion to abandon his lyre for arms, Hermes now orders him to arm himself (ὡπλισμένον) with his lyre.[13]

[10] This passage is mostly preserved on a papyrus (P. Petrie 1–2) which contains about 120 lines of the play and was recovered in 1891. See further Diggle (1996) with full bibliography.

[11] θήσει is the reading of the papyrus, with δένδρη as subject. Collard, following Diggle, reads θήσῃ (2nd singular future middle), the subject being Amphion.

[12] Snell (1971) believes that this was a cosmogonic hymn presenting 'eine Lehre von den Elementen' (87) and 'hohe Philosophie' (88), but on the basis of one (relatively generic) fragment, this has to remain speculation: see Collard, Cropp, and Gilbert (2004), 299, *ad loc*.

[13] As far as we can judge on the basis of the fragmentary transmission, Amphion's achievement in the *Antiope* consists of transporting the stones to the building site. His song does not in itself accomplish the formation of stones into the wall, since workmen (τέκτονες) are still needed (although the phrasing may be taken to imply that his music also rendered the lifting into position of the building materials an easier task). Apollonius's brief mention also only concerns the transportation of stones. As far as I have been able to discover, the earliest definite mention of Amphion's power to form stones into a wall by means of his lyre occurs only in Prop. 3.2 (see n. 24 in this chapter). The state of transmission of the *Antiope*, as well as the potential loss of numerous versions of the myth, should, however, prevent us from drawing any conclusions about Roman (or Propertian) innovation on this point.

176 BUILDING IN WORDS

In Apollonius's *Argonautica*, Amphion and Zethus and the walls of Thebes feature as one of the seven scenes described in the ecphrasis of Jason's cloak (1.735–41):

> Ἐν δ' ἔσαν Ἀντιόπης Ἀσωπίδος υἱέε δοιώ,   735
> Ἀμφίων καὶ Ζῆθος, ἀπύργωτος δ' ἔτι Θήβη
> κεῖτο πέλας· τῆς οἵγε νέον βάλλοντο δομαίους
> ἱέμενοι· Ζῆθος μὲν ἐπωμαδὸν ἤρταζεν
> οὔρεος ἠλιβάτοιο κάρη, μογέοντι ἐοικώς·
> Ἀμφίων δ' ἐπὶ οἷ χρυσέῃ φόρμιγγι λιγαίνων   740
> ἤιε, δὶς τόσση δὲ μετ' ἴχνια νίσσετο πέτρη.

And on it were the two sons of Asopus's daughter Antiope, Amphion and Zethus, and nearby lay Thebes, still towerless. They were just now eagerly laying her foundation stones. Zethus was lifting the top of a high mountain on his shoulder, like someone working hard, but Amphion walked behind him, loudly playing his golden lyre, and a rock twice as big followed his footsteps.

The meaning of the scenes on the cloak of Jason is the subject of a continuing debate, since it is extremely difficult to find a theme connecting all seven of them or to link them all to the narrative of the epic.[14] One connection between the image of Amphion and Zethus and the narrative at least seems secure. The theme of the power of song and the superiority of song over physical strength, exemplified by the larger-size boulder that Amphion moves, is present in the main narrative in the person of Orpheus, the singer among the Argonauts. Orpheus is first introduced into the narrative, just after the invocation of the Muses, as the first Argonaut in the catalogue (1.27–31). He is described as moving stones, rivers, and trees through his song; here is the magical power of song over nature animate and inanimate, which is

---

[14] An eccentric reading is proposed by Shapiro (1980), who argues that the description has no relation to the narrative, but rather represents different techniques of (actual) Hellenistic art. Lawall (1966) has famously argued for reading the cloak as a 'didactic' present from Athena, designed to teach the 'anti-hero' Jason how to act in different situations. Merriam (1993) tries to tie the cloak to the important theme of cooperation between different kinds of forces in the epic (on Amphion and Zethus, see 75–6). Hunter (1993) has a more open reading of the cloak in general, drawing out suggestive interactions with Homeric and other models and suggesting that 'the cloak … presents scenes which are partial analogues of elements of the epic, with correspondences which are both oblique and polyvalent' (58).

picked up in the Amphion-scene.[15] The contest between Amphion's song and Zethus's physical strength parallels the contest between Orpheus's musical magic and the more traditional warrior skills of other Argonauts, such as Idas and Heracles.[16]

I also tentatively add another suggestion to the many possible (and in most cases complementary) readings of the cloak. It appears that the first three scenes, combined with the introduction of the cloak as the handiwork of Athena and a work of skill and craft to match the design of the Argo (1.721–9), offer a series of reflections on how art and artfully made objects come into being—a theme not out of place in an ecphrasis, the *locus classicus* of poetic and artistic self-reflection. In the first scene of the cloak (1.730–4), the Cyclopes are shown as forging a thunderbolt (with an echo of the shield of Achilles, which is famously being made as it is described).[17] Their work is unending (ἀφθίτῳ . . . ἔργῳ) and is accomplished through perseverance and skill as well as hard physical labour (πονεύμενοι). In the second scene, Amphion and Zethus (like the Cyclopes) cooperate in building the walls of Thebes, but their advantages of hard work and artistic inspiration are weighed against each other. While hard work is necessary, and Zethus's contribution is by no means worthless, Amphion's divine musical talent makes the more important contribution to their joint project.[18] Finally, their scene is followed by a depiction of Aphrodite studying her reflection in the shield of Ares. Perfect likeness is here achieved through an exact replication of reality, with neither skill nor hard work involved—but the ontological status of a mere reflection remains in doubt.[19] On such a reading of the first part of the ecphrasis of Jason's cloak, the wall-building of Amphion and Zethus can

[15] On Orpheus in the *Argonautica*, see Klooster (2011), 75–7 and 82–91. Cf. Fränkel (1968), 102, on the motif of the 'Zaubermacht der Lieder'.

[16] Merriam (1993), 75–6; Hunter (1993), 58; and Clauss (1993), 124, who likewise sees the contrast between Amphion's skill and Zethus's strength as recalling the contrast between Orpheus and Heracles in the catalogue at the beginning of book 1 and compares to this the sixth scene of the cloak (759–62), also a contest of strength versus skill.

[17] Cf. also Hunter (1993), 54, who reads the 'work in progress' of the Cyclopes and Amphion as highlighting the difference between Apollonius's ecphrasis of the 'finished' cloak and the making of the Homeric shield. On the representation of the making of ecphrases, including the shield of Achilles and (briefly) Jason's coat, see now the excellent treatment by De Jong (2015).

[18] Merriam (1993) also stresses that Zethus's part in the work is necessary and goes on to develop the theme of cooperation in the different scenes.

[19] Cf. Pl. *Resp.* 10.596d–e, where Socrates suggests that by carrying a mirror one could 'make' sun, sky, earth, oneself, and everything else, and that a painter produces the same kind of representation. Hunter (1993), 55, also reads this scene as artistically self-referential, but in terms of reception, not production. He argues that Apollonius uses the Aphrodite-scene to 'suggest ways of reading his

178 BUILDING IN WORDS

then be read as a reflection on the respective contributions of zeal and (divinely inspired) talent to the production of visual and poetic art.

In the versions of both Euripides and Apollonius, the myth of Amphion tells of the power of poetry to alter reality, to accomplish magical feats that simple physical effort cannot achieve. In Euripides, Amphion appears as a city-founder, and both authors stress Amphion's peaceful, harmonizing force, which contrasts with the efforts of the warrior Zethus, as does the power of Orpheus with the Argonautic warriors. However, any potential parallels between the power of Amphion's song and the power of the poetry in which his story is told remain—if they are present at all—implicit. In Roman poetry, this parallel and its implications become the subject of more explicit reflections.

Amphion in Rome

Amphion's appearances in Latin literature are relatively few. The hero sometimes appears in Latin poetry simply as a figure of Theban myth, with little or no reference to his wall-building magic. Propertius's elegy 3.15, for example, tells the story of the punishment of Dirce by Amphion and his brother Zethus.[20] In the Theban narrative of Ovid's *Metamorphoses*, Amphion features as the husband of the unhappy Niobe (*Met.* 6.178–9, 221, 271, 402), and he is also referred to in this capacity in Juvenal's sixth satire (172–7).[21]

Far more frequently, however, Amphion appears on account of his magical wall-building, quickly developing into a classic *exemplum* of the power of poetry. Most commonly, he forms part of a line-up of famous mythical poets alongside the more famous Orpheus and some other poet (often Arion). The heroes' mythical feats of taming beasts, and moving plants and rocks, are

own text . . . as the goddess is reflected in the shield, so we examine the shield of Homer and find reflections in our text'.

[20] Although the musical foundation of Thebes is not mentioned directly, Amphion's role as the 'poetic' brother is alluded to when he sings a paean of victory at Dirce's death (3.15.42). See Rutherford and Naiden (1996), who suggest that this paean has sinister associations and points forward to Amphion's death and the killing of the Niobids.

[21] In Ovid's Niobe episode, the poetic foundation is referred to fleetingly, as one of the things of which Niobe fatally boasts (3.178–9). Material on this dark side of the Amphion myth is collected by Rutherford and Naiden (1996).

employed to illustrate the power of song and poetry and its impact on the world outside it.[22] For example, Ovid in the third book of the *Ars Amatoria* suggests that women should learn to sing, since song has an alluring power (3.315): *res est blanda canor: discant cantare puellae*—'Song is a seductive thing—let girls learn to sing!' He illustrates this with a line-up of mythical singers, headed by the Sirens (3.311–14, a deliciously immoral model for female readers), followed by Orpheus, Amphion, and Arion (3.321–6), all of whom had the gift of especially powerful or magical song.[23] Similar groups of famous mythical poets are used to illustrate the power of song in Propertius 3.2.3–8 (Orpheus, Amphion, Polyphemus) and in Silius Italicus's *Punica* 11.440–82, where the bard Teuthras sings a song about the power of the lyre (Amphion, Arion, Cheiron, Orpheus).[24] Whatever the composition of these groups of mythical poets, Amphion and Orpheus are always among them. Perhaps they are coupled so often because their mythical feats ideally complement each other: while Orpheus sings to wild beasts and trees, Amphion's magic works on inanimate stones.[25] In Horace's *Odes* 3.11, however, Amphion is exceptionally invoked as a poetic *exemplum* in his own right. The speaker calls on Mercury to help with his song, using the god's gift of Amphion's magical powers as an argument for now obtaining the same

[22] In a late-antique epitaph for an architect from Hermoupolis Magna (Donderer A8 with commentary), Amphion and Orpheus also appear as a pair. There, however, they illustrate not the power of poetry, but the almost supernatural powers of the deceased architect, who was able to move and lift columns and heavy blocks of stone just as easily as the mythical singers.

[23] Implicit is the suggestion that not only the women's song, but also the song of love elegy, has magically persuasive powers. This concept of persuasive song is a key theme of love elegy: Stroh (1971). Ovid also plays on the fact that *carmen* can mean not only song but also magical incantation in Latin. On the double meaning of *carmen* and the *topos* of magic as an image of the poet's art, see also Ov. *Am.* 2.2.23–8 with Reitzenstein (1935), 79; Wimmel (1960), 304–5; and Booth (1991), 103; Verg. *Ecl.* 8.64–109 with Luck (1985), 77; and Erichtho in Lucan's *Bellum Civile* with Masters (1992), 206–7.

[24] In Prop. 3.2.5–6, Amphion is clearly described not only as moving building blocks to the site but actually as magicking them into position: *saxa Cithaeronis Thebas agitata per artem / sponte sua in muri membra coisse ferunt.*—'They say that the rocks of Cithairon, moved to Thebes by the art [of Amphion], spontaneously came together to form the parts of the wall.' See also n. 13 in this chapter on Amphion's transport vs. construction miracle. Fantham (1997), 124, reads the architectural metaphors in Prop. 4.1 (on which see pp. 117–123) as a backward look to Amphion in the earlier elegies: 'Propertius sees himself as another Amphion, the poet architect first mentioned in the second Ponticus elegy . . . then cited with Orpheus as a model for Propertius' creative power in 3.2.5–6.' On Teuthras's song and the role of Amphion in it, see Deremetz (1995), 419–20; Jourdan (2008), 111–15; Marks (2010), 192; Walter (2014), 293–5. Amphion himself seems to have sung a song about the lyre (and its development) in the Euripidean *Antiope* (fr. 190 Collard/*TrGF*) and the Pacuvian *Antiopa* (fr. 3 Schierl).

[25] This division is not always maintained: for example, in *Silv.* 3.1.16–17, the walls that have been constructed with magical speed are suspected to be the work of either Orpheus or Amphion (see pp. 140–1).

180   BUILDING IN WORDS

favour: *nam te docilis magistro / movit Amphion lapides canendo*—'for with
you as master, docile Amphion moved stones by singing' (3.11.1–2).[26]

In his *Ars Poetica*, Horace draws the most explicit connection between
Amphion's poetic feat and his role as a founder and bringer of civilization. In a
narrative of *Kulturentstehung*, the myth of Amphion (again coupled with that of
Orpheus) is interpreted as an allegory of the development of civilization (Hor.
Ars P. 391–401):

> silvestris homines sacer interpresque deorum   391
> caedibus et victu foedo deterruit Orpheus,
> dictus ob hoc lenire tigres rabidosque leones;
> dictus et Amphion, Thebanae conditor urbis,
> saxa movere sono testudinis et prece blanda   395
> ducere quo vellet. fuit haec sapientia quondam,
> publica privatis secernere, sacra profanis,
> concubitu prohibere vago, dare iura maritis,
> oppida moliri, leges incidere ligno.
> sic honor et nomen divinis vatibus atque   400
> carminibus venit.

> Orpheus, priest and interpreter of the gods, kept men, who were then still
> living in the woods, from murder and cannibalism; hence he was said to
> have tamed rabid tigres and lions. It is also said that Amphion, the founder
> of the city of Thebes, moved stones by the sound of his lyre and led them by
> alluring persuasion where he wanted. This, once, was wisdom, to divide public
> from private affairs and the sacred from the profane, to prohibit random inter-
> course, to lay down laws for married couples, to toil at cities, and to carve laws
> into wood. In such a way honour and renown came to the holy bards and
> their songs.

Horace argues that poets and poetry served as catalysts for the development
of civilization. Stories about the taming of wild beasts (Orpheus) and the
building of a city by song (Amphion) developed, he argues, as a reflection of
this civilizing influence of poetry—poetry and the wisdom of the inspired

---

[26] Amphion's wall-building is also referred to in a half-sentence in Ov. *Am.* 3.12.40, in a long list of
myths which Ovid introduces to illustrate the 'untruthfulness' of poets.

WALLS OF SONG 181

vates moved humans to stop behaving like wild beasts, to move to cities, and to live peacefully together.[27]

Amphion's characterization as a peaceful and harmonizing force is complemented by that of his brother Zethus as a warrior and man of action. The brothers' debate about their respective life choices, well-known from Euripides's *Antiope*, also appears in the Pacuvian play of the same title, which is in turn referred to by Cicero and the author of the *Rhetorica ad Herennium*.[28] The debate also features in Horace's first book of *Epistles*. There, the addressee (Lollius) is advised to gain the favour of his patron by yielding to the latter's interests, just as Amphion did to Zethus, and to leave poetry behind to join the patron's hunt (*Epist.* 1.18.39–43). The irony of using this particular mythical illustration is that Amphion's life choice, and not that of Zethus, eventually triumphs in the myth and that, furthermore, this sage advice is transmitted through the medium of poetry. The brothers also appear in Seneca's *Oedipus* 609–12, rising together from the underworld, again embodying the peaceful and the violent aspects of Theban foundation, respectively: Zethus emerges *ferocem . . . taurum premens*—'restraining the wild bull' (610) while Amphion is carrying the lyre that moves stones *dulci . . . sono* 'with sweet sound' (612).[29]

Amphion has thus become a standard *exemplum* for the power of poetry as well as a bringer of peace and civilization. However, where Amphion's roles as poet and as founder of the Theban walls are combined, the picture is complicated by the eventual fate of Amphion's city of Thebes and its walls. In two Theban plays, Seneca exploits the contrast between the walls' magical foundation and their (impending) destruction. In the *Hercules Furens*, Amphitryon (Hercules's foster father and husband of Alcmene) laments the present suffering of Thebes. Since Heracles has left to accomplish a labour in the underworld, the tyrant Lycus has usurped power. Amphitryon contrasts Thebes's sorry state with the great past of the city (*Her. F.* 258–63):

[27] The list of ancient famous poets then continues with Homer and Tyrtaeus. For this passage, see the analysis of Jourdan (2008), 104–11, especially on the link between civilization and the power of the poet. See also Kießling and Heinze (1959), 354–5 *ad* 391 on the (Stoic?) tradition of this allegorical reading, and Brink (1971), 388 *ad* 394 on Amphion as a civilizing poet (and possibly founder of Thebes). Lovatt (2007), 148–9, discusses this passage and the poet's political role.

[28] Cic. *Inv. rhet.* 1.94; *Rhet. Her.* 2.43: the debate is referred to in order to illustrate a particular weakness of argumentation of which Amphion is apparently guilty. For the fragments of Pacuvius's *Antiopa*, see Schierl (2006), 91–130 (also with a collection of testimonies for the Pacuvian tragedy, 104–5). See also Manuwald (2003), 95–7, on Pacuvius's treatment of the debate.

[29] See Segal (1983), 231: 'The pairing of Zethus and Amphion anticipates the ambiguous truth concealed beneath Oedipus' kingship: a murderous violence beneath the civilising act of killing the Sphinx (cf. 640f.). Oedipus holds in himself the potential of both Zethus and Amphion.'

182   BUILDING IN WORDS

> ... quis satis Thebas fleat?   258
> ferax deorum terra, quem dominum tremit?
> e cuius arvis eque fecundo sinu   260
> stricto iuventus orta cum ferro stetit
> cuiusque muros natus Amphion Iove
> struxit canoro saxa modulatu trahens, ...

Who could weep enough for Thebes? Before what master does the land that has brought forth gods now quake? From its fields and fertile bosom young men rose up and stood ready with drawn swords, and Amphion, Jupiter's son, built its walls, transporting stones with melodious composition...

Amphion's magical wall-building is numbered among the great achievements of Thebes—all the worse and all the more incomprehensible that the city has now been brought so low.[30] In Seneca's *Phoenissae*, the walls feature in a similar context. Iocasta has intervened on the battlefield and in a long speech tries to dissuade her sons Eteocles and Polynices from fighting each other. Here she is asking Polynices to desist from attacking his home, the city of Thebes (*Phoen.* 565–71):

> ... haec telis petes   565
> flammisque tecta? poteris has Amphionis
> quassare moles? nulla quas struxit manus
> stridente tardum machina ducens onus,
> sed convocatus vocis et citharae sono
> per se ipse summas venit in turres lapis;   570
> haec saxa franges?

These buildings you want to attack with weapons and flames? Can you batter these bastions of Amphion? No hand built them, raising a load slowly with a noisy crane; instead, the stone was summoned by the sound of his voice and lyre, and rose by itself to the top of the towers. Will you smash *these* stones?

---

[30] See Segal (1983), 233–4, who stresses the peaceful and harmonious associations of Amphion in contrast to the violent (dramatic) present. Segal also points to the conspicuous absence of peaceful Amphion from Hercules's invocation of the founders of Thebes when his madness begins to take hold: he only refers to warlike Zethus (*Her. F.* 915–6).

Iocasta uses the origin of the walls as an argument in her attempt to convince her son to spare the city. She suggests both that the destruction of such walls may be beyond Polynices's power (*poteris*, 566), but also that the walls should somehow be respected, since no human hand, no crane, but song and the lyre lifted the stones into position. The power of the music of Amphion is contrasted with the ugly noise of the inferior crane.[31] But Iocasta's arguments are of no avail—the point is precisely that Polynices does *not* respect the special status of these walls, and that their magical-poetic origin is *not* good enough to render them immune to the Seven's assault.[32] In Seneca's plays, therefore, Amphion symbolizes not so much the power as the (eventual) *powerlessness* of poetry. Although the building of the walls was a powerful act of poetic magic, this magic cannot protect them now that the city is threatened. Furthermore, while the founder-hero Amphion is 'a reminder of civilising order in Thebes' past', these passages, by showing the ineffectiveness of his magic in the present, develop a 'larger contrast between the civilising art of song and the destructive savagery of war'.[33]

In Roman literature, Amphion has developed into an illustration of the power of poetry and its peaceful and civilizing force. Often, he is mentioned without any reference to the city of Thebes at all. Seneca's Theban plays, however, problematize the contrast between the magical-poetic construction of the Theban walls and their fate of destruction. This contrast also forms the catalyst for Statius's treatment of Amphion in his *Thebaid*.

Chelys Thebais: Statius and Amphion

In the previous chapter, I analysed the use that Statius makes of the building metaphor in some of his *Silvae*. The special interest in the metaphorical potential of construction also leads to a special interest in the myth of Amphion. In *Silvae* 2.2 and 3.1, two poems about building projects of Statius's friend Pollius Felix, Amphion and Orpheus appear in their familiar double act.[34] Since

---

[31] Cf. Statius's use of the noise of the building site, discussed in Chapter 4, pp. 154–62.

[32] Segal (1983), 230, points out that civilizing hero Amphion serves as a foil for Polynices. Barchiesi (1988), 126, suggests that the reference to Amphion may be a nod towards the harmonious joint reign of the brothers Amphion and Zethus, in contrast to that of Polynices and Eteocles.

[33] Segal (1983), 230–1. Frank (1994), 228, *ad loc.*, also points out that, in accordance with the themes of the play, Seneca generally 'devotes more attention to legendary figures of destruction' than foundation.

[34] *Silvae* 3.1 is discussed in Chapter 4.

184   BUILDING IN WORDS

Pollius Felix is both a poet and a builder, they illustrate his admirable civilizing control over nature at the same time as hinting at his poetic prowess.[35]

For Statius, however, Amphion is not just one among several mythical poets, second best to the more famous Orpheus. Since Statius is the author of a *Thebaid*, he, too, is a 'Theban' poet, and he constructs Amphion as a literary ancestor. This association is made explicit, for example, in the proem to Statius's final, unfinished epic project, the *Achilleid*, when the poet asks Apollo for new inspiration after finishing the *Thebaid* (*Achil.* 1.8–13):

> tu modo, si veterem digno deplevimus haustu,   8
> da fontes mihi, Phoebe, novos ac fronde secunda
> necte comas: neque enim Aonium nemus advena pulso   10
> nec mea nunc primis augescunt tempora vittis.
> scit Dircaeus ager meque inter prisca parentum
> nomina cumque suo numerant Amphione Thebae.

> You, Phoebus, grant me new springs, if I have drunk the old one dry with a worthy draught, and bind my hair with a second wreath; for I do not knock on the Aonian grove as a newcomer, nor are my temples for the first time honoured by your fillets. The land of Dirce knows it, and Thebes numbers me among the ancient names of her founding fathers, together with her own Amphion.

Statius claims that he is now a 'poetic' founder of Thebes, alongside Amphion, implicitly setting up his own poetic edifice, the *Thebaid*, as parallel to Amphion's Theban walls. The suggestion is that he has refounded Thebes through a song comparable to that of Amphion.[36] In the *Silvae*, too, 'there is play with the equation of Amphion and Statius as poetic founders of Thebes'.[37] In *Silvae* 3.2, the poet prays for a safe journey for Maecius Celer. Among a series of invocations of sea deities, he asks the sea-god Palaemon

---

[35] See *Silv.* 2.2.60–2 and 3.1.16–17 and 117, discussed earlier (pp. 168–9). Newlands (2011), 136 *ad Silv.* 2.2.60–1, sees in the mention of Amphion there, between Arion and Orpheus, all of whom are surpassed by Pollius Felix, a playful reference to Statius's own *Thebaid* (*Silv.* 2.2.60–1: *chelys Thebais*). On Amphion and Orpheus as civilizers in this passage, see Lovatt (2007), 149–52.

[36] See Heslin (2005), 102: 'Statius is like Amphion because he "constructed Thebes" with his lyre, building the city in the imagination of the audience of his previous epic, stone by stone, word by word. . . . Other poets might use this metaphor of city building, or compare themselves to Amphion and Orpheus; but because Statius has written an epic about Thebes, he can claim a much closer analogy with the lyre of Amphion.'

[37] Cowan (2002), 197.

and his mother Leucothea, who are of Theban origin, for a safe voyage (*Silv.* 3.2.39–41):

Tu tamen ante omnes diva cum matre, Palaemon,
annue, si vestras amor est mihi pandere Thebas
nec cano degeneri Phoebeum Amphiona plectro.

But you above all, Palaemon, together with your divine mother, grant your support, if I desire to tell of your Thebes and I sing Apollo's Amphion with a lyre not unworthy.

Since Ino, Palaemon, and Amphion also all feature in the proem of the *Thebaid* (1.13–14, 1.9–10), Statius seems to be nodding towards the opening of his epic, while adducing his composition of the *Thebaid* as a reason for divine favour from Ino and Palaemon. Furthermore, by juxtaposing the words *Amphiona* and *plectro*, the poet effectively associates his own Theban poetics with Amphion's achievements and suggests that his own *plectrum* and lyre are not inferior to those of the first Theban bard.

In the *Silvae* and the *Achilleid*, Amphion thus appears in his now-familiar role, symbolizing the power of poetry and its civilizing force. However, Statius goes further than the poets already discussed since he represents Amphion as his mythical (Theban) predecessor and draws a comparison between his own poetic powers and those of the legendary Theban founder. With this parallel between Amphion and the poet in mind, we turn to Statius's *Thebaid*.

'When Song Was Great': Amphion's Walls
in Statius's *Thebaid*

The close association between the two 'Theban' poets might be expected to lend special force and relevance to the poetic *exemplum* of Amphion in the *Thebaid*.[38] However, the relationship between poet and hero in the *Thebaid* differs substantially from that constructed by the proem of the *Achilleid* or

---

[38] The title of this section derives from the poem 'Amphion' by Alfred, Lord Tennyson (1809–1892), beginning 'Oh, had I lived when song was great, / In days of old Amphion . . '. The poem consists of nostalgic reflections on the mythical Amphion's legendary skill, humorously contrasted with the speaker's own impractical talents. On poets and their mythical counterparts in the narrative cf. also. Klooster (2011) on Apollonius in the *Argonautica* presenting himself 'as a latter-day embodiment of the Apollo-related singer/religious expert Orpheus' (91).

186   BUILDING IN WORDS

the comparisons between Pollius Felix and Amphion in the *Silvae*. While Amphion and his walls feature prominently in the epic (as does a homonymous descendant of Amphion, one of the Theban leaders),[39] I argue that the founder-poet here appears as a deeply ambiguous figure, an emblem of the power of poetry as well as its ultimate lack of power.[40] Amphion's combination of magical singing and of civilizing force is turned back on itself when the *Thebaid* explores the fate of the creative, poetic magic of Amphion in a world of *nefas*, war, and city-destruction. Statius's narrative mercilessly explores the tension, already brought out by Seneca in the *Hercules Furens* and the *Phoenissae*, between the peace and harmony of the past foundation and the destructive present of Thebes.

The poet of the *Thebaid* gradually dismantles the walls and their magic as the narrative of the epic proceeds. But while Amphionic poetry is shown to lose its power in the world of the *Thebaid*, Statius's own poetic achievement is thereby implicitly raised to new heights. While Amphion sang Thebes into existence, Statius sings it into defeat, disintegration, and destruction, and as Amphion's power crumbles, Statius demonstrates his mastery of the destructive poetics of the *Thebaid*.[41]

Moving Mountains: Amphion in the Proem

We encounter Amphion for the first time in the proem of the epic. The poet professes to feel overwhelmed by the richness of Theban mythical history, does not know where to begin, and asks the Muses for guidance. One of the events which he says he is unable to sing about in his epic is the building of the walls of Thebes by song (1.9–10): *quo carmine muris / iusserit Amphion*

---

[39] Amphion the younger appears several times in the later books of the epic: in 7.278–81 (catalogue of Theban warriors), 9.776–801 (fighting Parthenopaeus) and 10.387–492 (discovering Hopleus and Dymas). See further discussion later in this chapter.

[40] Cf. Walter (2014), 112–13, who argues that the destruction of Amphion's walls in the *Thebaid* symbolizes the epic's attack on traditional modes of epic storytelling. See also Lovatt (2007), on Orpheus in Statius's *Silvae*, concluding that Orpheus, too, serves to demonstrate the failure of poetry as well as its power (see esp. 153–61).

[41] I take a different view from Cowan (2002), who argues that 'to narrate the story of Thebes from its origin is similar to the action of founding it' (197). It seems to me that, in spite of numerous delays and deviations, Statius is narrating the city into destruction—he is un-founding Thebes. For the destructive teleology of the *Thebaid*, cf. McNelis's (2007) reading of the *Thebaid*, which explores the tension between two opposed narrative forces in the *Thebaid*: the 'teleological' tendency of the martial epic to move to its (destructive) conclusion, and a 'Callimachean' strand of the narrative that impedes and delays this movement. Walter (2014) sees the epic narrator as giving in to the forces of *furor* in the course of the epic, when traditional modes of epic inspiration fail him.

Tyriis accedere montes—'with what song Amphion ordered the mountains to approach the Tyrian walls'.[42] This first appearance leads into the story of Amphion's walls in the *Thebaid*. The word *carmen* that is used for the song that Amphion sings in order to charm the rocks is repeated only a few lines further on, when the poet calls his own epic, likewise, *carmen* (1.16).[43] This is the first hint that Amphion's work is in some way parallel to the epic work of Statius, and that the mythical founder should be seen as a poet in a similar sense to the author of the *Thebaid*.[44] At this point, Amphion seems to have the upper hand in any comparison. While the proem conveys a stance of doubt and disorientation, Amphion's song, in the hyperbolic expression of the poet, could move mountains. Furthermore, the author claims that his epic is unable to include the larger mythical history of Thebes (part of which is the wall-building of Amphion)—the Statian *carmen* cannot contain the Amphionic one.

At a much later point in the epic, the proem is, in a sense, reprised (*resonant*, 8.224) when the Thebans, delighted by the death of Amphiaraus, sing paeans about the origins of Thebes (8.223–36), including those events of early Thebes which the poet had decided to exclude from his epic in the proem.[45] It is not surprising that this moment of (misguided) Theban confidence in an eventual victory and the safety of the city is the only instance in the poem, besides the proem, where Amphion's powers are simply depicted as awe-inspiring and unchallenged.[46]

Don't Play It Again: Amphion in *Thebaid* 2

However, the next appearance of Amphion's walls in book 2 of the epic already begins to reveal their essential weakness. Tydeus has been sent to Eteocles from Argos to negotiate, but Eteocles refuses to surrender the power to his brother. Tydeus departs on a threat (2.452–6):

---

[42] The text of the *Thebaid* is taken from Hill (1983) unless otherwise noted.

[43] *Carmen* is the conventional word for poets to use of their own epic (cf. e.g. *perpetuum carmen* in Ov. *Met.* 1.4), which makes an appearance of the word in a proem while *not* referring to the poet's own work all the more marked. Again, Amphion's *carmen* seems to unite the meanings of song and magic (see n. 23 in this chapter).

[44] Cowan (2002), 197, also suggests that *nunc tendo chelyn* (1.33) 'may just resonate' because of the earlier mention of Amphion.

[45] Augoustakis (2016), 159, *ad* 226–36.

[46] *Theb.* 8.232–3: *Tyriam reptantia saxa / ad chelyn et duras animantem Amphiona cautes*—'the stones, crawling along to the sound of the Tyrian lyre, and Amphion, who made the hard rocks come alive'.

188   BUILDING IN WORDS

> 'reddes',
> ingeminat 'reddes; non si te ferreus agger
> ambiat aut triplices alio tibi carmine muros
> Amphion auditus agat, ...'

> 'You will return it [i.e. power]', and he repeats, 'You will return it! Not even if an
> iron rampart surrounded you, or Amphion were heard and with another song
> made threefold walls for you ...'

Tydeus here, for the first time and still implicitly, utters what will become more
and more apparent throughout the epic. He claims that the walls of Amphion,
once the pride of Thebes, built by the musical magic of a son of Zeus, no longer
function in the present times. They will not afford Eteocles protection, and even
if Amphion returned to sing another song and erect a threefold wall, this would
not be enough to keep Thebes safe.[47] Amphion's magic song appears out of place
in the present. Amphion's status as the personification of the power of poetry is
drawn into doubt: even a triple effort from him would not be heeded by Tydeus.
As war threatens, the peaceful magic of Amphion loses its relevance.

Patch-up Work: Amphion in *Thebaid* 4

Amphion's walls fare steadily worse as the epic proceeds. In book 4, we learn
that his walls and mighty towers are crumbling and falling down, and are
therefore being patched up, albeit without the magical help of Amphion
(4.356–60):

> ipsa vetusto   356
> moenia lapsa situ magnaeque Amphionis arces
> iam fessum senio nudant latus, et fide sacra
> aequatos caelo surdum atque ignobile muros
> firmat opus.   360

---

[47] On *alio* here see Mulder (1954) *ad loc.* (arguing that it has the force of *altero*) and Gervais (2017),
who also considers 'a different [i.e. greater] song': 229, *ad loc.* On the word *alius* in Latin epic, see
Hardie (1993), 17–18.

WALLS OF SONG   189

The very walls have collapsed with long neglect, and the great towers of Amphion expose a flank weakened with age. Mute ignoble labour [or: deaf ignoble work][48] fortifies the walls that the sacred lyre once raised to heaven.

When Amphion first built the walls with his divine talent (*fide sacra*), they reached to the heavens.[49] But the time of Amphion's magic has passed. The walls are no longer strong but in danger of collapse.[50] The necessary repair works have to proceed without song: a *surdum atque ignobile opus*.[51] The passage conveys a nostalgic longing for the times when Amphion's song still functioned and his walls were still strong and magical.[52]

The doom hanging over the weakened walls is also brought out by the hyperbolic phrase *aequatos caelo*—'made equal to heaven', which recalls book 4 of Vergil's *Aeneid*.[53] There, Dido, crazed by her love for Aeneas, neglects the building of her city, Carthage (*Aen.* 4.86–9):

> non coeptae adsurgunt turres, non arma iuventus
> exercet portusve aut propugnacula bello
> tuta parant: pendent opera interrupta, minaeque
> murorum ingentes aequataque machina caelo.

The towers that she had begun do not rise, the young men do not exercise in arms, or prepare harbours or safe bulwarks for war; the works are broken off and stand idle—the huge merlons of the walls and the crane[54] soaring to the sky.

---

[48] *opus* can mean either the labour of the workmen, or the product of the labour, i.e. the repair works. The meaning of *surdus* changes accordingly: In the first case, the workmen's toil is mute, because they do not sing as Amphion did. In the second, the repairs to the walls are called 'deaf', since they do not hear the song of Amphion. The latter is endorsed by an authority cited in Barth (1664) *ad* 359: '*surdum*: Schol. Vet.: *non enim audiebant saxa sonum testudinis, ut priora illa*.'

[49] On the literary tradition of this hyperbole, see Parkes (2012), 201, *ad loc.*

[50] That the walls are weakened by age is also already implied by Tydeus in 2.700.

[51] Cf. Sen. *Phoen.* 568–9, discussed earlier, pp. 182–3, where the building of the walls with song and lyre is contrasted not with the *silence* of 'regular' building, but with the ugly noise of a creaking crane.

[52] The walls have disintegrated at an alarming speed, bearing in mind the chronology of the epic. Barth (1664) notes (*ad* 356) that it is simply impossible that these walls should already be crumbling: Amphion, he argues, was the predecessor of Laius, the father of Oedipus, whose sons are the cause of war. On this passage in the context of the theme of decline, cf. Micozzi (2015), 328.

[53] The parallel is noted by Barth (1664), *ad loc.*

[54] Commentators since Servius have disagreed about the meaning of *machina*. The word is more often translated as 'crane' (see the exhaustive discussion of Pease (1967), 160 *ad loc.*, and Austin (1955), 49 *ad loc.*), but could also refer simply to the 'structure' of the fortified walls rather than to machinery (Williams (1972), 341 *ad loc.*, agreeing with Servius). See also Chapter 4, n. 8, about the interpretation of *machina* in *Silvae* 1.1.64.

190 BUILDING IN WORDS

The allusion suggests a connection between Vergilian Carthage and Statian Thebes, strengthened by the use of the adjective 'Sidonian', which is used frequently for Carthage in Vergil's *Aeneid*.[55] Both passages describe a scene of construction and city-fortification, and in both cases, there is a problem with the process of construction: in the case of Thebes, it proceeds with difficulty; in Carthage, it has come to a temporary halt. Both cities are ultimately doomed to destruction, although disaster is a lot closer for Thebes, where the period of hopeful initial construction has long passed. The shoddy repair works to the Amphionic walls, a pale recollection of the bustling building site described in the *Aeneid*, are a late attempt to stave off destruction which will come, and soon.

The eventual destruction of Carthage is also already prefigured in a famous simile, in which the panic in the city after Dido's suicide is compared to the panic in a city taken by enemies and on fire (*Aen.* 4.669–71).[56] This simile is likewise recalled by Statius at *Thebaid* 7.599–601,[57] and while in the *Aeneid*, the simile hints at events in the remote future, for Thebes, imminent destruction is a terrible reality.[58]

Times of War: Amphion in *Thebaid* 7

In book 7, the Argives have finally arrived outside Thebes, and they pitch their camp on a hill near the city (7.441–51):

> haud procul inde iugum tutisque accommoda castris   441
> arva notant, unde urbem etiam turresque videre
> Sidonias; placuit sedes fidique receptus
> colle per excelsum patulo quem subter aperto
> arva sinu, nullique aliis a montibus instant   445
> despectus; nec longa labor munimina durus
> addidit: ipsa loco mirum natura favebat.

---

[55] Statius frequently calls Thebes the 'Sidonian' city, alluding to the Phoenician origin of Cadmus (on which see e.g. *Theb.* 1.5, 180–5, 3.181–2, 300, 8.229–32, 11.210–14). He uses the adjective as synonymous to 'Theban' at 3.656, 4.648, 7.632, 8.330, 696, 9.144, 567, 709, 10.125, 297, 306. For *Sidonius* as referring to the city, see *Theb.* 7.443, 7.600, 8.218, 10.481, 11.303.

[56] . . . *non aliter, quam si immissis ruat hostibus omnis / Karthago aut antiqua Tyros, flammaeque furentes / culmina perque hominum volvantur perque deorum.* See also pp. 128–9.

[57] See Smolenaars (1994), 269–70, *ad loc.*, who points to *Il.* 22.410–11 (Priam's lament for Hector) as the ultimate source of the motif. In the *Iliad*, of course, the destruction of the city is nearly as imminent as it is in the *Thebaid*.

[58] For the destruction of the walls see 10.877–82 (on which see later in this chapter) and 12.703–6.

WALLS OF SONG 191

in vallum elatae rupes devexaque fossis
aequa et fortuito ductae quater aggere pinnae;
cetera dant ipsi, donec sol montibus omnis   450
erepsit rebusque dedit sopor otia fessis.

Not far from there they notice a ridge and fields suitable for a safe camp, from which they can even see the city and her Sidonian towers. The position pleased them, and the reliable place for shelter, on a hill with a broad summit, beneath which there were fields sloping without cover, and which could not be viewed from other mountains. And hard toil did not have to add long fortifications; nature herself miraculously favoured the site. Rocks rose to form an enclosure, the slopes were as good as ditches, and four merlons had been shaped from the rampart which happened to be there. The rest they add themselves, until all sunlight crept from the mountains and sleep brought rest to their wearied fortunes.

While the Argives seem to have found the ideal situation for their camp, their arrival causes panic in the city of Thebes (7.452–9):[59]

quis queat attonitas dictis ostendere Thebas?   452
urbem in conspectu belli suprema parantis
territat insomnem nox atra diemque minatur.
discurrunt muris; nil saeptum horrore sub illo,   455
nil fidum satis, invalidaeque Amphionis arces.
rumor ubique alius plures adnuntiat hostes,
maioresque timor; spectant tentoria contra
Inachia externosque suis in montibus ignes.

Who could show in words how stunned Thebes was? In sight of an army which was preparing their end, black night terrifies the unsleeping city and holds out the menace of day. They run about on the walls. In that state of panic, nothing appears enclosed, nothing is sufficiently safe, and Amphion's towers are weak. Everywhere another rumour announces that there are more enemies, and fear says that they are more powerful. They

---

[59] The description of the panic-stricken city belongs to an entire category of similar descriptions in epic (perhaps this tradition is hinted at in the phrase *quis queat . . . dictis ostendere*). The typology of such descriptions and the specific links of the Statian passage with different models are analysed by Smolenaars (1994), 199–202.

192 BUILDING IN WORDS

observe opposite them the Inachian tents and the fires of strangers on their own hills.

Once again, the walls of Amphion are weak, *invalidae*. For the terrified Thebans, they seem to offer no protection against the enemy. The striking contrast between the two passages offers further illustration of why and how this is the case. The effortless erection of the Argive camp is described at length. The place is naturally so well suited to a fortification (*ipsa loco mirum natura favebat*) that the Argives can turn it into their camp without a *labor durus*. Once upon a time, the walls of Amphion had also been built without effort and physical toil, and the description of the natural features of the site evokes this Amphionic magical wall-building, since rocks have been raised (*elatae*) by nature, rather than man, to form the fortifications of the camp (*vallum*). *Natura* has done most of the work, allowing the Argives to build their camp in only one day. But while there is miraculously fast building (*mirum*) for the Argives, and they are sure of *fidique receptus*, the Thebans had to toil to patch up their walls (4.359–60) and still, they now doubt that their walls can protect them (*nil fidum satis*).[60]

This contrast between ease and hard work is also strengthened by the close intertextual relation between the Argives' camp building and a scene from the third book of Lucan's *Bellum Civile*. There, Caesar's soldiers also fortify a hill, which lies next to the city of Massilia, in order to capture that city; they then try to connect fortification and city by a huge rampart.[61] The verbal parallels between the two passages are used to highlight an essential difference: Lucan especially stresses the huge amount of work, the *immensus labor* (Luc. 3.381) that the Caesarian soldiers have to carry out. The Argives, in contrast, are specifically said *not* to require a *labor durus*. Once, Amphion, too, built the walls of Thebes without a *labor durus*. But in the *Thebaid*'s

---

[60] The magical creation of the camp through the cooperation of nature is reminiscent of the villa poems in Statius's *Silvae*: Amphion is explicitly evoked as an *exemplum* in *Silv*. 2.2 and 3.1, and the idea of nature herself favouring the spot is present e.g. in *Silv*. 1.3.15–17 or *Silv*. 2.2.52. On the cooperation between builder and nature in building projects, see also n. 60 in Chapter 1, and Reitz (2013).

[61] The parallels are noted by Smolenaars (1994), 195–8. Luc. 3.375–87 is the most important intertext, although *in the Bellum Civile* the fortifications are not finished until 3.458. The description of the fortification-hill begins with *haud procul*, just as the Statian description. *Tutis accomoda castris* in the *Thebaid* recalls the Lucanian *tutis . . . aptissima castris* (3.378). The lexical parallels are specifically employed to bring out the difference between the two superficially similar situations. Caesar's soldiers are supposed to surround the hill with fortifications (*longo munimine cingi*, Luc. 3.377). The hill chosen by the Argives is already fortified: *nec longa labor munimina durus addidit* (*Theb.* 7.446). The Argives' easy progress contrasts with *tunc res inmenso placuit statura labore* (Luc. 3.381). Furthermore, terrified Thebes is a far cry from brave Massilia (*urbem / haud trepidam*, 3.372–3).

destructive world of war, it is only camp building that is accomplished with magical ease. Amphion's peaceful, civilizing magic of city and wall-building has lost its power and become irrelevant.

Armed with a Lyre: Amphion the Younger

Before the arrival of the Argives, book 7 also features the catalogue of Theban troops, viewed by Antigone and Phorbas, Laios's aged armour-bearer, from the walls of Thebes. One of the warriors introduced in the course of this catalogue is also called Amphion, and we learn that he is a descendant of the famous Theban founder. Phorbas describes him as follows (7.277–9):

> hos regis egenos
> Amphion en noster agit (cognoscere pronum,
> virgo) lyra galeam tauroque insignis avito.

> Since they [a band of rustic warriors] lack a king, see, our Amphion leads them (easy to recognise, maiden), his helmet marked with a lyre and the bull of his ancestor.[62]

The description of the present-day Amphion further serves to establish the *Thebaid* as an epic of war in which the peaceful magic of the more famous Amphion has no place. In the *Antiope*, Hermes had pointedly asked Amphion to arm himself with his lyre.[63] Now, Amphion's descendant has reverted to bearing real arms (more of a Zethus than an Amphion), while Amphion's lyre, instrument of peace and civilization, has been demoted to a piece of military decoration.[64]

[62] The group of warriors led by Amphion is made up of three contingents whose origin is described in *Theb.* 7.271–5: those from Onchestos; those from the region of Mycalessos, the river Melas, and the spring Gargaphie; and the ones from Haliartus. See Smolenaars (1994), 135–6.

[63] *Antiope* fr. 223.91 (Collard)/223.120 (*TrGF*). See p. 175.

[64] While the image of the lyre on Amphion's helmet is easily identifiable as referring to the elder Amphion, the significance of the *taurus avitus* is less clear. The phrase could refer to Zeus, who abducted Europa in the form of a bull (see *Theb.* 1.5: *Sidonios raptus*), forcing her brother Cadmus to go in search of her and to found Thebes (suggested by Shackleton Bailey (2003), 40 n. 1), or possibly to the river-god Asopos, in some versions called the father of Antiope, though not by Statius himself (see Smolenaars (1994), 138 *ad* 279). It seems simpler to read *avitus* as meaning 'of his ancestors' (*OLD* 2, also supported by Smolenaars), in which case the bull could simply refer to the punishment of Dirce, and probably evoke Amphion's twin Zethus. The same division of the symbols (lyre-Amphion and bull-Zethus) also appears in Sen. *Oed.* 609–12 (see p. 181 and n. 29 in this chapter).

194   BUILDING IN WORDS

Un-founding Thebes: Amphion in *Thebaid* 10

The story of the failure of Amphionic poetry reaches its climax in book 10 of the *Thebaid*. In this episode, one of the seven Argive leaders, Capaneus, is accorded a very special *aristeia*, in an episode full of drama and hyperbole, which has aroused both the admiration and the wrath of commentators.[65] Capaneus is tired of earthly battles and begins to climb towards heaven. First with the help of a ladder, then simply through thin air, he climbs first above the battlements of the walls of Thebes, then continues towards heaven. Missiles cannot hurt him; for a moment he seems invincible and determined to fight the gods themselves, until Jupiter finally kills him with one of his thunderbolts.

On his way towards heaven, Capaneus in passing deals the death blow to Amphion's walls, reversing Amphion's poetic foundation with brute force. Capaneus is towering above the city of Thebes (10.870–82):

> utque petita diu celsus fastigia supra   870
> eminuit trepidamque adsurgens desuper urbem
> vidit et ingenti Thebas exterruit umbra,
> increpat attonitos: 'humilesne Amphionis arces?[66]
> pro pudor! hi faciles carmenque imbelle secuti,
> hi, mentita diu Thebarum fabula, muri?   875
> et quid tam egregium prosternere moenia molli
> structa lyra?' simul insultans gressuque manuque
> molibus obstantes cuneos tabulataque saevus
> restruit:[67] absiliunt pontes, tectique trementis
> saxea frena labant, dissaeptoque aggere rursus   880
> utitur et truncas rupes in templa domosque
> praecipitat frangitque suis iam moenibus urbem.

---

[65] Leigh (2006), *passim*, and esp. 238–9 on Barth.

[66] I follow the punctuation supported by Williams (1972). Hill (1983) punctuates differently but obelizes 873–5. Shackleton Bailey (1983), 58–9, argues for Capaneus' speech beginning in 874, at *pro pudor!*. These three lines present numerous textual problems (Barth (1664), *ad* 10.867: *impeditus est sermo, non spirat Papinium*): see Williams (1972), 129–30 *ad* 873–4, Cowan (2002), 240 n. 495. Hall, Ritchie, and Edwards (2007) print *haene illae* instead of *humilesne* at 10.873, a reading that Barth claimed to have seen in *ille optimis melior antiquissimus Codex*.

[67] The unparalleled *restruit* is corrected in several MSS to *destruit*, which Shackleton Bailey (2003) prints. Hill (1983) retains *restruit*, also defended by Williams (1972), 130, *ad loc*. If correct, *restruit* is a striking expression of Capaneus's reversal of the construction of the Theban walls, just like *dissaepto*, 880: likewise unparalleled in the meaning 'stop from surrounding', i.e. reversing the process of *aggere saepire* (cf. e.g. *Aen*. 9.70 or Var. *R.R.*1.14.2) by destroying the *agger*.

And when he loomed high above the roofs he had long sought and, rising up, saw the town quaking below and terrified Thebes with his huge shadow, he roared at the dismayed inhabitants: 'Are the citadels of Amphion so insignificant then? What an embarrassment! These are the walls that were so willing and followed an unwarlike song, these the walls about which the legend of Thebes has long been falsely told? And what is so special about knocking down walls built by a soft lyre?' At the same time, leaping upon the fortifications with foot and hand, he fiercely unbuilds stones and platforms[68] standing in his way. Bridges burst apart, the stone stays of the shaking roof fall down, and the destroyed rampart he uses again. He hurls mutilated rocks down upon temples and houses and is already smashing the city with her own walls.

In this passage, the walls of Thebes are for the final time explicitly called the walls of Amphion. The passage also contains the clearest statement of the dysfunctionality of Amphionic poetics in the world of the *Thebaid*. The poetic *opus* of Amphion is now completely humiliated and powerless, derided and destroyed by Capaneus. This scene had already briefly been foreshadowed in an episode in *Thebaid* 7.649–87, where Capaneus kills the Bacchic priest Eunaeus. Eunaeus there entreats the Argives to spare the sacred walls of Thebes, adducing their mythical construction as an argument (7.665): *parcite, in haec ultro scopuli venere volentes*—'spare these walls, to which willing rocks came of their own accord'.[69] Capaneus, armed with an *aeria . . . hasta* (7.669), which already points to his later ascent towards heaven, derides Eunaeus's arguments, and kills the priest while expressing his scorn of the prophet's song (7.679): *haec Tyriis cane matribus!*—'Sing that to Theban mothers!'

The hero's scorn for the walls' sanctity and his disbelief in their poetic history is then given free reign in book 10. The brutal demolition of the walls literally reverses Amphion's civilizing wall-building and city-foundation. The elements of the city that Capaneus destroys are precisely those one would expect to be built and set up in a description of city foundation (a number of which were discussed in Chapter 3): city walls, fortifications, houses, roofs,

[68] The language is specific and technical: *cunei* are wedge-shaped stones used for the construction of stone arches (cf. Vitr. 6.8.3–4; *pace OLD* s.v. *cuneus* 1b, where it is suggested that *cuneus* here refers to a splitting tool used by Capaneus); *tabulata* are the wooden floors or platforms of (military) towers, as in Caes. *Gal.* 6.29.3 (a four-storey defence tower).

[69] Eunaeus's words recall those of Jocasta in Sen. *Phoen.* 566–71 (cited on p. 182): Smolenaars (1994), 308, *ad loc.*

196 BUILDING IN WORDS

and temples. Capaneus is un-founding Thebes—further emphasized by the striking vocabulary of *restruere* and *dissaepire*, which highlight his reversal of the foundational activities of *struere* and *(aggere) saepire*.[70] Where the archetypal founding activity is the building of walls to keep a city safe, Capaneus turns the walls of Thebes against herself, smashing her with the very fortifications which were to protect her (*frangit suis iam moenibus urbem*). Civilization deteriorates and reverts back to uncultivated rawness: stones which had long ago been shaped and built up into civilized structures like walls, roofs, bridges, and ramparts now turn back into bare rocks (*rupes*).[71] But Capaneus is not only an un-founder in a general sense; he is specifically undoing the Amphionic foundation of the Theban walls.[72] In response to Amphion's song, the stones built themselves up and joined together of their own accord. Now that his poetic magic has gone, the stones fall down and split apart of their own accord as well: *absiliunt pontes . . . saxea frena labant*.

In the taunts that he hurls at the walls, Capaneus gives vent to his utter contempt for the poetic magic of Amphion. The stones followed a *carmen . . . imbelle*, an 'unwarlike song', and they were *molli / structa lyra*—'built by an unmanly lyre'. The suggestion that Amphion's song was *mollis* perhaps has a specific generic ring to it (*mollis* is regularly used to describe poetry that is not epic, and in particular love-poetry), but more importantly, it is a broad swipe at the weakness of Amphion's peaceful music.[73] Capaneus's taunts have already been proving correct throughout the epic. Amphion's *carmen* was indeed *imbelle*, in that it was a song that brought about foundation peacefully,

---

[70] See n. 67 in this chapter.

[71] In this sense, Capaneus's un-founding also reverses Amphion's civilizing role as depicted in Horace's *Ars Poetica*: see pp. 180–1 in this chapter.

[72] There is also a sense in which he undoes Menoeceus recent 're-foundation' of Thebes (10.786–8: *omni / concinitur vulgo Cadmum atque Amphiona supra / conditor*—'and he [i.e. Menoeceus] is sung by the whole people as their founder above Cadmus and Amphion'); see also Vessey (1973), 123 with n. 5, for Menoeceus's death as a re-foundation. When Capaneus prepares to attack the walls, he feels drawn to the place 'where the tower is slippery with the blood of Menoeceus' (*Menoeceo qua lubrica sanguine turris, Theb.* 10.846), marking his action also as an undoing of Menoeceus actions: Cowan (2002), 238–9. On Menoeceus and Capaneus, see also Heinrich (1999), 184–9.

[73] Combined with *lyra*, Capaneus perhaps conveys a suggestion that Amphion sang a lyric song about amatory themes. The word *mollis* is used by Propertius in a poem which deals with the drawbacks of writing a *Thebaid*: in poem 1.7, Propertius warns his poet-colleague Ponticus, who is composing an epic *Thebaid*, that such poetry will not help him to win over his love. He suggests that Ponticus should really be busy *mollem componere versum* (1.7.19), contrasting this with the *carmen grave* (1.9.9) that Ponticus *is* in fact writing, and which deals with the walls of Amphion: *quid tibi nunc misero prodest grave dicere carmen / aut Amphioniae moenia flere lyrae*, 1.9.9–10). Capaneus's attack here subverts the distinctions between genres in suggesting that the quintessentially (ktistic) epic hero Amphion only composed love-poetry himself. See generally Edwards (1993), ch. 2, for an analysis of the language of *mollitia* as used in Roman political discourse not to sexual ends, but as a means of verbal power play.

WALLS OF SONG 197

and the *Thebaid*'s inhuman war has robbed it of its strength. The moment of complete civilizatory reversal, of un-foundation, coincides with the final disappearance of the last trace of Amphion's magic.

Capaneus also taunts the walls as *mentita diu Thebarum fabula*—'the long-told lying tale of Thebes', implying, even more explicitly than in the earlier confrontation with Eunaeus, that the entire story of the walls' foundation is a lie.[74] When Capaneus verbally denigrates and at the same time (*simul*, 877) physically rips apart Amphion's walls, Statius demonstrates how architectural deconstruction can be performed both in deed and in words. Capaneus is physically destroying the walls and simultaneously verbally destroying their magical history, which his words render both worthless and untrue.[75]

An implicit contrast has been building up throughout the epic between, on the one hand, the disturbing destruction of Amphion's walls and the weakening of the powers of Amphionic song in the face of war, and, on the other hand, the power of Statian poetry to tell of this war and destruction.[76] To tell of the transgressions of Capaneus, the narrator had asked the Muses for further, greater inspiration (10.829–31):

> non mihi iam solito vatum de more canendum;
> maior ab Aoniis poscenda amentia lucis:
> mecum omnes audete deae!

> I must no longer sing in the usual fashion of bards; I must ask for a higher lunacy from Aonian groves. All you goddesses, dare with me!

While one poet's song is ground into the dust, another's rises to new 'furious' heights.[77] While Amphion's poetic magic of foundation and civilization has gradually been dismantled and proven ineffective, Statius's own song soars further and further above the ordinary to tell the story of war and

---

[74] Cowan (2002), 240, remarks that Capaneus may here be '[e]schewing consistency for rhetorical and poetic effect . . .'. It is also possible that *mentita fabula* refers to a legendary special magical impregnability of the walls due to their mythical origins, perhaps 'by analogy with those of Troy built by Apollo and Neptune', which Capaneus is about to finally disprove through his act of destruction.

[75] Leigh (2006) has suggested that, through the theme of sublimity, Statius creates a connection between the figure of Capaneus and the poet himself. The parallel activities of verbal and the verbal-physical destruction of the city by narrator-poet and hero may reinforce his point.

[76] Parkes (2012), 200 *ad* 356–60, also points to 10.703–6 and 12.9–10 for the theme of the destroyed Theban walls.

[77] For a slightly different interpretation of this scene, see Walter (2014), 137–41, who argues that it signifies the narrator's loss of control of his epic.

198   BUILDING IN WORDS

destruction. In the *Silvae* and the *Achilleid*, Statius encourages comparison between Amphion and himself. At the end of the *Thebaid*, Statius is the last man singing, while Amphion's *opus* has been destroyed.

Conclusion

In Chapter 3, where I investigated city-building as a poetological metaphor, I concluded that one aspect of the city-building metaphor that poets particularly exploit is the cultural prestige of (city) *foundation*. Suggesting an analogy between their own poetic composition and the foundation of a city serves to enhance the status of their poetic creation. In the story of Amphion, the metaphor is both mythologized and literalized: the mythical poet really *is* a founder. Most of the treatments of the Amphion-myth in Latin literature seize upon this identification of foundation and poetic composition, exploiting it as an illustration of the power of poetry to impact reality. In the *Thebaid*, however, we see the opposite mechanism at work. There, Statius increases his own poetic prestige precisely by dissociating himself from the founder-poet Amphion. By describing the ultimate failure of Amphion's peaceful poetry in a world of war, Statius implicitly raises himself above his mythical predecessor as the poet who is able to *un*-found Amphionic Thebes through song.

Seneca and Statius both highlight the discrepancy between Amphion's poetic foundation and the ultimately fragile, ephemeral nature of his poetic *opus*. The myth allows for uncomfortable questions about the implications of the architectural metaphor for the production of literary text. The myth can function as an optimistic story about the power of poetry, but in Statius's *Thebaid*, the destruction wrought upon the Theban walls of song leaves us with a disconcerting sense of the fragility of (poetic) constructs. If texts can be 'built', can they also be destroyed? This theme of destruction, both physical and poetic, will be further explored in the concluding chapter.

6

Conclusion

Construction in Reverse

Introduction

In the preceding five chapters, I investigated different strategies of representing construction in ancient Rome, and analysed how these representations relate to finished physical as well as literary constructs. I propose to recapitulate and contextualize my results by considering construction 'in reverse': I conclude this study with a brief discussion of *de*struction, investigating whether strategies similar or analogous to those discussed with respect to construction are also to be found in representations of the process of destruction.

While representing construction adds new dimensions to the ways in which its finished product is or should be perceived (knowing where something has come from changes how we think about it), representing *de*struction changes the way in which we look at—what? The point of destruction is that as soon as it is complete, its object is either unrecognizable or gone. Nevertheless, destruction always leaves something behind: a lacuna, a ruin, a reconstruction, a new building in the place of the old one.[1] I have argued that representations of construction in different media are used to create or manipulate a viewer-reader's mental image of the construction process in order to heighten the impact of the monument. Can a representation of destruction then also influence the way in which the reader thinks about, and even looks at, the *absence* of a monument formerly there or a new structure that has taken the place of the old one? What representational strategies are used in creating images of destruction? And do such representations

---

[1] Cf. my opening example of the construction at Ground Zero, where new buildings have now risen while the lacuna has been monumentalized in the 9/11 Memorial. On the power of defaced or destroyed objects and buildings to function as monuments, see Elsner (2003). On the site of the destroyed World Trade Center as a monument, see specifically Nelson and Olin (2003).

Building in Words. Bettina Reitz-Joosse, Oxford University Press. © Oxford University Press 2021.
DOI: 10.1093/oso/9780197610688.003.0007

200 BUILDING IN WORDS

also aim to influence the reader's impression of the durability and stability of monuments that still exist?

I have also analysed how representations of construction can be made to impact the reader's assessment of the text itself. We have already seen that a similar effect can also be observed in connection with destruction: I argued in Chapter 5 that Statius's portrayal of the destruction of Amphion's walls prompts reflections about the power and powerlessness of poetry. In this chapter I investigate more closely how representations of destruction can influence readers' responses to the text they are reading, or to 'text' more generally.

Construction—Destruction—Reconstruction

Representations of destruction derive much of their power from creating an awareness of the 'constructive' prequel of making, and the (possible) sequel of reconstruction. In the same way, representations of construction can gain additional meaning from being juxtaposed or in some way connected with (the possibility of) destruction. Rebuilding-inscriptions, which I briefly touched upon in Chapter 1, are a case in point.[2] Apart from recording the act of rebuilding, they frequently provide details of the destruction that necessitated the repairs, such as the extent to which destruction had occurred, or the means by which it had happened (e.g. *vetustate, terrae motu, vi ignis, vi maris, vi torrentium, vi tempestatis* or *longa incuria ... conlapsum*).[3] The detail sketches the events preceding the constructive intervention of the builder, setting off his or her prestigious activity against the destructive past.

Visual representations, too, make use of the juxtaposition of destruction and construction as a way of giving added meaning to both activities. I considered the representations of building on the Column of Trajan, arguing that they serve to enhance the viewer's appreciation of the monument and surrounding architecture.[4] However, I did not in that context pay much attention to the numerous scenes of destruction on the column. In the scheme of the spiral relief, the sculptors regularly juxtapose the construction of Roman camps with the destruction of Dacian buildings, using this interplay to stress

---

[2] See pp. 18–20.
[3] Horster (2001), 52–3; and see p. 19 n. 11.
[4] See pp. 43–8.

CONCLUSION   201

Roman superiority.[5] Roman buildings are shown under construction, while Dacian buildings are torched and demolished by Roman troops or by the Dacians themselves.[6] Construction is the mark of the superior party, the victors' prerogative.[7]

The juxtapositions of construction and destruction or the activation of the one in the context of the description of the other is an equally effective device in literary representations. In the Introduction, I mentioned the temple of Jupiter Optimus Maximus on the Capitoline, destroyed in the civil war of AD 69.[8] Tacitus's famous description of its destruction in the course of the fighting between the followers of Vespasian and Vitellius (Tac. *Hist.* 3.71) is followed by an 'obituary' of the temple, in which Tacitus recalls the monument's venerable history (3.72.2–3): it was vowed by Tarquinius Priscus, built under Servius Tullius and Tarquinius Superbus, completed after the institution of the republic, and restored and renovated several times.[9] Setting off the description of the temple's senseless burning against its construction-rich past heightens the pathos and significance of the event. At the same time, Tacitus's juxtaposition of the physical destruction and his literary reconstruction of the temple implicitly contrasts the durability and stability of architectural and literary monuments.

I have so far discussed destruction only as the negative equivalent of construction. Tacitus's Vitellians impiously destroy the temple built by (mostly) venerable ancestors; Statius's Capaneus is shown to transgress human

[5] See Wolfram Thill (2011) for a detailed analysis of destruction of architecture on the columns of Trajan and Marcus Aurelius 'as a metaphor for cultural erasure' (283).

[6] Examples of the former are scenes XXV, XXX, LVII–LVIII, CXVI, and CLII–CLIV; examples of the latter LXXV–LXXVI, CXIX. Numbers refer to the scene numbering of Cichorius (1896–1900). Scenes of destruction and construction are often horizontally or vertically adjacent, their position on the column further enhancing their contrasting effect: for example XXV (destruction) is placed directly above XIX–XX (Roman construction). LVII–LVIII (Roman destruction of Dacian buildings) is framed by LV–LVI (bridge construction) and LX (construction). The scheme in Wolfram Thill (2011), 288, fig. 2, shows the position of destruction sequences on the column. She analyses the contrasting effect of construction and destruction on the column in some detail (297–9), stressing the 'equation between architecture and culture' (299).

[7] This contrast is also expressed through the way the artists combine construction and deconstruction with other elements. For example, XXXIX–XL shows soldiers building the wall of a camp. Along the left-hand wall, a file of Dacian old men, women, and children descends (XXXIX), while within the encampment, Trajan accepts the surrender of three Dacian leaders. By contrast, CXIX shows a group of Dacians destroying their own buildings, and breaking down their walls. The significance of this action is emphasized by the adjoining scene (CXX) of Dacians committing suicide by poison. While construction represents energy and strength, destruction signals weakness, failure, and death.

[8] See p. 1 with bibliography there.

[9] Specifically on this 'Nekrolog', see e.g. the historical discussion of Heubner (1972), 151–3; Edwards (1996), 79–82 (who argues that Tacitus's description of the history of the Capitol, by evoking Livy's early Rome, encapsulates the history of the entire city of Rome); Döpp (2003); Ash (2007), 232–7; Flower (2008), 89–92.

202 BUILDING IN WORDS

boundaries in undoing the work of Amphion and unfounding Thebes.[10] I now turn to a passage from Pliny's *Panegyricus* where the interplay of construction and destruction works very differently. There, the act of construction is depicted as transgressive, while its undoing is praised; the reversal of construction is used retrospectively to discredit the original construction. The passage offers further insight into the interplay of destruction and construction, especially given that Pliny's text deconstructs a monument built up in a text also discussed at length in this study: Statius's *Silvae*. As such, Pliny's representation of destruction allows us to revisit a number of the key strategies of representing construction that I have identified in the previous chapters, most importantly the double functionality of construction on a literal and a metaliterary level.

Toppling the Statue: Pliny's *Panegyricus*

In Chapter 4, I discussed the opening poem of Statius's first book of *Silvae*: the description of the colossal equestrian statue of Domitian in the Forum Romanum, which he represents as a symbol of imperial power and control, as well as an embodiment of his own panegyric poetry.[11] This equestrian statue and many other images of Domitian were obliterated in accordance with a decree passed by the senate after the emperor's assassination.[12] The object of these powerful, officially enforced memory sanctions was, however, not the obliteration of all recollection of the emperor Domitian. Mutilated images, but also sudden and often extremely conspicuous *lacunae* in the visual and epigraphic landscapes of the empire (at least initially) preserved and heightened awareness of the disgraced, unspeakable emperor.[13]

---

[10] See pp. 194–8.

[11] On *Silvae* 1.1 see especially pp.137–40, 150, and 154–5.

[12] On the so-called *damnatio memoriae* of Domitian, see Suet. *Dom.* 23; Cass. Dio 68.1.1; Flower (2006), 234–71. The term *damnatio memoriae* is a modern coinage, usually used to refer to large-scale memory sanctions which could include the banning of the condemned's *praenomen* within the *gens*, the erasure of his name from inscriptions, the confiscation of his property, the prohibition of mourning for his death, the destruction of his houses (on which see Roller (2010)), or the removal or mutilation of his portraits. These actions could be officially mandated by senate, emperor, or army, or they could be 'spontaneous' actions. See in general Vittinghoff (1936), 12–51, 64–74; Flower (2006); and on Domitian's portraits Varner (2004), 112–35.

[13] See Carey (2003), 165–71; Stewart (2003), 279–83 ('the point is not that the population should forget, but that the victim should be obviously unworthy of social existence'); Elsner (2003), esp. 209–19, on the inherent memory of mutilated objects; and Vout (2008), who interrogates the aesthetics of recarved images as well as erasures and deletions. Cf. also the Domitianic inscription from Puteoli (discussed in Chapter 4, p.144 n. 24), which was for some years displayed in its mutilated state before the block of stone was reused for a Trajanic monument. Varner (2004), 133, argues that the erased

CONCLUSION 203

The *damnatio memoriae* created an 'anti-memory' of the emperor, devoid of all positive aspects of Roman *memoria*.[14]

Pliny's Memory of Destruction

The *process* of this destruction of the emperor's images is represented in Pliny the Younger's *Panegyricus*, a speech delivered in the senate AD 100 and then published, in which Pliny praised the new emperor Trajan for his political activities (chief among them his excellent relationship with the senate), his *munera* to the people, and his virtuous private life. I argue that Pliny's representation of the obliteration of the emperor's images is designed to impact on the audience's response to the absent Domitianic images, as well as to the images that (in part) replaced them.[15]

Pliny's describes the destruction of the statues of Domitian as follows (52.4–5):

(4) Ergo istae quidem aereae et paucae manent manebuntque quam diu templum ipsum, illae autem <aureae> et innumerabiles strage ac ruina publico gaudio litaverunt. Iuvabat illidere solo superbissimos vultus, instare ferro, saevire securibus, ut si singulos ictus sanguis dolorque sequeretur. (5) Nemo tam temperans gaudii seraeque laetitiae, quin instar ultionis videretur cernere laceros artus truncata membra, postremo truces horrendasque imagines obiectas excoctasque flammis, ut ex illo terrore et minis in usum hominum ac voluptates ignibus mutarentur.

Therefore, these statues, made of bronze and few in number, stand and will stand as long as the temple itself, but those, made of gold and countless in number, have served, through their overthrow and fall, as a propitiating sacrifice to the public rejoicing. It was pleasurable to dash the very arrogant

---

inscription remained on display 'as a visual marker of Domitian's posthumous humiliation and repudiation'.

[14] On 'memory games' as a political tool in Rome, see Flower (2006), *passim*. Cf. also Pliny's claim that an emperor will always be remembered—the question is only *how* he is remembered: Plin. *Pan.* 55.9: *Praeterea ut quisque factus est princeps, extemplo fama eius, incertum bona an mala, ceterum aeterna est.*—'Furthermore, as soon as anyone is made princeps, it is in any case immediately clear that his reputation is eternal, although it is uncertain whether it will be good or bad.'

[15] Stewart (2003), 280, points out that 'the melting of the bronze image of a face . . . has the disadvantage of leaving no trace of mutilation', a shortcoming of the procedure which a description such as Pliny's, in preserving a memory of the destruction, can compensate to some extent.

Figure 6.1. The statue of Saddam Hussein is toppled in Baghdad's Firdos Square, 9 April 2003.
Photo by Gilles Bassignac/Gamma-Rapho via Getty Images.

faces to the ground, to attack them with the sword, to rage against them with axes, as if blood and pain might really follow from every blow. No one was so moderate in their joy and long-delayed happiness that it did not seem like revenge to see the mangled limbs, the body parts hacked in pieces, and finally the savage and dreadful portraits thrown into the flames and melted down, so that they might be changed in the flames from such terror and menaces to something useful and pleasant for humankind.

On first reading this passage, more recent images may occur to the modern reader, such as the toppling of the statues of communist dictators after the end of the cold war, or the destruction of the images of Saddam Hussein after the surrender of Iraq (Figure 6.1).[16] It is no accident that the image of the

---

[16] Cf. also the written account of the toppling of this statue on the website of BBC News (source: http://news.bbc.co.uk/onthisday/hi/dates/stories/april/9/newsid_3502000/3502633.stm, accessed 23 July 2012): 'The metal plaque at the base of the statue was torn off and the statue's marble plinth attacked with a sledgehammer. The men scaled the statue to secure a noose around its neck but were unable to pull it down. Then US troops joined in, and used an armoured vehicle to gradually pull down the statue.... As the statue fell to the ground at last, the crowd surged forward and jumped on it. Chanting and jeering, they danced on the fallen effigy, kicking it and hitting it with their shoes in a symbolic gesture of contempt as it was torn to pieces. They then severed the head, tied chains

CONCLUSION   205

falling colossal statue of Saddam has become so well-known. The moment was skillfully staged and captured by carefully directed footage to create a modern, powerful representation of destruction.[17] Similarly, Pliny's representation of the destruction of the statues of Domitian, disturbing and gruesome as it reads at first sight, with its fantasies of bloody revenge projected upon the images of the emperor, is carefully designed and calculated to create or manipulate his audience's mental image of this process of destruction.

The representation of the statue's destruction is prefaced by a comparison (characteristic of the *Panegyricus*) between Trajan and his reprehensible pre-predecessor. Pliny praises Trajan's admirable restraint in having only a few statues of himself set up in the entrance court of the temple of Jupiter Capitolinus and compares this frugality favourably to the profusion of golden images of Domitian with which the emperor had allegedly crammed the temple (*Pan.* 52.3):

> Itaque tuam statuam in vestibulo Iovis optimi maximi unam alteramve et hanc aeream cernimus. At paulo ante aditus omnes, omnes gradus, totaque area hinc auro hinc argento relucebat, seu potius polluebatur ...

> Of your statues, we see only one or two in the vestibule of the temple of Jupiter Optimus Maximus, and these are made of bronze. But a little while ago all entrances and all steps and the whole space shone, here with gold, there with silver, or I should rather say it was polluted by them ...

Here, Pliny introduces the destruction that follows (52.4–5) with a description of the present aspect of the sanctuary, now devoid of Domitian's golden images. The representation of destruction is used to construct a model interpretation of the newly 'bare' sanctuaries and the visible absence of Domitian from the cityscape. We are to read the absences as a sign of the piety of the new emperor and the contrast between him and his predecessor.[18]

Pliny's representation of the destruction proper, too, carefully manipulates his audience's image of the event. For example, Pliny stresses repeatedly that

---

around it, and dragged it through the streets.' Stewart (2004), 28, also compares ancient *damnatio memoriae* to the destruction of the images of Saddam Hussein.

[17] The extent to which the toppling of Saddam's statue in front of the Palestine Hotel was staged and/or the footage (immorally?) instrumentalized by the US government has been hotly debated. For a thoughtful analysis, see Maass (2011).

[18] On descriptions of construction as part of 'model interpretations', see pp. 136–45 on the *Silvae*.

206   BUILDING IN WORDS

the destruction gave expression to general public rejoicing about the death of the tyrant and the new freedom (*publico gaudio . . . iuvabat . . . gaudii seraeque laetitiae*). This feature of his account of the destruction may well address a potential embarrassment: it appears (from our scarce sources) that the general populace was by no means as unequivocally delighted at the murder of Domitian and the *damnatio memoriae* as was the senatorial class.[19] The process of destruction is turned by Pliny into a performance of the general populace's passionate hatred of Domitian and their joy at his murder.

The representation of the beheading, dismemberment, and melting down of the statues is shocking in its bloodthirstiness and violence: the frenzied populace hacks away at the statues as if they could bleed and feel pain.[20] The description also activates disturbing intertexts. There is some epic battle terminology,[21] but the dismemberment and subsequent cooking of the emperor's limbs are rather eerily reminiscent of dismemberment and even the cooking of human flesh in (Senecan) revenge tragedies, as is the focus on the pleasure of viewing the terrible deed (*cernere*).[22] Representing this violence as *revenge* (*instar ultionis*) suggests that it represents retribution for similarly terrible deeds committed by the emperor, a 'tit for tat' that can now at least be played out on statues. The violent scene therefore becomes a mirror of Domitian's own violence, allowing Pliny to re-enact Domitian's cruel and murderous reign through the description of destruction. At the same time, Pliny makes it clear that while Domitian may have tortured real people, this retribution is only visited upon statues, not human beings; when he stresses that the statues were attacked *ut si singulos ictus sanguis dolorque sequeretur*, it is clear that in fact they do *not* feel pain.[23]

---

[19] Suet. *Dom.* 23.1: *Occisum eum populus indifferenter, miles gravissime tulit statimque Divum apellare conatus est . . .*—'The people bore the fact that he had been killed with indifference, but the military took it very badly and immediately tried to call him *Divus* . . .'. See Flower (2006), 239, on the people's reaction; and Varner (2004), 113, on the senatorial bias of Pliny's account of the event.

[20] Varner (2001) relates the destruction of the statues to corpse mutilation (*poena post mortem*), see esp. 49 on Pliny's description.

[21] The phrase *laceros artus* is found in Ov. *Met.* 9.169, Luc. 2.165, 2.177, Man. 1.911, 4.185, Sil. *Pun.* 3.433, and Stat. *Theb.* 5.605, 12.411) as well as at Sen. *Oed.* 440; *truncata membra* appears in Sil. *Pun.* 17.149.

[22] E.g. Sen. *Thy.* 60–2, 755–67. See also [Sen.] *Oct.* 794–9 on the savage dismemberment of the statues of Octavia by an angry mob, foreshadowing her impending death. On the internal and external audience of performances of extreme violence in Seneca's tragedies, see e.g. Mowbray (2012).

[23] However, the thrill lies precisely in the fact that the statue is so close to the 'real thing'. Roman imperial portraits were not only representations of the emperor but also objects of veneration that were garlanded and received prayers and sacrifices (e.g. Stewart (2004), 27–8, with bibliography on responses to Roman portraits). For attacks on imperial images as 'mutilation in effigy', see Varner (2001), esp. 47. While these ways of responding to imperial portraits suggest that the 'presence' of the emperor in his image was somehow felt, in this instance Pliny clearly demarcates these images as different from a living thing.

CONCLUSION 207

The word *litaverunt* (52.4) fulfils an important function in Pliny's description. The destruction of the statues is framed in terms of religious observance, as a pious sacrifice, perhaps also necessary for purifying the polluted temple (*polluebatur*, 52.1).[24] Turning the destruction into a religious act renders it morally and religiously unimpeachable. The sanctity of the Domitianic dedications themselves is definitively denied,[25] while the violent removal and destruction of temple dedications is in itself a ritual act of atonement.

Pliny's representation of the process of destruction thus frames the statues' destruction as evidence of the public hatred of Domitian and the general rejoicing at his death. The violence re-enacts Domitian's own excesses, and is doubly justified as deserved retribution and in being confined to statues. Religious overtones, too, render the destruction of the images morally acceptable. This representation of destruction as a whole is designed to influence the reader-viewer's interpretation of the visible absence of Domitian from the cityscape.

The Destruction of Praise: The *Panegyricus* and the *Silvae*

Domitian's images are destroyed, and Pliny's description of their destruction offers a pro-Trajanic interpretation of their absence. However, while physical statues can be destroyed, texts and the ideas they preserve may initially appear more resistant to obliteration. In Chapter 4, I argued that *Silvae* 1.1 offered a model interpretation of the equestrian statue of Domitian in the Forum Romanum (part of which was awareness of the effort of erecting it). Even though the statue itself had been removed, texts like that of Statius, and presumably others like it, were still in circulation.[26] On another level, then, Pliny's description of the destruction of the images of Domitian also aims to invalidate or overwrite Domitianic panegyric, foiling the efforts of texts like *Silvae* 1.1 to perpetuate the monument and its originally opportune interpretation. Pliny's description of destruction specifically addresses and contradicts many of the points of Statius's poem. A poem cannot be toppled

---

[24] Pliny claims that the images of the gods in and around the temple had been polluted by the images of Domitian, since he was guilty of incest with his niece (52.3): . . . *cum incesti principis statuis permixta deorum simulacra sorderent.*

[25] For a dedication of a statue of the emperor by a private individual represented as an act of extreme piety, see Stat. *Silv.* 5.1.189–90.

[26] Cf. Griffin (2000), 88; Sullivan (1991), 44–52; and Coleman (1998b) on Martial's unsuccessful efforts to withdraw his pro-Domitianic poems from circulation.

208 BUILDING IN WORDS

and melted down, but Pliny's text constitutes a determined literary attack on the Statian poetic statue. This is indicated by broader thematic links, as well as more specific correspondences between the two passages.[27]

Both passages deal with sculptures of Domitian, made of precious metal and placed in the centre of Rome. Statius's poem specifically emphasizes the process of the statue's erection, while Pliny's passage contains a complementary focus on the process of destruction. The actual equestrian statue which is the subject of *Silvae* 1.1 specifically features in the *Panegyricus* as well, forming, according to Pliny, a hindrance to the oldest Roman religious practices, just as the statues in front of the temple in reality polluted it (52.7):[28]

> Ante quidem ingentes hostiarum greges per Capitolinum iter magna sui parte velut intercepti devertere via cogebantur, cum saevissimi domini atrocissima effigies tanto victimarum cruore coleretur, quantum ipse humani sanguinis profundebat.

> Yet previously huge herds of sacrificial animals were forced to turn away from their road, a large part of them intercepted, as it were, on the Capitoline way, so that the most savage image of the cruellest tyrant might be worshipped with as much blood of sacrificial animals as he himself had spilt of human blood.

The central, controlling position of the equestrian statue in the Forum Romanum, represented as a great advantage and a reason for praise in Statius's *Silvae* 1.1, is here associated with impiety.[29] The presence of the statue next to the *clivus Capitolinus* serves to interrupt the victims' progress up to the temple on the Capitoline (already defiled by Domitian's golden images). Instead, many of them are slaughtered in honour of the emperor's *genius* at the foot of his equestrian statue.[30]

---

[27] Cf. Cordes (2017), 50–2, who investigates Pliny's 'Umkodierung' of the liberal use of gold for Domitian's statues in response to Domitianic panegyric.

[28] Commentators agree that Domitian's equestrian statue is meant here: see Durry (1938), 164 *ad loc.*; Kühn (1985), 192 *ad loc.*; Moreno Soldevila (2010), 68 n. 400. The statue forms a hindrance to piety: cf. Suet. *Dom.* 15.2.

[29] See p. 138, especially n. 5, on viewing and control in *Silvae* 1.1.

[30] That the animals are slaughtered in honour of the *genius* of Domitian can be deduced from the immediately preceding mention of Trajan forgoing any veneration of his own *genius* (52.6: *non apud genium tuum . . .*). Domitian's behaviour is then contrasted unfavourably. Cf. also *Silv.* 1.1.57–8, where the earth is said to pant under the weight of the emperor's *genius*: *nec ferro aut aere, laborat / sub genio.*

CONCLUSION   209

Both texts connect the representation of the emperor closely to the man himself, dwelling on questions of the presence of the emperor (or his *genius*) in the sculpture.[31] For the workmen in Statius, the 'presence' of the emperor in his image renders their labour easier (*iuvat ipsa labores / forma dei praesens*, Silv. 1.1.61–2). In Pliny's version, imagining the emperor as present in his image heightens the pleasure of destruction.

When Pliny stresses that it gives particular pleasure to dash the heads of the statues with their proud faces to the ground (*iuvabat illidere solo superbissimos vultus, instare ferro, saevire securibus, Pan.* 52.4), he prompts readers to recall that Statius had emphasized the pleasure of gazing at the face of the statue of Domitian in the forum (*Silv.* 1.1.15–6): *iuvat ora tueri.*[32] Similarly, Pliny describes the joy of the populace in viewing the vengeance wrought on the statues (*nemo tam temperans gaudii seraeque laetitiae . . .*), in contrast with the joy felt by Curtius when he gazes upon the emperor (*laetus mox praeside viso*, 107).[33]

Finally, irony is a powerful means of attacking an earlier text. In Statius's poem, Domitian's power and control over fire and flames is stressed (*Silv.* 1.1.33–5):

> . . . prospectare videris,
> an nova contemptis surgant Palatia flammis
> pulchrius, an tacita vigilet face Troicus ignis . . .

> You seem to gaze before you, [observing] whether the new palace rises more beautiful than ever, despising the flames, or whether the Trojan fire keeps vigil with silent flame . . .

The emperor himself carries certain fire-like qualities in Statius's poem: he is said to shine above the temples (*superfulges*, 1.1.33); his eyes imitate the flames of the stars (*tua sidereas imitantia flammas / lumina*, 103–4). How ironic that a ruler with such complete control over flames both harmful and holy could end up melted down in flames (*postremo truces horrendasque imagines obiectas excoctasque flammis*)!

This passage is not the only place in the *Panegyricus* where Pliny attempts to reinterpret features of Domitianic self-presentation and therefore also has

---

[31] Varner (2004), 112–13, analyses this aspect of Pliny's description.

[32] Noted by Trisoglio (1973), 1274 n. 19.

[33] The expression of the countenance, described as mild and peaceful by Statius (*mitis, Silv.* 1.1.15 and bringing *placidam pacem*, 25), is called *superbissimus, trux,* and *horrendus* by Pliny.

210   BUILDING IN WORDS

to engage with the panegyric texts which codified Domitianic ideology.[34] However, I argue that Pliny's representation of the destruction of Domitian's images is of particular importance, in that the destruction of the statues also functions as an image of Pliny's (literary) undertaking in the *Panegyricus*. In the *Silvae*, the equestrian statue functioned as a programmatic image of Statius's own panegyric poetry, and its construction also represented, on a metaphorical level, the composition of this poetry.[35] His poetry, like the statue, presented a supposedly faithful portrait of the glorious emperor, aesthetically pleasing and impressive in artistic execution, produced at astounding speed. Conversely, in Pliny's text, the destruction of these statues is linked to the overwriting and invalidating of texts like *Silvae* 1.1. In describing the smashing of the statues, Pliny argues against the praise of the *Silvae* while at the same time metaphorically representing their literary demolition.

In *Silvae* 1.1, Statius made some large claims regarding the longevity of the equestrian statue (*Silv.* 1.1.91–4):

Non hoc imbriferas hiemes opus aut Iovis ignem
tergeminum, Aeolii non agmina carceris horret
annorumve moras: stabit, dum terra polusque,
dum Romana dies.

This work fears not rainy winters nor the three-forked fire of Jupiter, not the troops of Aeolus's prison nor the long-drawn years: it shall stand, as long as earth and heaven and Roman day.

Through his choice of words, Statius activates the famous Horatian ode about the poet's *monumentum aere perennius* (Hor. *Carm.* 3.30.1) and Ovid's reworking of the Horatian passage (Ov. *Met.* 15.871–9), both of which deal with the longevity of the poetic *opus* which exceeds that of any physical

[34] Another example is Pliny's reinterpretation of the theme of the imperial gaze and of seeing the emperor. The controlling gaze of the emperor in *Silvae* 1.1 (see chapter 4, n. 5) is reinterpreted in *Pan.* 50.1, where it is suggested that Domitian wanted to own whatever he saw, while Trajan can look without wanting to possess; 51.3–4 develops the theme of seeing and being seen with respect to the circus. Cf. also the accounts of dining with the emperor in *Silvae* and *Panegyricus*: in *Silvae* 4.2, it is a particular honour and pleasure to be allowed to gaze upon the emperor himself (4.2.14–16, 40, 52); compare to this *Pan.* 49.4–8. For a full discussion of the reinterpretation of Domitian's building activities in the *Panegyricus*, see Roche (2011b).

[35] On the process of building as an image of poetic production in *Silvae* 1.1, see pp. 150 and 154–5. On the equestrian statue generally as a programmatic image of Statius's poetry, see Geyssen (1996), esp. ch. 2, and Newlands (2002), esp. 49–50, 69–73, who argues that the poem sets up a competition between poetry and monumental sculpture.

CONCLUSION 211

monument.[36] But unlike Ovid and Horace, Statius does not stress the superiority of poetic monuments, but rather ties the longevity of the statue to that of his poetry, using the intertextual references to stress that *both* statue *and* the authoritative reading of it, Statius's text, will last forever.

Pliny's description of destruction simultaneously dispels both the statue's and the poem's claims to eternity—the statue is smashed, the poem overwritten. Superior claims of eternity are instead formulated for the images of the emperor Trajan. The new bronze statues of Trajan placed (modestly) only in the vestibule of the temple of Jupiter will be eternal, unlike those of Domitian (*Pan.* 52.4): *ergo istae quidem aereae et paucae manent manebuntque quam diu templum ipsum.* However, these new claims to eternity seem more brittle than those of Statius. Association with the temple and cult of Jupiter on the Capitoline is a well-established motif of eternity, but the evident failure of Domitian's attempt at self-memorialization on the Capitoline shows the fragility of these claims.[37] Moreover, a little further on, Pliny stresses the short-lived nature of physical monuments and their unsuitability for the preservation of memory (*Pan.* 55.9): *Arcus enim et statuas, aras etiam templaque demolitur et obscurat oblivio, neglegit carpitque posteritas—*'For oblivion demolishes and obscures arches and statues, even altars and temples, and posterity neglects and destroys them'. Trajan's praise, on the other hand, does not suffer from a similar transience. This, Pliny suggests, is not due to the durability of the literary medium (Domitian's praise, as he demonstrated, is not eternal at all), but to the *content* of that praise—the virtue of Trajan himself. The reputation and popularity of a good princeps are inviolable. The *fama* of the emperor's virtues (or possibly of his lack of virtues), not his monuments, will be truly eternal (*Pan.* 55.9–10), and a good emperor will therefore be praised forever.

Pliny ends his description of the frenzied, vengeful destruction with a positive image of reconstitution and healing. The broken bits of statuary are

---

[36] The correspondences between Statius and Horace are particularly strong (Hor. *Carm.* 3.30.1–5): *Exegi monumentum aere perennius / regalique situ Pyramidum altius, / quod non imber edax, non Aquilo impotens / possit diruere aut innumerabilis / annorum series et fuga temporum.* Statius's mention of the *Iovis ignem*, on the other hand, refers to *Met.* 15.871, where the Ovidian *opus* is said to be susceptible to nec *Iovis ira nec ignis* (871). See Geyssen (1996), 122–3, and Newlands (2002), 69–73.

[37] On the Capitoline and the cult of the temple of Jupiter Optimus Maximus as a trope of eternity, see Edwards (1996), 86–8. Pliny's promise that Trajan's statues will last *quam diu templum ipsum* again recalls Hor. *Carm.* 3.30.8–9, where the durability of the poetic *opus* is assured *dum Capitolium / scandet cum tacita Virgine pontifex*—'as long as the *pontifex* climbs the Capitoline with the silent virgin', i.e. as long as the cult of Jupiter Optimus Maximus on the Capitoline is still intact. Horace's phrase is both abbreviated and universalized by the Statian *dum terra polusque, / dum Romana dies* (*Silv.* 1.1.93–4).

212 BUILDING IN WORDS

melted down *ut ex illo terrore et minis in usum hominum ac voluptates ignibus mutarentur*—'so that they might be changed in the flames from that terror and those menaces to something useful and pleasant for humankind' (*Pan.* 52.5). Cassius Dio (68.1.1) reports that the images were melted down into coins, but Pliny's description rises above such mundane realism. While actual melting down into coins would presumably have occurred at a mint rather than in a public space, the transformation is in Pliny's account a pleasure to *watch* for the populace. There is also a more general meaning to be sought behind this formulation. The process of destruction ends with reconstitution and a new, better beginning. The process of literary destruction, too, in reality provides the *materia* for a new, and better, literary construction. Statius's statue may have been smashed, but from the fragments, the praise of a new and better emperor has been constituted *in usum hominum ac voluptates*.[38]

Conclusion

This short glance at destruction demonstrates to what extent representations of construction and destruction depend on one another—only the existence of the alternative can give each activity its full meaning. At the same time, this excursion has allowed us to revisit some of the crucial results of this study.

The meaning of monuments is not fixed. Whatever the intentions of a builder (if we can ever know them)—once a structure exists, it is subject to debate and interpretation. Ancient texts that deal with monuments do not allow us easy access to the way in which a monument was looked at—instead, they participate in a never-ending contest of interpretation. Pliny's account of destruction once more demonstrates how telling the story of the making or unmaking of a structure is an extremely important way of participating in this process of meaning-making, of reinterpreting and reframing finished projects. Representing creation can raise awareness of the 'madeness' of a monument and encourage admiration of artistry, cost, speed, or effort (Chapter 1). On the other hand, both construction and destruction constitute

---

[38] In his tenth satire, Juvenal describes a comparable scene of statue destruction (*Juv.* 10.61–4). There, the head of Sejanus is melted down and turned into *urceoli pelves sartago matellae* –'pitchers, basins, a frying-pan, piss-pots' (64). Juvenal may be responding to Pliny's sanctimonious conclusion: in *Sat.* 10 the melting down of the images of Sejanus—and possibly also historiographical accounts of this event?—is being 'cooked down' to furnish the classic material of satire.

CONCLUSION 213

alterations of the status quo, and by representing them in certain ways, such alterations can be endowed with complex moral dimensions (Chapters 2 and 4).

Representing the process of creating architecture allows writers to reflect on their own activity, to consider the process of creation—and its reversal. Different chapters have explored the polyvalence of the poetological image of construction. In writing about architectural processes, writers can think through the aesthetics or ambition of their literary work (Chapters 4 and 3, respectively) and question or assert the power and durability of literature (Chapter 5 and this Conclusion).

The literal and metaphorical dimensions of building processes are not confined to distinct texts, nor do they exist within the same text independently of each other. Pliny's representation of statue-destruction reveals his own deep understanding of the way in which architectural and literary construction are tied together in the *Silvae* (explored in Chapter 4). In his reversal of the (physical and literary) erection of the statue, he represents architectural destruction in order to perform—and reflect on—a simultaneous process of literary destruction.

Epilogue

Constructing *Romanità*

The Obelisk at the Foro Mussolini

Roman representations of construction and destruction give meaning to the physical world in which they function, and they engage with each other in contests of interpretation and memory-making. Since antiquity, these representations have undergone two thousand years of reception, strategic reinterpretation, and reuse. Our understanding of how Roman construction looked and what it signified has, in part, been shaped by this process. This afterword offers some reflections on one particular moment in the history of this reception. How have ancient Roman representations of construction shaped modern conceptions of architecture and 'Romanness'? Conversely, how have modern receptions of ancient Roman building influenced our image of what ancient construction looked like and what it meant? We remain in the city of Rome, but travel forward in time to the twentieth century and the Fascist regime of Benito Mussolini (1922–1943).

Constructing and Deconstructing the City of Rome

The architectural and urbanistic transformation of Rome during the Fascist era was staggering in its scale and speed.[1] It continued (and largely subsumed) a comprehensive reconfiguration of urban spaces begun in post-unification Rome after 1870.[2] The impact of these Fascist transformations was partly due to the effective staging and representation of the *processes* of demolition and construction. Modern (mass) media allowed for the communication of the impact of construction projects in progress to a large audience almost in 'real time': through newspapers and other print publications, sometimes

---

[1] This process of transformation has been well studied. See e.g. Cederna (2006), originally published in 1979, for a pioneering and highly critical analysis of the Fascist interventions; Painter (2005) for an accessible overview; Kallis (2012) for important methodological reflections and (2014) for a fuller treatment; and the recent study of Marcello (2018) with up-to-date bibliography.

[2] Kallis (2012), esp. 43–4, 47–51.

Building in Words. Bettina Reitz-Joosse, Oxford University Press. © Oxford University Press 2021.
DOI: 10.1093/oso/9780197610688.003.0008

EPILOGUE 215

accompanied by illustrations, via the radio, and most innovatively, through film, which reached mass audiences in the form of newsreels, shown before feature films in cinemas.[3] The latter were produced by LUCE (L'Unione Cinematografica Educativa), founded in 1924 and generously endowed with state funding for the production of documentaries and newsreels, which were to articulate the transformation and modernization of Italy under the beneficial leadership of 'Il Duce'.

Certain rhetorical gestures tend to characterize this media coverage. The striking and sustained focus on the violence and physicality of the demolitions which usually preceded construction, especially in densely built-up urban locations, is staged almost in terms of an attack on the city's urban fabric. It serves to communicate Fascism's 'violent and assertive' character, as well as the 'revolutionary nature of the regime'.[4] Furthermore, both the staging and the coverage of demolition and construction processes often focus on Mussolini's personal involvement, especially for the most prestigious projects. Emblematic of this are the many representations, in photography and film, of Mussolini himself wielding the pickaxe (*piccone*) and thereby beginning the process of demolition (Figure E.1).[5] Mussolini's involvement in the physical processes of demolition and construction is presented as very 'hands on': images of Mussolini joining forces with workmen are intended to show 'Il Duce' as close to the people and not afraid of getting his hands dirty, to emphasize his impressive physical prowess— an important characteristic of the Fascist 'New Man'—and his political responsibility for the process as a whole.[6] This aspect of the rhetoric of these images becomes especially noticeable when compared to ancient Roman strategies of communicating a builder's personal involvement and agency, as investigated in Chapter 1. There, I considered Roman building inscriptions' use of *fecit*, and visual representations of the patron watching the proceedings of construction. In Roman antiquity, agency was usually constructed without any suggestion of physical involvement in manual labour, a difference which highlights the highly divergent connotations of manual labour projected by the ancient Roman elite, on the one hand, and Fascist leadership

---

[3] Pilat (2016) analyses the visual rhetoric of photographs and illustrations in the coverage of demolition and construction around the imperial fora and the Mausoleum of Augustus during the *ventennio*. On newsreels (*cinegiornali*) during the *ventennio*, see Dalla Pria (2012); Pomeroy (2018), 265–6.

[4] Pilat (2016), 336, 339, and *passim*.

[5] Dalla Pria (2012), 145; Pilat (2016), esp. 336–8.

[6] Cf. Della Pria (2012), 186–7, on Mussolini's comparable depiction during agricultural labour. On the importance of the body of the workers in construction images, see Pilat (2016), 331–3.

Figure E.1. Mussolini wielding the *piccone*.
Photo: Istituto Luce.

in twentieth-century Italy, on the other, as well as the difference between the constituencies which the leaders in question chiefly had to rely on for political support.[7]

Romanizing Obelisks

In what follows, I focus on one particularly high-profile engineering project of the *ventennio fascista*. Since 1927, a complex of mostly sports-related buildings was under construction in the north of Rome, on a previously swampy terrain next to the Tiber. As the space developed, it became an important arena for Fascist political representation and was christened the 'Foro Mussolini' (today,

---

[7] However, representations of direct physical involvement of the ruler or patron are not entirely without parallel in ancient Rome: compare, for example, Vespasian carrying the first bucket of rubble on his shoulders during the commencement of the reconstruction of the temple of Jupiter Capitolinus (p. 1), or the Basilica Aemilia frieze, with a patron or his ancestor possibly portrayed as lifting stones himself (pp. 41–2).

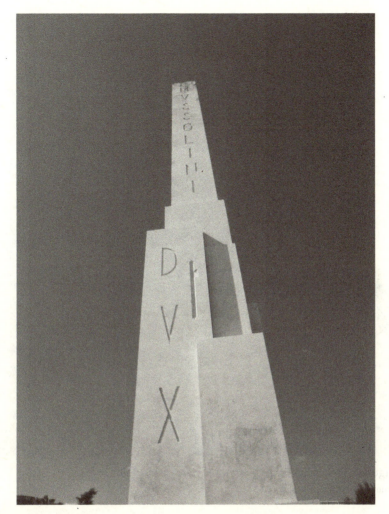

Figure E.2. Obelisk as it stands in the Foro Italico today.
Photo: author.

it is called the Foro Italico).[8] The entrance to the Foro Italico is dominated by a huge monolithic marble obelisk, which to this day bears the inscription *MVSSOLINI DVX* (Figure E.2).[9] The idea of placing an obelisk dedicated to Mussolini at the entrance of the complex was conceived by Renato Ricci, the

---

[8] On the Foro Mussolini complex, see e.g. Painter (2005), 40–9; Kallis (2014), 163–70; and Caporilli and Simeoni (1990).

[9] D'Amelio (2009) offers a thorough investigation of the history of the obelisk. See also briefly Benton (2001), 97–8, and more extensively Lamers and Reitz-Joosse (2016), 28–61, on the Foro and the obelisk.

Figure E.3. Obelisk in the quarries of Carrara in 1928.
From Opera Nazionale Balilla (1937), 238.

president of the Fascist youth organization Opera Nazionale Balilla, the headquarters of which were situated at the Foro Mussolini.[10]

The obelisk was to be made entirely of white Carrara marble, with the tip to be covered in gold. In 1928 a suitably large block of marble, free of imperfections and cracks, was identified in the quarries of Carrara. The block was then extracted, cut, and covered with a protective encasing of wood and iron (Figure E.3). Thus prepared for transport, the monolith,

---

[10] On Ricci, see Setta (1986); Zanzanaini (2004). On Ricci as the driving force behind the obelisk, see Benton (2001), 97; D'Amelio (2009), *passim*.

weighing almost 300 tons (excluding its heavy cover), began its precarious journey from the quarry in the mountains to the marina of Forte dei Marmi, transported on sleighs and dragged by sixty-six oxen. Floating between two pontoons, it was conveyed to Rome by sea and the river Tiber, and finally arrived there in June 1929. Three years later, it was transported from Farnesina to the site of the Foro, erected by means of a specially erected lifting tower (Figure E.4), and inaugurated in the presence of Mussolini and

Figure E.4. Erection of the obelisk.
From Opera Nazionale Balilla (1937), 241.

220 BUILDING IN WORDS

Figure E.5. Benito Mussolini and Renato Ricci at the inauguration of the obelisk.
From Opera Nazionale Balilla (1937), 7.

Ricci on 4 November 1932 as part of the decennial celebrations of the March on Rome (Figure E.5).[11]

The obelisk and its architectural surroundings have to be understood in the context of the ideal of 'Romanness' (*romanità*), which the Fascists moulded into a constitutive element of their political ideology.[12] Ancient Rome (the city, the empire, and the 'idea') became a crucial reference point

---

[11] For details of this process, see D'Amelio (2009), 41–83.
[12] They did not, however, 'invent' the ideal of *romanità*: cf. e.g. De Haan (2015) on the role of *romanità* in the formation and consolidation of the Italian nation in the late nineteenth century.

EPILOGUE 221

for Italian Fascism, in particular for its symbols, institutions, values, and forms of expression. However, *romanità* was also an extremely flexible notion: in Fascist Italy, the Roman past could be activated through carefully selected references and general gestures towards Roman aesthetics, *mores*, or history.[13] The flexible nature of Fascist *romanità* is well exemplified by the Foro Italico itself, initially known as the Foro Mussolini. The name given to the complex clearly evokes the newly excavated imperial fora in the city centre, most of them named after the emperors under whose reign they were built.[14] The label 'Foro Mussolini' therefore communicates a message about Mussolini's own position within the Fascist regime, as well as the imperialistic ambitions that he nurtured for Italy. However, similarities between the imperial fora and the Foro Mussolini remained largely confined to the name: in terms of use, layout, and aesthetics, the sports complex had little in common with the commercial and legal centres of imperial Rome. Instead, its architectural layout and function rather recalled large-scale imperial bath complexes.[15]

Likewise, the erection of an obelisk serves in itself as a reference to antiquity, since these monuments were conspicuous displays of the emperor's power in imperial Rome.[16] But a whole range of features further surrounded the Mussolini obelisk with an aura of *romanità*, though none of them, strictly speaking, had an ancient Roman precedent:[17] the placing of the obelisk in the context of a (neo-)imperial forum, the Latin inscription on the obelisk itself, and the material of the obelisk: Carrara marble rather than, like its ancient forebears, Egyptian granite. The choice of material could be used to forge a new link with the ancient Roman past: since the quarries at Carrara had first been exploited in antiquity and had allowed Augustus to transform Rome into a city of marble, Carrara marble was a Roman as well as an 'Italian' choice, and conveyed a general sense of

[13] On Fascism and the cult of *romanità*, see e.g. Visser (1992); Stone (1999); Giardina and Vauchez (2000); Nelis (2007a, 2007b, and 2011); Arthurs (2012).

[14] On the Fascist exploration of the imperial fora and the construction of the new Via dell'Impero across them, see the individual chapters in Cardilli Alloisi (1995). Accessible overviews are Tamassia (1985), 181–194; Schieder (2006), 717–20; Painter (2005), 22–5. A selection of the photographic documentation by the Istituto Luce can be found in Insolera (2001), 132–59.

[15] See further Lamers and Reitz-Joosse (2016), 38–42. On the appropriation of Roman architectural forms in the architecture of the Fascist period in general, see Welge (2005).

[16] On the obelisks of Rome and their histories, see Iversen (1968) and D'Onofrio (1992); on the cultural history of obelisks generally, see e.g. Curran et al. (2009).

[17] On the connection of Mussolini's obelisks (including the Foro Mussolini obelisk and the Axum stele) with Roman, especially Augustan, displays of power, see Wilkins (2005), 61–2.

222   BUILDING IN WORDS

romanità. All of these measures served to radically 'romanize' the obelisk. Its Egyptian origins were precisely what had rendered obelisks such prestigious objects in ancient Rome. The strong emphasis by the Fascist regime and media on the 'Italian' story of this particular obelisk, on its impressive process of manufacture and transportation, can partly be explained as an attempt to compensate for the loss of the 'foreign' prestige of this type of monument.[18]

The Journey of the Obelisk

Hardly any type of monument depends for its impact so much upon its 'madeness' as an obelisk. In Chapter 1, I discussed how in antiquity inscriptions, visual representations, and literary texts were employed to activate and manipulate a viewer-reader's awareness of the effort, difficulty, and spectacle of the transportation and erection of an obelisk. Comparable strategies can be identified in the many depictions of the Mussolini obelisk's creation, transportation, and erection in a variety of media. Additionally, many of these representations strategically 'Romanize' the process of the obelisk's creation in a variety of ways.

Every step of the obelisk's journey and erection was meticulously documented and reported in the national press, in newspapers, weeklies, and specialized journals. These publications were often lavishly illustrated with photographic documentation (cf. Figures E.3, E.4, E.6). The Istituto Luce also filmed the proceedings, using the material for documentaries and newsreels.[19] In the last category a striking twenty-five items on the obelisk alone were produced and presented to the Italian public.[20] Via all these different channels, the long duration, the cost, the technical hazards, and the allegedly 'superhuman' achievement of the project were documented and

---

[18] The imperialist claim communicated by the import of foreign, especially African, obelisks was of course also not lost on Mussolini, who had the so-called stele of Axum transported to Rome in 1937 and erected in front of the Ministry of the Colonies in the Piazza di Porta Capena. The stolen monument was only returned to Ethiopia in 2008. See Curran et al. (2009), 291–3.

[19] On the Luce coverage of the obelisk transportation, see Tiberi (2009). Films and photographs of the process can be viewed on the website of Archivio Luce (www.archivioluce.com) and in D'Amelio (2009).

[20] D'Amelio (2009), 10.

Figure E.6. Demolition of the concrete structure used for erection.
From Opera Nazionale Balilla (1937), 242.

extolled. For example, an article which appeared in 1933 in the architectural design magazine *Casabella* on the subject of the obelisk begins:[21]

> When one is admiring, nose in the air, this white block of Carrara marble, which will recall for centuries the name of Mussolini, and if one roughly estimates the dimensions and weights, one cannot avoid one very simple

[21] The article, written by the editor, the rationalist architect Giuseppe Pagano (1896–1945), appeared in the first installment of January 1933 (22–3), and is here quoted from its reproduction in Insolera and Sette (2003), 30–1.

224 BUILDING IN WORDS

and legitimate question: how was this Cyclopian monolith brought here and raised on its base?[22]

The opening of this article shows a certain similarity to the opening of *Silvae* 1.1, which also begins with a sequence of questions about the manufacturing history of the colossal statue of Domitian.[23] When Pagano calls the obelisk a *ciclopico monolito*, with its suggestions of colossality and mythical proportions, he evokes mythical workmen familiar from ancient sources—like Statius, whose opening lines also reflected (more explicitly) on a potential involvement of the Cyclopes in manufacturing the work (*Silv.* 1.1.3–4). It is unlikely that Pagano was an avid reader of Statius. Rather, this overlap shows how certain elements of the rhetoric of making transcend their political contexts and times, and also that Pagano (like many of his contemporaries) embues his representation with a deliberate sense of 'Romanness'. In what follows, further categories of praise which we have frequently encountered in this study are activated. Pagano stresses the speed at which the work was executed (*una velocità veramente esemplar[e]*), and devotes much attention to the immense difficulty of the work, describing in detail the design of the lifting mechanism, the dangers and crises of the actual lifting process, and the ways in which they were solved. Renato Ricci is praised for his exceptional daring in attempting the raising, in ways which are somewhat reminiscent of the inscription, discussed in Chapter 1, which praises Constantius II for finally erecting an abandoned obelisk:[24]

> For one and a half years, the obelisk remained lying there (i.e. on the shore), waiting for the one who would dare to raise it. Through the decision of His Excellency Renato Ricci, the leading force of ever new daring undertakings, the honour of this most difficult undertaking became the responsibility of the architect Costantino Costantini....[25]

[22] 'Quando si sta ad ammirare col naso in aria quel candido blocco di marmo di Carrara che ricorderà nei secoli il nome di Mussolini, e se ne valutano ad occhio le misure e i pesi, non si può evitare una domanda molto semplice e legittima: come fu trasportato fin lassù e innalzato sulla sua base questo ciclopico monolito?'

[23] Discussed earlier, pp. 137–8.

[24] See pp. 28–9.

[25] Per un anno e mezzo è rimasto [l'obelisco] coricato in attesa di chi osasse innalzarlo. Per decisione di S. E. Renato Ricci, animatore di sempre nuovi ardimenti, l'onore di questa arditissima impresa è spettata all'architetto Costantino Costantini....

EPILOGUE   225

This presentation of events uses the three-year delay to advantage and at the same time smoothly elides the fact that Ricci, as the one who had commissioned the obelisk, could hardly escape the responsibility of raising it, and that it required no special daring on his part to organize it. Finally, the article directly addresses the theme of memory and future recollections of the raising. Of the moment when the concrete construction used for the raising is spectacularly shattered and the obelisk freed from the concrete scaffolding (Figure E.6), Pagano writes:

> The final collapse of the last pier will never be deleted from the memory of those who experienced the good fortune of being present.[26]

Those who attended this spectacular moment would never forget it—but how about those who did not? The dramatic blow-by-blow account in the article, which stresses the aural and visual impact of the process, is combined with photographs showing its different stages. The most dramatic moments of the raising are recreated for the readers' imagination, as in the description of a near-disaster during the demolition:

> The pier leaned, was on the point of tipping over, leaned; but when one was already expecting the thunder of collapse, the engine made a strange noise, and the support swayed worryingly towards the monolith: the ropes held three times.[27]

The question suggested in the first sentence of the article, and the dramatic representation of its answer, are made part of the reader's appreciation of the obelisk.[28] Although the possibilities of modern media render the communicative situation somewhat different from that of antiquity, the same basic attempt to create or manipulate a 'memory' of construction is clearly recognizable.[29]

[26] 'Il crollo finale dell'ultima stilata non sarà mai cancellato dalla memoria di chi ebbe l'avventura di assistervi.'

[27] 'La trave . . . si inclina, sta per ribaltarsi, si inclina; ma quando si attende già lo scroscio della caduta, il motore 'rata' e la stilata oscilla paurosamente verso il monolito: le funi, per tre volte, resistono.'

[28] Cf. D'Amelio (2009), 13, discussing the impact of the media coverage of the obelisk: 'Con un'abile operazione di propaganda, l'epopea della sua realizzazione diventa parte integrante dell'obelisco stesso.'

[29] Other examples of media coverage of the transportation and raising of the obelisk include Maccaroni (1929); Brigante Colonna (1929); and Caffarelli (1938).

226 BUILDING IN WORDS

Media coverage of the obelisk also explicitly stressed the connection between Roman and Fascist engineering achievements, in particular regarding the technical mastery and the enormous effort of raising an obelisk. For example, in the publication accompanying the official opening of the Foro Mussolini in 1937, it was suggested that the Carrara workmen had in the Fascist era renewed a typically Roman enterprise.[30] Just like the Egyptian pedigree of the monument itself, the fact that Egyptians had already erected obelisks successfully long before the Romans was conveniently left unmentioned. Instead, tangible connections between the ancient and the Fascist effort were inventively 'discovered': in a Luce documentary of May 1929, for example, a large square marble block, destined for the podium of the obelisk, was shown from two sides, one of them cut smoothly with modern methods of marble working, one allegedly showing the incisions of chisels used by ancient Roman workmen.[31] In another newsreel, the opening legend read:[32] 'The transportation of the block of marble took place by land, by sea and by river, lasted almost four years, and renewed the ancient achievements of the transportation and raising of obelisks in Rome.' The obelisk was presented to the public as an achievement directly linked to the engineering achievements of the ancient Romans. In this way, the obelisk is 'Romanized', while the emphasis on the parallel between Roman and Fascist engineering also impacts the viewers' image of the ancient Romans themselves. The ancient Romans are constructed as a people of able engineers and brave, passionate workmen, whose indomitable spirit lives on in the Italians of the Fascist age.

Making Memories for the Future: The *Codex fori Mussolini*

One unique document particularly underlines how the regime attempted to tie the Mussolini obelisk to (their version of) Roman antiquity. The document also offers particular insights into the conscious creation, in 1932, of memories for a different age in the distant future. This document is called the

[30] Opera Nazionale Balilla (1937), 86: 'L'esperienza fu inventata, l'ingegno e la tenacia ebbero ragione di tutti: i carraresi rinnovarano in tempo fascista l'impresa tipicamente romana.'

[31] See D03470 on www.archivioluce.it, with the following text: 'Due lati di un medesimo blocco di marmo: uno fu tagliato dagli antichi romani, l'altro con i moderni sistemi elettrici' (at TCR 00:17:49). Cf. also D'Amelio (2009), 10 with n. 15.

[32] In D03470, which opens with the text 'Il trasporto del blocco di marmo avvenne per terra, per mare e per fiume, durò quasi quattro anni e rinnovò le antiche imprese del trasferimento e dell'innalzamento degli obelischi a Roma' (at TCR 00:06:06).

EPILOGUE 227

Codex fori Mussolini.[33] It is a Latin text, which, together with a number of gold coins, was immured in the marble base of the obelisk before its inauguration. The text had been composed by Aurelio Giuseppe Amatucci (1867–1960), an eminent Latinist of the time,[34] and executed on parchment in medieval-style calligraphy with illuminations.[35] While the original document presumably remains buried under the obelisk, the text was also published (though never translated) several times in the 1930s: in a newsletter of the Opera Nazionale Balilla (1932), a journal for schoolteachers (1933), and an expensively produced book on the Foro Mussolini (1937).[36]

The text of ca. 1,200 words is written in a classical, highly emphatic style, and comprises three sections. The first and longest of these (i–lvi; 1–69)[37] deals with the political career of Benito Mussolini, the second with the Opera Nazionale Balilla and its president Renato Ricci (lvii–lxxxii, 69–97), while the final section (lxxxiii–cxviii, 98–141) is devoted to the construction of the Foro Mussolini, and especially to the quarrying, transportation, and erection of the obelisk. Since the text is entombed in the podium of the obelisk, inaccessible to anyone as long as the obelisk stands, it was not, or at least not primarily, intended for an audience of contemporaries. Instead, as a 'time capsule', it was intended to communicate an authorized version of history to those who might, in a remote future, (re-)discover the Forum complex, or seek to move the Mussolini obelisk. Perhaps recent archaeological discoveries relating to the Roman emperors and their building projects inspired Fascist leaders to consider and 'stage' their own future rediscovery in this particular way. Through Amatucci's text, the Fascist regime was attempting to mould its own future reception. The *Codex* was strategically placed under a monument which served as a concentrated statement of Fascism's power and dominance, as well as that of its leader.[38]

---

[33] Several sections of the *Codex* are cited and discussed in the groundbreaking Aicher (2000), 130–2 and 134. Since I first analysed the closing section of the *Codex* in my dissertation in 2012, I have undertaken a detailed investigation of it, together with Han Lamers, now published as Lamers and Reitz-Joosse (2016). Many of the improvements to the argument since the dissertation stage are owed to this fruitful collaboration. For an easily accessible version of the text see https://flt.hf.uio.no/, an online library of Latin texts of Italian Fascism, edited by Han Lamers and myself.

[34] On Amatucci, see Nazzaro (2009).

[35] See Lamers and Reitz-Joosse (2016), 75–81.

[36] For details on these publications, see Lamers and Reitz-Joosse (2016), 8–9.

[37] Line numbers refer to Lamers and Reitz-Joosse (2016). Roman numerals refer to the Latin texts, Arabic numerals to the translation.

[38] Another point in support of this hypothesis is the fact that the text supplies information that a contemporary reader would not have required, such as the date of the First World War (ii, 2). See further Lamers and Reitz-Joosse (2016), esp. 62–81.

228 BUILDING IN WORDS

The story of the creation of the obelisk under which the text lies forms the climax and conclusion of the entire *Codex*. Amatucci tells the story of the obelisk chronologically (*Codex* xcviii–cxiii, 116–41):[39]

Quo vero studio, quibus adsiduis conatibus, qua anxia cura Carariae montes longe lateque temptati atque pervestigati sint ut marmor reperiretur ex quo obeliscus monolithus DVCI dicaretur haud facile enarrari potest. Denique candida moles, quae in altitudinem LX, in latitudinem X fere pedes egrederetur, reperta est solisque lumine refulsit. Sed huius inventionis gaudio nova cura successit, cum moles illa ex monte in aequum, Cararia Romam transvehenda esset. Quod quidem nulla antea gens nisi Romani perfecerant; neque qua ratione Romani perfecerint satis constat. Vicit tamen architectorum nostrorum acre ingenium, fabrorum singularis peritia, omnium patriae DVCISQUE ingens amor. Quo factum est ut illa moles ferro lignoque mira arte contexto inclusa fabris molientibus viam primum ex monte in urbem atque ex urbe ad mare inter civium, qui floribus ornaverant, gratulationes precesque veheretur, deinde duobus iunctis novo artificio ratibus, quae inter se onus illud |XII| fere pondo acciperent atque transveherent, quam difficillimo cursu mari Tyrrheno et per flumen Tiberim Romam ad divi Pauli portum perveniret.

In divi Pauli portu quinque fere menses stetit navigium illud, cui nomen "Apuanum" inditum erat, dum flumen augeret. Denique a.d. X Kal. Dec. a. MCMXXX ad Farnesinam adduxerunt atque opportunam tempestatem nacti obeliscum exposuerunt. Qui, a. d. V Kal. Nov. a. X. a fasc. instaur. machinis instrumentisque idoneis basi quadratae impositus, altitudine pedum fere CXXX, cuspide aurea, marmoris candore ceteros omnes vincit.

It is not an easy task to describe the genuine dedication, the unremitting attempts, the solicitous attention with which the mountains of Carrara were tested and searched far and wide, to find marble from which a monolithic obelisk might be dedicated to the LEADER. Finally a shining mass was found, which exceeded in height sixty feet, in width almost ten feet, and glittered in the sunlight. But upon the joy of discovery followed a new task, because this mass had to be transported from the mountains to the plain and from Carrara to Rome. This indeed no people except the Romans had earlier managed, and how they managed it is not sufficiently clear. But nevertheless the strong talent of our architects, the singular skill of our craftsmen, and the huge love of all for the fatherland and for the LEADER prevailed. Thus it was achieved that that

[39] Text, line numbers, and translations according to Lamers and Reitz-Joosse (2016).

EPILOGUE   229

mass, encased in iron and wood woven together by miraculous skill, as a result of craftsmen's toil, travelled first the road from the mountain into the city and from the city to the sea amid the rejoicing and good wishes of the citizens who had decorated it with flowers. By means of two pontoons that had been connected to each other by a new system and which between them supported and conveyed that load of almost 400 tons, it then travelled by the most difficult route possible, over the Tyrrhenian sea and via the river Tiber, and arrived in Rome at the harbour of San Paolo.

In the harbour of San Paolo, that raft, which was called 'Apuano', stood for almost five months, until the river swelled. Finally, on 22 November 1930 (VIII), they transported it to Farnesina, and, when excellent weather conditions had arrived, they offloaded the obelisk. On 27 October in the tenth year after the restoration of the Fasces, it was placed on its square base with suitable machines and tools, and with its height of almost 130 feet, with its gold tip, and with the shine of its marble, it surpasses all others.

In relation to the text as a whole, the amount of space and detail lavished on the obelisk is striking. In total, it receives a stunning twenty-four lines, compared to, for example, three lines spent on the entire building activity of Mussolini and on his excavation of ancient monuments (xliii–xlv, 53–6). Furthermore, the story of the obelisk is treated last in the text. The reader is invited to consider the obelisk as the pinnacle and culmination of all achievements of Fascism, the Italian people, and their leader.

Most of the representative strategies employed in this paragraph are familiar from the news coverage of the time. Amatucci, too, stresses the skill of the architects, the love for Il Duce which apparently inspired all those involved to superhuman efforts, and the almost unsurmountable *difficultas* of the task. The achievement is again deliberately 'Romanized', Egyptian predecessors passed over.[40] While the text explicitly and implicitly (by its language and diction) constructs the achievement as 'Roman', Amatucci does not, in this passage, obviously refer to specific Roman literary models.[41] Although some of the themes prominent in the accounts of obelisks in Pliny the Elder and Ammianus Marcellinus (such as the size and novelty of the ships used for transportation) also occur in Amatucci's text,

---

[40] Cf. *Quod quidem nulla antea gens nisi Romani perfecerant; neque qua ratione Romani perfecerint satis constat* (civ–cv, 123–4), with Lamers and Reitz-Joosse (2016), *ad loc.*

[41] The text does activate several ancient models elsewhere; see Lamers and Reitz-Joosse (2016), 23–7.

230 BUILDING IN WORDS

clear intertextual links to those passages are absent, as are links with other prominent descriptions of Roman engineering.[42] Instead, a general impression of *romanità* created by the language and classical style is combined with rhetoric and themes which unite contemporary media coverage and ancient models.

The relation between this text and its memorial function is somewhat complex. On the one hand, the text elides its own memorial function. It is the obelisk itself, and not the text, which is to serve as a lasting memory of the greatness of Fascism, as the conclusion of the text makes clear (cxix–cxxi, 142–6):

> Stat in ipso aditu *Fori Mussolini* et patriae fata per DVCEM renovata, DVCIS in patriam excelsum invictumque animum, civium erga DVCEM immotam fidem, res per Fasces praeclare gestas in perpetuum consecrabit.

> It stands in the very entrance to the *Foro Mussolini* and it will immortalize in eternity the fortunes of the fatherland, restored by the LEADER, the excellent and unconquered spirit of the LEADER regarding the fatherland, the immovable loyalty of the citizens to the LEADER, the outstanding achievements of Fascism.

The competition between architectural and textual monumentalization and memorialization has been prominent throughout this investigation. The *Codex* has no need of asserting its own memorial powers, since the very fact of its ever being read (in its original version on the buried parchment) requires the obelisk's removal, relocation, or collapse. At the moment of reading, the text's claims about the eternity of the obelisk will already have been proven false, but they will have been superseded by the eternity of the text itself. Through the medium of the *Codex*, the memories of the obelisk's making are set up to outlast the monument itself.

This short Epilogue has shone a spotlight on one moment in the reception of Roman construction. It serves to create a context for my conclusions about construction in ancient Rome in a number of ways. First, it helps us to appreciate the extent to which our modern image of Roman building is

---

[42] Except perhaps for the relatively generic *topos* of the impossibility of description, on which see pp. 52–8.

shaped not only by its physical remains or its ancient literary representations, but also, inescapably, by the story of reception which separates us from—and at the same time connects us with—ancient Rome. Spectacular stagings and representations of constructions, and, in the Italian Fascists' case, the explicit claim to the *romanità* of such undertakings, influence our own image of ancient construction. More broadly, the case of Fascist Italy highlights the fact that the ancient Romans' reputation as a people of skilled builders and engineers is not only a result of their achievements in this area during the Roman Empire, but also of later constructions of what it meant to be 'Roman'. Second, the similarities and differences between ancient and modern strategies of representing construction bring into focus the specificities of either period: for example, the *piccone*-wielding Duce alerts us to the specific value placed on manual labour in different types of societies. Third, while ancient Rome's builders, rulers, and elites are separated from us by a sometimes all-too-comfortable temporal distance, the *ventennio fascista* is not. Appreciating how stagings and representations of construction contributed to the hold on power of a totalitarian regime in living memory brings home to us in a powerfully immediate way the emotional force and the manipulative potential of ancient Roman construction, of its staging and representation.

Bibliography

Adam, J. (1984), *La construction romaine, materiaux et techniques*, Paris.

Adams, J. N. (2016), *An Anthology of Informal Latin, 200 BC–AD 900: Fifty Texts with Translations and Linguistic Commentary*, Cambridge.

Ahl, F. (1984a), 'The Art of Safe Criticism in Greece and Rome', *AJPh* 105, 174–208.

Ahl, F. (1984b), 'The Rider and the Horse: Politics and Power in Roman Poetry from Horace to Statius', *ANRW* II.32.1, 40–124.

Aicher, P. (2000), 'Mussolini's Forum and the Myth of Augustan Rome', *Classical Bulletin* 76, 117–39.

Albertson, F. C. (1990), 'The Basilica Aemilia Frieze. Religion and Politics in Late Republican Rome', *Latomus* 49, 801–15.

Alföldy, G. (1990), *Der Obelisk auf dem Petersplatz in Rom. Ein historisches Monument der Antike*, Heidelberg.

Alföldy, G. (1991), 'Augustus und die Inschriften: Tradition und Innovation. Die Geburt der imperialen Epigraphik', *Gymnasium* 98, 289–324.

Alfonsi, L. (1944), 'Aurelio Giuseppe Amatucci', *Aevum* 18, 7–12.

Almar, K. P. (1990), *Inscriptiones Latinae*, Odense.

Altekamp, S., Marcks-Jacobs, C., and Seiler, P. (2013) (eds.), *Perspektiven der Spolienforschung (1): Spoliierung und Transposition*, Berlin; Boston.

Amatucci, A. (1937), 'Il Codice di Foro Mussolini', in Opera Nazionale Balilla (1937), 103–4.

Ambrosetti, G. (1960), 'Monumento degli Haterii', in Bianchi Bandinelli, R. (ed.), *Enciclopedia dell'Arte Antica, Classica e Orientale* 3, 1112–15.

Anderson, J. C. (1997), *Roman Architecture and Society*, Baltimore, MD.

Anderson, W. S. (1969), *The Art of the* Aeneid, Englewood Cliffs, NJ.

André, J., Bloch, R., and Rouveret, A. (1981), *Pline l'Ancien: Histoire Naturelle, livre XXXVI*, Paris.

Armstrong, D. (1995), 'The Impossibility of Metathesis: Philodemus and Lucretius on Form and Content in Poetry', in Obbink, D. (ed.), *Philodemus and Poetry*, Oxford, 210–32.

Armstrong, R. (2009), 'Against Nature? Some Augustan Perspectives on Man-Made Marvels', in Hardie, P. (ed.), *Paradox and the Marvellous in Augustan Literature and Culture*, Oxford, 75–94.

Arthurs, J. (2012), *Excavating Modernity: The Roman Past in Fascist Italy*, Ithaca, NY.

Ash, R. (2007), 'Victim and Voyeur: Rome as a Character in Tacitus' *Histories* 3', in Larmour and Spencer (2007), 211–37.

Asper, M. (1997), *Onomata allotria: Zur Genese, Struktur und Funktion poetologischer Metaphern bei Kallimachos*, Stuttgart.

Asper, M. (2004), *Kallimachos / Werke: griechisch und deutsch*, Darmstadt.

Assmann, J. (1999), *Das kulturelle Gedächtnis: Schrift, Erinnerung und politische Identität in frühen Hochkulturen*, Munich.

Augoustakis, A. (2016), *Statius*, Thebaid 8, Oxford.

234 BIBLIOGRAPHY

Austin, R. G. (1955), *P. Vergili Maronis Aeneidos Liber Quartus*, Oxford.

Austin, R. G. (1971), *P. Vergili Maronis Aeneidos Liber Primus*, Oxford.

Bailey, D. M. (1996), 'Honorific Columns, Cranes, and the Tuna Epitaph', in Bailey, D. M. (ed.), *Archaeological Research in Roman Egypt* (JRA Supp. 19), Ann Arbor, 155–68.

Barchiesi, A. (1988), *Seneca: Le Fenicie*, Venice.

Barchiesi, A. (1997), *The Poet and the Prince: Ovid and Augustan Discourse*, Berkeley, CA.

Barker, S. (2018), 'The Demolition, Salvage, and Recycling Industry in Imperial Rome', *Aedificare* 4, 37–88.

Barth, C. (1664), *P. Papinii Statii opera quae extant. Casp. Barthius recensuit et animadversationibus locupletissimis illustravit*, Zwickau.

Bartoli, A. (1950), 'Il fregio figurato della Basilica Emilia', *BdA* 35, 289–94.

Beagon, M. (1992), *Roman Nature: The Thought of Pliny the Elder*, Oxford.

Beagon, M. (1996), 'Nature and Views of Her Landscapes in Pliny the Elder', in Shipley and Salmon (1996), 284–309.

Beard, M. (2003), 'The Spectator and the Column: Reading and Writing the Language of Gesture', in Huet and Scheid (2003), 265–79.

Becker, A. S. (1995), *The Shield of Achilles and the Poetics of Ekphrasis*, Lanham, MD, and London.

Benndorf, O., and Schöne, R. (1867), *Die antiken Bildwerke des Lateranensischen Museums*, Leipzig.

Benton, T. (2001), 'Humanism and Fascism', in Schaffer, E. S. (ed.), *Humanist Traditions in the Twentieth Century* (*Comparative Critisism* 23), Cambridge, 69–115.

Berlan-Bajard, A. (2006), *Les spectacles aquatiques Romains*, Rome.

Berman, D. W. (2004), 'The Double Foundation of Boiotian Thebes', *TAPhA* 134, 1–22.

Bernard, S. (2013), 'The Transport of Heavy Loads in Antiquity: Lifting, Moving, and Building in Ancient Rome', in Altekamp, Marcks-Jacobs, and Seiler (2013), 99–122.

Bernard, S. (2018), *Building Mid-Republican Rome: Labor, Architecture, and the Urban Economy*, Oxford/New York.

Biermann, V. (2013), 'Ortswechsel: Überlegungen zur Bedeutung der Bewegung schwerer Lasten für die Wirkung und Rezeption monumentaler Architektur am Beispiel des Vatikanischen Obelisken', in Altekamp, Marcks-Jacobs, and Seiler (2013), 123–56.

Bisconti, F. (2004), 'Il programma decorativo dell'ipogeo di Trebio Giusto tra attitudine e autorappresentazione', in Rea (2004), 133–44.

Boatwright, M. (1987), *Hadrian and the City of Rome*, Princeton, NJ.

Boatwright, M. (2000), *Hadrian and the Cities of the Roman Empire*, Princeton, NJ.

Böhm, G., and Pfotenhauer, H. (1995), *Beschreibungskunst, Kunstbeschreibung: Ekphrasis von der Antike bis zur Gegenwart*, Munich.

Bol, P. C. (1985), *Antike Bronzetechnik*, Munich.

Bonifazi, A. (2001), *Mescolare un cratere di canti: Pragmatica della poesia epinicia in Pindaro*, Alessandria.

Booth, J. (1991), *Ovid: Amores II*, Warminster.

Bowra, C. M. (1964), *Pindar*, Oxford.

Boyle, A. J. (2003), *Ovid and the Monuments: A Poet's Rome*, Victoria.

Boyle, A. J., and Dominik, W. J. (2003), *Flavian Rome: Culture, Image, Text*, Leiden.

Brigante Colonna, G. (1929), 'Mentre l'obelisco dedicato al Duce viaggia verso Roma', *Capitolium*, 1929.5, 270–7.

Briggs, W. W. (1980), *Narrative and Simile from the Georgics in the Aeneid*, Leiden.

Bright, D. (1980), *Elaborate Disarray: The Nature of Statius' 'Silvae'*, Meisenheim am Glan.

BIBLIOGRAPHY   235

Brilliant, R. (1984), *Visual Narratives: Storytelling in Roman and Etruscan Art*, Ithaca, NY; London.

Brink, C. O. (1971), *Horace on Poetry: The Ars Poetica*, Cambridge.

Brisse, A., and de Rotrou, L. (1876), *Dessèchement du Lac Fucino exécuté par S. E. le prince Alexandre Torlonia: précis historique et technique / The Draining of Lake Fucino accomplished by His Excellency Prince Alexander Torlonia: an abridged account historical and technical*, Rome.

Bruck, S. (1993), *Labor in Vergils Aeneis*, Frankfurt.

Bruns, G. (1935), *Der Obelisk und seine Basis auf dem Hippodrom zu Konstantinopel*, Istanbul.

Buchheit, V. (1963), *Vergil über die Sendung Roms: Untersuchungen zum Bellum Poenicum und zur Aeneis*, Heidelberg.

Burri, E. (1994a) (ed.), *Sulle rive della memoria: Il lago Fucino e il suo Emissario*, Pescara.

Burri, E. (1994b), 'Analisi topografica dell'emissario Claudio-Torlonia', in Burri (1994a), 234–61.

Burri, E. (2001), 'Il Fucino e l'emissario antico', in Campanelli (2001), 9–11.

Burri, E. (2011), *Il prosciugamento del lago Fucino e l'emissario sotterraneo*, Pescara.

Busch, S. (2005), 'Who Are 'We'? Towards Propagandistic Mechanism and Purpose of Caesar's *Bellum Gallicum*', in Enenkel, K. A. E., and Pfeijffer, I. L. (2005) (eds.), *The Manipulative Mode. Political Propaganda in Antiquity: A Collection of Case Studies*, Leiden, 143–66.

Bussels, S. (2013), *The Animated Image: Roman Theory on Naturalism, Vividness and Divine Power*, Berlin.

Byvanck, A. W. (1960), *De Obelisk van Constantinopel, Mededeelingen der Koninklijke Nederlandse Akademie van Wetenschappen, Afd. Letterkunde*, 23.11 (n.s.), Amsterdam.

Caffarelli, G. (1938), 'Il trasporto dell'obelisco di Piazza S. Pietro e di quello del Foro Mussolini', in Galassi Paluzzi, C. (ed.), *Atti del 4. Congresso nazionale di studi romani*, Bologna, 120–31.

Cairoli, R., Torrieri, V., and Agostini, S. (1994), 'Il Complesso archeologico di età imperiale noto come "i cunicoli di Claudio"', in Burri (1994a), 214–33.

Calza, G. (1934), 'The Via dell'Impero and the Imperial Fora', *Journal of the Royal Institute of British Architects*, March 1934, 489–508.

Cameron, A. (1966), 'A Biographical Note on Claudian', *Athenaeum* 44, 32–40.

Cameron, A. (1995), *Callimachus and His Critics*, Princeton, NJ.

Campanelli, A. (2001) (ed.), *Il Tesoro del Lago: l'archeologia del Fucino e la Collezione Torlonia*, Pescara.

Campanelli, A. (2003) (ed.), *La Collezione Torlonia di Antichità del Fucino*, Pescara.

Campbell, B. (2012), *Rivers and the Power of Ancient Rome*, Chapel Hill.

Capelli, R. (1993), 'La leggenda di Enea nel racconto figurato degli Aemilii', *Ostraka* 2, 57–71.

Capelli, R. (1998), 'Il fregio dipinto dell'Esquilino e la propaganda augustea del mito delle origine', in La Regina, A. (ed.), *Museo Nazionale Romano. Palazzo Massimo alle terme*, Milan, 51–8.

Caporilli, M., and Simeoni, F. (1990), *Il foro italico e lo stadio olimpico. Immagini dalla storia*, Rome.

Cardilli Alloisi, L. (1995), *Gli anni del governatorato (1926-1944): Interventi urbanistici, scoperte archeologiche, arredo urbano, restauri*, Rome.

Carettoni, G. F. (1961), 'Il fregio figurato della Basilica Aemilia', *RIA* 10, 5–78.

236 BIBLIOGRAPHY

Carey, S. (2003), *Pliny's Catalogue of Culture: Art and Empire in the Natural History*, Oxford.

Carney, E. D. (1986), 'City-Founding in the *Aeneid*', in Deroux, C. (ed.), *Studies in Latin Literature and Roman History IV*, Brussels, 422–30.

Casali, S. (2006), 'The Making of the Shield: Inspiration and Repression in the *Aeneid*', *G&R* 53, 185–204.

Catalli, F. (2011), 'Cod. 2', http://www.avezzanodigitale.it/archeologia/museo-lapidario-comunale/epigrafi-provenienti-dal-territorio-di-alba-fucens/cod-2 (last accessed 28 August 2012).

Cederna, A. (2012), *Mussolini urbanista. Lo sventramento di Roma negli anni del consenso*, Bari.

Cichorius, C. (1896–1900), *Die Reliefs der Trajanssäule*, Berlin; Leipzig.

Citroni Marchetti, S. (1982), '*Iuvare mortalem*. L'ideale programmatico della *Naturalis Historia* di Plinio nei rapporti con il moralismo stoico-diatribico', *Atene e Roma* 27, 124–48.

Claridge, A. (1993), 'Hadrian's Column of Trajan', *JRA* 6, 5–22.

Claridge, A. (2007), 'Hadrian's Lost Temple of Trajan', *JRA* 20, 54–94.

Clarke, M. J., Currie, B. G. F., and Lyne, R. O. A. M. (2006) (eds.), *Epic Interactions: Perpectives on Homer, Virgil and the Epic Tradition*, Oxford.

Clauss, J. J. (1993), *The Best of the Argonauts: The Redefinition of the Epic Hero in Book One of Apollonius' Argonautica*, Berkeley, CA.

Coarelli, F. (1979), 'La riscoperta del sepolcro degli Haterii: una base con dedica a Silvano', in Kopcke, G., and Moore, M. B. (eds.), *Studies in Classical Art and Archaeology: A Tribute to Peter Heinrich von Blanckenhagen*, New York.

Coarelli, F. (1996), 'La costruzione del porto di Terracina in un rilievo storico tardo-repubblicano', in Coarelli, F., *Revixit ars. Arte e ideologia a Roma. Dai modelli ellenistici alla tradizione repubblicana*, Roma, 434–54.

Coarelli, F. (2000), *The Column of Trajan*, Rome.

Coleman, K. M. (1988), *Statius: Silvae IV*, Oxford.

Coleman, K. M. (1990), 'Fatal Charades: Roman Executions Staged as Mythological Enactments', *JRS* 80, 44–73.

Coleman, K. M. (1993), 'Launching into History: Aquatic Displays in the Early Empire', *JRS* 83, 48–74.

Coleman, K. M. (1998a), 'The *liber spectaculorum*: Perpetuating the Ephemeral', in Grewing, F. (1998) (ed.), *Toto notus in orbe: Perspektiven der Martial-Interpretation*, Stuttgart, 15–36.

Coleman, K. M. (1998b), 'Martial Book 8 and the Politics of A.D. 93', *Papers of the Leeds International Latin Seminar* 10, 337–57.

Coleman, K. M. (2008), 'Stones in the Forest: Epigraphic Allusion in the *Silvae*', in Smolenaars, van Dam, and Nauta (2008), 19–43.

Collard, C., Cropp, M. J., and Gilbert, J. (2004), *Euripides: Selected Fragmentary Plays*, Volume II, Warminster.

Conrad, D. (1987) (ed.), *Domenico Fontana: Die Art wie der vatikanische Obelisk transportiert wurde*, Düsseldorf.

Conte, G. B. (1992), 'Proems in the Middle', *YCS* 29, 147–59.

Corbier, M. (2006), *Donner à voir, donner à lire. Mémoire et communication dans la Rome ancienne*, Paris.

Cordes, L. (2014), 'Preferred Readings: von Seneca zu Statius', in Bönisch, S., Cordes, L., Schulz, V., Wolsfeld, A., and Ziegert, C. (eds.), *Nero und Domitian. Mediale Diskurse der Herrscherrepräsentation im Vergleich*, Munich, 341–78.

BIBLIOGRAPHY 237

Cordes, L. (2017), *Kaiser und Tyrann: Die Kodierung und Umkodierung der Herrscherrepräsentation Neros und Domitians*, Berlin; Boston.

Coulston, J. C. N. (1990), 'The Architecture and Construction Scenes on Trajan's Column', in Henig, M. (ed.), *Architecture and Architectural Sculpture in the Roman Empire*, Oxford, 39–50.

Courtney, E. (1990), *P. Papinii Stati Silvae*, Oxford.

Courtney, E. (1995), *Musa Lapidaria*, Atlanta, GA.

Cowan, R. (2002), *In My Beginning Is My End: Origins, Cities, and Foundations in Flavian epic*, diss. Oxford.

Cowling, D. (1998), *Building the Text: Architecture as Metaphor in Late Medieval and Early Modern France*, Oxford.

Cozzo, G. (1928), *Ingegneria Romana*, Rome.

Cuomo, S. (2011), 'A Roman Engineer's Tales', *JRS* 101, 143–65.

Cuomo, S., and Formisano, M. (2016), *Vitruvius: Text, Architecture, Reception, Arethusa* Special Issue 49.2.

Curran, B. A., Grafton, A., Long, P. O., and Weiss, B. (2009), *Obelisks: A History*, Cambridge, MA.

Dällenbach, L. (1977), *Le récit spéculaire: essai sur la mise en abyme*, Paris.

Dalla Pria, F. (2012), *Dittatura e immagine: Mussolini e Hitler nei cinegiornali*, Roma.

D'Amato, S. (1980), *Il primo prosciugamento del Fucino*, Avezzano.

D'Amelio, M. G. (2009), *L'obelisco marmoreo del Foro Italico a Roma: Storia, immagini e note techniche*, Roma.

Dams, P. (1970), *Dichtungskritik bei nichtausgusteischen Dichtern*, diss. Marburg.

Darmesteter, J. (1968), 'Eine grammatikalische Metapher des Indogermanischen', in Schmitt, R. (ed.), *Indogermanische Dichtersprache*, Darmstadt, 26–9.

Darwall-Smith, R. H. (1996), *Emperors and Architecture: A Study of Flavian Rome*, Brussels.

David-Guignard, S. (2004), 'Bâtir en musique: l'exemple d'Amphion à Thèbes', in Mortier-Waldschmidt, O. (ed.), *Musique & Antiquité: actes du colloque d'Amiens, 25–26 octobre 2004*, Paris, 247–66.

Davies, P. (2004), *Death and the Emperor*, Austin, TX.

DeBrohun, J. B. (2003), *Roman Propertius and the Reinvention of Elegy*, Ann Arbor, MI.

De Haan, N. (2015), 'Fare gli italiani. Het Romeinse verleden in modern Italië', *Lampas* 48, 395–410.

De Jong, I. J. F. (2015), 'Pluperfects and the Artist in Ekphrases: From the Shield of Achilles to the Shield of Aeneas (and Beyond)', *Mnemosyne* 68, 889–916.

de Jonge, C. C. (2008), *Between Grammar and Rhetoric: Dionysius of Halicarnassus on Language, Linguistics and Literature*, Leiden.

de Jonge, P. (1977), *Philological and Historical Commentary on Ammianus Marcellinus XVII*, Groningen.

DeLaine, J. (1997), *The Baths of Caracalla: A Study in the Design, Construction and Economics of a Large-Scale Building Project in Imperial Rome*, Portsmouth, RI.

DeLaine, J. (1999), 'Benefactions and Urban Renewal: Bath Buildings in Italy', in DeLaine, J., and Johnston, D. E. (eds.), *Roman Baths and Bathing: Proceedings of the First International Conference on Roman Baths* (2 vols.), *JRA* Suppl. 37, Portsmouth, 67–74.

DeLaine, J. (2002), 'The Temple of Hadrian at Cyzicus and Roman Attitudes to Exceptional Construction', in *PBSR* 70, 205–30.

238 BIBLIOGRAPHY

DeLaine, J. (2006), 'The Cost of Creation: Technology at the Service of Construction', in Lo Cascio, L. (ed.), *Innovazione tecnica e progresso economico nel mondo romano*, Bari.

Della Portella, I. (2004), *The Appian Way*, Verona.

De Nuccio, M., and Ungaro, L. (2002) (eds.), *I Marmi Colorati della Roma Imperiale*, Venice.

Deremetz, A. (1995), *Le Miroir des Muses: Poétiques de la réflexivité à Rome*, Villeneuve d'Ascq.

Deremetz, A. (2000), 'Le livre II de l'Énéide et la conception virgilienne de l'épopée: épopée et tragédie dans l'Énéide', *REL* 78, 76–92.

Deremetz, A. (2001), 'Énée aède: tradition auctoriale et (re)fondation d'un genre', in Schmidt (2001), 143–81.

Dessales, H. (2017), 'The Archaeology of Construction: A New Approach to Roman Architecture', *Annales. Histoire, Sciences Sociales: English Edition* 72, 69–86.

Dewar, M. (1994), 'Laying It on with a Trowel: The Proem to Lucan and Related Texts', *CQ* 44, 199–211.

Dewar, M. (2008), 'The Equine Cuckoo: Statius' *Ecus maximus Domitiani imperatoris* and the Flavian Forum', in Smolenaars, van Dam, and Nauta (2008), 65–83.

Dickison, S. K. (1977), 'Claudius, Saturnalicius Princeps', *Latomus* 36, 634–47.

Dietrich, N., and Squire, M. J. (2018) (eds.), *Ornament and Figure in Graeco-Roman Art: Rethinking Visual Ontologies in Classical Antiquity*, Berlin; Boston.

Diggle, J. (1996), 'P. Petrie 1.1-2: Euripides, *Antiope* (fr. 223 [Nauck] Kannicht, XLVIII Kambitsis', *PCPhS* 42, 106–26.

Dirschedl, U. (2003) (ed.), *Die Stadt als Großbaustelle: von der Antike bis zur Neuzeit. Deutsches Archäologisches Institut, Internationaler Kongreß vom 7. bis 11. November 2001 im Auswärtigen Amt*, Berlin.

Dodds, E. R. (1959), *Plato: Gorgias*, Oxford.

Dodington, P. M. (1980), *The Function of the References to Engineering in Caesar's 'Commentaries'*, diss. University of Iowa.

Dominik, W. J., Newlands, C. E., and Gervais, K. (eds.) (2015), *Brill's Companion to Statius*, Leiden.

Donderer, M. (1996), *Die Architekten der späten römischen Republik und der Kaiserzeit: epigraphische Zeugnisse*, Erlangen.

Döpp, S. (2003), 'L'incendio del Campidoglio. Sullo stile di Tacito, *Hist.* III 72', *Eikasmos* 14, 231–41.

D'Onofrio, C. (1992), *Gli obelischi di Roma. Storia e urbanistica di una città dall'età antica al XX secolo*, Rome.

Dufallo, B. (2013), *The Captor's Image: Greek Culture in Roman Ecphrasis*, Oxford; New York.

Durry, M. (1938), *Pline le Jeune: Panégyrique de Trajan*, Paris.

Edmondson, J. (2006), 'Cities and Urban Life in the Western Provinces of the Roman Empire 30 BCE–250 CE', in Potter, D. S. (ed.), *A Companion to the Roman Empire*, Malden MA; Oxford, 250–80.

Edwards, C. (1993), *The Politics of Immorality*, Cambridge.

Edwards, C. (1996), *Writing Rome: Textual Approaches to the City*, Cambridge.

Effe, B. (2003), 'Der Held als Gott: Die Apotheose des Herakles in der alexandrinischen Dichtung', in Binder, G., Effe, B., and Glei, R. F. (eds.), *Gottmenschen: Konzepte existentieller Grenzüberschreitung im Altertum*, Trier, 27–43.

Egelhaaf-Gaiser, U. (2007), 'Kolossale Miniaturen. Der Holzfäller Hercules in Statius' 'Wäldern' (Silve 3,1)', *Millennium* 4, 63–92.

BIBLIOGRAPHY   239

Egelhaaf-Gaiser, U. (2008), 'Werkstattbesuch bei Vulcanus: Triumphale Geschichtsbilder aus Vergils intertextueller Waffenschmiede (*Aen.* 8,407–453)', in Krasser, H., Pausch, D., and Petrovic, I. (eds.), *Triplici invectus triumpho: Der römische Triumph in Augusteischer Zeit*, Stuttgart, 209–37.

Elsner, J. (1994), 'Constructing Decadence: The Representation of Nero as Imperial Builder', in Elsner, J., and Masters, J. (eds.), *Reflections of Nero*, Chapel Hill, 112–27.

Elsner, J. (1996a) (ed.), *Art and Text in Roman Culture*, Cambridge.

Elsner, J. (1996b), 'Inventing Imperium: Texts and the Propaganda of Monuments in Augustan Rome', in Elsner (1996a), 32–54.

Elsner, J. (2002) (ed.), *The Verbal and the Visual: Cultures of Ekphrasis in Antiquity*, *RAMUS* 31.

Elsner, J. (2003), 'Iconoclasm and the Preservation of Memory' in Nelson, R. S., and Olin, M. (eds.), *Monuments and Memory, Made and Unmade*, Chicago; London.

Elsner, J. (2005), 'Art and Text', in Harrison, S. J. (ed.), *A Companion to Latin Literature*, Malden MA; Oxford; Victoria, 300–18.

Elsner, J., and Meyer, M. (2014) (eds.), *Art and Rhetoric in Roman Culture*, Cambridge.

Erickson, B. (2002), 'Falling Masts, Rising Masters: The Ethnography of Virtue in Caesar's Account of the Veneti', *AJPh* 123, 601–22.

Eriksen, R. (2001), *Building in the Text: Alberti to Shakespeare and Milton*, University Park, PA.

Erll, A., and Rigney, A. (2009) (eds.), *Mediation, Remediation, and the Dynamics of Cultural Memory*, Berlin; Boston.

Erman, A. (1914), 'Die Obeliskenübersetzung des Hermapion', *Sitz. Ak. Wissensch. Berlin (Ph.-Hist. Kl.)*, 245–73.

Ertel, C., and Freyberger, K. S. (2007), 'Nuove indagini sulla Basilica Aemilia nel Foro Romano', *ArchClass* 58, 109–42.

Ertel, C., Freyberger, K. S., Lipps, J., and Bitterer, T. (2007), 'Im Zentrum der Macht: Zur Baugeschichte, Rekonstruktion und Funktion der Basilica Aemilia auf dem Forum Romanum in Rom', *RM* 113, 493–552.

Ewald, B. C., and Noreña, C. F. (2010), *The Emperor and Rome: Space, Representation, and Ritual*, Cambridge.

Facenna, D. (2003), 'I rilievi Torlonia dal Fucino', in Campanelli (2003), 69–79.

Fagan, G. G. (1996), 'The Reliability of Roman Rebuilding Inscriptions', *PBSR* 64, 81–93.

Fagan, G. G. (1999), *Bathing in Public in the Roman World*, Ann Arbor, MI.

Fant, J. C. (2008), 'Quarrying and Stoneworking', in Oleson (2008), 121–35.

Fantham, E. (1997), 'Images of the City: Propertius' New-Old Rome', in Habinek, T., and Schiesaro, A. (eds.), *The Roman Cultural Revolution*, Cambridge, 122–35.

Fantham, E. (1998), *Ovid: Fasti. Book 4*, Cambridge.

Fantuzzi, M., and Hunter, R. (2004), *Tradition and Innovation in Hellenistic Poetry*, Cambridge.

Favro, D. (1996), *The Urban Image of Augustan Rome*, Cambridge.

Favro, D. (2011), 'Construction Traffic in Imperial Rome: Building the Arch of Septimius Severus', in Laurence, R., and Newsome, D. (eds.), *Rome, Ostia, Pompeii: Movement and Space*, Oxford, 332–60.

Favro, D. (2017), 'Reading Augustan Rome: Materiality as Rhetoric *In Situ*', *Advances in the History of Rhetoric* 20.2, 180–95.

Fedeli, P. (2006) (ed.), *Sextus Propertius: Elegiarum Libri IV*, München; Leipzig.

Feeney, D. (1991), *The Gods in Epic*, Oxford.

240 BIBLIOGRAPHY

Feldherr, A. (1998), *Spectacle and Society in Livy's History*, Berkeley; Los Angeles; London.

Feraboli, S., Flores, E., and Scarcia, R. (1996), *Il poema degli astri (Astronomica)*, Volume I, Milan.

Feraboli, S., Flores, E., and Scarcia, R. (2001), *Il poema degli astri (Astronomica)*, Volume II, Milan.

Fitch, J. G. (2002–4), *Seneca: Tragedies* (2 vols.), Cambridge, MA; London.

Fletcher, K. F. B. (2014), *Finding Italy: Travel, Colonization, and Nation in Vergil's Aeneid*, Ann Arbor, MI.

Flower, H. I. (2001), 'A Tale of Two Monuments: Domitian, Trajan, and Some Praetorians at Puteoli', *AJA* 105, 625–48.

Flower, H. I. (2006), *The Art of Forgetting: Disgrace and Oblivion in Roman Political Culture*, Chapel Hill, NC.

Flower, H. I. (2008), 'Remembering and Forgetting Temple Destruction: The Destruction of the Temple of Jupiter Optimus Maximus in 83 BC', in Gardner, G., and Osterloh, K. (eds.), *Antiquity in Antiquity: Jewish and Christian Pasts in the Greco-Roman World*, Tübingen.

Fontana, D. (1590), *Della trasportatione dell'obelisco Vaticano et delle fabriche di Nostro Signore Papa Sisto V, fatte dal caualier Domenico Fontana architetto di Sua Santita*, Rome.

Ford, A. (2002), *The Origins of Criticism: Literary Culture and Poetic Theory in Classical Greece*, Princeton, NJ; Oxford.

Fowler, D. (1991), 'Narrate and Describe: The Problem of Ecphrasis', *JRS* 81, 25–35.

Frank, M. (1994), *Seneca's Phoenissae*, Leiden.

Fränkel, H. (1968), *Noten zu den Argonautika des Apollonios*, München.

Fredrick, D. (2003), 'Architecture and Surveillance in Flavian Rome', in Boyle and Dominik (2003), 199–227.

Frere, S., and Lepper, F. (1988), *Trajan's Column*, Glouchester.

Freyberger, K. S., and Ertel, C. (2016), *Die Basilica Aemilia auf dem Forum Romanum in Rom*, Wiesbaden.

Frischer, B. (2017), with technical appendices by P. Albèri Alber, D. Dearborn, J. Fillwalk, M. Kajava, and S. Floris, 'Edmund Buchner's Solarium Augusti: New Observations and Simpirical Studies', *Atti della Pontificia Accademia Romana di Archeologia (Serie III). Rendiconti 89*, 3–90.

Fritz, H.-J. (1995), *Vitruv: Architekturtheorie und Machtpolitik in der römischen Antike*, Münster.

Furuhagen, H. (1961), 'Some Remarks on the Sculptured Frieze of the Basilica Aemilia in Rome', *Opuscula Romana* 3, 139–55.

Gale, M. (2004), 'The Story of Us: A Narratological Analysis of Lucretius' *De Rerum Natura*', in Gale, M. (ed.), *Latin Epic and Didactic Poetry: Genre, Tradition and Individuality*, Swansea, 49–71.

Gall, D. (2006), *Die Literatur in der Zeit des Augustus*, Darmstadt.

Gaggiotti, M. (1996), 'Un'insospettabile fonte d'ispirazione per Giotto: nota sul fregio della Basilica Aemilia', in Casale, V., Coarelli, F., and Toscano, B. (eds.), *Scritti di archeologia e storia dell'arte in onore di Carlo Pietrangeli*, Rome, 11–21.

Gervais, K. (2017), *Statius, Thebaid 2*, Oxford.

Geyssen, J. W. (1996), *Imperial Panegyric in Statius: A Literary Commentary on Silvae 1.1*, New York.

Giardina, A., and Vauchez, A. (2000), 'Ritorno al futuro: la romanità fascista', in Giardina, A., and Vauchez, A., *Il mito di Roma. Da Carlo Magno a Mussolini*, Bari, 212–96.

BIBLIOGRAPHY   241

Gibson, B. (2006a), 'The *Silvae* and Epic', in Nauta, van Dam, and Smolenaars (2006), 163–83.

Gibson, B. (2006b), *Statius. Silvae 5. Edited with Introduction, Translation and Commentary*, Oxford.

Gibson, R. K., and Morello, R. (2011) (eds.), *Pliny the Elder: Themes and Contexts*, Leiden.

Giuliani, C. F. (2003a), 'Note sulla composizione dei rilievi Torlonia', in Campanelli (2003), 79–80.

Giuliani, C. F. (2003b), 'La rappresentazione degli argani', in Campanelli (2003), 81–2.

Goldhill, S. (2007), 'What Is Ekphrasis For?', *CPh* 102, 1–19.

Goldhill, S. (2020), *Preposterous Poetics: The Politics and Aesthetics of Form in Late Antiquity*, Cambridge.

Goold, G. P. (1977), *Manilius: Astronomica*, Cambridge, MA; London.

Goold, G. P. (1983), 'The Great Lacuna in Manilius', *PACA* 17, 64–8.

Goold, G. P. (1998^2) (ed.), *M. Manilii Astronomica*, Stuttgart; Leipzig.

Goold, G. P. (1999^2), *Propertius: Elegies*, Cambridge, MA; London.

Gordon, A. (1983), *Illustrated Introduction to Latin Epigraphy*, Berkeley; London.

Gowers, E. (1993), *The Loaded Table: Representations of Food in Roman Literature*, Oxford.

Grandazzi, A. (2009), '*Summa difficultas faciendi pontis*: César et le passage du Rhin en 55 av. J.-C. (B.G., IV, 17). Une analyse sémiologique', *Mélanges de l'école française de Rome* 121, 545–70.

Greco, A., and Santuccio, S. (1991), *Foro Italico*, Rome.

Green, S. (2004), *Ovid, Fasti I: A Commentary*, Leiden.

Green, S. J. (2009), '*Arduum ad astra*: The Poetics and Politics of Horoscopic Failure in Manilius' *Astronomica*', in Greek, S. J., and Volk, K. (eds.), *Forgotten Stars: Rediscovering Manilius'* Astronomica, Oxford, 120–38.

Gregori, G. L. (1987–88), 'Horti sepulchrales e cepotaphia nelle iscrizioni urbane', *BullCom* 92, 175–88.

Griffin, M. (1987^2), *Nero: The End of a Dynasty*, New York.

Griffin, M. (1990), 'Claudius in Tacitus', *CQ* 40, 482–501.

Griffin, M. (2000), 'Nerva to Hadrian', in Bowman, A. K., Garnsey, P., and Rathbone, D. (eds.), *Cambridge Ancient History: The High Empire, A.D. 70–192*, Cambridge, 84–131.

Günther, H.-C. (2006), 'The Fourth Book', in Günther, H.-C. (ed.), *Brill's Companion to Propertius*, Leiden, 353–95.

Hall, J. B., Ritchie, A. L., and Edwards, M. J. (2005), *Thebaid and Achilleid / P. Papinius Statius*, Cambridge.

Hammer, D. (2010), 'Roman Spectacle Entertainments and the Technology of Reality', *Arethusa* 43, 63–86.

Hamon, P. (1988), 'Texte et architecture', *Poétique* 73, 3–25.

Hanoune, R. (2003), 'Représentations de construction et d'architecture sur la colonne Aurélienne', in Huet and Scheid (2003), 205–11.

Harder, A. (2012), *Callimachus'* Aetia (2 vols.), Oxford.

Hardie, A. (1983), *Statius and the* Silvae: *Poets, Patrons, and Epideixis in the Greco-Roman World*, Liverpool.

Hardie, P. R. (1986), *Virgil's Aeneid: Cosmos and Imperium*, Oxford.

Hardie, P. R. (1993), *The Epic Successors of Virgil*, Cambridge.

Hardie, P. R. (1998), *Virgil*, Oxford.

242 BIBLIOGRAPHY

Harrison, S. J. (2006), 'The Epic and the Monuments: Interactions between Virgil's *Aeneid* and the Augustan Building Programme', in Clarke, Currie, and Lyne (2006), 159–83.

Haselberger, L. (2011), 'A Debate on the Horologium of Augustus: Controversy and Clarifications, with Responses by P. J. Heslin and M. Schütz and Additional Remarks by R. Hannah and G. Alföldy', in *JRA* 24, 47–98.

Haskins, C. E. (1887), *M. Annaei Lucani Pharsalia / ed. with Engl. notes by C. E. Haskins, with an introd. by W. E. Heitland*, London.

Hausmann, M. (2009), *Die Leserlenkung durch Tacitus in den Tiberius- und Claudiusbüchern der "Annalen"*, Berlin.

Heerink, M. A. J. (2015), *Echoing Hylas: A Study in Hellenistic and Roman Metapoetics*, Madison, WI.

Heinrich, A. J. (1999), 'Longa retro series: Sacrifice and Repetition in Statius' Menoeceus episode', *Arethusa* 32, 165–95.

Heirman, J., and Klooster, J. (2013) (eds.), *Ideologies of Space: Ancient and Modern*, Gent.

Henig, M. (1990), *Architecture and Architectural Sculpture in the Roman Empire*, Oxford.

Heslin, P. J. (2005), *The Transvestite Achilles: Gender and Genre in Statius' Achilleid*, Cambridge.

Heslin, P. J. (2007), 'Augustus, Domitian and the So-Called *Horologium Augusti*', *JRS* 97, 1–20.

Heubner, H. (1972), *P. Cornelius Tacitus, Die Historien III. Kommentar*, Heidelberg.

Heubner, H. (1994), *Cornelii Taciti libri qui supersunt*, Stuttgart.

Heyworth, S. J. (1995), 'Propertius: Division, Transmission and the Editor's Task', *Papers of the Leeds International Latin Seminar* 8, 165–85.

Heyworth, S. J. (2007), *Cynthia: A Companion to the Text of Propertius*, Oxford.

Hill, D. E. (1983), *P. Papini Stati Thebaidos libri XII*, Leiden.

Hill, D. E. (1985), *Ovid: Metamorphoses I–IV*, Warminster.

Hillier, B., and Hanson, J. (1984), *The Social Logic of Space*, Cambridge.

Hillier, B., and Penn, A. (2004), 'Rejoinder to Carlo Ratti', *Environment and Planning B: Planning and Design* 31, 501–11.

Hinds, S. J. (1998), *Allusion and Intertext: Dynamics of Appropriation in Roman Poetry*, Cambridge.

Hinds, S. J. (2001), 'Cinna, Statius and "Immanent Literary History" in the Cultural Economy', in Schmidt (2001), 221–65.

Hölkeskamp, K.-J., and Stein-Hölkeskamp, E. (2006), *Erinnerungsorte der Antike: Die römische Welt*, München.

Holleran, C., and Claridge, A. (2018) (eds.), *A Companion to the City of Rome*, Hoboken, NJ.

Hoogma, R. P. (1959), *Der Einfluss Vergils auf die Carmina Latina epigraphica: eine Studie mit besonderer Berücksichtigung der metrisch-technischen Grundsätze der Entlehnung*, Amsterdam.

Horsfall, N. (1989), 'Aeneas the Colonist', *Vergilius* 35, 8–27.

Horsfall, N. (1999), *Virgil, Aeneid 7: A Commentary*, Leiden.

Horsfall, N. (2006), *Virgil, Aeneid 3: A Commentary*, Leiden.

Horster, M. (2001), *Bauinschriften römischer Kaiser: Untersuchungen zu Inschriftenpraxis und Bautätigkeit in Städten des westlichen Imperium Romanum in der Zeit des Prinzipats*, Stuttgart.

Housman, A. E. (1912), *M. Manilii astronomicon liber secundus*, London.

Hude, K. (1927³), *Herodoti Historiae*, Oxford.

BIBLIOGRAPHY 243

Huet, V. (1996), 'Stories One Might Tell of Roman Art: Reading Trajan's Column and the Tiberius Cup', in Elsner (1996a), 9–31.

Huet, V., and Scheid, J. (2003) (eds.), *Autour de la Colonne Aurélienne*, Turnhout.

Hunter, R. (1993), *The Argonautica of Apollonius: Literary Studies*, Cambridge.

Hunter, R. (2006), *The Shadow of Callimachus*, Cambridge.

Hurley, D. W. (2001), *Suetonius: Divus Claudius*, Cambridge.

Hurst, A. (2000), 'Bâtir les murailles de Thèbes', in Angeli Bernardini, P. (ed.), *Presenza e funzione della città di Tebe nella cultura Greca*, Pisa; Rome, 63–81.

Hutchinson, G. (1984), 'Propertius and the Unity of the Book', *JRS* 74, 99–106.

Hutchinson, G. (2006), *Propertius: Elegies Book IV*, Cambridge.

Ingold, T. (2013), *Making: Anthropology, Archaeology, Art and Architecture*, London.

Insolera, I. (2001), *Roma fascista nelle fotografie dell'Istituto Luce*, Roma.

Insolera, I., and Sette, A. M. (2003) (eds.), *Roma tra le due guerre: Cronache da una città che cambia*, Rome.

Iversen, E. (1961), *The Myth of Egypt and its Hieroglyphs in European Tradition*, Copenhagen.

Iversen, E. (1968), *Obelisks in Exile (1): The Obelisks of Rome*, Copenhagen.

Iversen, E. (1972), *Obelisks in Exile (2): The Obelisks of Istanbul and England*, Copenhagen.

Jaeger, M. K. (1993), '*Custodia fidelis memoriae*: Livy's Story of M. Manlius Capitolinus', *Latomus* 52, 350–63.

Jaeger, M. K. (1997), *Livy's Written Rome*, Ann Arbor, MI.

Jensen, W. M. (1978), *The Sculptures from the Tomb of the Haterii*, diss. Ann Arbor, MI.

Johannsen, N. (2006), *Dichter über ihre Gedichte: Die Prosavorreden in den "Epigrammaton libri" Martials und in den "Silvae" des Statius*, Göttingen.

Jouan, F., and van Looy, H. (1998), *Euripide. Fragments, première partie: Aigeus-Autolykos*, Paris, 213–74.

Jourdan, F. (2008), 'Vertus iréniques et civilisatrices du chant sur le chant: l'association poétique des citharèdes légendaires (Amphion, Arion et Orphée) chez Horace et Silius Italicus', *REA* 110, 103–16.

Kallis, A. (2012), 'The "Third Rome" of Fascism: Demolitions and the Search for a New Urban Syntax', *The Journal of Modern History* 84, 40–79.

Kallis, A. (2014), *The Third Rome, 1922-1943: The Making of the Fascist Capital*, Basingstoke.

Kambitsis, J. (1972), *L'Antiope d'Euripide*, Athens.

Keitel, E. (1977), *The Structure of Tacitus' Annals 11 and 12*, diss. Univ. of North Carolina, Chapel Hill.

Keitel, E. (2009), ' "Is dying so very terrible?" The Neronian *Annals*', in Woodman (2009a), 127–43.

Keith, A. (2004), 'Ovid's Theban Narrative in Statius' *Thebaid*', in *Hermathena* 177/8, 177–202.

Kelly, G. (2003), 'The New Roman and the Old: Ammianus Marcellinus' Silences on Constantinople', *CQ* 53, 588–607.

Kelly, G. (2008), *Ammianus Marcellinus: The Allusive Historian*, Cambridge.

Kennedy, D. (1993), *The Arts of Love*, Cambridge.

Keppie, L. (1991), *Understanding Roman Inscriptions*, London.

Kießling, A., and Heinze, R. (1959[6]), *Q. Horatius Flaccus. Briefe*, Berlin.

Kierdorf, W. (1992), *Sueton: Leben des Claudius und Nero*, Paderborn.

244   BIBLIOGRAPHY

Kiilerich, B. (1998), *The Obelisk Base in Constantinople: Court Art and Imperial Ideology*, Rome.

Kleiner, F. S. (1990), 'The Arches of Vespasian in Rome', *RM* 97, 127–36.

Kleiner, F. S. (1991), 'The Trophy on the Bridge and the Roman Triumph over Nature', *L'Antiquité Classique* 60, 182–92.

Klinnert, T. C. (1970), *Capaneus—Hippomedon: Interpretationen zur Heldendarstellung in der Thebais des P. Papinius Statius*, diss. Heidelberg.

Klodt, C. (1998), 'Platzanlagen der Kaiser in der Beschreibung der Dichter', *Gymnasium* 105, 1–38.

Klodt, C. (2001), *Bescheidene Größe. Die Herrschergestalt, der Kaiserpalast und die Stadt Rom: literarische Reflexionen monarchischer Selbstdarstellung*, Göttingen.

Klooster, J. (2011), *Poetry as Window and Mirror: Positioning the Poet in Hellenistic Poetry*, Leiden.

Koestermann, E. (1967), *Annalen: Band III, Buch 11–13*, Heidelberg.

Kövecses, Z. (2010²), *Metaphor: A Practical Introduction*, Oxford.

Kofler, W. (2003), *Aeneas und Vergil. Untersuchungen zur poetologischen Dimension der Aeneis*, Heidelberg.

Kolb, F. (1984), *Die Stadt im Altertum*, Munich.

Kränzle, P. (1991), *Die zeitliche und ikonographische Stellung des Frieses der Basilica Aemilia*. Hamburg.

Kraus, C. S. (1994a), *Livy. Ab urbe condita: Book VI*, Cambridge.

Kraus, C. S. (1994b), ' "No Second Troy": Topoi and Refoundation in Livy, Book V', *TAPhA* 124, 267–89.

Kraus, C. S. (2006), 'Bellum Gallicum', in Griffin, M. (ed.), *A Companion to Julius Caesar*, Chichester; Malden, MA; Oxford, 159–74.

Kretzschmer, F. (1958), *Bilddokumente römischer Technik*, Düsseldorf.

Krevans, N. (1983), 'Geography and the Literary Tradition in Theocritus 7', *TAPhA* 113, 201–20.

Kühn, W. (1985), *Plinius der Jüngere: Panegyrikus*, Darmstadt.

Kyriakidis, S. (1998), *Narrative Structure and Poetics in the Aeneid: The Frame of Book 6*, Bari.

Laguna, G. (1992), *Estacio: Silvas III*, Madrid.

Laird, A. (1996), '*Ut figura poesis*: Writing Art and the Art of Writing in Augustan Poetry', in Elsner (1996a), 75–102.

Lakoff, G., and Johnson, M. (1980), *Metaphors We Live By*, Chicago.

Lakoff, G., and Johnson, M. (2003²), *Metaphors We Live By*, Chicago.

Lakoff, G., and Turner, M. (1989), *More than Cool Reason: A Field Guide to Poetic Metaphor*, Chicago; London.

Lamers, H., and Reitz-Joosse, B. (2016), *The Codex Fori Mussolini: A Latin Text of Italian Fascism*, London.

Lancaster, L. C. (1998), 'Building Trajan's Markets', *AJA* 102, 283–308.

Lancaster, L. C. (1999), 'Building Trajan's Column', *AJA* 103, 419–39.

Lancaster, L. C. (2000), 'Building Trajan's Markets 2: The Construction Process', *AJA* 104, 755–85.

Lancaster, L. C. (2005), *Concrete Vaulted Construction in Imperial Rome*, Cambridge.

Lancaster, L. C. (2008), 'Roman Engineering and Construction', in Oleson (2008), 256–84.

Lancaster, L. C. (2015), *Innovative Vaulting in the Architecture of the Roman Empire, 1st to 4th Centuries CE*, Cambridge.

BIBLIOGRAPHY 245

Landolfi, L. (1990), 'Manilio e le ansie dell' insegnamento: *L'excursus* metodologico (Astr. II,750–787)', *Pan* 10, 27–37.

Larmour, H. J., and Spencer, D. (2007), *The Sites of Rome: Time, Space, Memory*, Oxford.

Laurence, R. (1999), *The Roads of Roman Italy: Mobility and Cultural Change*, London; New York.

Lawall, G. (1966), 'Apollonius' *Argonautica*: Jason as Anti-Hero', *YCS* 19, 119–69.

Lazzaro, C., and Crum, R. J. (2005) (eds.), *Donatello among the Blackshirts*, Ithaca, NY.

Leach, E. W. (2006), 'Freedmen and Immortality in the Tomb of the Haterii', in D'Ambra, E., and Métraux, G. P. R. (eds.), *The Art of Citizens, Soldiers and Freedmen in the Roman World*, Oxford, 1–18.

Leberl, J. (2004), *Domitian und die Dichter. Poesie als Medium der Herrschaftsdarstellung*, Göttingen.

Leeman, A. D. (1982), 'Bomen vellen. Vergilius als schakel in de antieke epische traditie', *Lampas* 15, 1–27.

Lehmann-Hartleben, K. (1926), *Die Trajanssäule*, Berlin; Leipzig.

Leigh, M. (2006), 'Statius and the Sublimity of Capaneus', in Clarke, Currie, and Lyne (2006), 217–41.

Lesueur, R. (1994), *Stace: Thébaïde. Livres IX–XII*, Paris.

Letta, C. (1972), *I Marsi e il Fucino nell'antichità*, Milan.

Letta, C. (1994), 'Rileggendo le fonti antiche sul Fucino', in Burri (1994a), 202–13.

Letta, C. (2001), 'Un lago e il suo popolo', in Campanelli (2001), 139–55 = Letta, C. (2003) in Campanelli (2003), 26–37.

Leveau, P. (1993), 'Mentalité économique et grands travaux hydrauliques. Le drainage du lac Fucin. Aux origines d'un modèle', *AnnEconSocCiv* 48, 3–16.

Levick, B. (1990), *Claudius*, London.

Liberman, G. (2010) (ed.), *Stace: Silves*, Paris.

Lichtheim, M. (1976), *Ancient Egyptian Literature: A Book of Readings*, Vol. 2, Berkeley, CA.

Lieberg, G. (1956), 'Der Begriff 'Structura' in der Lateinischen Literatur', *Hermes* 84, 455–77.

Lieberg, G. (1982), *Poeta creator: Studien zu einer Figur der antiken Dichtung*, Amsterdam.

Lieberg, G. (1985), *Zu Idee und Figur des dichterischen Schöpfertums*, Bochum.

Lipps, J. (2011), *Die Basilica Aemilia am Forum Romanum: der kaiserzeitliche Bau und seine Ornamentik*, Wiesbaden.

Loftus, E. F., and Palmer, J. C. (1974), 'Reconstruction of Automobile Destruction: An Example of the Interaction between Language and Memory', *Journal of Verbal Learning & Verbal Behavior* 13, 585–9.

Lorenz, T. (1987), *Römische Städte*, Darmstadt.

Lovatt, H. (2007), 'Statius, Orpheus, and the Post-Augustan *vates*', *Arethusa* 40, 145–63.

Luck, G. (1985), *Arcana mundi: Magic and the Occult in the Greek and Roman Worlds*, Baltimore, MD.

Maass, P. (2011), 'The Toppling: How the Media Inflated a Minor Moment in a Long War', in *The New Yorker*, 3 January 2011, accessed at http://www.newyorker.com/reporting/2011/01/10/110110fa_fact_maass (last accessed 16 September 2012).

Maccaroni, C. R. (1929), 'La Colonna del Duce verso il mare di Roma', *Il Carlino della Sera* (Bologna, 16 January 1929).

Macleod, C. (1983), 'Propertius 4.1', in *Collected Essays*, Oxford, 141–53.

MacMullen, R. (1959), 'Roman Imperial Building in the Provinces', *HSPh* 64, 207–35.

246 BIBLIOGRAPHY

MacMullen, R. (1982), 'The Epigraphic Habit in the Roman Empire', *AJP* 103, 233–46.

Malloch, S. J. V. (2009), 'Hamlet without the Prince? The Claudian *Annals*', in Woodman (2009a), 116–26.

Manacorda, D., and Tamassia, R. (1985), *Il piccone del regime*, Rome.

Manuwald, G. (2003), *Pacuvius: summus tragicus poeta*, München; Leipzig.

Marcello, F. (2018), '*Forma Urbis Mussolini*: Vision and Rhetoric in the Designs for Fascist Rome', in Roche and Demetriou (2018), 370–403.

Marks, R. D. (2003), 'Hannibal in Liternum', in Thibodeau, P., and Hershell, H. (eds.), *Being There Together: Essays in Honor of Michael C. J. Putnam on the Occasion of His Seventieth Birthday*, Afton, 128–44.

Marks, R. D. (2010), 'The Song and the Sword: Silius' *Punica* and the Crisis of Early Imperial Song', in Konstan, D., and Raaflaub, K. A. (eds.), *Epic and History*, Malden MA, 185–211.

Martin, R. H. (1981), *Tacitus*, London.

Masters, J. (1992), *Poetry and Civil War in Lucan's 'Bellum Civile'*, Cambridge.

McCarter, S. (2012), 'The Forging of a God: Venus, the Shield of Aeneas, and Callimachus's "Hymn to Artemis"', *TAPhA* 142, 355–81.

McEwen, K. I. (2003), *Vitruvius: Writing the Body of Architecture*, Cambridge, MA.

McNelis, C. (2007), *Statius' Thebaid and the Poetics of Civil War*, Cambridge.

Meban, D. (2008), 'Temple Building, *Primus* Language and the Proem to Virgil's Third *Georgic*', *CPh* 103.2, 150–74.

Mehl, A. (1974), *Tacitus über Kaiser Claudius: die Ereignisse am Hof*, diss. Gießen.

Meijer, E. (2021), *All Roads Lead to Home: Navigating Self and Empire in Early Imperial Latin Poetry*, diss. Durham.

Meneghini, R. (2009), *I Fori Imperiali e i Mercati di Traiano: Storia e descrizione dei monumenti alla luce degli studi e degli scavi recenti*, Rome.

Meneghini, R., and Santangeli Valenzani, R. (2006), *Formae Urbis Romae*, Rome.

Mercati, M. (1589), *De gli obelischi di Roma*, Rome.

Merriam, C. U. (1993), 'An Examination of Jason's Cloak (Apollonius Rhodius, *Argonautica* 1.730-68)', *Scholia* 2 (n.s.), 69–80.

Messineo, G. (1979), 'Un'opera titanica: l'Emissario di Claudio', in *Fucino cento anni: 1877–1977. Atti degli incontri e dei convegni svoltisi per il Centenario del prosciugamento del Fucino e per il Venticinquennale della Riforma Agraria*, L'Aquila, 139–67.

Meyer, E. (1973), *Einführung in die lateinische Epigraphik*, Darmstadt.

Meyer, E. (1990), 'Explaining the Epigraphic Habit in the Roman Empire: The Evidence of Epitaphs', *JRS* 80, 74–96.

Micozzi, L. (2015), 'Statius' Epic Poetry: A Challenge to the Literary Past', in Dominik, Newlands, and Gervais (2015), 325–42.

Millar, F. (1964), *A Study of Cassius Dio*, Oxford.

Millar, F. (1983), 'Epigraphy', in Crawford, M. (ed.), *Sources for Ancient History*, Cambridge, 80–136.

Mogetta, M. (2015), 'A New Date for Concrete in Rome', *JRS* 105, 1–40.

Moreno Soldevila, R. (2010), *Plinio el Joven: Panegírico de Trajano*, Madrid.

Morgan, K. (2015), *Pindar and the Construction of Syracusan Monarchy in the Fifth Century B.C.*, Oxford; New York.

Morgan, L. (2000), 'Metre Matters: Some Higher-Level Metrical Play in Latin Poetry', *PCPS* 46, 99–120.

Morwood, J. (1991), 'Aeneas, Augustus, and the Theme of the City', *G&R* 38, 212–23.

Morzadec, F. (2009), *Les Images du monde: structure, écriture et esthétique du paysage dans les oeuvres de Stace et Silius Italicus*, Brussels.

Mottershead, J. (1986), *Suetonius: Claudius*, Bristol.

Mowbray, C. (2012), 'Captive Audience? The Aesthetics of *Nefas* in Senecan Drama', in Sluiter and Rosen (2012), 393–420.

Müller, D. (1974a), *Handwerk und Sprache: die sprachlichen Bilder aus dem Bereich des Handwerks in der griechischen Literatur bis 400 v. Chr.*, Meisenheim am Glan.

Müller, D. (1974b), 'Die Verspottung der metaphorischen Ausdrucksweise durch Aristophanes', in Reinhardt, U., and Sallmann, K. (eds.), *Musa iocosa*, Hildesheim, 29–41.

Mulder, H. M. (1954), *Publii Papinii Statii Thebaidos liber secundus*, Groningen.

Mundt, F. (2012) (ed.), *Kommunikationsräume im kaiserzeitlichen Rom*, Berlin; Boston.

Mynors, R. A. B. (1969), *P. Vergili Maronis Opera*, Oxford.

Nash, E. (1962), *Pictorial Dictionary of Ancient Rome*, Tübingen.

Nauta, R. (2002), *Poetry for Patrons: Literary Communication in the Age of Domitian*, Leiden.

Nauta, R. (2006), 'The *Recusatio* in Flavian Poetry', in Nauta, van Dam, and Smolenaars (2006), 21–40.

Nauta, R. (2010), '*Flavius ultimus, caluus Nero*. Einige Betrachtungen zu Herrscherbild und Panegyrik unter Domitian', in Kramer, N., and Reitz, C. (eds.), *Tradition und Erneuerung: Mediale Strategien in der Zeit der Flavier*, Berlin; New York, 239–72.

Nauta, R., van Dam, H.-J., and Smolenaars, J. J. L. (2006) (eds.), *Flavian Poetry*, Leiden.

Nazzaro, A. V. (ed.) (2009), *Aurelio Giuseppe Amatucci: Avellino 2 settembre 1867–Roma 22 aprile 1960*. Atti della giornata di studi, Sorbo Serpico 26 maggio 2007, Avellino.

Nelis, D. (2001), *Vergil's* Aeneid *and the* Argonautica *of Apollonius Rhodius*, Leeds.

Nelis, D. (2015), 'Vergilian Cities: Visions of Troy, Carthage and Rome', in Fuhrer, T., Mundt, F., and Stenger, J. (eds.), *Cityscaping: Constructing and Modelling Images of the City*, Berlin; Boston, 19–45.

Nelis, J. (2007a), 'Constructing Fascist Identity: Benito Mussolini and the Myth of "Romanità"', *The Classical World* 100, 391–415.

Nelis, J. (2007b), 'La romanité (romanità) fasciste: Bilan des recherches et propositions pour le futur', *Latomus* 66, 987–1006.

Nelis, J. (2011), *From Ancient to Modern: The Myth of* Romanità *during the* ventennio fascista: *The Written Imprint of Mussolini's Cult of the 'Third Rome'*, Brussels; Rome.

Nelson, R. S., and Olin, M. (2003), 'Epilogue. The Rhetoric of Monument Making: The World Trade Center', in Nelson, R. S., and Olin, M. (eds.), *Monuments and Memory, Made and Unmade*, Chicago; London, 305–23.

Newlands, C. E. (1991), '*Silvae* 3.1 and Statius' Poetic Temple', *CQ* 41, 438–52.

Newlands, C. E. (2002), *Statius' Silvae and the Poetics of Empire*, Cambridge.

Newlands, C. E. (2011), *Statius: Silvae Book II*, Cambridge.

Newlands, C. E. (2013), 'The 'Good Life' in Statius: Baucis and Philemon on the Bay of Naples', in Labate, M., and Rosati, G. (eds.), *La costruzione del mito augusteo*, Heidelberg, 241–66.

Newmyer, S. T. (1979), *The Silvae of Statius: Structure and Theme*, Leiden.

Newsome, D. J. (2009), 'Centrality in Its Place: Defining Urban Space in the City of Rome', in Driessen, M., Heeren, S., Hendriks, J., Kemmers, F., and Visser, R. (eds.), *TRAC 2008: Proceedings of the Eighteenth Annual Theoretical Roman Archaeology Conference*, Oxford, 25–38.

248 BIBLIOGRAPHY

Nichols, M. F. (2017), *Author and Audience in Vitruvius'* De architectura, Cambridge.

Nightingale, A. W. (1992), 'Plato's *Gorgias* and Euripides' *Antiope*: A Study in Generic Transformation', *ClAnt* 11, 121–41.

Nisbet, R. G. M. (1990), '*Aeneas imperator*: Roman Generalship in an Epic Context', in Harrison, S. J. (ed.), *Oxford Readings in Vergil's* Aeneid, Oxford, 378–89.

Nisbet, R. G. M., and Rudd, N. (2004), *A Commentary on Horace, Odes, Book III*, Oxford.

Nora, P. (1989), 'Between Memory and History: Les Lieux de Mémoire', *Representations* 26, 7–25.

Norden, E. (1957[4]), *P. Vergilius Maro: Aeneis Buch VI*, Darmstadt.

Nünlist, R. (1998), *Poetologische Bildersprache in der frühgriechischen Dichtung*, Stuttgart; Leipzig.

O'Gorman, E. (2000), *Irony and Misreading in the Annals of Tacitus*, Cambridge.

Oksanish, J. (2019), *Vitruvian Man: Rome under Construction*, Oxford; New York.

Oleson, J. P. (2008) (ed.), *The Oxford Handbook of Engineering and Technology in the Ancient World*, Oxford.

Olivieri, O. (2011), *Miti e culti Tebani nella poesia di Pindaro*, Pisa; Rome.

Opera Nazionale Balilla (1937), *Il foro Mussolini*, Milan.

Osborne, J. F. (2014) (ed.), *Approaching Monumentality in Archaeology*, Albany, NY.

Osgood, J. (2011), *Claudius Caesar: Image and Power in the Early Roman Empire*, Cambridge.

Owens, E. J. (1991), *The City in the Greek and Roman World*, London.

Pagano-Pogatschnig, G. (1933), 'L'Obelisco di Mussolini', in Insolera and Sette (2003), 30–1.

Painter, B. W. (2005), *Mussolini's Rome*, New York.

Parker, G. (2007), 'Obelisks Still in Exile: Monuments Made to Measure', in Bricault, L., Versluys, M. J., and Meyboom, P. G. P. (eds.), *Nile into Tiber: Egypt in the Roman World*, Leiden, 209–22.

Parker, G. (2014), 'Mobile Monumentality: The Case of Obelisks', in Osborne (2014), 273–87.

Parkes, R. (2012), *Statius, Thebaid 4*, Oxford.

Paul, G. M. (1991), 'Symposia and Deipna in Plutarch's *Lives* and in Other Historical Writings', in Slater, W. J. (ed.), *Dining in a Classical Context*, Ann Arbor, MI, 157–69.

Pavlovskis, Z. (1973), *Man in an Artificial Landscape: The Marvels of Civilisation in Imperial Roman Literature*, Leiden.

Payne, A. A. (1999), *The Architectural Treatise in the Italian Renaissance: Architectural Invention, Ornament, and Literary Culture*, Cambridge.

Pearcy, L. T. (1973), *Tacitus' Use of* Species, Imago, Effigies, *and* Simulacrum, diss. Bryn Mawr.

Pease, A. S. (1967[2]), *Publi Vergili Maronis Aeneidos Liber Quartus*, Darmstadt.

Pfeiffer, R. (1949–53), *Callimachus: Fragmenta* (2 vols.), Oxford.

Pilat, S. Z. (2016), 'La Parola al Piccone: Demonstrations of Fascism at the Imperial Fora and the Mausoleum of Augustus', in Christie, J. J., Bogdanović, J., and Guzmán, E. (eds.), *Political Landscapes of Capital Cities*, Boulder, CO, 319–46.

Pizzolato, L. F. (2007), 'Aurelio Giuseppe Amatucci studioso di letteratura cristiana antica', *Aevum: Rassegna di scienze storiche linguistiche e filologiche* 81 (n.s.), 227–53.

Pomeroy, A. J. (2018), 'Classical Antiquity, Cinema and Propaganda', in Roche and Demetriou (2018), 264–85.

Purcell, N. (1987), 'Town in Country and Country in Town', in MacDougall, E. B. (ed.), *Ancient Roman Villa Gardens*, Washington, DC, 187–203.

Purcell, N. (1996), 'Rome and the Management of Water: Environment, Culture and Power', in Shipley and Salmon (1996), 180–212.

Race, W. H. (2008), *Argonautica, Apollonius Rhodius*, Cambridge, MA.

Rea, J. (2007), *Legendary Rome: Myth, Monuments, and Memory on the Palatine and Capitoline*, London.

Rea, R. (2004) (ed.), *L'Ipogeo di Trebio Giusto sulla Via Latina: Scavi e restauri*, Vatican City.

Rebenich, S. (1989), 'Beobachtungen zum Sturz des Tatianus und des Proculus', *ZPE* 76, 153–65.

Rebenich, S. (1991), 'Zum Theodosiusobelisken in Konstantinopel', *IstMitt* 41, 447–76.

Reed, J. D. (2007), *Virgil's Gaze: Nation and Poetry in the* Aeneid, Princeton, NJ.

Reed, J. D. (2010), 'Vergil's Roman', in Farrell, J., and Putnam, M. J. C. (eds.), *A Companion to Vergil's* Aeneid *and Its Tradition*, Malden, MA; Oxford, 66–79.

Reitz, B. L. (2012), '*Tantae molis erat*: On Valuing Roman Imperial Architecture', in Sluiter and Rosen (2012), 315–44.

Reitz, B. L. (2013), 'Nature's Helping Hand: Cooperation between Builder and Nature as a Rhetorical Strategy in Vitruvius, Statius and Pliny the Elder', in Heirman, J., and Klooster, J. (eds.) *Ideologies of Space: Ancient and Modern*, Gent, 109–24.

Reitz-Joosse, B. L. (2016), 'The City and the Text in Vitruvius' De Architectura', *Arethusa* 49, 183–97.

Reitzenstein, E. (1935), 'Das neue Kunstwollen in den Amores Ovids', *RhM* 84, 62–88.

Richards, I. A. (1936), *The Philosophy of Rhetoric*, London; Oxford; New York.

Richmond, I. A. (1935), 'Trajan's Army on Trajan's Column', *PBSR* 13, 1–40.

Riesenweber, T. (2007), *Uneigentliches Sprechen und Bildermischung in den Elegien des Properz*, Berlin.

Riggsby, A. M. (2006), *Caesar in Gaul and Rome: War in Words*, Austin, TX.

Rimell, V. (2009), *Martial's Rome: Empire and the Ideology of Epigram*, Cambridge.

Robinson, M. (2006), 'Augustan Responses to the *Aeneid*', in Clarke, Currie, and Lyne (2006), 185–216.

Robinson, O. F. (1992), *Ancient Rome: City Planning and Administration*, London.

Roby, C. (2016), *Technical Ekphrasis in Greek and Roman Science and Literature: The Written Machine between Alexandria and Rome*, Cambridge.

Roche, H., and Demetriou, K. (2018) (eds.), *Brill's Companion to the Classics, Fascist Italy and Nazi Germany*, Leiden.

Roche, P. (2011a) (ed.), *Pliny's Praise: The* Panegyricus *in the Roman World*, Cambridge.

Roche, P. (2011b), 'The *Panegyricus* and the Monuments of Rome', in Roche (2011a), 45–66.

Romano, E. (2016), 'Between Republic and Principate: Vitruvius and the Culture of Transition', *Arethusa* 49, 335–51.

Römer, F. (1994), 'Mode und Methode in der Deutung panegyrischer Dichtung der nachaugusteischen Zeit', *Hermes* 122, 95–113.

Rolfe, J. C. (1963), *Ammianus Marcellinus* (3 vols.), Cambridge, MA; London.

Roller, M. B. (2010), 'Demolished Houses, Monumentality, and Memory in Roman Culture', *ClAnt* 29, 117–80.

Rossi, A. (2000), 'The *Aeneid* Revisited: The Journey of Pompey in Lucan's *Pharsalia*', *AJPh* 121, 571–91.

Rossi, L. (1978), 'Technique, Toil and Triumph on the Danube in Trajan's Propaganda Programme', *AntJ* 58, 81–7.

Russell, B. (2013), *The Economics of the Roman Stone Trade*, Oxford.

250 BIBLIOGRAPHY

Russell, B. (2018), ' "Difficult and Costly": Stone Transport, Its Constraints, and Its Impact', in Coquelet, C., Creemers, G., Dreesen, R., and Goemare, É. (eds.), *Roman Ornamental Stones in North-Western Europe: Natural Resources, Manufacturing, Supply, Life & After-Life*, Namur, 131–50.

Russell, B., and Wootton, W. (2017), 'Makers and Making: Classical Art in Action', in Lichtenberger, A., and Raja, R. (eds.), *The Diversity of Classical Archaeology*, Turnhout.

Rutherford, I. C., and Naiden, F. (1996), 'Amphion's Paean: A Note on Propertius 3.15.42', *MD* 37, 231–8.

Saastamoinen, A. (2010), *The Phraseology of Latin Building Inscriptions in Roman North Africa*, Helsinki.

Saatmann, K., Jüngst, E., and Thielscher, P. (1939), *Caesars Rheinbrücke*, offprint from *Bonner Jahrbücher* 143, 83–212, Berlin.

Sabbah, G. (1970), *Ammien Marcellin, Histoire II, Livres XVII–XIX*, Paris.

Sallmann, K. (1986), 'La responsabilité de l'homme face à la nature', *Helmantica* 37, 251–66.

Santoro L'Hoir, F. (2008), *Tragedy, Rhetoric and the Historiography of Tacitus'* Annales, Ann Arbor, MI.

Sapirstein, P. (2018), 'Picturing Work', in Lytle, E. (ed.), *A Cultural History of Work in Antiquity*, London, 33–56.

Scarola, M. (1987), 'Il muro di Avaricum: lettura di Cesare, *B. G.* 7,23', *MD* 18, 183–204.

Scheid, J., and Svenbro, J. (1996), *The Craft of Zeus: Myths of Weaving and Fabric*, Cambridge, MA.

Scheithauer, A. (2000), *Bautätigkeit in Rom: das Echo in der antiken Literatur*, Stuttgart.

Schieder, W. (2006), 'Rom: die Repräsentation der Antike im Faschismus', in Hölkeskamp and Stein-Hölkeskamp (2006), 701–21.

Schierl, P. (2006), *Die Tragödien des Pacuvius*, Berlin.

Schindler, C. (2000), *Untersuchungen zu den Gleichnissen im römischen Lehrgedicht*, Göttingen.

Schmidt, E. A. (2001) (ed.), *L'histoire littéraire immanente dans la poésie latine, Entretiens* 47, Geneva.

Schmitt, R. (1967), *Dichtung und Dichtersprache in indogermanischer Zeit*, Wiesbaden.

Schmitzer, U. (2016), *Rom im Blick. Lesarten der Stadt von Plautus bis Juvenal*, Darmstadt.

Schraven, M. (2009), 'Out of Sight, Yet Still in Place: On the Use of Italian Renaissance Portrait Medals as Building Deposits', *Res* 55–56, 182–93.

Schraven, M. (2012), 'Founding Rome Anew: Pope Sixtus IV and the Foundation of Ponte Sisto, 1473', in Delbeke, M., and Schraven, M. (eds.), *Foundation, Dedication and Consecration in Early Modern Europe*, Leiden, 129–51.

Seelentag, G. (2006), 'Die Trajanssäule: Bilder des Sieges', in Hölkeskamp and Stein-Hölkeskamp (2006), 401–18.

Segal, C. (1983), 'Dissonant Sympathy: Song, Orpheus, and the Golden Age in Seneca's Tragedies', in Boyle, A. J. (ed.), *Seneca Tragicus: Ramus Essays on Senecan Drama*, Berwick, 229–51.

Segenni, S. (2003), 'Il prosciugamento del lago Fucino e le scoperte archeologiche', in Campanelli (2003), 56–62.

Seif, K. P. (1973), *Die Claudiusbücher in den Annalen des Tacitus*, diss. Mainz.

Senseney, J. R. (2011), *The Art of Building in the Classical World*, Cambridge.

Setta, S. (1986), *Renato Ricci: dallo squadrismo alla Repubblica sociale italiana*, Bologna.

BIBLIOGRAPHY 251

Settis, S. (1988), 'La Colonna' in Settis, S., La Regina, A., Agosti, G., and Farinella, V. (eds.), *La Colonna Traiana*, Turin, 45–255.

Settis, S. (1991), 'La Colonne Trajane: l'empereur et son public', *RA* 1 (n.s.), 186–98.

Seyfarth, W. (1968–71), *Ammianus Marcellinus: Römische Geschichte. Lateinisch und Deutsch und mit einem Kommentar versehen*, Berlin.

Seyfarth, W. (1978), *Ammiani Marcellini Rerum gestarum libri qui supersunt*, Leipzig.

Shackleton Bailey, D. R. (1949), 'Propertiana', *CQ* 43, 22–9.

Shackleton Bailey, D. R. (1983), 'Notes on Statius' *Thebaid*', *MH* 40, 51–60.

Shackleton Bailey, D. R. (2003), *Statius* (3 vols.), Cambridge, MA; London.

Shannon, K. (2012), 'Memory, Religion, and History in Nero's Great Fire: Tacitus *Annals* 15.41–7', *CQ* 62, 749–65.

Shapiro, H. A. (1980), 'Jason's Cloak', *TAPhA* 110, 263–86.

Shipley, G., and Salmon, J. B. (1996) (eds.), *Human Landscapes in Classical Antiquity: Environment and Culture*, London; New York.

Silk, M. S. (1974), *Interaction in Poetic Imagery: With Special Reference to Early Greek Poetry*, Cambridge.

Simon, E. (1966), 'Fragmente from Fries der Basilica Aemilia', in Helbig, W., *Führer durch die öffentlichen Sammlungen klassischer Altertümer in Rom* II⁴, Tübingen, 834–43.

Sinn, F., and Freyberger, K. (1996), *Museo Gregoriano Profano. Katalog der Skulpturen I.2: Die Ausstattung des Hateriergrabes*, Mainz.

Sjöblad, A. (2009), *Metaphors Cicero Lived By: The Role of Simile and Metaphor in* De senectute, Lund.

Sluiter, I., and Rosen, R. (2012) (eds.), *Aesthetic Value in Classical Antiquity*, Leiden.

Smolenaars, J. J. L. (1994), *Statius Thebaid VII: A Commentary*, Leiden.

Smolenaars, J. J. L. (2006), 'Ideology and Poetics along the Via Domitiana: Statius' *Silvae* 4.3', in Nauta, van Dam, and Smolenaars (2006), 223–44.

Smolenaars, J. J. L., van Dam, H.-J., and Nauta, R. (2008) (eds.), *The Poetry of Statius*, Leiden; Boston.

Snell, B. (1971), *Szenen aus griechischen Dramen*, Berlin.

Snyder, J. M. (1980), *Puns and Poetry in Lucretius'* De Rerum Natura, Amsterdam.

Spencer, D. (2010), *Roman Landscape Culture and Identity*, Cambridge.

Spencer, D. (2018), 'Written Rome: Ancient Literary Responses', in Holleran and Claridge (2018), 621–42.

Squire, M. (2009), *Image and Text in Greco-Roman Antiquity*, Cambridge.

Squire, M. (2013), 'Ekphrasis at the Forge and the Forging of Ekphrasis: The "Shield of Achilles" in Graeco-Roman Word and Image', *Word & Image* 29: 157–91.

Squire, M. (2015), 'Ecphrasis: Visual and Verbal Interactions in Ancient Greek and Latin Literature'. *Oxford Handbooks Online*. https://doi.org/10.1093/oxfordhb/9780199935390.013.58.

Stärk, E. (1995), *Kampanien als geistige Landschaft*, München.

Steen, G. J. (2011), 'The Contemporary Theory of Metaphor: Now New and Improved', *Review of Cognitive Linguistics* 9, 26–64.

Steiner, D. (1986), *The Crown of Song: Metaphor in Pindar*, London.

Stenger, J. (2015), 'Ammian und die Ewige Stadt. Das spätantike Rom als Heterotopie', in Fuhrer, T. (ed.), *Rom und Mailand in der Spätantike*, Berlin; Boston, 189–216.

Stewart, P. (2003), *Statues in Roman Society: Representation and Response*, Oxford.

Stewart, P. (2004), *Roman Art*, Oxford.

252 BIBLIOGRAPHY

Stieber, M. (2011), *Euripides and the Language of Craft*, Leiden.

Stöger, H. (2011), *Rethinking Ostia: A Spatial Enquiry into the Urban Society of Rome's Imperial Port-Town*, Leiden.

Stone, M. (1999), 'A Flexible Rome: Fascism and the Cult of Romanità', in Edwards, C. (ed.), *Roman Presences: Receptions of Rome in European Culture, 1789–1945*, Cambridge, 205–20.

Stover, T. (2010), 'Rebuilding Argo: Valerius Flaccus' Poetic Creed', *Mnemosyne* 63, 640–50.

Stroh, W. (1971), *Die römische Liebeselegie als werbende Dichtung*, Amsterdam.

Sullivan, J. P. (1991), *Martial: The Unexpected Classic*, Cambridge.

Syme, R. (1958), *Tacitus* (2 vols.), Oxford.

Taisne, A.-M. (1994), *L'Esthétique de Stace: la peinture des correspondances*, Paris.

Taisne, A.-M. (1996), 'Échos épiques dans les *Silves* de Stace', in Delarue, F., Georgacoupolou, S., Laurens, P., and Taisne, A.-M. (eds.), *Epicedion: Hommage à P. Papinus Statius*, Poitiers, 215–34.

Tamassia, R. (1985), 'Dall'ideologia al saccheggio', in Manacorda, C., and Tamassia, R., *Il piccone del regime*, Rome.

Taylor, R. (2003), *Roman Builders: A Study in Architectural Process*, Cambridge.

Thomas, E. (2007), *Monumentality in The Roman Empire: Architecture in the Antonine Age*, Oxford.

Thomas, E. (2010), 'Architecture', in Barchiesi, A., and Scheidel, W. (eds.), *The Oxford Handbook of Roman Studies*, Oxford, 838–58.

Thomas, E. (2014), 'The Monumentality of Text', in Osborne (2014), 57–82.

Thomas, E., and Witschel, C. (1992), 'Constructing Reconstruction: Claim and Reality of Roman Rebuilding Inscriptions in the Latin West', *PBSR* 60, 135–77.

Thomas, M. L. (2004), '(Re)Locating Domitian's Horse of Glory: The Equus Domitiani and Flavian Urban Design', *MAAR* 49, 21–46.

Thomas, R. (1983), 'Callimachus, the *Victoria Berenices* and Roman Poetry', *CQ* 33, 92–113.

Thomas, R. (1988), 'Tree Violation and Ambivalence in Virgil', *TAPhA* 118, 261–73.

Thornton, M. K. (1986), 'Julio-Claudian Building Programs: Eat, Drink, and Be Merry', *Historia* 35, 28–44.

Thornton, M. K., and Thornton, R. L. (1985), 'The Draining of the Fucine Lake: A Quantitative Analysis', *AncW* 12, 105–20.

Tiberi, L. (2009), 'L'istituto Luce a la sua documentaristica', in D'Amelio (2009), 169–70.

Torelli, M. (1995), 'Innovations in Roman Construction Techniques between the 1st Century BC and the 1st Century AD', in Torelli, M. (ed.), *Studies in the Romanization of Italy*, Edmonton, 212–45.

Toynbee, J. M. C. (1971), *Death and Burial in the Roman World*, London.

Traina, G. (1988), 'Da Dinocrate a Vitruvio', *Civiltà classica e cristiana* 9, 303–49.

Trisoglio, F. (1973), *Opere di Plinio Cecilio Secundo* (2 vols.), Turin.

Tutton, M. (2021), *Construction as Depicted in Western Art: From Antiquity to the Photograph*, Amsterdam.

Ulrich, R. (2008), 'Representations of Technical Processes', in Oleson (2008), 35–61.

van Dam, H.-J. (1984), *P. Papinius Statius, Silvae Book II: A Commentary*, Leiden.

van Dam, H.-J. (2006), 'Multiple Imitation of Epic Models in the *Silvae*', in Nauta, van Dam, and Smolenaars (2006), 185–205.

van Hook, L. (1905), *The Metaphorical Terminology of Greek Rhetoric and Literary Criticism*, diss. Chicago.

BIBLIOGRAPHY   253

van Tilburg, C. (2007), *Traffic and Congestion in the Roman Empire*, New York.

Varner, E. R. (2001), 'Punishment after Death: Mutilation of Images and Corpse Abuse in Ancient Rome', *Mortality* 6, 45–64.

Varner, E. R. (2004), *Mutilation and Transformation: Damnatio Memoriae and Roman Imperial Portraiture*, Leiden; Boston 2004.

Ventre, F. (2004), 'From the Pontine Plain to Benevento', in Della Portella (2004), 106–45.

Vessey, D. W. T. C. (1971), 'Thoughts on Tacitus' Portrayal of Claudius', *AJPh* 92, 385–409.

Vessey, D. W. T. C. (1973), *Statius and the Thebaid*, Cambridge.

Veyne, P. (1988), 'Conduct without Belief and Works of Art without Viewers', *Diogenes* 143, 1–22.

Visser, R. (1992), 'Fascist Doctrine and the Cult of the *Romanità*', *Journal of Contemporary History* 27.1, 5–22.

Vittinghoff, F. (1936), *Der Staatsfeind in der römischen Kaiserzeit: Untersuchungen zur damnatio memoriae*, Berlin.

Volk, K. (2002), *The Poetics of Latin Didactic*, Oxford.

Volk, K. (2009), *Manilius and his Intellectual Background*, Oxford.

Vollmer, F. (1898), *P. Papini Statii Silvarum Libri*, Leipzig.

Vout, C. (2008), 'The Art of "Damnatio Memoriae"', in Benoist, S., and Daguet-Gagey, A. (eds.), *Un discours en images de la condamnation de mémoire*, Metz, 153–72.

Vout, C. (2012), *The Hills of Rome: Signature of an Eternal City*, Cambridge.

Wagoner, B. (2017), 'Introduction', in Wagoner, B. (ed.), *Handbook of Culture and Memory*, Oxford, 1–16.

Wallace-Hadrill, A. (1983), *Suetonius: The Scholar and His Caesars*, London.

Wallace-Hadrill, A. (1990), 'Pliny the Elder and Man's Unnatural History', *G&R* 37, 80–96.

Walter, A. (2014), *Erzählen und Gesang im Flavischen Epos*, Berlin; Boston.

Ward-Perkins, J.-B. (1992), 'Nicomedia and the Marble Trade', in Dodge, H., and Ward-Perkins, B. (eds.), *Marble in Antiquity: Collected Papers of J. B. Ward-Perkins, Archaeological Monographs of the British School at Rome* 6, London, 61–105.

Webb, R. (1999), 'The Aesthetics of Sacred Space: Narrative, Metaphor, and Motion in "Ekphraseis" of Church Buildings', *Dumbarton Oaks Papers* 53, 59–74.

Webb, R. (2001), 'Ekphrasis, Amplification and Persuasion in Procopius' *Buildings*', *Antiquité Tardive* 8, 67–71.

Webb, R. (2009), *Ekphrasis, Imagination and Persuasion in Ancient Rhetorical Theory and Practice*, Farnham.

Welch, T. S. (2005), *The Elegiac Cityscape: Propertius and the Meaning of Roman Monuments*, Columbus, OH.

Welge, J. (2005), 'Fascism Triumphans: On the Architectural Translation of Rome', in Lazzaro and Crum (2005), 83–94.

Wellesley, K. (1981), 'What Happened on the Capitol in December AD 69?', *AJAH* 6, 166–90.

Werth, P. (1994), 'Extended Metaphor: A Text-World Account', *Language and Literature* 3, 79–103.

Wilkins, A. T. (2005), 'Augustus, Mussolini and the Parallel Imagery of Empire', in Lazzaro and Crum (2005), 53–65.

Williams, R. D. (1972), *P. Papini Stati Thebaidos Liber Decimus. Edited with a Commentary*, Leiden.

254 BIBLIOGRAPHY

Wilson, A. I. (2005), 'The Economic Impact of Technological Advances in the Roman Construction Industry', in Lo Cascio, E. (ed.), *Innovazione tecnica e progresso economico nel mondo romano*, Bari, 225–36.

Wilson Jones, M. (1993), 'One Hundred Feet and a Spiral Stair: The Problem of Designing Trajan's Column', *JRA* 6, 23–38.

Wilson Jones, M. (2000), *Principles of Roman Architecture*, New Haven, CT.

Wimmel, W. (1960), *Kallimachos in Rom: Nachfolge seines apologetischen Dichtens in der Augusteerzeit*, Wiesbaden.

Wimmel, W. (1973), *Die technische Seite von Caesars Unternehmen gegen Avaricum (B. G. 7, 13 ff.)*, Wiesbaden.

Wirsching, A. (2006), 'Wie die Obelisken um die Zeitenwende und im 4. Jahrhundert aufgerichtet wurden', *Gymnasium* 113, 329–58.

Wirsching, A. (2010), 'Wie die Obelisken Rom erreichten', *Gymnasium* 117, 255–73.

Wirsching, A. (2013), *Obelisken transportieren und aufrichten in Ägypten und in Rom*, Norderstedt.

Wiseman, T. P. (1978), 'Flavians on the Capitol', *AJAH* 3, 163–78.

Wiseman, T. P. (1991), 'Review of Thornton, M. K. and Thornton, R. L. (1989), *Julio-Claudian Building Programs. A Quantitative Study in Political Management*, Wauconda', *Classical Review* 41.1, 255–6.

Wiseman, T. P. (1998), 'The Publication of *De Bello Gallico*', in Welch, K., and Powell, A. (eds.), *Julius Caesar as Artful Reporter*, London, 1–9.

Wolfram Thill, E. (2010), 'Civilization under Construction: Depictions of Architecture on the Column of Trajan', *AJA* 114, 27–43.

Wolfram Thill, E. (2011), 'Aurelius', *JRA* 24, 283–312.

Wolpert, A. (2002), *Remembering Defeat*, Baltimore, MD; London.

Woodman, A. J. (2004), *Tacitus: The Annals*, Indianapolis.

Woodman, A. J. (2009a) (ed.), *The Cambridge Companion to Tacitus*, Cambridge.

Woodman, A. J. (2009b), 'Tacitus and the Contemporary Scene', in Woodman (2009a), 31–46.

Woolf, G. (1995), *Becoming Roman: The Origins of Provincial Civilization in Gaul*, Cambridge.

Woolf, G. (1996), 'Monumental Writing and the Expansion of Roman Society in the Early Empire', *JRS* 86, 22–39.

Wray, D. (2007), 'Wood: Statius' *Silvae* and the Poetics of Genius', *Arethusa* 40, 127–43.

Wrede, H. (1966), 'Zur Errichtung des Theododiusobelisken in Istanbul', *IstMitt* 16, 178–98.

Wrede, H. (1971), 'Das Mausoleum der Claudia Semne', *RM* 78, 125–66.

Wrede, H. (1981), *Consecratio in Formam Deorum. Vergöttlichte Privatpersonen in der römischen Kaiserzeit*, Mainz.

Zanker, P. (1987), *Augustus und die Macht der Bilder*, München.

Zanker, P. (1997), *Der Kaiser baut fürs Volk*, Opladen.

Zanzanaini, G. (2004), *Renato Ricci, fascista integrale*, Mursia.

Zimmer, G. (1982), *Römische Berufsdarstellungen, Archäologische Forschungen* 12, Berlin.

Index Locorum

Amatucci, Aurelio Giuseppe
  Codex fori Mussolini
    1-69, 69-97, 98-141: 227
    xliii-xlv, 53-56: 229
    xcviii-cxiii, 116-141: 228
Ammianus Marcellinus
  Res Gestae
    16.10.17: 54
    17.4: 53–61
    17.4.7-11: 57n135
    17.4.12: 54–7
    17.4.12–13: 60–1
    17.4.13: 55, 57
    17.4.14: 58
    17.4.15: 58–9
    17.4.19, 21, 23: 54n125
Apollonius of Rhodes
  Argonautica
    1.27-31: 176
    1.721-9: 177
    1.730-4: 177
    1.735-41: 174n2, 176–8
    1.759-62: 177n16
Aratus of Soloi
  Phaenomena
    1: 104n16
Aristophanes
  Frogs
    1004: 105n20
  Peace
    749-50: 104

Caesar [Gaius Iulius Caesar]
  De Bello Gallico
    4.17.1-2: 48–50, 81n53
    4.17.3: 51
    4.18.1: 50–1
    4.18–4.19: 51
    4.19.4: 51
    6.29.3: 195n68
    7.23: 50n111
    7.72-3: 49n108

Callimachus of Cyrene
  Aetia
    fr.1.3-4, 1.17-18: 149n39
    fr.1.16: 152n50
    fr.1.20: 157, 160n79
    fr.1.25-8: 163n90
    fr.1.29-30: 158n68
    fr.1.30-2: 105n23
    fr.1.30: 157
    fr.118: 151–2
  Epigrams
    27: 149n39
    27.2-4: 152n50
    28: 162
  Hymn to Apollo
    106: 163
    108-12: 162
    110-12: 162
  Hymn to Artemis
    46-86: 160–1
Cassius Dio [Dio Cassius]
  Roman History
    60.2.5-7: 97n95
    60.11.5: 68n22, 72
    60.33.3-5: 72
    60.33.3: 94n87
    60.33.4: 94n89
    60.33.5: 86n66
    64.17.3: 1n1
    65.10.2: 1
    68.1.1: 212
    68.16.3: 24n27
Catullus
  Carmina
    64: 128n98
    95.1-3: 149n39, 149n40
Cicero [Marcus Tullius
    Cicero]
  De inventione
    1.94: 181n28
  Orator
    3.12: 164n96

256 INDEX LOCORUM

Democritus
  fr.21: 112n52
Dionysius of Halicarnassus
  Roman Antiquities
  1.88: 122n81
Dio of Prusa [Dio Chrysostomus]
  Orations
  32.62: 174n2

Ennius [Quintus Ennius]
  Annales
  175-9: 167n111
Eumelos
  fr.13: 174n2, 174n5
Euripides
  Antiope: 174–5
  fr.182a: 175
  fr.190: 179n24
  fr.223.90-7: 175, 193n63

Herodotus
  Histories
  2.124.1-3, 5: 13–14
  2.125.6-7: 14–15
Hesiod
  Fragmenta Hesiodea
  182: 174n2
Homer
  Iliad
  22.410-1: 190n57
  Odyssey
  8.489, 8.492-3: 112n52
  11.260-5: 174n2
  12.183: 102n11
  24.197: 102
Homeric Hymns
  6.20: 102n11
Horace [Quintus Horatius
  Flaccus]
  Ars poetica
  291-4, 386-90: 149n39
  391-401: 180–1
  Epistles
  1.18: 174n9
  1.18.39-43: 181
  1.19.20-1: 153n54
  2.2.72-3: 154n56
  2.2.123: 168n112

Odes
  3.1.45-6: 104n18
  3.11: 179–80
  3.30: 104n18, 169
  3.30.1: 100, 210
  3.30.1-5: 211n36
  3.30.8-9: 211n37
  3.30.15-6: 170n122
Satires
  1.4.9-10: 149n39, 149n40
  1.10: 149n40

Josephus [Titus Flavius Josephus]
  Bellum Judaicum
  4.648: 1n1
Julian [Flavius Claudius Julianus]
  Epistulae
  58: 27n38
Juvenal [Decimus Junius Juvenalis]
  Satires
  3.236-8, 254-61: 154n56
  6.169-72: 178
  10.61-4: 212n38

Livy [Titus Livius]
  Ab urbe conditae
  4.6: 122n82
  39.13.13: 35n69
Lucan [Marcus Annaeus Lucanus]
  Civil War
  2.165, 2.177: 206n21
  2.261-2: 167n111
  2.679: 112n47
  3.375-458: 192n62
  3.432-45: 167n111
Lucian of Samosata
  Imagines
  14: 174n2
  Quomodo historia conscribenda sit
  20: 93n85
Lucretius [Titus Lucretius Carus]
  De rerum natura
  1.925-6: 153n54
  4.513-21: 111n46
Lycophron
  Alexandra
  604: 174n2
  1275-80: 68n20

INDEX LOCORUM 257

Manilius [Marcus Manilius]
Astronomica
1.20-2: 112n49
1.113: 112n47
1.911, 4.185: 206n21
2.751-4: 111n44
2.752-3: 109
2.755-71: 109–113
2.772, 782: 111
2.772-87: 113–17
2.780-1: 115
2.784: 115
5.709: 109n39
Menander Rhetor
368.21-369.2: 80n51
Minyas
fr.3: 174n2, 174n5

Ovid [Publius Ovidius Naso]
Amores
1.1: 159n73
1.1.17: 111n47
2.2.23-8: 179n23
3.12.40: 180n26
Ars amatoria
3.311-4, 315, 321-6: 179
3.467-8: 153n54
Fasti
1.1: 152n51
5.111, 4.830: 111n47
Metamorphoses
1.4: 187n43
1.330-9, 341-7: 95–7
6.178-9, 221, 271, 402: 178
8.626-720: 150n44
9.169: 206n21
11.156: 29
15.871-9: 210–11
Tristia
2.559-60: 111n47

Pacuvius [Marcus Pacuvius]
Antiopa
fr.3: 179n24
Pausanias
Description of Greece
9.5.7-8: 174n2
10.5.9-13: 152n49

Philostratus
Imagines
1.10: 174n2
Pindar
Isthmian Odes
4.38: 103n12, 104n17
Nemean Odes
3.3-5: 104n17
Olympian Odes
3.3: 103n12, 104n17
6: 104n18
6.1-5: 103–4
6.27: 103n15
Pythian Odes
3.113: 104n17
6.5-9: 104n17
6.10-18: 104
7.1-4, 4.138, fr.194.1-3: 104n17
Plato
Gorgias
485e-486a: 174n8
485e-486c: 174n2
Republic
10.596d-e: 177n19
Pliny the Elder [Gaius Plinius Secundus]
Natural History
4.75: 89n76
9.14-5: 88n72
16.190: 89n75
33.1-2: 81–2
33.63: 88n73
34.38: 1n1
36.1-2: 82–3
36.64: 57n135
36.69-70: 52–3, 57–8, 81n53
36.71: 56
36.121: 79
36.122: 80
36.123: 79n48, 89n77
36.124: 79–81, 89n77, 92
Pliny the Younger [Gaius Plinius Caecilius
Secundus]
Epistles
1.16.6: 168n113
10.41: 66–67
Panegyricus
16.5, 36.1: 142n17
49.4-8: 210n34

258 INDEX LOCORUM

Pliny the Younger [Gaius Plinius Caecilius
    Secundus] (cont)
  50.1: 210n34
  51: 154n56
  51.3-4: 210n34
  52.3: 205
  52.4: 209, 211
  52.4-5: 203-7
  52.5: 212
  52.6: 208n30
  52.7: 208-9
  55.9: 203n14, 211
  Poetae Comici Graeci
  fr.100: 105n20
  fr.657: 105n20
Propertius [Sextus Aurelius
    Propertius]
  Elegies
  1.9.9-10: 121n78, 196n73
  2.1.40: 159n75
  2.10.2: 153n54
  3.2.3-8: 179
  3.2.5-6: 121n78, 179n24
  3.3.40-2: 157n66
  3.9.49-52: 120n71
  3.15: 178
  4.1.1-70: 118
  4.1.5-6: 119
  4.1.37-8: 119
  4.1.39-54: 118
  4.1.55-8: 118-121
  4.1.67-8: 121-2
Pseudo-Apollodorus
  Bibliotheca
  3.5.5: 174n2
Pseudo-Seneca
  Octavia
  794-9: 206n22

Quintilian [Marcus Fabius
    Quintilianus]
  Institutio oratoria
  7 pr.1: 120n73
  10.3.17: 164
  11.3.128: 95n91
  Rhetorica ad Herennium
  2.43: 181n28

Scriptores Historiae Augustae
  Hadrian
  22.12: 69n25
Seneca the Younger [Lucius Annaeus
    Seneca]
  Apocolocyntosis
  1.2, 5.3: 95n91
  8.2: 97n95
  Hercules furens
  258-63: 181-2
  915-6: 182n30
  Oedipus
  440: 206n21
  609-12: 181, 193n65
  Phoenissae
  565-71: 182-3, 195n69
  Quaestiones naturales
  3.3.1: 68n20
  Thyestes
  60-2, 755-67: 206n22
Servius
  In Vergilii Aeneidos Libros
  praef. 2-4: 128n98
Silius Italicus
  Punica
  3.433: 206n21
  11.440-82: 179
Statius [Publius Papinius Statius]
  Achilleid
  1.8-13: 184
  Silvae
  Praef. 1.3-4: 150
  Praef. 1.1-5: 146-7
  Praef. 1.11-5: 147, 168n114
  Praef. 1.13-14: 150
  Praef. 1.22-3: 149
  Praef. 1.24-7: 147
  1.1, 3.1, 4.3: 11
  1.1: 136-43, 144n26, 145n31,
      148n36, 150, 154-7, 172, 202, 207-
      11, 224
  1.1.1-7: 137-40, 141
  1.1.2-3: 150
  1.1.3-4: 159, 224
  1.1.15-6: 209
  1.1.33-5: 209
  1.1.56-7: 208n30

INDEX LOCORUM 259

1.1.57: 138n6
1.1.61-70: 138–40
1.1.61-2: 150, 209
1.1.63-70: 154–5
1.1.64-5: 156, 189n55
1.1.74-5: 155
1.1.91-4: 210–11
1.1.103-4: 209
1.2.1: 155–6
1.2.222-4: 156n60
1.3.15-7: 192n60
1.5.23-29, 215–16: 163n90
2.1.17-8: 155n59
2.2: 143n23, 158, 169n119,
  183, 192n60
2.2.36-42: 158n69
2.2.56: 141n16
2.2.60-2: 169n117, 184n35
2.2.72-84: 156n62
2.2.124-5: 141n16
2.7: 165
2.7.12-13: 165
Praef. 3: 151n45, 163n92, 170
3.1: 136, 137n3, 140–3, 148n36,
  150–2, 161, 164n94, 166, 169–
  171, 192n60
3.1.1-15: 140–1
3.1.2: 152n51
3.1.16-7, 115: 169n117,
  179n25, 184n35
3.1.19-22: 141, 150, 159n75
3.1.29-30: 151n44, 152n51
3.1.32-3: 150n44
3.1.49-51: 152n51, 158–9, 170
3.1.54: 138n6
3.1.82: 150n44
3.1.91-102: 158
3.1.91-116: 142
3.1.117-38: 142, 150n42
3.1.118-20: 166–8
3.1.125-34: 159–160, 170
3.1.128-9: 156
3.1.134-5: 141n15
3.1.139-40: 165
3.1.147-53: 156n62, 165–6
3.1.166-83: 170n123
3.1.168-9: 141n16, 169
3.1.180-1: 169

3.1.184-6: 169–171
3.2.39-41: 185
3.3.102: 158n69
3.5.35-6: 149n39
4.2: 138n5, 210n34
4.3: 136, 137n3, 142–6, 153–4, 156–
  7, 162–4, 166–9, 172
4.3.1-3: 142–3
4.3.4-8: 144
4.3.9-26: 143–4
4.3.27-39: 143, 153n53
4.3.32-3: 153n53
4.3.49-53: 166–8
4.3.49-55: 153
4.3.56-60: 144–5
4.3.61: 169n117
4.3.62-71: 143n20, 156–7
4.3.71: 159n75
4.3.72-94: 143n21, 143n23, 162–3
4.3.79-80: 168
4.3.119-20, 141-4: 155n59
4.3.124-63: 143n21
4.3.135-7: 144, 145n31
4.4.51-5: 166
4.4.90: 165n102
4.4.96: 160n81
4.6: 172
4.7.11-12: 163n90
4.7.26: 149n39
4.8.35-41: 155n59
5.1.189-90: 207n25
Thebaid
1.5: 193n64
1.9-10: 186–7
1.13-14, 9-10: 185
1.33: 187n44
1.295: 29n47
2.273-4: 161n84
2.452-6: 187–8
2.700: 189n50
4.356-60: 188–190
4.823-30: 163n90
5.605, 12.411: 206n21
6.84-117: 169n118
7.271-5: 193n62
7.277-9: 193
7.278-81: 186n39
7.441-51: 132n104, 190–3

260 INDEX LOCORUM

Statius [Publius Papinius Statius] (cont)
  7.452-60: 191–3
  7.599-601: 190
  7.649-87: 195
  8.223-36: 187
  8.232-3: 187n46
  9.776-801: 186n39
  10.387-492: 186n39
  10.445: 111n47
  10.703-6, 12.9-10: 197n76
  10.786-8: 196n72
  10.829-31: 197–8
  10.846: 196n72
  10.870-82: 194–7
  10.877-82, 12.703-6: 190n58
  12.810-12: 149n39
Strabo
  Geography
  5.3.13: 68n20
  9.3.9: 152n49
Suetonius [Gaius Suetonius
        Tranquillus]
  Divus Augustus
  9: 90
  Gaius Caligula
  19.2: 88n74
  19.3: 89n76
  21: 144n28
  Divus Claudius
  10-25: 90n78
  20, 21, 32: 90
  20.1-3: 68n18, 91–3
  20.2: 69n23
  21.2: 94n88
  21.6: 93–7
  26-42: 90n78
  30, 41, 45: 95n91
  32: 97
  33.1: 97n95
  Domitianus
  23: 202n12, 206n19
  Divus Iulius
  44.3: 68n18, 144n28
  Nero
  19.2, 37.3: 144n28
  Tiberius
  73: 73n33

Divus Vespasianus
  8.5: 1

Tacitus [Publius Cornelius Tacitus]
  Annals
  12.56-7: 84–90
  12.64.2: 97n95
  15.42: 66, 89n77
  15.46.2: 66n12
  Histories
  3.71: 201
  3.72.2-3: 1n1, 201
Theocritus of Syracuse
  Idylls
  7.45-8: 105
Tibullus [Albius Tibullus]
  2.3.43-4: 154n56
Tragicorum Graecorum Fragmenta
  159: 104n19

Vacca
  Vita Lucani
  165n104
Varro [Marcus Terentius Varro]
  Res rusticae
  1.14.2: 194n67
Vergil [Publius Vergilius Maro]
  Aeneid
  1.1-11, 7.37-45: 124n84
  1.5: 124
  1.7: 126
  1.12: 126
  1.33: 28–9, 115, 126
  1.125-96, 6.756-886,
      8.626-728: 133n110
  1.263-4: 127
  1.265-79: 92n84
  1.276-7: 129
  1.278-9: 169n120
  1.421-9: 125–7
  1.430-6: 126n92
  1.436: 117
  1.437: 126
  1.522-3: 126–7
  1.573: 127
  3.13: 129
  3.16-8: 129

3.78: 129n101
3.132-7: 130
3.350: 130n103
4.74-5: 127n94
4.86-9: 127n94, 139n8, 189–90
4.233, 7.127, 7.290: 133n107
4.259-61: 127
4.265-7: 127–8
4.667-71: 128–9, 190
5.633: 131
5.755-8: 131
6.128: 29n47
6.177-82: 167n111
6.179-80: 115–16
6.781-3: 115
6.853: 127
7.61, 7.169-91: 132n105
7.157-9: 131–2
7.160-1: 132
8.285-8: 170
8.424-53: 159–60

8.443: 150n42
8.626-738: 150n42
9.70: 194n67
Eclogues
  4.3: 164n100
  8.64-109: 179n23
Georgics
  1.143: 115
  2.207-10: 116
  2.534-5: 115
  2.541-2: 153n54
  3.13: 116
  3.12-6: 124n83, 151n46
  3.16: 133
  4.169: 116
  4.170-5: 160n79
  4.486: 29n47
Vitruvius [Marcus Vitruvius Pollio]
  De architectura
    6.8.3-4: 195n68
    10.2.5-7: 37n73, 139n8

General Index

For ancient authors and their works see the *index locorum*.
Figures are indicated by *f* following the page number.

absence, visible, 199, 205, 207. *See
      also* lacuna
Acesta, 131–2
Acestes, 130–1
Achilles, 102
   shield of, 8n27, 160, 161n84, 177
Aemilii, 41–3
Aemilius Lepidus, 41–2n83
Aeneas, 40n81, 42, 167, 189
   as city-founder, 28–9, 108, 115, 121,
      123, 125–34
   shield of, 150n42, 159, 161n84
Aeolus, 210
aesthetics
   of architecture, 6, 103–6, 134,
      137, 151–2
   Callimachean, 118, 152, 157–63, 171
      (*see also* sound; speed)
   of construction, 102, 148–71
   and ecphrasis, 7
   of Fascist *romanità*, 220–2
   of texts, 8–9, 103–6, 134, 137, 148, 151–
      72, 213
Aetna, 160
agon, 174
Alba Fucens, 68n19
Alba Longa, 41
Albucia Candida, 18–19
Alcmene, 181
Alesia, 49n108
Alessandro di Torlonia, 68
Alexandria, 26–7, 55, 57
Algeria, 21, 22*f*
Amatucci, Aurelio Giuseppe, 227–9
Amphiaraus, 187
Amphion, 7, 10, 102, 121n78, 141, 168–9,
      173–98, 200, 202
Amphion the Younger, 186, 193

Amphitryon, 181
Anchises, 115, 127, 131, 133n107
Andromache, 130n103
Antigone, 193
Antiope, 176
   play by Euripides, 174–5, 179n24,
      181, 193
   play by Pacuvius, 179n24, 181
Antoninus Pius, 39
Aphrodite, 177. *See also* Venus
Apollo, 152, 156, 184–5, 197n74. *See also*
      Phoebus
aqueduct, 20n14, 163n90
   Aqua Claudia, 79–81, 89n77
   at Lambaesis, 21–2
arch, 79n48, 195n68, 211
   Septimius Severus, 5
architect, 20–1, 42
   Celer, 66
   Costantino Costantini, 224
   Domenico Fontana, 25
   Eupalinus, 21n23
   Giuseppe Pagano, 223–5
   Narcissus, 85–6, 90
   poet, 121n78, 179n22
   Severus, 66
Ares, 177. *See also* Mars
Argives, 190–5
Argo, 177
Argonauts, 176–8
Argos, 187
Aries. *See* zodiac
Arion, 178–9, 184n35
aristeia, 194
Artemis, 160–1.
ashlar masonry, 40, 46
Asia, 72n31
Asopus, 176

264 GENERAL INDEX

Augustus (Octavian), 42, 52–61, 68n18,
 84–5, 87, 91–2, 94n88, 121, 124–5,
 133, 215n3, 221
Avaricum, walls of. *See* walls
Avestan, 101n3
Avezzano, 69*f*, 74
Axum stele, 221–2

Baiae, 88n74, 144
Basilica Aemilia, 39–43, 40*f*, 45n99, 46–7,
 51, 216n7. *See also* frieze
Baths of Caracalla, 4
Béjaïa, 2*f*, 21–2
Beroë, 131
Bithynia, 66–7
Boeotia, 165
brick, 4
bridge, 20n15, 75, 78, 195–6
 building, 65n9, 143n23, 201n6
 Caesar's Rhine, 22n24, 48–51,
  53n121, 63n1
 between Puteoli and Baiae,
  88n74, 144n24
 Xerxes's Hellespont, 89, 144–5
Britannia, 18–19
Brontes, 138, 159–160
building site
 Fucine lake, 72
 at Ground Zero, 1–5, 2*f*
 obelisk St. Peter, 25
 represented in texts, 114, 125–7, 134,
  154–5, 175, 183n31, 190
 Trajanic, 45, 47

Cadmus, 174n3, 190n55, 193n64, 196n72
Caesar
 Julius, 48–51, 68, 81n53, 91, 144n28,
  167, 192
 Rhine bridge (*see* bridge)
 title, 23, 74, 133
Caligula, 25, 88n74
Callimacheanism. *See* aesthetics
Calliope, 157n66, 158
camp, 131–2
 construction of, 43–4, 190–3,
  200, 201n7
campaign, 50
 Dacia, 43

Campania, 166
Campi Palentini, 68
Campus Martius, 52n120, 53–6
Capaneus, 194–7, 201
Cape of Misenum, 66, 166
Capitoline, 1–2, 201, 208, 211
Capri, 156, 160
capstan, 34*f*, 75–8, 77*f*, 81, 99
Carrara, 218, 221, 226, 228 (*see also* marble)
Carthage, 117, 125–30, 139n8, 189–90
Cassandra, 118, 122
Celaeno, 133n107
celeritas. See speed
Cheiron, 179
Cheops, 13
chlamys, 84–5, 88
Circus of Nero, 25
Circus Maximus, 27–8, 31, 52–9
Cithairon, 179n24
city-building
 metaphor, 102, 108–9, 111, 113–35
 political role of, 107–8, 135
Claudius, 57
 draining of Fucine Lake (*see*
  Fucine Lake)
Codex fori Mussolini, 226–31
column, 37n72, 103–4, 125–6, 179n22
 of Trajan, 21–4, 23*f*, 28n46, 43–7,
  44*f*, 200–1
 of Marcus Aurelius, 201n5
concrete, 1, 4, 223*f*, 225
Constantine, 27n40
 obelisk, 53–5, 58, 61 (*see also* obelisk of
  Constantius)
Constantinople
 obelisk, 24–8, 34n63, 39, 47, 55, 61 (*see
  also* obelisk of Theodosius)
Constantius II, 26–8, 53–8, 224
constellations, 109
Costantini, Costantino. *See* architect
crane, 1, 25
 on Haterii relief, 35–9, 36*f*, 78
 in literature, 127n94, 139, 189
  noise, 154, 182–3 (*see also* sound)
Cretan labyrinth, 52
Crete, 130
Cupid, 159n73
curia, 39

GENERAL INDEX 265

Curtius, 143, 155–6, 209
Cyclopes, 141, 150n42, 177, 224. *See also*
    Brontes; Steropes
Cyme, 156

Dacia, 23, 74, 138
    on Column of Trajan (*see* column)
    Dacian campaigns (*see* campaign)
damnatio memoriae. See memory sanctions
Decentius, 27n40
demolition, 4n14, 8, 10, 195, 201, 210–11
    in Fascist Italy 214–16, 216*f*, 223*f*, 225
    See also destruction
destruction, 1, 181–98, 199–213
    in building inscriptions, 19, 212
    of Caesar's Rhine bridge, 51of
        Carthage, 128–9
    of Dacian buildings, 43, 200–1
    in Fascist Italy, 214–16, 216*f*, 223*f*, 225
    of Fucine Lake tunnel, 71
    interplay with construction, 1, 10, 43,
        181–98, 200–13, 215
    as memory sanction (*see* memory
        sanctions)
    staging of, 205, 215
    of statues, 202–13
    of temple of Jupiter Capitolinus, 1–2, 201
    and text, 53, 181–98, 207–212
    of Thebes, 10, 181–98, 202*See also*
        fragility; lacuna
Deucalion, 95
Dido, 125–8, 189–90
difficulty (*difficultas*)
    of construction, 49, 80, 86, 91–2, 97–9
    of transport, 24n29, 26, 28, 52–4, 57–8,
        222, 224, 229
digging, 131, 156, 160
    basket, 45, 46*f*
    on Column of Trajan, 45 (*see also*
        column)
    at Fucine Lake, 67–8, 78, 89, 92
    moral implications of, 80–3
Dirce, 178, 184, 193n64
Domitian
    building activity of, 2, 143–4,
        154n56, 162
    damnatio memoriae, 144n24, 202–12
        (*see also* memory sanctions)

praising of, 142–3, 153, 207–12
    See also statue; via
Domus Aurea, 66
Duce. *See* Mussolini, Benito
durability
    of structures, 200–1
    of literature, 8–9, 106, 173, 201, 211, 213
Dymas, 186n39

ecphrasis, 7–8, 50n111, 138, 154, 166
    of Jason's cloak, 176–8
    and narrative delay, 150n42
    technical, 8n27
Egypt, 13–15, 66
    granite from, 221
    obelisks from, 27n37, 52, 54, 57, 61,
        221–2, 226, 229
    See also Heliopolis; Thebes (Egypt)
ephemerality, 6, 15, 51, 53, 172, 198
Epirus, 130n103
Erichtho, 179n23
Esquiline. *See* frieze
Eteocles, 182–3, 187–8
Eunaeus, 195, 197
Eupalinus. *See* architect
Euploea, 165–6
Evander, 121
exemplum, 144
    Amphion as, 178–9, 181, 185–6,
        192n60
    of interpretation, 137, 145, 171

Farnesina, 219, 228–9
Fascism, Italian, 5, 10, 214–31
Faustina, 39
Fontana, Domenico. *See* architect
Foro Italico, 216–22
    construction of, 227
    name of, 216–18, 221
    obelisk of (*see* Obelisk)
    opening, 226
    similarity with imperial fora, 221
Foro Mussolini. *See* Foro Italico
Forte dei Marmi, 219
forum
    Acesta's, 131
    Romanum, 5, 39
        Domitian's statue on (*see* statue)

266 GENERAL INDEX

forum (*cont.*)
    Trajanic, 24, 44–7, 142n17 (*see also* column)
foundation (act of establishment)
    of the Basilica Aemilia, 42–3
    of cities, 9, 40–3, 48, 107–35
        of Acesta, 131
        of Aenus, 129
        of Alba Longa, 41, 41*f*
        of Carthage, 125–9
        of Lavinium, 40–1, 40*f*, 41*f*
        of Pergamum (in Crete), 130
        of Rome, 40, 40*f*, 43, 108, 115–35
        of Thebes, 174–98
    as poetic metaphor, 106–35, 174–98
    reversal of, 185–98
    rituals of, 122, 129, 131
    See also foundation (part of building);
        refoundation
foundation (part of building), 110–11,
        125–8, 130n102, 133
    of a poem (κρηπίς), 104n17
    rebuilding from the, 19
    See also foundation (act of
        establishment)
fragility, 172, 198
frieze
    Basilica Aemilia, 39–43, 40*f*, 46–7,
        51, 216n7
    Esquiline, 45–7, 41*f*
    See also Column of Trajan
Fucine Lake (lago Fucino), 9, 63–99
    draining
        Augustan rejection, 92
        Claudian, 68–9, 78–98
        degree of completion of, 69, 74, 79–
            80, 92, 98
        economic implications, 80, 86, 92–
            3, 97–9
        Hadrianic maintenance, 78
        modern, 68, 71–2, 75
        moral implications, 81–3, 88–9
        potential benefits of, 68
        success of, 69, 74, 86–7, 92, 98
        Trajanic maintenance, 74–5
        See also digging; nature; relief
    plain, 68, 78
    spectacles (*see* spectacle)

Gaius Valerius Pansa, 18–19
Gallic war, 48–50
Gargaphie, 193n62
Gaurus, 156–7, 165–6
Germania, 23, 74
Germanicus, 138
Ground Zero. *See* 9/11

Hadrian, 3n5, 18
    maintenance of Fucine Lake tunnel (*see*
        Fucine Lake)
Haemus, 144n25
Haliartus, 193n62
Hannibal, 143–4
Harmonia, 161
Haterii relief. *See* relief
Haterius (Tychicus). *See* architect
Hector, 130n103, 190n57
Helenus, 130n103
Heliopolis
    obelisks from, 52, 54, 56
Helios, 54n125
Hellespont. *See* bridge; Xerxes
Heracles, 177, 181. *See also* Hercules
Hercules
    assisting in construction, 141n15,
        142n17, 150–1, 159–161 (*see*
        also sound)
    digging, 156.
    labours of, 141, 143n20
    as a poet, 158–9, 169–71
    statuette, 172
    See also Heracles; temple
Hermes, 127–8, 174–5, 193. *See also*
    Mercury
Hermoupolis Magna, 179n22
Hippodrome of Constantinople, 25
Hopleus, 186n39
hybris
    of emperor, 143–5
    of poet, 105, 142n17

Idas, 177
Ilioneus, 126
Inachia, 191–2
India, 144n25
Ino, 145, 185
Iocasta, 182–3

GENERAL INDEX 267

Iraq, 204
Iris, 131
irony, 61, 145n30–31, 181, 209
Isthmus of Corinth, 144–5
Italy, 3, 5, 9–10, 68, 125, 129, 215–19, 230
Iuvencus river. *See* river

Jason, 176–7
  cloak (*see* ecphrasis)
Julia Agrippina, 83–90
Julian, 27n38
Jupiter, 92n84, 95–6, 126–9, 133n107, 169,
    182, 194, 210–11. *See also* Zeus
  planet, 109n39
  temple of (*see* temple)

Kulturentstehung, 180

lacuna
  left by destruction, 199, 202
  textual, 109n39, 146n33
lacus Avernus. See lake
lacus Curtius. See lake
Laius, 189n52
lake
  Avernus, 66, 143n19
  Curtius, 143
  Fucine (*see* Fucine lake)
  Lucrine, 166
Lambaesis, 21–2
Liternian marsh, 156
Latian Forum, 138
Latini, 132
Latinus, 131–2
Latium, 137, 155
Lavinium, 40–1
Lemnian caves, 160
Leucothea, 185
librator, 20–1
Libya, 14, 144n25
Limon, 165–6
Liris. *See* river
Lollius, 181
LUCE, 215, 221n14, 222, 226
Lycus, 181
Lykidas, 105
lyre, 155, 179
  as decoration, 193

used in construction, 141, 173–6, 180–
    5, 189, 195–6

madeness, 8–9, 16–17, 20, 24, 100, 106,
    138, 146, 173, 212, 222
Maecius Celer, 184
Magnentius, 28, 55
marble, 4, 74n36
  Carrara, 218–29, 219*f*
  used in construction, 5n19, 46n101,
      114, 116
  obelisk (*see* obelisk of Mussolini)
  Pentelic, 39
  statue, 204n16
March on Rome, 220, 221*f*
Marcus Aurelius, 201n5
Marruvium, 78, 77*f*
Mars, 118, 129, 139, 154
  planet, 109n39
  See also Ares
Marsi, 68, 91
mass media, 214–15
Massicus, 156–7
Massilia, 192
Mausoleum of Augustus, 215n3
Maxentius, 27n40
Maximus (the usurper), 27
Mediolanum, 18
Melas. *See* river
memory
  of construction, 13–61, 137–148,
      214, 225
  cultural, 5n15, 15–16
  destruction of, 202–12 (*see also*
      memory sanctions)
  epigraphic, 16–29, 50–1
  of Fascism, 230
  mediation/remediation of, 15
  visual, 29–48, 51
memory sanctions, 144n24, 202–12
Menoeceus, 196n72
Mercury, 179
  planet, 109n39
  See also Hermes
Messalina, 83
Minerva, 140, 161. *See also* Pallas Athena
Misenus, 115, 166
mise en abyme, 7n23

268 GENERAL INDEX

Molorchus, 151n44, 152n51
Mons Salvianus, 68
monumentality, 5n16, 8n27, 11, 24n27,
    37–39, 53n122, 199n1, 210–1, 230
Mount Athos, 144–5
Mount Helicon, 165
Mulciber, 160. *See also* Vulcan
the Muses, 105, 110, 156, 165, 176, 186,
    197. *See also* Calliope
Mussolini, Benito, 10, 214, 217, 220*f*, 221,
    227, 229
    Foro (*see* Foro Italico)
    obelisk (*see* obelisk of Mussolini)
    personal involvement in construction,
        215, 216*f*
    See also *Codex fori Mussolini*
Mycalessos, 193n62

Naples, 68, 166
Narcissus. *See* architect
National Socialism, 5
nature, 140, 176, 191–2
    and boundaries, 9, 65–6, 82–3, 88–9,
        99, 142n17
    human control over, 5, 65, 69, 89–90, 97,
        99, 141–4, 184
    legitimacy of human intervention
        in, 9, 48n105, 63–7, 73–4, 143–
        4, 171
    metaphors drawn from, 59–60, 162–71
    relationship between man and, 74, 81–
        3, 88–90, 96–9
naumachia. *See* spectacle
Nautes, 130
Neptune, 95–6, 197
Nero, 83
    building activity of, 66–9, 80, 143–5
    circus of (*see* Circus of Nero)
Nerva, 22–3, 74
Nesis, 165–6
New Man (Fascism), 215
Nile. *See* river
Niobe, 178
Niobids, 178n20
Nonius Datus, 2*f*, 21–2
North Africa, 17n7, 20n14, 28n46
Novara, 18–19
Novius Vindex, 172

Obelisk
    of Constantius II, 27–8, 53–6, 224–5
    in front of Palazzo Montecitorio, 52–3
    of Mussolini, 216–31, 217*f*–221*f*
        transport of, 222–6
    in piazza S. Maria del Popolo, 52–3
    of Theodosius, 24–34, 26*f*–34*f*,
        39, 47, 51
    relief on (*see* relief)
Oedipus, 181n29, 189n52
Olympus, 115
One World Trade Center, 1
Onchestos, 193n62
Opera Nazionale Balilla, 218, 227
Opheltes, 169n118
Oromedon, 105
Orpheus, 141, 168, 169n117, 176–
    80, 183–6
Ostia, 66, 83, 88n72, 91–2, 143n19

paean, 178n20, 187
Pagano, Giuseppe. *See* architect
Palaemon, 184–5
Palatine, 132n105, 138n5
Pallas Athena, 138, 141, 160. *See also*
    Minerva
paludamentum, 88
panegyric, 9, 55n128, 143, 145, 154, 157,
    162, 171, 202, 207–8, 210
Parthenopaeus, 186n39
Parthenope, 165–6. *See also* Naples
patron, 11, 17, 20, 136, 147, 169, 181
    active participation in construction, 42,
        48, 51, 160, 215, 216n7
    deity, 140n11
Pentelic marble. *See* marble
Pergamum, 130
Persia, 31, 88, 149n39
Phoebus, 96, 184. *See also* Apollo
Phorbas, 193
piccone, 215, 216*f*, 231
planets, 109, 112n47. *See also* Jupiter;
    Mars; Mercury; Saturn; Venus
plectrum, 141, 185
Pollius Felix, 136–7, 140–2, 151n45, 156,
    158, 169, 183–6
Polycrates, 22n23
Polydorus, 129

GENERAL INDEX 269

Polynices, 182–3
Polyphemus, 179
Ponticus, 179n24, 196n73
Pontus, 66n14
Porta Maggiore, 88n72
pozzi, 70–1, 70*f*
Priam, 190n57
Proculus (Proclus), 25–9
propaganda, 5, 31n51, 225n28
Puteoli, 52–3, 66, 88n74, 136,
    144n24, 202n13
pyramids, 13–14, 52
Pyrrha, 95

rebuilding. *See* reconstruction
reconstruction, 199–212
    of Basilica Aemilia, 41–3
    in building inscriptions, 18–20
    of Caesar's Rhine bridge, 51
    of cities, 107
    of temple of Jupiter Capitolinus, 1–2,
        201, 216n7
    See also refoundation
recusatio, 157–9
redemptor, 37, 39.
    Haterius (Tychicus), 37
re-foundation, 108, 121, 125n89, 135,
        196n72. *See also* reconstruction
relief
    on Column of Marcus Aurelius (*see*
        Column of Marcus Aurelius)
    on Column of Trajan (*see* Column of
        Trajan)
    Haterii, 34–39, 36*f*–38*f* (*see also* crane)
    on obelisk of Theodosius, 25, 30–4
    Torlonia, x, 75–7, 76*f*–77*f*, 81, 99
Remus, 119–20, 131
Renaissance, 3n3, 25, 28, 101n7. *See also*
    reception
Renato Ricci, 217–18, 220*f*, 224–5, 227. *See
    also* Opera Nazionale Balilla
Rhine bridge. *See* bridge
river
    Iuvencus, 78
    Liris, 68, 69*f*–70*f*, 85, 162
    Melas, 193
    Nile, 13–14, 55, 57–8

Tiber, 56n132, 58, 65, 84–5, 87–8,
    143n21, 216, 219, 228–9
Styx, 170
Xanthus, 130n103
romanità, 220–22, 229–30
Romanization, 108, 222, 226, 229
Rome
    Antonine, 3n5, 5n16, 8n27,
        11n29, 21n21
    Augustan, 3n5, 5, 108, 118, 125n89,
        133n110
    Fascist, 5, 10, 214, 216–18, 226
    Flavian, 38, 64
    post-unification, 214
Romulus, 40n81, 65n8, 108, 119–22,
    129, 131

Saddam Hussein, 204–5
    statue of (*see* statue)
Saldae, 21n22
Salii, 170
Samos, 22n23
San Bartolomeo, 74
San Paolo, 229
Savo, 156
scaffolding, 5, 59, 139n8, 225
Sejanus, 212n38
senses, 2, 154. *See also* sound
Septicius Clarus, 72n31
Septimius Severus. *See* arch
Serviu Tullius, 201
Severus. *See* architect
Sicily, 93, 130, 138, 159, 161
Sidonian, 190–1
Simichidas, 105
Sinuessa, 136
Sirens, 179
sound
    of construction, 139, 142–6,
        148, 154–62
    effects, 60n141
    of poetry, 118, 120, 148, 154–62, 170
    of song, 180–2
    See also lyre
spectacle
    of construction, 4–5, 38, 47–8, 231
    of engineering, 45n96, 87, 99

270 GENERAL INDEX

sound (*cont.*)
  gladiatorial, 84–90, 99
  and mythological reenactment, 95–7
  naumachia, 84–90, 93–8
  of raising an obelisk, 24–5, 31–4, 58–60,
      222, 225
  of transportation, 4n14, 53, 57, 222
  vocabulary of, 87
speed
  in building inscriptions, 19, 29of
      construction, 4, 29, 47, 50, 99,
      140–2, 146–7, 149–53, 171,
      179n25, 210, 212, 214, 224
  of poetic composition, 146–8, 149–53,
      171statue
  base, restoration of Fucine lake tunnel,
      72, 74–5 (*see also* Fucine lake)
  of Domitian
    destruction of, 202–12
    erection of, 139–40, 150
    provenance of, 137–8, 141, 154–5,
      159, 224of Saddam Hussein,
      204, 204f
  of Triton, 95
Stella, Lucius Arruntius, 146, 156
Steropes, 138, 159–60
St Peter's basilica, 25
Styx. *See* river
Suebi, 51
Sugambri, 51
Surrentum, 140, 151n45
Sybil of Cumae, 143

Tarquinius Priscus, 201
Tarquinius Superbus, 201
Taurubulae, 156, 160
Taurus. *See* zodiac
Telchines, 161n84
temple, 196
  of Antoninus Pius and Faustina, 39
  of Apollo (Delphi), 152
  in Egypt, 13, 61
  of Hercules on the estate of Pollius Felix
      (*see* Pollius Felix)
  of Juno at Carthage, 7n24
  of Jupiter Optimus Maximus
      (Capitoline), 132n105, 205, 207–
      8, 211

destruction of, 1, 201
  reconstruction of, 1–2, 216n7
  poetic, 7, 100, 105n23, 106, 114, 116,
      119, 123–4, 152
Teuthras, 179
Thebes (Egypt), 54, 57
Thebes (Greece), 7, 10, 102, 173–98, 202
Theodosius I, 25–7, 31n51, 34n63
  obelisk of (*see* obelisk)
Thrace, 129
Tiber. *See* river
Tibur, 147
Titus, 2, 72n31
tomb
  of Anchises, 131
  of Claudia Semne, 39n77
  of the Flavii, 8n27
  of the Haterii, 34–9 (*see also* relief)
  of Hector, 130n103
  of Trebius Iustus, 45
  of Vergil, 166
topos
  of cooperation between builder and
      nature, 83n60
  of eating at inappropriate times, 97
  of foundation, 123, 135
  of impossibility of description,
      80, 230n42
  of innumerability, 80n51
  of poetry as magic, 179n23
  of temple building, 151
Torlonia relief. *See* relief
Trajan, 18, 43, 47, 66–7, 74–5,
      88, 201n7, 203, 205, 207,
      210n34, 211
  column of (*see* column)
  forum of (*see* forum)
  markets of, 46
Triton, 93, 95–7
Troy, 126, 197n74
  refoundation, 121–2, 131
  See also Epirus
tunnel. *See* Fucine lake: draining
Tydeus, 187–9
Tyre, 128
Tyrrhenian sea, 229

utilitas, 66, 83, 92, 142–3

GENERAL INDEX 271

Valentinian II, 31n51
vates, 155n59, 181
vaulting, 4
Vedic, 100n1, 101n3
ventennio. See Fascism
Venus, 92n84, 122, 127, 131, 165–6
   planet, 109
   See also Aphrodite
Vercellae, 18
Verona, 19n14
Vespasian, 1, 18, 201, 216n7
Via
   Appia, 45n96, 142
   dell'Impero, 221n14
   Domitiana, 7, 136–7, 142, 144n27,
      153, 163n90
   Labicana, 35
Victor (the usurper), 27
Villa of Manlius Vopiscus, 147
violence, 74–5, 82–3, 85, 89, 97, 99,
      169n118, 181n29, 206–7, 215
Violentilla, 156
Vitellius, 1, 201
Volturnus, 143, 153, 156, 159n75, 162–
      3, 168
Vulcan, 141, 150n42, 159–61. *See also*
   Mulciber

walls
   of Aeneadae, 129
   of Avaricum, 50n111
   forum, 46
   of Pergamum, 130
   of Rome, 58, 115, 118–21, 126–7
   of Thebes, 7, 10, 102, 173–98 (*see also*
      Amphion; lyre)
   of Troy, 131
   of Verona, 19n14
water engineering, 11, 64–7, 73, 78. *See*
      also Fucine Lake
World Trade Center. *See* 9/11

Xanthus. *See* river
Xerxes, 88–9, 144–5. *See also* bridge

Zethus, 173–8, 181–3, 193
Zeus, 158n68, 175, 188, 193n64. *See also*
   Jupiter
zodiac signs
   Aries, 109n39
   Taurus, 109

9/11
   Ground zero, 1–2, 2f, 5, 199n1
   World Trade Center, 199n1
   See also One World Trade Center